The **WILEY** *advantage*

Dear Valued Customer,

We realize you're a busy professional with deadlines to hit. Whether your goal is to learn a new technology or solve a critical problem, we want to be there to lend you a hand. Our primary objective is to provide you with the insight and knowledge you need to stay atop the highly competitive and ever-changing technology industry.

Wiley Publishing, Inc., offers books on a wide variety of technical categories, including security, data warehousing, software development tools, and networking — everything you need to reach your peak. Regardless of your level of expertise, the Wiley family of books has you covered.

- For Dummies – The *fun* and *easy* way to learn
- The Weekend Crash Course –The *fastest* way to learn a new tool or technology
- Visual – For those who prefer to learn a new topic *visually*
- The Bible – The *100% comprehensive* tutorial and reference
- The Wiley Professional list – *Practical* and *reliable* resources for IT professionals

The book you hold now, *Official Red Hat Linux Administrator's Guide,* is the Red Hat–reviewed and approved guide no Linux administrator should be without. If you manage a small LAN, or an enterprise Linux installation, here is everything you need to keep your network running smoothly. Beginning with Kickstart installations and creating networking scripts, the experts at Red Hat guide you through all the essentials with coverage of Tripwire, PAM, Samba, and even RAID. Not just another Linux book, *Official Red Hat Linux Administrator's Guide* is the official source for Red Hat system administrators.

Our commitment to you does not end at the last page of this book. We'd want to open a dialog with you to see what other solutions we can provide. Please be sure to visit us at www.wiley.com/compbooks to review our complete title list and explore the other resources we offer. If you have a comment, suggestion, or any other inquiry, please locate the "contact us" link at www.wiley.com.

Finally, we encourage you to review the following page for a list of Wiley titles on related topics. Thank you for your support and we look forward to hearing from you and serving your needs again in the future.

Sincerely,

Richard K. Swadley

D1614031

Richard K. Swadley
Vice President & Executive Group Publisher
Wiley Technology Publishing

Bible

DUMMIES

Independent Thinkers

more information on related titles

The Next Level of Red Hat Press Books

— Available from Wiley Publishing

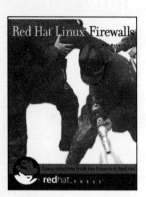

0-7645-2463-1
Everything needed
to construct
firewalls that
protect networks
from attacks and
intrusions.

0-7645-3632-X
Delivers all the know-
how needed to set up
and manage a state-
of-the-art Linux
network.

0-7645-4754-2
Delivers all the know-
how needed to
improve the
performance of your
Red Hat Linux system
— and protect it from
attacks and break-ins.

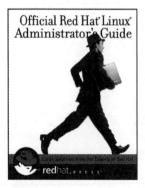

0-7645-1695-7
The most complete
coverage available —
focusing on
configuration and
administration of
Red Hat Linux 8.

ADVANCED

INTERMEDIATE

Official
Red Hat® Linux®
User's Guide

Official
Red Hat® Linux®
User's Guide

Red Hat

Contributors:

Sandra A. Moore • Tammy Fox • Johnray Fuller
John Ha • Edward C. Bailey

WILEY

Wiley Publishing, Inc.

Official Red Hat® Linux® User's Guide

Published by
Wiley Publishing, Inc.
10475 Crosspoint Boulevard
Indianapolis, IN 46256
www.wiley.com

Copyright © 2003 by Red Hat, Inc.

Published by Wiley Publishing, Inc., Indianapolis, Indiana

Published simultaneously in Canada

Library of Congress Control Number: 2002110254

ISBN: 0-7645-4967-7

Manufactured in the United States of America

10 9 8 7 6 5 4 3 2 1

1B/SS/RQ/QS/IN

Credits

Acquisitions Editor
Debra Williams Cauley

Project Editor
Sara Shlaer

Writer
James H. Russell

Editorial Manager
Mary Beth Wakefield

Vice President & Executive Group Publisher
Richard Swadley

Vice President and Publisher
Joseph B. Wikert

Executive Editorial Director
Mary Bednarek

Project Coordinator
Maridee Ennis

Proofreader
Anne Owen

Indexer
Virginia Bess Munroe

Cover Design
Michael J. Freeland

Red Hat Press Documentation Team
Sandra A. Moore, Product Documentation Manager and Technical Writer
Tammy Fox, Product Documentation Technical Lead and Technical Writer
Johnray Fuller, Technical Writer
John Ha, Technical Writer
Edward C. Bailey, Technical Writer

Red Hat Press Liaisons
Lorien Golaski
Chris Grams

Special Red Hat Assistance
Kathleen Langhi
Jeremy Hogan
Jonathan Opp

Preface

Welcome to the *Official Red Hat Linux User's Guide*! From installation to navigation and instructions on performing common tasks, this book is designed to help new and intermediate Linux users get up and running with Red Hat Linux.

If you need more advanced coverage of Red Hat Linux, see the companion book to this one: the *Official Red Hat Linux Administrator's Guide* (Red Hat Press/Wiley, 2003).

As you read this book, keep in mind that Linux looks, feels, and performs differently from other operating systems you may have used, such as Windows or Mac OS. Our advice is to forget about the conventions of those other operating systems, and with an open mind, approach Red Hat Linux as a new, interesting, and versatile alternative.

Conventions Used in this Book

As you read this book you will see that certain words are represented in different fonts and styles. These conventions are designed to help you easily navigate the book so that you can find whatever you need fast. The following sections discuss the major typographical conventions used in this book.

Commands and File Names

Linux commands (and other operating system commands, when used) are represented in a monofont style; for example: `boot: linux console=device`. This style indicates to you that you can type the word or phrase on the command line and press Enter to invoke a command.

File names, directory names, and paths are also represented in monofont to set them visually apart from normal text; for example: `/test/new/RedHat`.

Computer Output

Computer output is displayed by the computer as text on the command line. You will see this output, which includes responses to commands you typed in, error messages, and interactive prompts for your input during scripts or programs, displayed in monofont against a gray background, as follows:

```
$ ls
Desktop axhome logs paulwesterberg.png
Mail backupfiles mail reports
```

User Input

Text that the user has to type, either on the command line or into a text box on a GUI screen, is displayed in bold font; for example: To boot your system into the text based installation program, type **text** at the `boot:` prompt.

Navigational Callouts

Throughout this book, we use several methods of calling out important or otherwise noteworthy information. In order of how critical the information is to your system, these items will be marked as Note, Tip, Important, Caution, or Warning. Following are examples of each of these items:

> **NOTE** Remember that Linux is case sensitive. In other words, a rose is not a ROSE is not a rOsE.

> **TIP** The directory `/usr/share/doc` contains additional documentation for packages installed on your system.

> **IMPORTANT** If you modify the DHCP configuration file, the changes will not take effect until you restart the DHCP daemon.

> **CAUTION** Do not perform routine tasks as root. Use a regular user account unless you need to use the root account for system administration tasks.

> **WARNING** If you choose not to partition manually, a server installation will remove all existing partitions on all installed hard drives. Do not choose this installation class unless you are sure you have no data you need to save.

How This Book Is Organized

The chapters in this book are grouped by topic into seven parts. The following sections give you a brief description of each of the book's parts.

Part I: Installing Red Hat Linux

This part is ideal for users (both new and experienced) who want a quick and simple installation solution. From fundamental concepts such as installation preparation to the step-by-step installation procedure, this part will be a valuable resource as you install Red Hat Linux. Once you have completed the installation as outlined in this manual, you will have a fully functioning system. This part also contains useful information to assist you before and after installing Red Hat Linux.

Part II: The Basics

This part is task-oriented, showing you useful tips, hints, warnings, and screenshots. These chapters help users learn the basics of using Red Hat Linux, including navigating the graphical user interface, working from the shell prompt, dealing with removable media, working with files and directories, and managing users and groups.

Part III: Getting the Most from Your Red Hat Linux System

This part shows you how to use your Red Hat Linux system for the most common user tasks, such as using office-productivity software, listening to music, getting online, and working with graphics.

Part IV: Configuring Your Red Hat Linux System

This part shows you how to configure Red Hat Linux to recognize (and be able to print from) your printer, as well as how to set up a firewall to protect your private information from hackers, and setting your system's time and date.

Part V: Updating and Adding Packages to Red Hat Linux

There are two methods to installing new packages (the Linux term for applications) and updating old ones: using RPM files or using the rpm command. This part shows you how to perform both of these methods.

Part VI: Additional References

This part includes a lot of really handy information, such as keyboard shortcuts, a comparison of similar MS-DOS and Linux commands, a chapter including the most frequently asked questions about Red Hat Linux, and a breakdown of the system directories used by your Red Hat Linux system. Also included is a chapter showing you how you can monitor your system's performance and status.

Part VII: Appendixes

This final part contains some of the less commonly needed information about Red Hat Linux, for example: rescue mode, KDE, how to configure a dual-boot system, the logistics of disk partitioning, the basics of the X Window System, and information about the CD-ROMs that accompany this book.

Where to Go from Here

After you feel comfortable using and navigating your Red Hat Linux system, you may find yourself needing more information. The *Official Red Hat Linux Administrator's Guide*, which is the companion to this book, covers more technical aspects and options of your Red Hat Linux system than this book does.

There are also many good resources available on the Internet. The following sections provide you with good online resources for Linux-related information.

Linux Websites

Following are a few recommended websites about Red Hat Linux. (Note that some sites will discuss other Linux distributions as well.)

- `http://www.redhat.com` — On the Red Hat website you can find links to the Linux Documentation Project (LDP), online versions of the Red Hat Linux manuals, FAQs (Frequently Asked Questions), a database which can help you find a Linux Users Group near you, technical information in the Red Hat Support Knowledge Base, and more.

- `http://www.linuxheadquarters.com` — The Linux Headquarters website features easy to follow, step-by-step guides for a variety of Linux tasks.

- `http://www.slashdot.org` — Slashdot is a site that is run by many people, a good number of which are Linux users and administrators, on topics such as open-source development, Linux, and new technology.

Linux Newsgroups

You can participate in newsgroups by watching the discussions of others attempting to solve problems, or by actively asking or answering questions. Experienced Linux users are known to be extremely helpful when trying to assist new users with various Linux issues — especially if you are posing your questions in the right venue. If you do not have access to a news reader application (note that you can use Mozilla Mail for newsgroups), you can access this information via the Web at `http://www.deja.com`. Dozens of Linux-related newsgroups exist, including the following:

- `linux.help` — A great place to get help from fellow Linux users.

- `linux.redhat` — This newsgroup primarily covers Red Hat Linux-specific issues.

- `linux.redhat.install` — Pose installation questions to this newsgroup or search it to see how others solved similar problems.

- `linux.redhat.misc` — Questions or requests for help that do not really fit into traditional categories go here.

- `linux.redhat.rpm` — A good place to go if you are having trouble using RPM to accomplish particular objectives.

Contents

Part I

Installing Red Hat Linux

Installing Red Hat Linux has never been easier than with Red Hat Linux 8.0.

This part shows you how to determine whether or not your hardware is compatible with Red Hat Linux as well as whether or not your system has enough space to hold the operating system. It also shows you how to install Red Hat Linux, taking you through all of the major options that you can use to do so, and shows you how to use the Setup Agent to set up your new Red Hat system as well as other tasks that you might want to perform after installing Red Hat Linux.

Chapter 1: Installation Options and System Requirements

Chapter 2: Installing Red Hat Linux

Chapter 3: Upgrading Your Current System

Chapter 4: After Installation . . .

Chapter 1

Installation Options and System Requirements

Before installing Red Hat Linux on your system, you first need to make sure that your hardware is compatible with Linux. This chapter provides instructions for learning about your hardware and details the requirements for your hardware depending on the installation type you choose when you install Red Hat Linux.

NOTE See Chapter 2 for instructions on how to install Red Hat Linux.

Although this chapter reflects the most current information possible, you should read the Red Hat Linux Release Notes for information that may not have been available prior to the documentation being finalized. The Release Notes can be found on the Red Hat Linux CD #1 and online at:

```
http://www.redhat.com/docs/manuals/linux
```

Do You Have the Right Red Hat Linux Components?

If you have purchased this book new, you have the Red Hat Linux distribution on the accompanying CD-ROMs. If not, you can download Red Hat Linux by visiting `http://www.redhat.com` and clicking the Download link in the upper-right corner of the screen.

Is Your Hardware Compatible?

Hardware compatibility is particularly important if you have an older system or a system that you built yourself. Red Hat Linux 8.0 is compatible with most hardware in systems that were factory built within the last two years. However, hardware specifications change almost daily, so it is difficult to guarantee that your hardware will be 100 percent compatible.

The most recent list of supported hardware can be found online at:

```
http://hardware.redhat.com/hcl/
```

Learning About Your Hardware with Windows

If your computer is running Windows, you can find information about your hardware by using the Device Manager. The Device Manager's location differs depending on the version of Windows you are running. The following sections describe how to find your hardware information in the two main versions of Windows: Windows 95/98/Me (these DOS-based versions of Windows are often collectively referred to as Windows 9x) and Windows NT/2000/XP.

Finding your hardware information in Windows 9x

If your computer is already running one of the versions of Windows 9x, you can use the following steps to get additional configuration information:

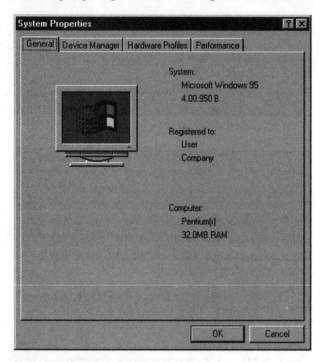

Figure 1-1. Windows 9x System Properties

1. In Windows, click the My Computer icon using the secondary (normally the right) mouse button. A pop-up menu should appear.

2. Select Properties. The System Properties window should appear. Note the information listed under Computer — in particular the amount of RAM listed.

3. Click on the Device Manager tab. You will then see a graphical representation of your computer's hardware configuration.

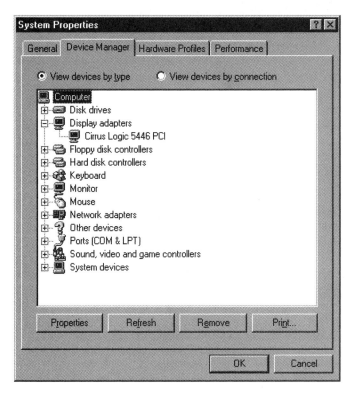

Figure 1-2. Windows 9x Device Manager

4. At this point, you can either double-click on the icons or single-click on the plus sign (**+**) to look at each entry in more detail. Look under the following icons for more information:

    - *Disk drives* — The type (IDE or SCSI) of hard drive will be found here. (IDE drives will normally include the word "IDE," while SCSI drives will not.)

    - *Hard disk controllers* — Information about your hard drive controller.

    - *CD-ROM* — Information about any CD-ROM drives connected to your computer.

> **NOTE** In some cases, there may be no CD-ROM icon, yet your computer has a functioning CD-ROM drive. This is normal, depending on how Windows was originally installed. In this case, you may be able to learn additional information by looking at the CD-ROM driver loaded in your computer's `config.sys` file.

    - *Mouse* — The type of mouse present on your computer.

    - *Display adapters* — If you are interested in running the X Window System, you should write down the information you find here.

    - *Sound, video, and game controllers* — If your computer has sound capabilities you will find more information about them here.

- *Network adapters* — Information on your computer's network card (if you have one).

- *SCSI controllers* — If your computer uses SCSI peripherals, you will find additional information on the SCSI controller here.

This method is not a complete substitute for opening your computer's case and physically examining each component. However, in many cases it can provide sufficient information to continue with the installation.

> **NOTE** You can print this information by clicking on the Print button. A second window will appear, allowing you to choose the printer, as well as the type of report. The All Devices and System Summary report type is the most complete.

Finding your hardware information in Windows NT/2000/XP

If your computer is running Windows 2000 or Windows XP, you can use the following steps to get additional configuration information:

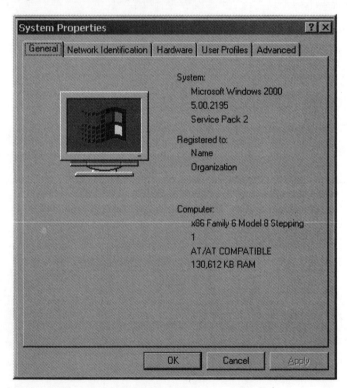

Figure 1-3. Windows 2000 System Properties

1. In Windows, click on the My Computer icon using the secondary (normally the right) mouse button. A pop-up menu should appear. (In Windows 2000, this icon is on the desktop; in Windows XP, it's on the Start Menu.)

2. Select Properties. The System Properties window should appear. Note the information listed under Computer — in particular the amount of RAM listed.

3. Click on the Hardware tab. You will then see your computer's hardware configuration options.

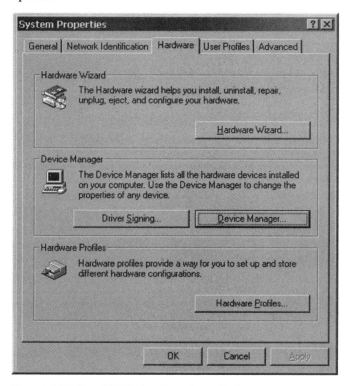

Figure 1-4. Windows 2000 System Properties — Hardware

4. Click on the Device Manager button. You will then see a graphical representation of your computer's hardware configuration. Make sure the View devices by type radio button is selected.

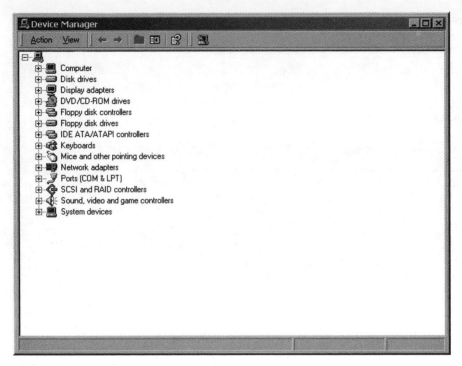

Figure 1-5. Windows 2000 Device Manager

At this point, you can either double-click on the icons or single-click on the plus sign to look at each entry in more detail. Look under the following icons for more information:

- *Disk drives* — The type (IDE or SCSI) of hard drive will be found here. (IDE drives will normally include the word "IDE," while SCSI drives will not.)
- *Hard disk controllers* — Information about your hard drive controller.
- *CD-ROM* — Information about any CD-ROM drives connected to your computer.
- *Mouse* — The type of mouse present on your computer.
- *Display adapters* — If you are interested in running the X Window System, you should write down the information you find here.
- *Sound, video, and game controllers* —If your computer has sound capabilities, you will find more information about them here.
- *Network adapters* — Information on your computer's network card (if you have one).
- *SCSI controllers* — If your computer uses SCSI peripherals, you will find additional information on the SCSI controller here.

This method is not a complete substitute for opening your computer's case and physically examining each component. However, in many cases it can provide sufficient information to continue with the installation.

Recording Your System's Hardware

Table 1-1 shows the information you need about your system's hardware to install Red Hat Linux. It's a good idea to write this information down as a handy reference to help make your Red Hat Linux installation go more smoothly.

Table 1-1. System Requirements Table

Hardware	Information Needed	Example
Hard drive(s)	Type, label, size	IDE `/dev/hda`=1.2 GB
Partitions	Map of partitions and mount points	`/dev/hda1=/home,` `/dev/hda2=/` (fill this in once you know where they will reside)
Memory	Amount of RAM installed on your system	64 MB, 128 MB
CD-ROM	Interface type	SCSI, IDE (ATAPI)
SCSI adapter	If present, make and model number	BusLogic SCSI Adapter, Adaptec 2940UW
Network card	If present, make and model number	Tulip, 3COM 3C590
Mouse	Type, protocol, and number of buttons	Generic 3 button PS/2 mouse, MouseMan 2 button serial mouse
Monitor	Make, model, and manufacturer specifications	Optiquest Q53, ViewSonic G773
Video card	Make, model number and size of VRAM	Creative Labs Graphics Blaster 3D, 8MB
Sound card	Make, chipset, and model number	S3 SonicVibes, Sound Blaster 32/64 AWE
IP, DHCP, and BOOTP addresses	Four numbers, separated by dots	10.0.2.15
Netmask	Four numbers, separated by dots	255.255.248.0
Gateway IP address	Four numbers, separated by dots	10.0.2.245
One or more name server IP addresses (DNS)	One or more sets of dot-separated numbers	10.0.2.1
Domain name	The name given to your organization	Red Hat's would be `redhat.com`

Hardware	Information Needed	Example
Hostname	The name of your computer; your personal choice of names	`cookie, southpark`

If any of these networking requirements or terms are unfamiliar to you, contact your network administrator for assistance.

Do You Have Enough Disk Space?

Nearly every modern-day operating system (OS) uses *disk partitions*, and Red Hat Linux is no exception. When you install Red Hat Linux, you may have to work with disk partitions. When you partition a disk, each partition will behave like a separate disk drive.

If Red Hat Linux will share your system with another OS, you will need to make sure you have enough available disk space on your hard drive(s) for this installation.

The disk space used by Red Hat Linux must be separate from the disk space used by other OSes you may have installed on your system, such as Windows or even a different version of Linux. At least two partitions (/ and `swap`) must be dedicated to Red Hat Linux.

Before you start the installation process, one of the following conditions must be met:

♦ Your computer must have enough disk space for the installation of Red Hat Linux. The available disk space must be either unpartitioned disk space or one or more partitions that you can delete.

♦ You must have one or more partitions that may be deleted so that you can free up enough disk space to install Red Hat Linux.

> **NOTE** These recommendations are based on an installation that only installs one language (such as English). If you plan to install multiple languages to use on your system, you should increase the disk space requirements.

The following list describes the installation types you can choose from during the Red Hat Linux installation along with the space requirements for each:

♦ *Personal Desktop* — A personal desktop installation, including a graphical desktop environment, requires at least 1.5GB of free space. Choosing both the GNOME and KDE desktop environments requires at least 1.8GB of free disk space.

♦ *Workstation* — A workstation installation, including a graphical desktop environment and software development tools, requires at least 2GB of free space. Choosing both the GNOME and KDE desktop environments requires at least 2.3GB of free disk space.

♦ *Server* — A server installation requires 1.3GB for a minimal installation without the X Window System (the graphical environment), at least 1.4GB of free space if all package groups other than X are installed, and at least 2.1GB to install all packages including the GNOME and KDE desktop environments.

♦ *Custom* — A Custom installation requires 400MB for a minimal installation and at least 4.5GB of free space if every package is selected.

Do I Need a Driver Disk?

A *driver disk* adds support for hardware that is not otherwise supported by the installation program. The driver disk could be produced by Red Hat, it could be a disk you make yourself from drivers found on the Internet, or it could be a disk that a hardware vendor includes with a piece of hardware.

> **NOTE** A driver disk is different than a boot disk. If you require a boot disk to begin the Red Hat Linux installation, you will still need to create that floppy and boot from it before using the driver disk. If you do not already have an installation boot disk and your system does not support booting from the CD-ROM, you should create an installation boot disk. For instructions on how make a boot disk, see Chapter 2.

While the Red Hat Linux installation program is loading, you may see a screen that asks you for a driver disk. The driver disk screen is most often seen in three scenarios:

- If you run the installation program in expert mode
- If you run the installation program by entering **linux dd** at the `boot:` prompt
- If you run the installation program on a computer that does not have any PCI devices

There is no need to use a driver disk unless you need a particular device in order to install Red Hat Linux. Driver disks are most often used for non-standard or very new CD-ROM drives, SCSI adapters, or NICs. These are the only devices used during the installation that might require drivers not included on the Red Hat Linux CD-ROMs (or boot disk, if you created an installation boot disk to begin the install process).

> **NOTE** If an unsupported device is not needed to install Red Hat Linux on your system, continue with the installation and add support for the new piece of hardware after the installation is complete.

How Do I Obtain a Driver Disk?

The Red Hat Linux CD-ROM #1 includes driver disk images (`images/drvnet.img` — network card drivers and `images/drvblock.img` — drivers for SCSI controllers) containing many rarely used drivers. If you suspect that your system may require one of these drivers, you should create the driver disk before beginning your Red Hat Linux installation.

Another option for finding specialized driver disk information is on Red Hat's website at

`http://www.redhat.com/support/errata`

under the section called Bug Fixes. Occasionally, popular hardware may be made available after a release of Red Hat Linux that will not work with drivers already in the installation program or included on the driver disk images on the Red Hat Linux CD-ROM #1. In such cases, the Red Hat website may contain a link to a current driver disk image.

Creating a Driver Disk from an Image File

If you have a driver disk image that you need to write to a floppy disk, this can be done from within DOS or Red Hat Linux.

To create a driver disk from a driver disk image using Red Hat Linux:

1. Insert a blank, formatted floppy disk into the first floppy drive.
2. From the same directory containing the driver disk image, such as `drvnet.img`, type **dd if=drvnet.img of=/dev/fd0** as root.

To create a driver disk from a driver disk image using MS-DOS:

1. Insert a blank, formatted floppy disk into the A: drive.
2. From the same directory containing the driver disk image, such as `drvnet.img`, type **d:\dosutils\rawrite drvnet.img a:** at the command line, where d: is the drive letter for the CD-ROM device.

Using a Driver Disk During Installation

Having a driver disk is not enough; you must specifically tell the Red Hat Linux installation program to load that driver disk and use it during the installation process.

After you have created your driver disk, begin the installation process by booting from the Red Hat Linux CD-ROM #1 (or the installation boot disk). At the `boot:` prompt, enter either `linux expert` or `linux dd`. See Chaper 2 for details on booting the installation program.

The Red Hat Linux installation program will ask you to insert the driver disk. After the driver disk is read by the installer, it can apply those drivers to hardware discovered on your system later in the installation process.

Can You Install Using the Red Hat Linux CD-ROM?

Most new computers will allow booting from the CD-ROM. If your system will support booting from the CD-ROM, it is an easy way to begin a local CD-ROM installation.

Your BIOS may need to be changed to allow booting from your CD-ROM drive. For more information about editing your BIOS and the installation process in general, see Chapter 2.

Alternative Boot Methods

If you cannot boot from the CD-ROM drive, you may need to use a boot diskette. A boot diskette can be a diskette you created to boot (or start) the installation program, or it can be a diskette you create during the installation process that can later be used to boot the operating system. Normally, your computer boots from a hard disk, but if the hard disk is damaged, you can boot the computer from a bootable diskette.

The following two types of boot disks are available:

♦ *Local Boot Diskette* — If you need a *local boot diskette*, you must create it. The local boot disk image file, `boot.img`, is located in the `images` directory on your Red Hat Linux CD-ROM. See the next section for more information on making a boot diskette.

♦ *PCMCIA Boot Diskettes* — You may need *PCMCIA boot diskettes* if you are using a PCMCIA device to install Red Hat Linux. If you need PCMCIA boot diskettes, you must create them. The following checklist can help you determine if you will need to create PCMCIA boot diskettes:

- You will install Red Hat Linux from a CD-ROM, and your CD-ROM drive is attached to your computer through a PCMCIA card.
- You will use a PCMCIA network adapter during the installation.

The PCMCIA boot diskette image files, `pcmcia.img` and `pcmciadd.img`, are located in the `images` directory on your Red Hat Linux CD-ROM #1.

> **NOTE** Although it is not required to boot your installation, you may occasionally find that a driver diskette is needed to continue with the installation. The "Do I Need a Driver Disk?" section earlier in this chapter explains why a driver diskette may be necessary for your installation, and how to obtain one If needed.

Making Installation Diskettes

You may need to create a diskette from an *image file*; for example, you may need to use updated diskette images obtained from the Red Hat Linux errata page:

```
http://www.redhat.com/apps/support/errata/
```

An image file contains an exact copy (or image) of a diskette's contents. Because a diskette contains file system information in addition to the data contained in files, the contents of the image file are not usable until they have been written to a diskette.

To start, you will need the following:

- A blank, formatted, high-density (1.44MB), 3.5-inch diskette.
- A computer with a 3.5-inch diskette drive. The computer must be able to run either an MSDOS program or the `dd` utility found on most Linux-like operating systems.

The `images` directory on your Red Hat Linux CD-ROM #1 contains the boot images for Red Hat Linux. After you select the proper image (such as `boot.img` for a CD-ROM-based installation or `bootnet.img` for a network installation), transfer the image file onto a diskette using one of the methods described in the following sections.

Using the rawrite Utility

To make a diskette using MS-DOS, use the `rawrite` utility included on the Red Hat Linux CD-ROM #1 in the `dosutils` directory. First, label a blank, formatted 3.5-inch diskette appropriately (such as "Boot Disk" or "Updates Disk"). Insert it into the diskette drive. Then, use the following commands (assuming your CD-ROM is drive `D:`):

```
C:\> d:
D:\> cd \dosutils
D:\dosutils> rawrite
Enter disk image source file name: ..\images\boot.img
Enter target diskette drive: a:
Please insert a formatted diskette into drive A: and
press --ENTER-- : [Enter]
```

First, `rawrite` asks you for the filename of a diskette image; enter the directory and name of the image you wish to write (for example, `..\images\boot.img`). Then `rawrite` asks for a diskette drive to write the image to; enter `a:`. Finally, `rawrite` asks for confirmation that a formatted diskette is in the drive you have selected. After pressing Enter to confirm, `rawrite` copies the image file onto the diskette. If you need to make another diskette, label that diskette, and run `rawrite` again, specifying the appropriate image file.

> **NOTE** The `rawrite` utility only accepts 8.3-type file names, such as `filename.img`. The 8.3-type file name originates from the naming convention of eight characters, a period, and three characters for a file name extension. This naming convention supports file names between 1 and 8 characters, which cannot have spaces, and may not contain ? or _ characters at the start of the name. If you download an update image from `http://www.redhat.com` named something similar to `update-anaconda-03292002.img`, you must rename it as `updates.img` before you run `rawrite`.

Using the dd Command

To make a diskette under Linux (or any other Linux-like operating system), you must have permission to write to the device representing a 3.5-inch diskette drive (known as `/dev/fd0` in Linux).

First, label a blank, formatted diskette appropriately (such as "Boot Disk" or "Updates Disk"). Insert it into the diskette drive, but do not mount the diskette (when you *mount* a floppy or CD-ROM, you make that device's contents available to you; see Chapter 8 for more information).

After mounting the Red Hat Linux CD-ROM, change to the directory containing the desired image file, and use the following command (changing the name of the image file and diskette device as appropriate):

```
# dd if=boot.img of=/dev/fd0 bs=1440k
```

To make another diskette, label that diskette and run `dd` again, specifying the appropriate image file.

Which Installation Class Is Best for You?

Usually, Red Hat Linux is installed on its own disk partition or set of partitions, or over another installation of Linux.

> **WARNING** Installing Red Hat Linux over another installation of Linux (including Red Hat Linux) does *not* preserve any information (files or data) from a prior installation. Make sure you save any important files! To preserve the current data on your existing system, you should back up your data and/or consider performing an upgrade instead (you can only upgrade from a previous Red Hat Linux installation — see Chapter 3 for more information).

The following installation types are available:

♦ *Personal Desktop* — A personal desktop installation is most appropriate if you are new to the world of Linux and would like to give it a try. This installation will create a system for your home, laptop, or desktop use. A graphical environment will be installed.

♦ *Workstation* — A workstation installation is most appropriate if you would like a graphical desktop environment and software development tools. This installation is good for Linux software developers who want to use the graphical desktop environment.

♦ *Server* — A server installation is most appropriate if you would like your system to function as a Linux-based server and you do not want to heavily customize your system configuration.

♦ *Custom* — A custom installation allows you the greatest flexibility during your installation. You choose your boot loader, which packages you want, and more. Custom installations are most appropriate for those users more familiar with Red Hat Linux installations and for those afraid of losing complete flexibility.

♦ *Upgrade* — If you already have a version of Red Hat Linux (6.2 or greater) running on your system and you want to quickly update to the latest packages and kernel version, then an upgrade is most appropriate for you.

These classes give you the option of simplifying the installation process, with some potential for loss of configuration flexibility, or retaining flexibility with a slightly more complex installation process.

The following sections give you a detailed look at each class so you can see which one is right for you.

Personal Desktop Installations

Most suitable for new users, the personal desktop installation will install a graphical desktop environment (the X Window System) and create a system ideal for home or desktop use.

Below are the minimum recommended disk space requirements for a personal desktop installation where only one language (such as English) will be installed.

♦ Personal Desktop: 1.5GB

♦ Personal Desktop choosing both GNOME and KDE: 1.8GB

> **NOTE** If you plan to choose all package groups (for example, Office/Productivity Applications are a group of packages), as well as select additional individual packages, you may want to allow 4GB or more of disk space.

If you choose automatic partitioning, a personal desktop installation will create the following partitions:

♦ The swap partition — The size of the swap partition is determined by the amount of RAM in your system and the amount of space available on your hard drive. For example, if you have 128MB of RAM, then the swap partition created can be 128MB to 256MB (twice your RAM), depending on how much disk space is available.

♦ /boot — A 100MB partition in which the Linux kernel and related files reside.

♦ / — This is the root partition — the partition within which all other files are stored (the exact size of this partition is dependent on your available disk space).

Workstation Installations

The workstation installation will install a graphical desktop environment and the X Window System, plus software development tools.

Following are the minimum recommended disk space requirements for a workstation installation where only one language (such as English) will be installed:

♦ Workstation: 2.0GB

♦ Workstation choosing both GNOME and KDE: 2.3GB

NOTE If you plan to choose all package groups (for example, Office/Productivity Applications are a group of packages), as well as select additional individual packages, you may want to allow 4GB or more of disk space. If you provide this extra space, you will have room for additional data, if needed.

If you choose automatic partitioning, a workstation installation will create the following partitions:

♦ The swap partition — The size of the swap partition is determined by the amount of RAM in your system and the amount of space available on your hard drive. For example, if you have 128MB of RAM, then the swap partition created can be 128MB to 256MB (twice your RAM), depending on how much disk space is available.

♦ /boot — A 100MB partition in which the Linux kernel and related files reside.

♦ / — This is the root partition within which all other files are stored (the exact size of this partition is dependent on your available disk space).

Server Installations

A server installation is most appropriate for you if you would like your system to function as a Linux-based server, and you do not want to heavily customize your system configuration.

Following are the minimum recommended disk space requirements for a server installation where only one language (such as English) will be installed:

♦ Server (minimum, no graphical interface): 1.3GB

♦ Server (choosing everything, no graphical interface): 1.4GB

♦ Server (choosing everything, including a graphical interface): 2.1GB

If you plan to choose all group packages, as well as select additional individual packages, you may want to allow 2.3GB or more of disk space.

NOTE During the server installation, the X Window System is not configured and no GUI will be loaded when the system boots unless you choose to install the appropriate packages during package selection.

If you choose automatic partitioning, the following partitions will be created during a server installation:

♦ The swap partition — The size of the swap partition is determined by the amount of RAM in your system and the amount of space available on your hard drive. For example, if you have 128MB of RAM, then the swap partition created can be 128MB to 256MB (twice your RAM), depending on how much disk space is available.

♦ / — A 384MB root partition.

- /usr — The exact size of this partition is dependent on your available disk space.
- /home —The exact size of this partition is dependent on your available disk space.
- /var — A 256MB partition.
- /boot — A 100MB partition in which the Linux kernel and related files are kept.

This disk partitioning scheme results in a reasonably flexible file system configuration for most server tasks.

Custom Installations

During a *custom installation*, you have complete control over the packages that will be installed on your system. The custom installation allows you the most flexibility during your installation. The personal desktop, workstation, and server installations automatically go through the installation process for you and omit certain steps.

The recommended disk space requirements for a custom installation are as follows:

- Custom (minimum): 400MB
- Custom (choosing everything): 4.5GB

As you might guess from the name, a custom installation puts the emphasis on flexibility. You have complete control over which packages will be installed on your system.

If you choose automatic partitioning, a custom installation will create the following partitions:

- The swap partition — The size of the swap partition is determined by the amount of RAM in your system and the amount of space available on your hard drive. For example, if you have 128 MB of RAM, then the swap partition created can be 128 MB - 256 MB (twice your RAM), depending on how much disk space is available.
- /boot — A 100 MB partition in which the Linux kernel and related files reside.
- / — The root partition within which all other files are stored (the exact size of this partition is dependent on your available disk space).

Upgrading Your System

Upgrading from Red Hat Linux 6.2 (or greater) will not delete any existing data. The installation program updates the modular kernel and all currently installed software packages. See Chapter 3 for instructions on upgrading your system.

Chapter 2

Installing Red Hat Linux

This chapter explains how to install Red Hat Linux from the CD-ROM. The following topics are discussed:

♦ Becoming familiar with the installation program's user interface

♦ Starting the installation program

♦ Selecting an installation method

♦ Configuration steps during the installation (language, keyboard, mouse, etc.)

♦ Finishing the installation

> **NOTE** If you already have another operating system installed and want to create a dual-boot system so that you can use both Red Hat Linux and the other operating system, please read Appendix C for more information.

The Graphical Installation Program User Interface

If you have used a *graphical user interface (GUI)* before, you will be familiar with this process; simply use your mouse to navigate the screens, "click" buttons, or enter text fields. You can also navigate through the installation using the Tab and Enter keys.

> **NOTE** If you do not wish to use the GUI installation program, the text mode installation program is also available. Use the boot command `boot: text` to start the text mode installation program. Please refer to the section "The Text Mode Installation Program User Interface" for an overview of text mode installation instructions.

A Note about Virtual Consoles

The Red Hat Linux installation program offers more than the dialog boxes of the installation process. Several different kinds of diagnostic messages are available to you, in addition to providing a way to enter commands from a shell prompt. The installation program displays these messages on five *virtual consoles*, among which you can switch using a single keystroke combination. These virtual consoles can be helpful if you encounter a problem while installing Red Hat Linux. Messages displayed on the installation or system consoles can help pinpoint a problem. See Table 2-1 for a listing of the virtual consoles, keystrokes used to switch to them, and their contents.

NOTE Generally, there is no reason to leave the default console (virtual console #7) unless you are attempting to diagnose installation problems.

Table 2-1: Virtual Consoles

Console #	Keystrokes	Contents
1	Ctrl-Alt-F1	Installation dialog
2	Ctrl-Alt-F2	Shell prompt
3	Ctrl-Alt-F3	Install log (messages from the installation program
4	Ctrl-Alt-F4	System-related messages
5	Ctrl-Alt-F5	Other messages
7	Ctrl-Alt-F7	X graphical environment

The Text Mode Installation Program User Interface

The Red Hat Linux text mode installation program uses a screen-based interface that includes most of the on-screen "widgets" commonly found on graphical user interfaces. Figure 2-1 and Figure 2-2 illustrate the screens you will see.

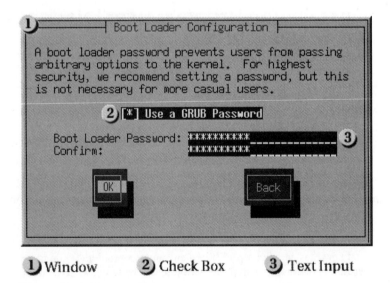

① Window   ② Check Box   ③ Text Input

Figure 2-1. Installation Program Widgets as Seen in Boot Loader Configuration

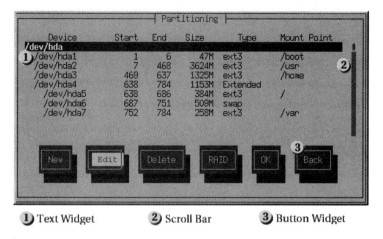

```
                        ┤ Partitioning ┤
     Device      Start    End    Size      Type      Mount Point
/dev/hda
 /dev/hda1          1      6      47M      ext3      /boot
 /dev/hda2          7    468    3624M      ext3      /usr
 /dev/hda3        469    637    1325M      ext3      /home
 /dev/hda4        638    784    1153M      Extended
   /dev/hda5      638    686     384M      ext3      /
   /dev/hda6      687    751     509M      swap
   /dev/hda7      752    784     258M      ext3      /var


        New      Edit      Delete     RAID      OK      Back
```

① Text Widget   ② Scroll Bar   ③ Button Widget

Figure 2-2. Installation Program Widgets as Seen in Disk Druid

Here is a list of the most important widgets shown in Figure 2-1 and Figure 2-2:

♦ *Window* — Windows will appear on your screen throughout the installation process. At times, one window may overlay another; in these cases, you can only interact with the window on top. When you are finished in that window, it will disappear, allowing you to continue working in the window underneath.

♦ *Checkbox* — Checkboxes allow you to select or deselect a feature. The box displays either an asterisk (selected) or a space (unselected). When the cursor is within a checkbox, press the spacebar to select an unselected feature or to deselect a selected feature.

♦ *Text Input* — Text input lines are regions where you can enter information required by the installation program. When the cursor rests on a text input line, you may enter and/or edit information on that line.

♦ *Text widget* — Text widgets are regions of the screen for the display of text. At times, text widgets may also contain other widgets, such as checkboxes. If a text widget contains more information than can be displayed in the space reserved for it, a scroll bar appears; if you position the cursor within the text widget, you can then use the Up and Down arrow keys to scroll through all the information available. Your current position is shown on the scroll bar by a hash mark (#) character that moves up and down the scroll bar as you scroll.

♦ *Scroll Bar* — Scroll bars appear on the side or bottom of a window to control which part of a list or document is currently in the window's frame. The scroll bar makes it easy to move to any part of a file.

♦ *Button widget* — Button widgets are the primary method of interacting with the installation program. You progress through the windows of the installation program by navigating these buttons using the Tab and Enter keys. Buttons can be selected when they are highlighted.

♦ *Cursor* — Although not a widget, the cursor is used to select (and interact) with a particular widget. As the cursor is moved from widget to widget, it may cause the widget to change color, or you may only see the cursor itself positioned in or next to the widget. In Figure 2-1, the cursor is positioned on the OK button. Figure 2-2 shows the cursor on the Edit button.

Navigation through the installation windows is performed through a simple set of keystrokes. To move the cursor, use the Left, Right, Up, and Down arrow keys. Use Tab and Alt-Tab to cycle forward or backward through each widget on the screen. Most screens display a summary of available cursor positioning keys along the bottom of the window.

To "press" a button, position the cursor over the button (using Tab, for example) and press the spacebar or the Enter key. To select an item from a list of items, move the cursor to the item you wish to select and press Enter. To select an item with a checkbox, move the cursor to the checkbox and press the spacebar to select an item. To deselect, press the spacebar a second time.

Pressing F12 accepts the current values and proceeds to the next dialog; it is equivalent to pressing the OK button.

> **CAUTION** Unless a dialog box is waiting for your input, do not press any keys during the installation process (doing so may result in unpredictable behavior).

Displaying Online Help

Once the installation program is loaded into memory, you can obtain information about the installation process and options by pressing F1 through F6. For example, press F2 to see general information about the online help screens.

Starting the Installation Program

To start the installation, you must first boot the installation program. Please make sure you have all the resources you will need for the installation. If you have already read through Chapter 1 and followed the instructions there, you should be ready to begin.

> **NOTE** Occasionally, some hardware components require a *driver diskette* during the installation. A driver diskette adds support for hardware that is not otherwise supported by the installation program. See Chapter 1 for more information.

Booting the Installation Program

You can boot the Red Hat Linux installation program using any one of the following media (depending upon what your system can support):

♦ *Bootable CD-ROM* — Your machine supports a bootable CD-ROM drive and you want to perform a local CD-ROM installation.

♦ *Local boot diskette* — Your machine will not support a bootable CD-ROM and you want to install from a local CD-ROM or a hard drive.

♦ *Network boot diskette* — Use a network boot diskette to install via NFS, FTP, and HTTP.

♦ *PCMCIA boot diskettes* — Use PCMCIA boot diskettes when you need PCMCIA support but your machine does not support booting from the CD-ROM drive or if you need PCMCIA support in order to make use of the CD-ROM drive on your system. The PCMCIA boot diskettes can be used for all installation methods (CD-ROM, hard drive, NFS, FTP, and HTTP).

To create a boot diskette, refer to Chapter 1.

Insert the boot diskette into your computer's first diskette drive and reboot (or boot using the CD-ROM, if your computer supports booting from it). Your BIOS settings may need to be changed to allow you to boot from the diskette or CD-ROM.

Changing Your BIOS Settings

To change your BIOS settings, watch the instructions provided on your display when your computer first boots. You will see a line of text telling you to press the Del or F1 key to enter the BIOS settings. Once you have entered your BIOS setup program, find the section where you can alter your boot sequence. The default is often "C, A" or "A, C" (depending on whether you boot from your hard drive C or a diskette in drive A). Change this sequence so that the CD-ROM is first in your boot order and that C or A (whichever is your typical boot default) is second. This instructs the computer to first look at the CD-ROM drive for bootable media; if it does not find bootable media on the CD-ROM drive, it will then check your hard drive or diskette drive. Save your changes before exiting the BIOS. For more information, refer to the documentation that came with your system.

After a short delay, a screen containing the boot: prompt should appear. The screen contains information on a variety of boot options. Each boot option also has one or more help screens associated with it. To access a help screen, press the appropriate function key as listed in the line at the bottom of the screen.

As you boot the installation program, be aware of two issues:

♦ Once you see the boot: prompt, the installation program will automatically begin if you take no action within the first minute. To disable this feature, press one of the help screen function keys.

♦ If you press a help screen function key, there will be a slight delay while the help screen is read from the boot media.

Normally, you only need to press Enter to boot the installation program. Watch the boot messages to see if the Linux kernel detects your hardware. If your hardware is properly detected, you can continue to the next section. If it does not properly detect your hardware, you may need to restart the installation in expert mode.

Additional Boot Options

While it is easiest for a user to boot from the CD-ROM and perform a graphical installation, sometimes there are installation scenarios where booting in a different manner may be needed. This section discusses addition boot options available for Red Hat Linux.

> **NOTE** See Table 2-2 in this section for additional boot options.

◆ If you do not wish to perform a graphical installation, you can start a text mode installation using the following boot command:

```
boot: linux text
```

◆ ISO images now have an md5sum embedded in them. To test the checksum integrity of an ISO image, at the installation boot prompt type:

```
boot: linux mediacheck
```

The installation program will prompt you to insert a CD or select an ISO image to test and select OK to perform the checksum operation. This checksum operation can be performed on any Red Hat Linux CD and does not have to be performed in a specific order (for example, CD #1 does not have the be the first CD you verify). It is strongly recommended to perform this operation on any Red Hat Linux CD that was created from downloaded ISO images. This procedure works with CD-based installations and hard drive and NFS installations using ISO images.

◆ If the installation program does not properly detect your hardware, you may need to restart the installation in expert mode. *Expert mode* disables most hardware probing and allows you to enter options for the drivers loaded during the installation. The initial boot messages will not contain any references to SCSI or network cards. This is normal; these devices are supported by modules that are loaded during the installation process. Enter expert mode using the following boot command:

```
boot: linux noprobe
```

For text mode installations, use:

```
boot: linux text noprobe
```

◆ If you need to perform the installation in serial mode, type the following command:

```
boot: linux console=device
```

For text mode installations, use:

```
boot: linux text console=device
```

In the above command, device should be the device you are using (such as ttyS0 or ttyS1). For example, linux text console=ttyS0,115200n8.

Table 2-2 shows more boot-time command arguments.

Table 2-2: Boot Options

Command	What It Does
askmethod	Asks you to select the installation method you would like to use when booting from the Red Hat Linux CD-ROM.
apic	Works around a bug commonly encountered in the Intel 440GX chipset BIOS and should only be executed with the installation program kernel.
apm=allow_ints	Changes how the suspend service is handled (and may be necessary for some laptops).
apm=off	Disables APM (Advanced Power Management). This is useful because some BIOSes have buggy power management (APM) and tend to crash.
apm=power_off	Makes Red Hat Linux shut down the system by default. This is useful for SMP systems that do not shut down by default.
apm=realmode_power_off	Some BIOSes crash when trying to shut down the machine. This command changes the method of how this is done from the Windows NT method to the Windows 95 method.
dd	Prompts you to use a driver disk during the installation of Red Hat Linux.
display=*IP*:0	Allows remote display forwarding. In this command, *IP* should be replaced with the IP address of the system you want the display to appear on. On the system you want the display to appear on, you must execute the command xhost +*remotehostname*, where *remotehostname* is the name of the host you are running the original display from. Using the command xhost +*remotehostname* limits access to the remote display terminal and does not allow access from anyone or any system not specifically authorized for remote access.
driverdisk	Performs the same function as the dd command and also prompts you to use a driver disk during the installation of Red Hat Linux.
expert	Allows partitioning of removable media and prompts for driver disk.
ide=nodma	Disables DMA on all IDE devices and may be useful when having IDE-related problems.
isa	Prompts you for ISA device configuration.
lowres	Forces the graphical (GUI) installation program to run at a lower resolution (640x480).

Command	What It Does
mediacheck	Gives you the option of testing the integrity of the installation source (if an ISO-based method). Verifying that the ISO images are intact before you attempt an installation will help to avoid problems that are often encountered during an installation.
mem=xxxM	Allows you to override the amount of memory the kernel detects for the machine. This may be necessary for some older systems where only 16MB is detected and for some new machines where the video card shares the video memory with the main memory. When executing this command, xxx should be replaced with the amount of memory in megabytes.
nmi_watchdog=1	Enables the built-in kernel deadlock detector. This command can be used to debug hard kernel lockups. By executing periodic NMI (Non Maskable Interrupt) interrupts, the kernel can monitor whether any CPU has locked up and print out debugging messages as needed.
noapic	Tells the kernel not to use the APIC chip. This command may be helpful for some motherboards with a bad APIC (such as the Abit BP6) or with a buggy BIOS.
noht	Disables hyperthreading (when available in SMP systems).
nomce	Disables self-diagnosis checks performed on the CPU. The kernel enables self-diagnosis on the CPU by default (called Machine Check Exception). On some older Compaq machines, this check is run too often and may need to be disabled.
nomount	This command disables automatic mounting of any installed Linux partitions in rescue mode.
nopass	Disables the passing of keyboard and mouse information to stage 2 of the installation program. This is good for testing keyboard and mouse configuration screens during stage 2 of the installation program when performing a network installation.
nopcmcia	Ignores any PCMCIA controllers in system.
noprobe	Disables hardware detection and instead prompts the user for hardware information.
noshell	Disables shell access on virtual console 2 during an installation.
nousb	Disables the loading of USB support during the installation. If the installation program tends to hang early in the process, this command may be helpful.

Command	What It Does
nousbstorage	Disables the loading of the usbstorage module in the installation program's loader. It may help with device ordering on SCSI systems.
reboot=b	Changes the way the kernel tries to reboot the machine. If a kernel hang is experienced while the system is shutting down, this command will allow the system to reboot.
rescue	Runs rescue mode. Refer to Appendix A for more information about rescue mode.
resolution=	Tells the installation program which video mode to run. It accepts any standard resolution, such as 640x480, 800x600, 1024x768, and so on.
serial	Turns on serial console support.
skipddc	Skips the ddc monitor probe, which causes problems on some systems.
text	Disables the graphical installation program and forces the installation program to run in text mode.
updates	Prompts you to insert a floppy diskette containing updates (bug fixes). This is not needed if you are performing a network installation and have already placed the updated image contents in RHupdates/ on the server.

Kernel Options

Options can also be passed to the kernel. For example, to instruct the kernel to use all the RAM in a system with 128MB of RAM, enter:

```
boot: linux mem=128M
```

For text mode installations, use:

```
boot: linux text mem=128M
```

After entering any options, press Enter to boot using those options.

If you need to specify boot options to identify your hardware, please write them down. The boot options will be needed during the boot loader configuration portion of the installation (see the "Boot Loader Configuration" section later in this chapter for more information).

Booting Without Diskettes

The Red Hat Linux CD-ROM can be booted by computers that support bootable CD-ROMs. Not all computers support this feature, so if your system cannot boot from the CD-ROM, there is one other way to start the installation without using a boot diskette. The following method is specific to x86-based computers only.

If you have MS-DOS installed on your system, you can boot directly from the CD-ROM drive without using a boot diskette. To do this (assuming your CD-ROM is drive d:), use the following commands:

```
C:\> d:
D:\> cd \dosutils
D:\dosutils> autoboot.bat
```

This method will not work if run in an MS-DOS Command Prompt window — the autoboot.bat file must be executed with MS-DOS as the only operating system; that is, Windows cannot be running.

If your computer cannot boot directly from CD-ROM (and you cannot use a MS-DOS-based autoboot.bat), you will have to use a boot diskette to start the installation.

Selecting an Installation Method

What type of installation method do you wish to use? The following installation methods are available:

♦ *CD-ROM* — If you have a CD-ROM drive and the Red Hat Linux CD-ROMs, you can use this method. You will need a boot diskette or a bootable CD-ROM. PCMCIA boot and driver diskettes may also be used. Refer to the next section for CD-ROM installation instructions.

♦ *Hard Drive* — If you have copied the Red Hat Linux ISO images to a local hard drive, you can use this method. You will need a boot diskette. PCMCIA boot and driver diskettes may also be used. See the "Installing from a Hard Drive" section later in this chapter for hard drive installation instructions.

♦ *NFS Image* — If you are installing from an NFS server using ISO images or a mirror image of Red Hat Linux, you can use this method. You will need a network boot diskette. PCMCIA boot and driver diskettes may also be used. See the "Installing via NFS" section later in this chapter for network installation instructions. Please note that NFS installations may also be performed in GUI mode.

♦ *FTP* — If you are installing directly from an FTP server, use this method. You will need a network boot diskette. PCMCIA boot and driver diskettes may also be used. See the "Installing via FTP" section later in this chapter for FTP installation instructions.

♦ *HTTP* — If you are installing directly from an HTTP (Web) server, use this method. You will need a network boot diskette. PCMCIA boot and driver diskettes may also be used. See the "Installing via HTTP" section in this chapter for HTTP installation instructions.

Installing from CD-ROM

To install Red Hat Linux from a CD-ROM, choose the CD-ROM option from the boot loader screen and select OK. When prompted, insert the Red Hat Linux CD into your CD-ROM drive (if you did not boot from the CD-ROM). When the CD is in the CD-ROM drive, select OK and press Enter.

> **NOTE** If you already have another operating system installed and want to create a dual boot system so that you can use both Red Hat Linux and the other operating system, read Appendix C for details.

The installation program will then probe your system and attempt to identify your CD-ROM drive. It will start by looking for an IDE (also known as an ATAPI) CD-ROM drive. If this is found, you will continue to the next stage of the installation process (see the "Welcome to Red Hat Linux" section later in this chapter).

> **NOTE** To abort the installation process at this time, reboot your machine and then eject the boot diskette or CD-ROM. You can safely cancel the installation at any point before the About to Install screen. See the "Preparing to Install" section later in this chapter for more information.

If your CD-ROM drive is not detected, and it is a SCSI CD-ROM, you can manually select the SCSI CD-ROM type when prompted. Select SCSI if your CD-ROM drive is attached to a supported SCSI adapter; the installation program will then ask you to choose a SCSI driver. Choose the driver that most closely resembles your adapter.

You may specify options for the driver if necessary; however, most drivers will detect your SCSI adapter automatically.

What If the IDE CD-ROM Was Not Found?

If you have an IDE (ATAPI) CD-ROM, but the installation program fails to find your IDE (ATAPI) CD-ROM and asks you what type of CD-ROM drive you have, restart the installation and at the boot: prompt enter **linux hdx=cdrom**. Replace the *x* with one of the following letters, depending on the interface the unit is connected to, and whether it is configured as master or slave (also known as primary and secondary):

a — First IDE controller, master

b — First IDE controller, slave

c — Second IDE controller, master

d — Second IDE controller, slave

If you have a third and/or fourth controller, continue assigning letters in alphabetical order going from controller to controller and master to slave.

Installing from a Hard Drive

Hard drive installations require the use of the ISO (or CD-ROM) images. An ISO image is a file containing an exact copy of a CD-ROM disk image. Because Red Hat Linux has so many packages included with its distribution, there are several ISO images available. After placing the required ISO images (the binary Red Hat Linux CD-ROMs) in a directory, choose to install from the hard drive.

> **NOTE** Hard drive installations only work from ext2, ext3, or FAT file systems. If you have a file system other than those listed here, such as reiserfs, you will not be able to perform a hard drive installation.

Next you will point the installation program at the directory where the ISO images reside to perform the installation. Verifying that the ISO images are intact before you attempt an installation will help to avoid problems that are often encountered during a hard drive installation. To verify the ISO images are intact prior to performing an installation, use an md5sum program (many md5sum programs are available for various operating systems). An md5sum program should be available on the same server as the ISO images.

> **NOTE** ISO images now have an md5sum embedded in them. To test the checksum integrity of an ISO image, at the installation boot prompt, type `linux mediacheck`.

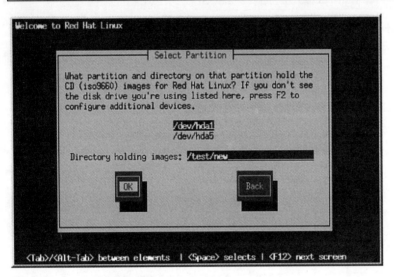

Figure 2-3. The Select Partition Dialog for Hard Drive Installation

The Select Partition dialog applies only if you are installing from a disk partition (that is, if you selected Hard Drive in the Installation Method dialog). This dialog allows you to name the disk partition and directory from which you are installing Red Hat Linux.

Enter the device name of the partition containing the Red Hat ISO images. There is also a field labeled Directory holding images. If the ISO images are not in the root directory of that partition, enter the path to the ISO images (for example, if the ISO images are in `/test/new/RedHat`, you would enter `/test/new`).

After you have identified the disk partition, you will see the Welcome dialog. See the "Welcome to Red Hat Linux" section later in this chapter to continue with the installation.

Installing via NFS

The NFS dialog (Figure 2-4) applies only if you are installing from an NFS server (if you booted from a network or PCMCIA boot disks and selected NFS Image in the Installation Method dialog).

Enter the fully-qualified domain name or IP address of your NFS server. For example, if you are installing from a host named `eastcoast` in the domain `redhat.com`, enter `eastcoast.redhat.com` in the NFS Server field.

Next, enter the name of the exported directory (the directory that contains the installation files).

If the NFS server is exporting a mirror of the Red Hat Linux installation tree, enter the directory that contains the `RedHat` directory. (If you do not know this directory path, ask your system administrator.) For example, if your NFS server contains the directory `/mirrors/redhat/i386/RedHat`, enter `/mirrors/redhat/i386`.

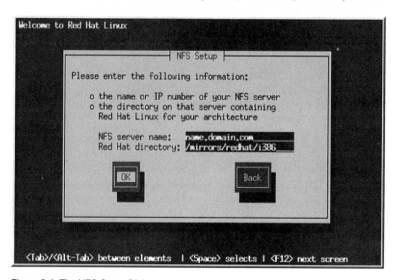

Figure 2-4. The NFS Setup Dialog

If the NFS server is exporting the ISO images of the Red Hat Linux CD-ROMs, enter the directory that contains the ISO images.

Next you will see the Welcome dialog. See the "Welcome to Red Hat Linux" section later in this chapter to continue with the installation.

Installing via FTP

The FTP dialog applies only if you are installing from an FTP server (if you selected FTP in the Installation Method dialog). This dialog allows you to identify the FTP server from which you are installing Red Hat Linux.

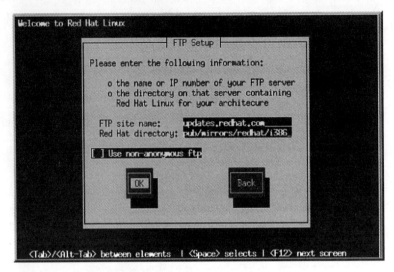

Figure 2-5. The FTP Setup Dialog

Enter the name or IP address of the FTP site you are installing from and the name of the directory containing the `RedHat` installation files for your architecture. For example, if the FTP site contains the directory `/mirrors/redhat/i386/RedHat`, enter `/mirrors/redhat/i386`.

If everything has been specified properly, a message box appears indicating that `base/hdlist` is being retrieved.

Next you will see the Welcome dialog. See the "Welcome to Red Hat Linux" section a bit later in this chapter to continue with the installation.

> **TIP** You can also install Red Hat Linux using ISO images without copying them into a single tree by loopback mounting them as: `disc1/`, `disc2/`, `disc3/`

Installing via HTTP

The HTTP dialog (Figure 2-6) applies only if you are installing from an HTTP server (if you selected HTTP in the Installation Method dialog). This dialog prompts you for information about the HTTP server from which you are installing Red Hat Linux.

Enter the name or IP address of the HTTP site you are installing from, and the name of the directory there containing the `RedHat` installation files for your architecture. For example, if

the HTTP site contains the directory /mirrors/redhat/i386/RedHat, enter
/mirrors/redhat/i386.

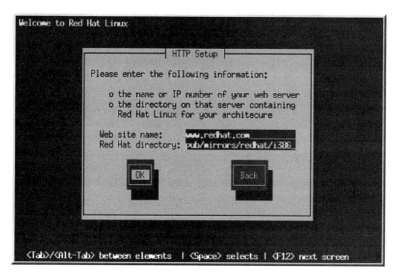

Figure 2-6. The HTTP Setup Dialog

If everything has been specified properly, a message box appears indicating that
base/hdlist is being retrieved.

Next you will see the Welcome dialog. See the next section to continue with the installation.

> **TIP** You can also install Red Hat Linux using ISO images without copying them into a single tree by
> loopback mounting them as: disc1/, disc2/, disc3/

Welcome to Red Hat Linux

The Welcome screen does not prompt you for any input. Feel free to read over the help text in
the left panel for additional instructions.

> **NOTE** Notice the Hide Help button at the bottom left corner of the screen. The help screen is open by
> default. If you do not want to view the help information, click on Hide Help to minimize the help portion of the
> screen.

Click on the Next button to continue.

Language Selection

Using your mouse, select the language you would prefer to use for the installation (see
Figure 2-7).

Selecting the appropriate language will also help target your time zone configuration later in the installation. The installation program will try to define the appropriate time zone based on what you specify on this screen.

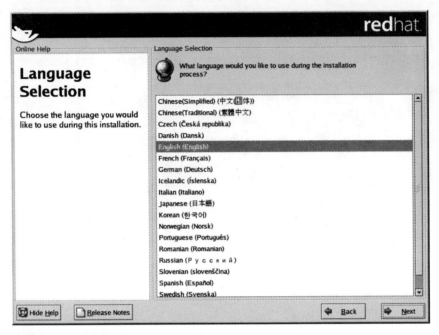

Figure 2-7. Language Selection

After selecting the appropriate language, click Next to continue.

Keyboard Configuration

Using your mouse, select the correct layout type (for example, U.S. English) for the keyboard you would prefer to use for the installation and as the system default (see Figure 2-7).

After making your selection, click Next to continue.

> **TIP** To change your keyboard layout type after you have completed the installation, click the Main Menu button and select System Settings ⇨ Keyboard (or type the `redhat-config-keyboard` command from a shell prompt) to launch the Keyboard Configuration tool. If you are not logged in as root, Linux will prompt you for the root password to continue.

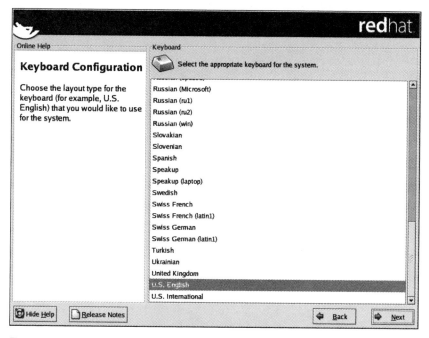

Figure 2-8. Keyboard Configuration

Mouse Configuration

Choose the correct mouse type for your system. If you cannot find an exact match, choose a mouse type that you are sure is compatible with your system (see Figure 2-10).

> **NOTE** If you are installing Red Hat Linux on a laptop computer, in most cases the pointing device will be PS/2 compatible.

To determine your mouse's interface, follow the mouse cable back to where it plugs into your system and use the following diagram to determine your mouse type.

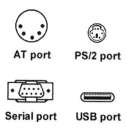

Figure 2-9. Determining Your Mouse Type

If you cannot find a mouse that you are sure is compatible with your system, select one of the Generic entries based on your mouse's number of buttons and its interface.

> **TIP** If you have a scroll mouse, select the MS Intellimouse entry (with your proper mouse port) as the compatible mouse type.

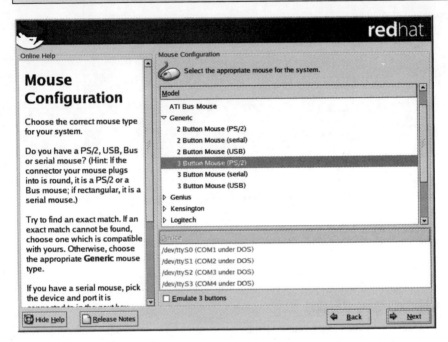

Figure 2-10. Mouse Configuration

If you have a PS/2, USB, or AT mouse, you do not need to pick a port and device. If you have a serial mouse, you should choose the correct port and device that your serial mouse is on.

The Emulate 3 buttons checkbox allows you to use a two-button mouse as if it had three buttons. In general, the graphical interface (the X Window System) is easier to use with a three-button mouse. If you select this checkbox, you can emulate a third, "middle" button by pressing both mouse buttons simultaneously.

To configure your mouse to work as a left-handed mouse, reset the order of the mouse buttons. To do this, after you have booted the system, type **gpm -B 321** at the shell prompt.

> **TIP** To change your mouse configuration after you have completed the installation, click the Main Menu button and select System Settings ⇨ Mouse (or type the `redhat-config-mouse` command from a shell prompt) to launch the Mouse Configuration tool. If you are not logged in as root, Linux will prompt you for the root password to continue.

Installation Type

Choose the type of installation you would like to perform. Red Hat Linux allows you to choose the installation type that best fits your needs. Your options are Personal Desktop, Workstation, Server, Custom, and Upgrade.

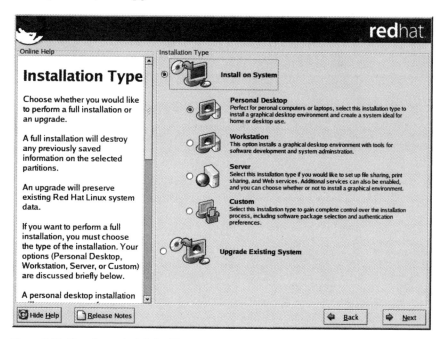

Figure 2-11. Choosing an Installation Type

To perform an upgrade, see Chapter 3.

For more information about the different installation classes, please refer to the "Selecting an Installation Method" section earlier in this chapter.

Disk Partitioning Setup

Partitioning allows you to divide your hard drive into isolated sections where each section behaves as if it were its own hard drive. Partitioning is particularly useful if you run more than one operating system. If you are not sure how you want your system to be partitioned, read Appendix D for more information.

On this screen, you can choose to perform automatic partitioning or manual partitioning using Disk Druid or `fdisk` (see Figure 2-12).

Automatic partitioning allows you to perform an installation without having to partition your drive(s) yourself. If you do not feel comfortable partitioning your system, it is recommended that you *do not* choose to partition manually and instead let the installation partition for you.

To partition manually, choose either the Disk Druid or `fdisk` (recommended for experts only) partitioning tool.

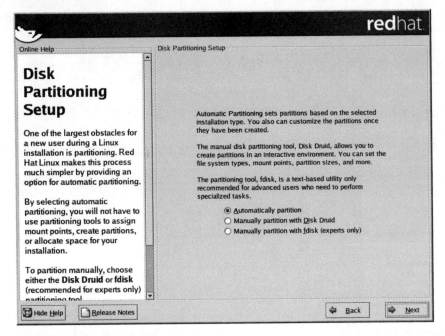

Figure 2-12. Disk Partitioning Setup

WARNING The Red Hat Update Agent downloads updated packages to `/var/spool/up2date` by default. If you partition the system manually and create a separate `/var` partition, be sure to create the partition large enough to download package updates.

If you chose to manually partition using Disk Druid, see the "Partitioning Your System Manually" section later in this chapter.

If you chose to manually partition using `fdisk`, see the "Partitioning with fdisk" section later in this chapter.

Automatic Partitioning

Automatic partitioning allows you to have some control concerning what data is removed (if any) from your system. Your options are:

♦ *Remove all Linux partitions on this system* — Select this option to remove only Linux partitions (partitions created from a previous Linux installation). This will not remove other partitions you may have on your hard drive(s) (such as VFAT or FAT32 partitions).

◆ *Remove all partitions on this system* — Select this option to remove all partitions on your hard drive(s) (this includes partitions created by other operating systems such as Windows' FAT or NTFS partitions).

> **CAUTION** If you select this option, all data on the selected hard drive(s) will be removed by the installation program. Do not select this option if you have information that you want to keep on the hard drive(s) where you are installing Red Hat Linux.

◆ *Keep all partitions and use existing free space* — Select this option to retain your current data and partitions, assuming you have enough free space available on your hard drive(s).

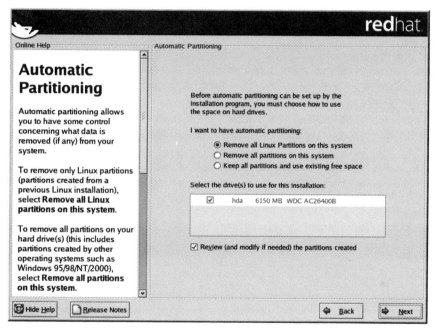

Figure 2-13. Automatic Partitioning

Using your mouse, choose the hard drive(s) on which you want Red Hat Linux to be installed. If you have two or more hard drives, you can choose which hard drive(s) should contain this installation.

> **NOTE** Unselected hard drives and any data on them will not be touched.

To review and make any necessary changes to the partitions created by automatic partitioning, select the Review option. After selecting Review and clicking Next to move forward, you will see the partitions created for you displayed in Disk Druid. You will also be able to make modifications to these partitions if they do not meet your needs.

Click Next to proceed after you have made your selections.

Partitioning Your System Manually

If you chose automatic partitioning and did not select Review, please skip ahead to the "Network Configuration" section.

If you chose to partition manually with Disk Druid, see the "Partitioning with Disk Druid" section a bit later in this chapter. If you chose to manually partition with fdisk, please skip ahead to the "Partitioning with fdisk" section.

Recommended Partitioning Scheme

Whether you use Disk Druid or fdisk, Red Hat recommends that you create the following partitions:

♦ *A swap partition (at least 32MB)* — Swap partitions are used to support virtual memory. In other words, data is written to a swap partition when there is not enough RAM to store the data your system is processing. The size of your swap partition should be equal to twice your computer's RAM, or 32MB, whichever amount is larger.

For example, if you have 1GB of RAM or less, your swap partition should be at least equal to the amount of RAM on your system, up to two times the RAM. For more than 1GB of RAM, a maximum of 2GB of swap is recommended.

♦ *A /boot partition (100MB)* — The partition mounted on /boot contains the operating system kernel (which allows your system to boot Red Hat Linux), along with files used during the bootstrap process. Due to the limitations of most PC BIOSes, creating a small partition to hold these files is a good idea. For most users, a 100MB boot partition is sufficient.

> **WARNING** Do not create your /boot partition as an LVM partition type. The boot loaders included with Red Hat Linux cannot read LVM partitions and you will not be able to boot your Red Hat Linux system.
>
> If your hard drive is more than 1024 cylinders (and your system was manufactured more than two years ago), you may need to create a /boot partition if you want the root (/) partition to use all of the remaining space on your hard drive.

♦ *A root (/) partition (1.5-4.5GB)* — This is where the root (/) directory will be located. In this setup, all files (except those stored in /boot) are on the root partition. A 1.5GB root partition will permit the equivalent of a personal desktop or workstation installation (with *very* little free space), while a 4.5GB root partition will let you install every package.

Partitioning with Disk Druid

The partitioning tool used by the installation program is Disk Druid. With the exception of certain esoteric situations, Disk Druid can handle the partitioning requirements for a typical installation. If you chose automatic partitioning and selected Review, you can either accept the current partition settings (click Next), or modify the setup using Disk Druid.

At this point you must tell the installation program where to install Red Hat Linux. This is done by defining mount points for one or more disk partitions in which Red Hat Linux will be installed. You may also need to create and/or delete partitions at this time (see Figure 2-14).

> **NOTE** As you plan how to set up your partitions, keep in mind that at a bare minimum you need an appropriately-sized root partition, and a swap partition equal to twice the amount of RAM you have on the system. See Chapter 1 for space requirements; see the "Recommended Partitioning Scheme" section later in this chapter if you want some suggestions on how to set up your partitions.

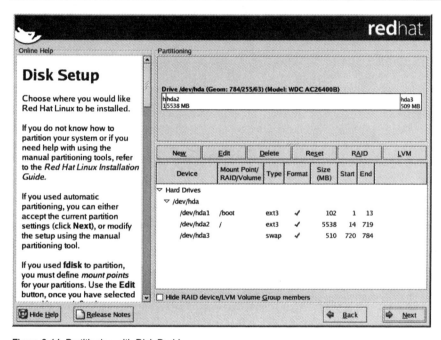

Figure 2-14. Partitioning with Disk Druid

Graphical Display of Hard Drive(s)

Disk Druid offers a graphical representation of your hard drive(s). Using your mouse, click once to highlight a particular field in the graphical display. Double-click to edit an existing partition or to create a partition out of existing free space.

Above the display, you will see the drive name (such as /dev/hda), the geom (which shows the hard disk's geometry and consists of three numbers representing the number of cylinders, heads, and sectors as reported by the hard disk), and the model of the hard drive as detected by the installation program.

Disk Druid's Buttons

Disk Druid's buttons control the utility's actions. These buttons are used to change the attributes of a partition (for example the file system type and mount point) and also to create

RAID devices. Buttons on this screen are also used to accept the changes you have made, or to exit Disk Druid. For further explanation, take a look at each button in order:

- ◆ *New* — Used to request a new partition. When selected, a dialog box appears containing fields (such as mount point and size) that must be filled in.

- ◆ *Edit* — Used to modify attributes of the partition currently selected in the Partitions section. Selecting Edit opens a dialog box. Some or all of the fields can be edited, depending on whether the partition information has already been written to disk. You can also edit free space as represented in the graphical display to create a new partition within that space. To do so, either highlight the free space and then select the Edit button or double-click on the free space to edit it.

- ◆ *Delete* — Used to remove the partition currently highlighted in the Current Disk Partitions section. You will be asked to confirm the deletion of any partition.

- ◆ *Reset* — Used to restore Disk Druid to its original state. All changes made will be lost if you reset the partitions.

- ◆ *RAID* — Used to provide redundancy to any or all disk partitions. It should only be used if you have experience using RAID. To read more about RAID, refer to the *Official Red Hat Linux Administrator's Guide* from Red Hat Press. To make a RAID device, you must first create software RAID partitions. After you have created two or more software RAID partitions, select RAID to join the software RAID partitions into a RAID device.

- ◆ *LVM* — Allows you to create an LVM logical volume. The role of LVM (Logical Volume Manager) is to present a simple logical view of underlying physical storage space, such as a hard drive(s). LVM manages individual physical disks — or to be more precise, the individual partitions present on them. It should only be used if you have experience using LVM. To create an LVM logical volume, you must first create partitions of type physical volume (LVM). Once you have created one or more physical volume (LVM) partitions, select LVM to create an LVM logical volume.

Partition Fields

Above the partition hierarchy are labels that display information about the partitions you are creating.

The labels are defined as follows:

- ◆ *Device* — This field displays the partition's device name.

- ◆ *Mount Point/RAID/Volume* — A mount point is the location within the directory hierarchy at which a volume exists; the volume is "mounted" at this location. This field indicates where the partition will be mounted. If a partition exists, but is not set, then you need to define its mount point. To do so, double-click on the partition or click the Edit button.

- ◆ *Type* — This field shows the partition's type (for example, ext2, ext3, or vfat).

- ◆ *Format* — This field shows if the partition being created will be formatted.

- ◆ *Size (MB)* — This field shows the partition's size in megabytes.

- ◆ *Start* — This field shows the sector on your hard drive where the partition begins.

♦ *End* — This field shows the sector on your hard drive where the partition ends.

♦ *Hide RAID device/LVM Volume Group members* — Select this option if you do not want to view any RAID device or LVM Volume Group members that have been created.

Adding Partitions

To add a new partition, select the New button. A dialog box appears.

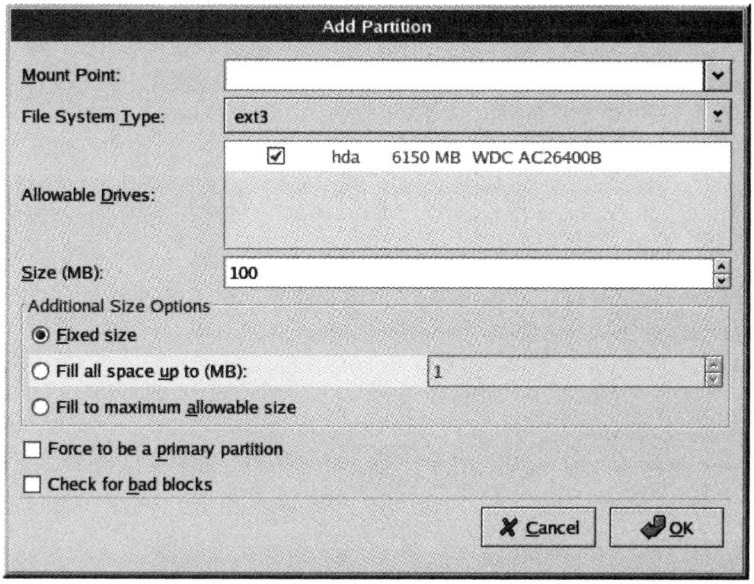

Figure 2-15. Creating a New Partition

The following list describes the major elements of the dialog box (refer to Figure 2-15).

♦ *Mount Point* — Enter the partition's mount point. For example, if this partition should be the root partition, enter /; enter /boot for the /boot partition, and so on. You can also use the pull-down menu to choose the correct mount point for your partition.

♦ *File System Type* — Using the pull-down menu, select the appropriate file system type for this partition. For more information on file system types, see the "File System Types" sidebar in this section.

♦ *Allowable Drives* — This field contains a list of the hard disks installed on your system. If a hard disk's box is highlighted, then a desired partition can be created on that hard disk. If the box is not checked, then the partition will never be created on that hard disk. By using different checkbox settings, you can have Disk Druid place partitions as you see fit, or let Disk Druid decide where partitions should go.

♦ *Size (Megs)* — Enter the size (in megabytes) of the partition. Note that this field starts with 100MB; unless changed, only a 100MB partition will be created.

◆ *Additional Size Options* — Choose whether to keep this partition at a fixed size, to allow it to *grow* (that is, fill up the available hard drive space) to a certain point, or to allow it to grow to fill any remaining hard drive space available. If you choose Fill all space up to (MB), you must give size constraints in the field to the right of this option. This allows you to keep a certain amount of space free on your hard drive for future use.

◆ *Force to be a primary partition* — Select whether the partition you are creating should be one of the first four partitions on the hard drive. If unselected, the partition created will be a logical partition. See Appendix D for more information.

◆ *Check for bad blocks* — Checking for bad blocks can help prevent data loss by locating the bad blocks on a drive and making a list of them to prevent using them in the future. If you wish to check for bad blocks while formatting each file system, please make sure to select this option.

> **NOTE** Because most newer hard drives are quite large in size, checking for bad blocks may take a long time; the length of time depends on the size of your hard drive. If you choose to check for bad blocks, you can monitor your progress on virtual console #6.

◆ *OK* — Select OK once you are satisfied with the settings and wish to create the partition.

◆ *Cancel* — Select Cancel if you do not want to create the partition.

File System Types

Red Hat Linux allows you to create different partition types, based on the file system they will use. The following is a brief description of the different file systems available and how they can be utilized.

ext2 — An ext2 file system supports standard Unix file types (regular files, directories, symbolic links, etc). It provides the ability to assign long file names, up to 255 characters. Versions prior to Red Hat Linux 7.2 used ext2 file systems by default.

ext3 — The ext3 file system is based on the ext2 file system and has one main advantage — journaling. Using a journaling file system reduces time spent recovering a file system after a crash as there is no need to fsck the file system (the fsck utility is used to check the file system for metadata consistency and optionally repair one or more Linux file systems). The ext3 file system will be selected by default and is highly recommended.

physical volume (LVM) — Creating one or more physical volume (LVM) partitions allows you to create an LVM logical volume.

software RAID — Creating two or more software RAID partitions allows you to create a RAID device. For more information regarding RAID, see the *Official Red Hat Linux Administrator's Guide* from Red Hat Press.

swap — Swap partitions are used to support virtual memory. In other words, data is written to a swap partition when there is not enough RAM to store the data your system is processing.

vfat — The VFAT file system is a Linux file system that is compatible with Windows long filenames on the FAT file system.

Editing Partitions

To edit a partition, select the Edit button or double-click on the existing partition.

> **NOTE** If the partition already exists on your hard disk, you will only be able to change the partition's mount point. If you want to make any other changes, you will need to delete the partition and recreate it.

Deleting a Partition

To delete a partition, highlight it in the Partitions section and click the Delete button. You will be asked to confirm the deletion.

Partitioning with fdisk

This section applies only if you chose to use fdisk to partition your system.

To partition your system without using fdisk, see the "Automatic Partitioning" or "Partitioning with Disk Druid" sections earlier in this chapter.

If you have already completed disk partitioning, skip to the "Boot Loader Configuration" section later in this chapter for further installation instructions.

> **CAUTION** Unless you have previously used fdisk and understand how it works, we do not recommend that you use it if you have any data on your computer that you do not want to lose. It is much easier for new users to accidentally corrupt or lose data using fdisk.

Disk Druid is easier to understand than fdisk. To exit fdisk, click Back to return to the previous screen, deselect fdisk, and then click Next.

If you have chosen to use fdisk, the next screen will prompt you to select a drive to partition using fdisk. After choosing which drive to partition, you will be presented with the fdisk command screen. If you do not know what command to use, type **m** at the prompt for help.

When you are finished making partitions, type **w** to save your changes and quit. You will be taken back to the original fdisk screen where you can partition another drive or continue the installation.

> **NOTE** None of the changes you make will take effect until you save them and exit fdisk using the **w** command. You can quit fdisk at any time without saving changes by using the **q** command.

After you have partitioned your drive(s), click Next. You will need to use Disk Druid to assign mount points to the partitions you just created with fdisk.

You will not be able to add new partitions using Disk Druid, but you can edit mount points for the partitions you have already created. For each partition created with fdisk, click on the Edit button, choose the appropriate mount point for that partition from the pull-down menu, and click OK.

Boot Loader Configuration

In order to boot the system without a boot diskette, you usually need to install a boot loader. A boot loader is the first program that runs when a computer starts. It is responsible for loading and transferring control to the operating system kernel software. The kernel, in turn, initializes the rest of the operating system.

The installation program provides two boot loaders for you to choose from:

♦ GRUB (GRand Unified Bootloader), which is installed by default, is a very powerful boot loader. GRUB can load a variety of free operating systems, as well as proprietary operating systems with chain-loading (the mechanism for loading unsupported operating systems by loading another boot loader, such as MS-DOS or Windows).

♦ LILO (LInux LOader) is a versatile boot loader for Linux. LILO does not depend on a specific file system, can boot Linux kernel images from floppy diskettes and hard disks, and can even boot other operating systems.

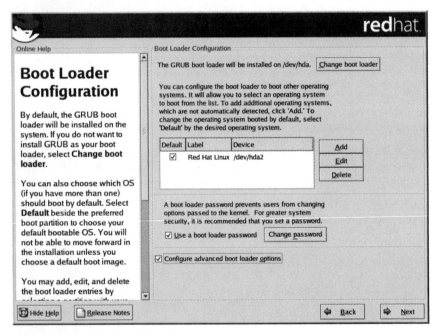

Figure 2-16. Boot Loader Configuration

If you do not want to install GRUB as your boot loader, click Change boot loader. You can then choose to install LILO or choose not to install a boot loader at all.

If you already have a boot loader that can boot Linux and do not want to overwrite your current boot loader, or if you plan to boot the system using boot diskettes, choose Do not install a boot loader by clicking on the Change boot loader button.

> **CAUTION** If you choose not to install GRUB or LILO for any reason, you will not be able to boot the system directly, and you will need to use another boot method (such as a boot diskette). Use this option only if you are sure you have another way of booting the system!

Every bootable partition is listed, including partitions used by other operating systems. The partition holding the system's root file system will have a label of Red Hat Linux (for GRUB) or Linux (for LILO). Other partitions may also have boot labels. If you would like to add or change the boot label for other partitions that have been detected by the installation program, click once on the partition to select it. Once selected, you can change the boot label by clicking the Edit button.

Select Default beside the preferred boot partition to choose your default bootable OS. You will not be able to move forward in the installation unless you choose a default boot image.

> **NOTE** The Label column lists what you must enter at the boot prompt in non-graphical boot loaders in order to boot the desired operating system.

After loading the GRUB boot screen, use the arrow keys to choose a boot label or type **e** for edit. You will be presented with a list of items in the configuration file for the boot label you have selected.

At the graphical LILO screen, press Ctrl-X to exit to the `boot :` prompt. If you forget the boot labels defined on your system, you can always press Tab at the prompt to display a list of defined boot labels.

Boot loader passwords provide a security mechanism in an environment where physical access to your server is available.

> **CAUTION** If you are installing a boot loader, you should create a password to protect your system. Without a boot loader password, users with access to your system can pass options to the kernel, which can compromise your system security. With a boot loader password in place, the password must first be entered in order to select any non-standard boot options.

If you choose to use a boot loader password to enhance your system security, be sure to select the checkbox labeled Use a boot loader password.

Once selected, enter a password and confirm it.

To configure more advanced boot loader options, such as changing the drive order or passing options to the kernel, be sure Configure advanced boot loader options is selected before clicking Next.

Advanced Boot Loader Configuration

Now that you have chosen which boot loader to install, you can also determine where you want the boot loader to be installed. You may install the boot loader in one of two places:

- *The master boot record (MBR)* — This is the recommended place to install a boot loader unless the MBR already starts another operating system loader, such as System Commander. The MBR is a special area on your hard drive that is automatically loaded by your computer's BIOS, and is the earliest point at which the boot loader can take control of the boot process. If you install it in the MBR, when your machine boots, GRUB (or LILO) will present a boot prompt. You can then boot Red Hat Linux or any other operating system that you have configured the boot loader to boot.

♦ *The first sector of your boot partition* — This is recommended if you are already using another boot loader on your system. In this case, your other boot loader will take control first. You can then configure that boot loader to start GRUB (or LILO), which will then boot Red Hat Linux.

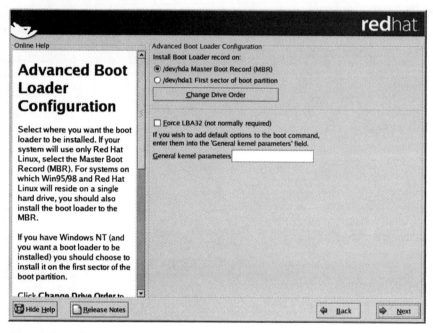

Figure 2-17. Boot Loader Installation

If your system will use only Red Hat Linux, you should choose the MBR. For systems with Windows 95/98, you should also install the boot loader to the MBR so that it can boot both operating systems.

> **WARNING** For systems with Windows NT/2000/XP, you should install the boot loader on the first sector of the partition or the Linux boot loader will overwrite the Windows boot loader and you will no longer be able to boot Windows.

Click the Change Drive Order button if you would like to rearrange the drive order. Changing the drive order may be useful if you have multiple SCSI adapters or both SCSI and IDE adapters and want to boot from the SCSI device.

The Force LBA32 (not normally required) option allows you to exceed the 1024 cylinder limit for the /boot partition. If you have a system that supports the LBA32 extension for booting operating systems above the 1024 cylinder limit and you want to place your /boot partition above cylinder 1024, you should select this option.

If you wish to add default options to the boot command, enter them into the Kernel parameters field. Any options you enter will be passed to the Linux kernel every time it boots.

Rescue Mode

If you need to use rescue mode, there are several options available to you:

♦ Using the CD-ROM to boot, type `linux rescue` at the `boot:` prompt.

♦ Booting your system from an installation boot diskette made from the `boot.img` image. This method requires that the Red Hat Linux CD-ROM #1 be inserted as the rescue image or that the rescue image reside on the hard drive as an ISO image. After booting using this diskette, type `linux rescue` at the `boot:` prompt.

♦ Booting from a network diskette made from the `bootnet.img` or PCMCIA boot diskettes made from `pcmcia.img`. After booting using this diskette, type `linux rescue` at the `boot:` prompt. You can only do this if your network connection is working. You will need to identify the network host and transfer type.

For more information on Rescue Mode, see Appendix A.

Alternative Boot Loaders

If you do not wish to use a boot loader, you have several alternatives:

♦ *Boot diskette* — You can use the boot diskette created by the installation program (if you create one).

♦ *LOADLIN* — You can load Linux from MS-DOS. Unfortunately, this requires a copy of the Linux kernel (and an initial RAM disk, if you have a SCSI adapter) to be available on an MS-DOS partition. The only way to accomplish this is to boot your Red Hat Linux system using some other method (for example, from a boot diskette) and then copy the kernel to an MS-DOS partition. LOADLIN is available from the following URL and associated mirror sites:

```
ftp://metalab.unc.edu/pub/Linux/system/boot/dualboot/
```

♦ *SYSLINUX* — SYSLINUX is an MS-DOS program very similar to LOADLIN. It is available from the following URL and associated mirror sites:

```
ftp://metalab.unc.edu/pub/Linux/system/boot/loaders/
```

♦ *Commercial boot loaders* — You can load Linux using commercial boot loaders. For example, System Commander and Partition Magic are able to boot Linux (but still require GRUB or LILO to be installed in your Linux root partition).

NOTE Boot loaders such as LOADLIN and System Commander are considered to be third-party boot loaders and are not supported by Red Hat.

Network Configuration

If you do not have a network device, you will not see this screen. In that case, you can skip ahead to the next section.

If you have a network device and you have not already configured your networking (such as booting from a network boot disk you created and entering in your network information as prompted), you now have the opportunity to do so.

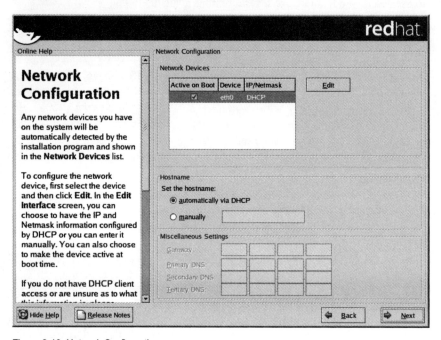

Figure 2-18. Network Configuration

The installation program will automatically detect any network devices you have and display them in the Network Devices list.

After selecting your network device, click Edit. From the Edit Interface dialog you can choose to configure the IP address and netmask of the device via DHCP (or manually if DHCP is not selected) and you can choose to activate the device at boot time. If you select Activate on Boot, your network interface will be started when you boot. If you do not have DHCP client access or you are unsure what to provide here, contact your network administrator.

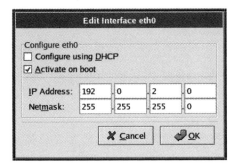

Figure 2-19. Editing a Network Device

NOTE Do not use the numbers shown in the figure's sample configuration. These values will not work for your own network configuration. If you are not sure what values to enter, contact your network administrator for assistance.

If you have a hostname (fully qualified domain name) for the network device, you can choose to have DHCP (Dynamic Host Configuration Protocol) automatically detect it or you can manually enter the hostname in the field provided.

TIP Even if your computer is not part of a network, you can enter a hostname for your system. If you do not take this opportunity to enter a name, your system will be known as localhost.

Finally, if you entered the IP and netmask information manually, you may also enter the gateway address and the primary, secondary, and tertiary DNS addresses.

TIP To change your network configuration after you have completed the installation, click System Settings ⇨ Network Device Control (or type the redhat-config-network command from a shell prompt) to launch the Network Administration tool. If you are not logged in as root, Linux will prompt you for the root password to continue.

Firewall Configuration

Red Hat Linux offers firewall protection for enhanced system security. A firewall exists between your computer and the network, and determines which resources on your computer remote users on the network can access. A properly configured firewall can greatly increase the security of your system.

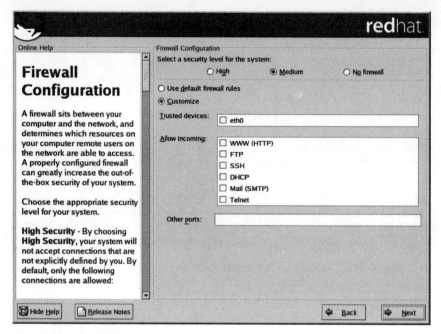

Figure 2-20. Firewall Configuration

Choose the appropriate security level for your system. The following sections discuss the three choices: High, Medium, and No Firewall.

> **TIP** To change your firewall configuration after you have completed the installation, click the Main Menu button and select System Settings ⇨ Security Level (or type the `redhat-config-securitylevel` command from a shell prompt) to launch the Security Level Configuration tool. If you are not logged in as root, Linux will prompt you for the root password to continue.

High

If you choose High, your system will not accept connections (other than the default settings) that are not explicitly defined by you. By default, only the following connections are allowed:

- ◆ DNS replies
- ◆ DHCP (so that any network interfaces that use DHCP can be properly configured)

If you choose High, your firewall will not allow the following:

- ◆ Active mode FTP (passive mode FTP, used by default in most clients, should still work)
- ◆ IRC DCC file transfers
- ◆ RealAudio
- ◆ Remote X Window System clients

If you are connecting your system to the Internet but do not plan to run a server, this is the safest choice. If additional services are needed, you can choose Customize to allow specific services through the firewall.

> **NOTE** If you select a medium or high firewall to be setup during this installation, network authentication methods (NIS and LDAP) will not work.

Medium

If you choose Medium, your firewall will not allow remote machines to have access to certain resources on your system. By default, access to the following resources are not allowed:

♦ Ports lower than 1023 — The standard reserved ports, used by most system services, such as FTP, SSH, telnet, HTTP, and NIS.

♦ The NFS server port (2049) — NFS is disabled for both remote severs and local clients.

♦ The local X Window System display for remote X clients.

♦ The X Font server port (by default, xfs does not listen on the network; it is disabled in the font server).

If you want to allow resources such as RealAudio while still blocking access to normal system services, choose Medium. Select Customize to allow specific services through the firewall.

> **NOTE** If you select a medium or high firewall to be set up during this installation, network authentication methods (NIS and LDAP) will not work.

No Firewall

No firewall provides complete access to your system and does no security checking. Security checking is the disabling of access to certain services. This should only be selected if you are running on a trusted network (not the Internet) or plan to do more firewall configuration later.

Choose Customize to add trusted devices or to allow additional incoming services.

♦ *Trusted Devices* — Selecting any of the Trusted Devices allows access to your system for all traffic from that device; it is excluded from the firewall rules. For example, if you are running a local network but are connected to the Internet via a PPP dialup, you can check eth0 and any traffic coming from your local network will be allowed. Selecting eth0 as trusted means all traffic over the Ethernet is allowed, put the ppp0 interface is still protected by the firewall. If you want to restrict traffic on an interface, leave it unchecked.

> **CAUTION** It is not recommended that you make any device that is connected to public networks, such as the Internet, a trusted device.

♦ *Allow Incoming* — Enabling these options allow the specified services to pass through the firewall. Note, during a workstation installation, the majority of these services are *not* installed on the system.

♦ *DHCP* — If you allow incoming DHCP queries and replies, you allow any network interface that uses DHCP to determine its IP address. DHCP is normally enabled. If DHCP is not enabled, your computer can no longer get an IP address.

♦ *SSH* — Secure Shell (SSH) is a suite of tools for logging into and executing commands on a remote machine. If you plan to use SSH tools to access your machine through a firewall, enable this option. You need to have the `openssh-server` package installed in order to access your machine remotely using SSH tools.

♦ *Telnet* — Telnet is a protocol for logging into remote machines. Telnet communications are unencrypted and provide no security from network snooping. Allowing incoming Telnet access is not recommended. If you do want to allow inbound Telnet access, you will need to install the `telnet-server` package.

♦ *WWW (HTTP)* — The HTTP protocol is used by Apache (and by other Web servers) to serve Web pages. If you plan on making your Web server publicly available, enable this option. This option is not required for viewing pages locally or for developing Web pages. You will need to install the `httpd` package if you want to serve Web pages.

> **NOTE** Enabling WWW (HTTP) will not open a port for HTTPS. To enable HTTPS, specify it in the Other ports field.

♦ *Mail (SMTP)* — If you want to allow incoming mail delivery through your firewall so that remote hosts can connect directly to your machine to deliver mail, enable this option. You do not need to enable this if you collect your mail from your ISP's server using POP3 or IMAP, or if you use a tool such as `fetchmail`. Note that an improperly configured SMTP server can allow remote machines to use your server to send spam (*spam* is a term for unsolicited email).

♦ *FTP* — The FTP protocol is used to transfer files between machines on a network. If you plan on making your FTP server publicly available, enable this option. You need to install the `wuftpd` (and possibly the `anonftp`) package for this option to be useful.

♦ *Other ports* — You can allow access to ports that are not listed here by listing them in this field. Use the following format: `port:protocol`. For example, if you want to allow IMAP access through your firewall, you can specify `imap:tcp`. You can also explicitly specify numeric ports; to allow UDP packets on port 1234 through the firewall, enter `1234:udp`. To specify multiple ports, separate them with commas.

> **TIP** To change your security level configuration after you have completed the installation, click the Main Menu button and select System Settings ⇨ Security Level (or type the `redhat-config-securitylevel` command from a shell prompt) to launch the Security Level Configuration tool. If you are not logged in as root, Linux will prompt you for the root password to continue.

Language Support Selection

Red Hat Linux can install and support multiple languages for use on your system.

You must select a language to use as the default language. The default language will be used on the system once the installation is complete. If you choose to install other languages during this installation, you can change your default language after the installation.

If you are only going to use one language on your system, selecting only that language will save significant disk space. The default language is the language you selected to use during the installation.

CAUTION If you select only one language, you will only be able to use that specified language after the installation is complete.

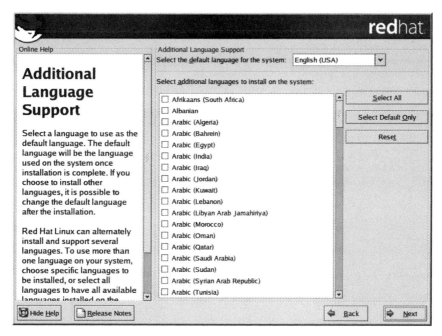

Figure 2-21. Language Support Selection

To use more than one language on your system, choose specific languages to be installed or select all languages to have all available languages installed on your Red Hat Linux system.

Use the Reset button to cancel your selections. Resetting will revert to the default; only the language you selected for use during the installation will be installed.

TIP To change the language configuration after you have completed the installation, use the Language Configuration Tool. System Settings ⇨ Language (or type the `redhat-config-language` command from a shell prompt) to launch the Language Selection tool. If you are not logged in as root, Linux will prompt you for the root password to continue.

Time Zone Configuration

You can set your time zone by selecting your computer's physical location or by specifying your time zone's offset from Universal Time, Coordinated (UTC).

Notice the two tabs at the top of the screen (see Figure 2-22). The first tab allows you to configure your time zone by your location.

On the interactive map, you can also click on a specific city, which is marked by a yellow dot; a red X will appear indicating your selection. You can also scroll through a list and choose a time zone.

The second tab allows you to specify a UTC offset. The tab displays a list of offsets to choose from, as well as an option to set daylight saving time.

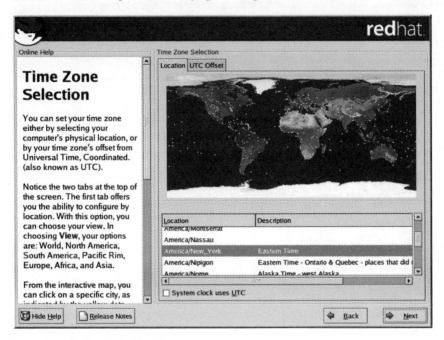

Figure 2-22. Configuring the Time Zone

On both tabs, you can select System Clock uses UTC. Please select this if you know that your system is set to UTC.

> **TIP** To change your time zone configuration after you have completed the installation, click the Main Menu button and select System Settings ⇨ Date and Time (or type the `redhat-config-date` command from a shell prompt) to launch the Date/Time Properties tool. If you are not logged in as root, it will prompt you for the root password to continue.

Account Configuration

The Account Configuration screen allows you to set your root password. Additionally, you can set up user accounts for you to log in to once the installation is complete.

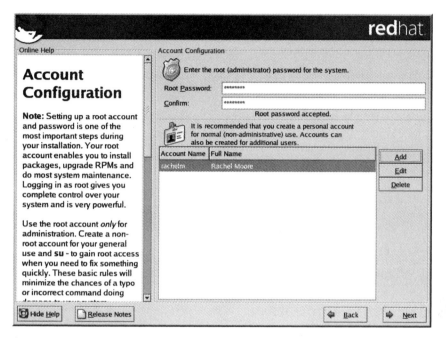

Figure 2-23. Account Creation

Setting the Root Password

Setting up a root account and password is one of the most important steps during your installation. The root account (sometimes called the *superuser*) is similar to the administrator account used on Windows NT machines. The root account is used to install packages, upgrade RPMs, and perform most system maintenance. Logging in as root gives you complete control over your system.

WARNING Because the root user has complete access to the entire system, logging in as the root user is best done *only* to perform system maintenance or administration. The root account does not operate within the restrictions placed on normal user accounts, so changes made as root can have implications for your entire system. Following this important rule will minimize the chances of a typo or an incorrect command damaging your system.

To become root when logged into another account, for instance if you need to fix something quickly, you can type **su** - at the shell prompt in a terminal window and then press Enter; then enter the root password and press Enter.

The installation program will prompt you to set a root password2 for your system. A *root password* is the administrative password for your Red Hat Linux system. You must enter a root password; the installation program will not let you proceed to the next section without entering a root password.

The root password must be at least six characters long; the password you type is not echoed to the screen. You must enter the password twice; if the two passwords do not match, the installation program will ask you to enter them again.

You should make the root password something you can remember, but not something that is easy for someone else to guess. Your name, your phone number, `qwerty`, `password`, `root`, `123456`, and `anteater` are all examples of bad passwords. Good passwords mix numerals with upper and lower case letters and do not contain dictionary words: `Aard387vark` or `420BMttNT`, for example. Remember that the password is case-sensitive. It is recommended that you do not write down this or any password you create; if you do write down your password, keep it in a secure place.

CAUTION Do not use one of the example passwords offered in this book. Using one of these passwords could be considered a security risk.

TIP To change your root password after you have completed the installation, use the Root Password Tool. Type the `redhat-config-rootpassword` command in a shell prompt to launch the Root Password Tool. If you are not logged in as root, it will prompt you for the root password to continue.

Setting Up User Accounts

If you choose to create a user account now, you will have an account to log in to once the installation has completed. This allows you to safely and easily log into your computer without having to be root to create your user account.

Figure 2-24. Creating a User Account

Click the Add button to add a new, non-root, user. Enter a user name for the user account. Next, enter and confirm a password for that user account. Enter the full name of the account user and click OK. Your account information will be added to the account list. You can also Edit or Delete the user accounts you have created and no longer want.

> **TIP** To change your user account configuration after you have completed the installation, click the Main Menu button and choose System Tools ⇨ User Manager (or, at the command prompt, enter the `redhat-config-users` command) to launch the User Manager. If you are not logged in as root, your system will prompt you for the root password to continue.

Authentication Configuration

If you are performing a personal desktop, workstation, or server installation, please skip ahead to the next section. You may skip this section if you will not be setting up network passwords. If you do not know whether you should do this, ask your system administrator for assistance.

Unless you are setting up NIS *(Network Information Service)* authentication, you will notice that only MD5 and shadow passwords are selected (see Figure 2-25). We recommend you use both to make your machine as secure as possible.

To configure the NIS option, you must be connected to an NIS network. If you are not sure whether you are connected to an NIS network, ask your system administrator.

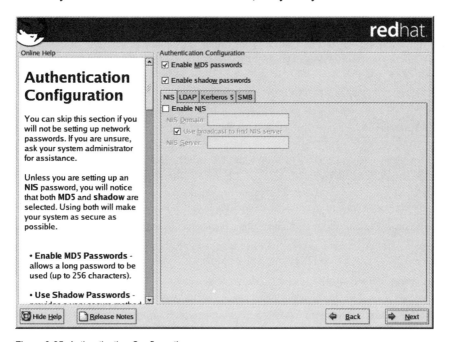

Figure 2-25. Authentication Configuration

The following list describes the options you can configure on the Authentication Configuration screen:

◆ *Enable MD5 passwords* — Allows a long password to be used (up to 256 characters), instead of the standard eight characters or less.

◆ *Enable shadow passwords* — Provides a secure method for retaining passwords. The passwords are stored in /etc/shadow, which can only be read by root.

◆ *Enable NIS*— Allows you to run a group of computers in the same NIS domain with a common password and group file. You can choose from the following options:

   • **NIS Domain:** Allows you to specify the domain or group of computers your system belongs to.

   • **Use broadcast to find NIS server:** Allows you to broadcast a message to your local area network to find an available NIS server.

   • **NIS Server:** Causes your computer to use a specific NIS server, rather than broadcasting a message to the local area network asking for any available server to host your system.

> **NOTE** If you have selected a medium or high firewall to be set up during this installation, network authentication methods (NIS and LDAP) will not work.

◆ *Enable LDAP* — Tells your computer to use LDAP for some or all authentication. LDAP consolidates certain types of information within your organization. For example, all of the different lists of users within your organization can be merged into one LDAP directory. For more information about LDAP, see the *Official Red Hat Linux Administrator's Guide* from Red Hat Press. You can choose from the following options:

   • **LDAP Server:** Allows you to access a specified server (by providing an IP address) running the LDAP protocol.

   • **LDAP Base DN:** Allows you to look up user information by its Distinguished Name (DN).

   • **Use TLS (Transport Layer Security) lookups:** Allows LDAP to send encrypted user names and passwords to an LDAP server before authentication.

◆ *Enable Kerberos* — Kerberos is a secure system for providing network authentication services. For more information about Kerberos, see the *Official Red Hat Linux Administrator's Guide* from Red Hat Press. There are three options to choose from here:

   • **Realm:** Allows you to access a network that uses Kerberos, composed of one or a few servers (also known as KDCs) and a potentially large number of clients.

   • **KDC (Key Distribution Center):** Allows you access to the KDC, a machine that issues Kerberos tickets (sometimes called a Ticket Granting Server or TGS).

   • **Admin Server:** Allows you to access a server running kadmind.

◆ *Enable SMB Authentication* — Configures PAM to use an SMB server to authenticate users. You must supply two pieces of information here:

   • **SMB Server:** Indicates which SMB server your workstation will connect to for authentication.

   • **SMBWorkgroup:** Indicates which workgroup the configured SMB servers are in.

TIP To change your authentication configuration after you have completed the installation, click the Main Menu button and choose System Settings ➪ Authentication (or type the `authconfig` command from a shell prompt) to launch the Authentication Configuration tool. If you are not logged in as root, Linux will prompt you for the root password to continue.

Package Group Selection

After your partitions have been selected and configured for formatting, you are ready to select packages for installation.

NOTE Unless you choose a custom installation, the installation program will automatically choose most packages for you.

You can select package groups, which group components together according to function (for example, the X Window System), individual packages, or a combination of the two.

To select a component, check the checkbox beside it so that a check appears the checkbox (see Figure 2-26).

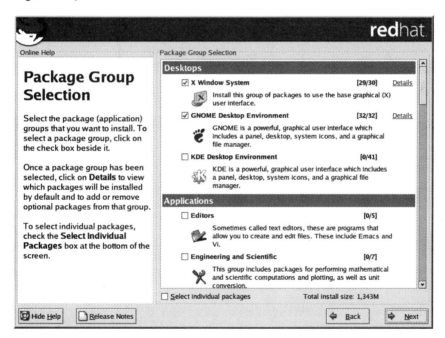

Figure 2-26. Package Group Selection

Select each component you wish to install. Selecting Everything (at the end of the component list) during a custom installation installs all packages included with Red Hat Linux.

After selecting a package group, click on Details to view which packages will be installed by default and feel free to add or remove optional packages from that group.

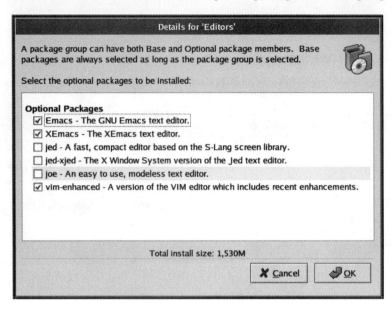

Figure 2-27. Package Group Details

To select packages individually, check the Select Individual Packages box at the bottom of the screen.

Selecting Individual Packages

After selecting the components you wish to install, you can select or deselect individual packages using your mouse (see Figure 2-28).

You can choose to view the individual packages in Tree View or Flat View. *Tree View* allows you to see the packages grouped by application type. When you expand this list (by double-clicking on the folder arrow beside a package group name) and pick one group, the list of packages in that group appears in the panel on the right. *Flat View* allows you to see all of the packages in an alphabetical listing on the right of the screen.

> **TIP** To sort packages alphabetically, click on the Package tab. To sort packages by size, click on the Size (MB) tab.

To select an individual package, double-click the checkbox beside the package name. A check mark in the box means that a package has been selected.

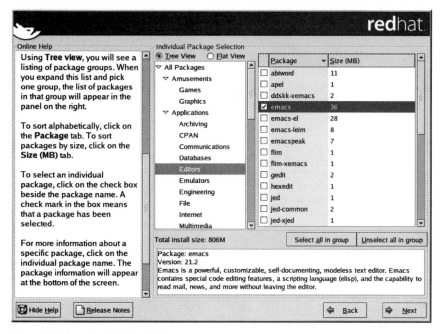

Figure 2-28. Selecting Individual Packages

For more information about a specific package, click on the individual package name. The package information will appear at the bottom of the screen.

You can also select or deselect all packages listed within a particular group by clicking on the Select all in group or Unselect all in group buttons.

> **NOTE** Some packages (such as the kernel and certain libraries) are required for every system and are not available to select or deselect. These base packages are selected by default.

Unresolved Dependencies

In order to work correctly, many software packages depend on other software packages that must be installed on your system. For example, many of the graphical Red Hat system administration tools require the python and pythonlib packages. To make sure your system has all the packages it needs in order to be fully functional, the installation program checks these package *dependencies* each time you install or remove software packages. If any package requires another package which you have not selected to install, the program presents a list of these unresolved dependencies and gives you the opportunity to resolve them (see Figure 2-29).

> **NOTE** The Unresolved Dependencies screen appears only if you are missing packages that are needed by the packages you have selected.

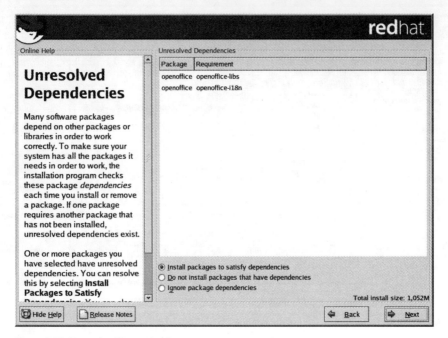

Figure 2-29. Unresolved Dependencies

TIP At the bottom of the screen, under the list of missing packages, an Install Packages to Satisfy Dependencies checkbox is selected by default. If you leave this checked, the installation program will resolve dependencies automatically by adding all required packages to the list of selected packages.

If you do not wish to install packages that require other packages, select the Do not install packages that have dependencies option.

To install only the packages you have selected and leave the dependencies unresolved, select Ignore package dependencies.

TIP To install or remove packages after you have completed the installation, click the Main Menu button and choose System Settings ⇨ Packages (or type the `redhat-config-packages` command from a shell prompt) to launch the Package Management tool. If you are not logged in as root, Linux will prompt you for the root password to continue.

Preparing to Install

You should now see a screen preparing you for the installation of Red Hat Linux. For your reference, a complete log of your installation can be found in `/root/install.log` after you reboot your system.

> **WARNING** If, for some reason, you would rather not continue with the installation process, this is your last opportunity to safely cancel the process and reboot your machine without any changes being made to your system. After pressing the Next button, partitions will be written and packages will be installed — and your hard drive(s) will be rewritten. If you wish to abort the installation, you should reboot now before any existing information on any hard drive is rewritten.

To cancel this installation process, press your computer's Reset button or use the Control-Alt-Delete key combination to restart your machine.

Installing Packages

At this point there is nothing left for you to do until all the packages have been installed. How quickly the package installation process happens depends on the number of packages you have selected and your computer's processor speed, available RAM, and other hardware.

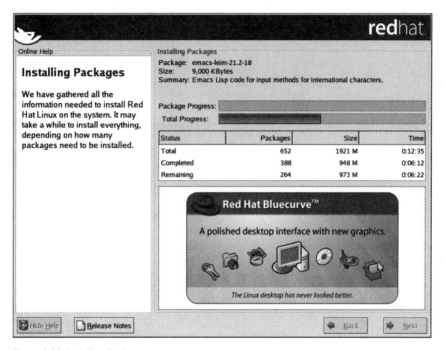

Figure 2-30. Installing Packages

Boot Disk Creation

To create a boot disk, insert a blank, formatted diskette into your diskette drive (see Figure 2-31) and click Next. It is highly recommended that you create a boot disk. If, for some reason, your system were not able to boot properly using GRUB, LILO, or a third-party boot loader, a boot disk would enable you to properly boot your Red Hat Linux system.

After a short delay, your boot disk will be created; remove it from your diskette drive and label it clearly.

> **TIP** If you want to create a boot disk after the installation, you will be able to do so. For more information, please see the mkbootdisk man page, by typing **man mkbootdisk** at the shell prompt.

If you do not want to create a boot disk, make sure to select the appropriate option before you click Next.

> **CAUTION** If you boot your system with the boot disk (instead of GRUB or LILO), make sure you create a new boot disk whenever you make any changes to your kernel (including the installation of a new kernel). Recovering with a boot disk that includes an archaic kernel on it can be a scarring experience.

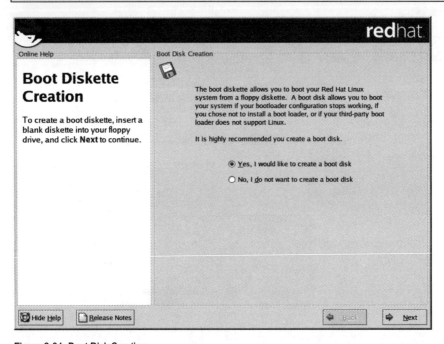

Figure 2-31. Boot Disk Creation

X Configuration — Monitor and Customization

In order to complete X configuration, you must configure your monitor and customize your X settings.

Video Card Configuration

If you decided to install the X Window System packages, you now have the opportunity to configure an X server for your system. If you did not choose to install the X Window System packages, skip ahead to the "Installation Complete!" section later in this chapter.

If your video card does not appear on the list, X may not support it. However, if you have technical knowledge about your card, you may choose Unlisted Card and attempt to configure it by matching your card's video chipset with one of the available X servers.

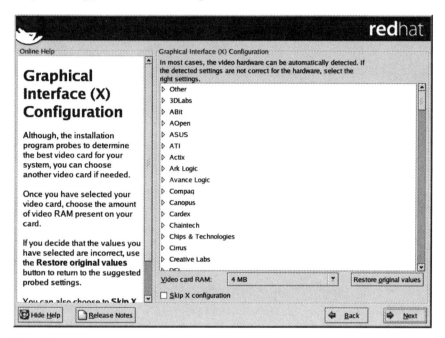

Figure 2-32. X Configuration

Next, enter the amount of video memory installed on your video card. If you are not sure, consult the documentation accompanying your video card.

> **NOTE** You will not damage your video card by choosing more memory than is available, but the X server may not start correctly if you do.

If you decide that the values you have selected are incorrect, you can click the Restore original values button to return to the suggested settings.

You can also select Skip X Configuration if you would rather configure X after the installation or not at all. If you do, skip ahead to the "Installation Complete!" section later in this chapter.

> **TIP** To change your X configuration after you have completed the installation, type the `redhat-config-xfree86` command from a shell prompt to launch the X Configuration Tool. If you are logged in as root, Linux will prompt you for the root password to continue.

Configuring Your Monitor

The installation program will present you with a list of monitors to select from. From this list, you can either use the monitor that is automatically detected for you or choose another monitor.

> **NOTE** If you are installing Red Hat Linux on a laptop with an LCD screen, you should select the most appropriate Generic model available.

If your monitor does not appear on the list, select the most appropriate Generic model available. If you select a Generic monitor, the installation program will suggest horizontal and vertical sync ranges. These values are generally available in the documentation which accompanies your monitor or from your monitor's vendor or manufacturer; check your hardware documentation to ensure these values are set correctly.

> **CAUTION** Do not select a monitor similar to your monitor unless you are certain that the monitor you are selecting does not exceed the capabilities of your monitor. Doing so may overclock your monitor and damage *or destroy* it.

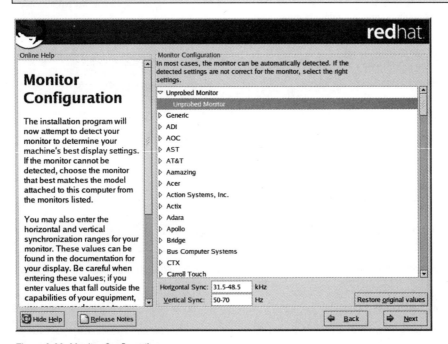

Figure 2-33. Monitor Configuration

The horizontal and vertical ranges that the installation program suggests for the selected monitor are also displayed below the list of monitors.

If you decide that your monitor selection or the horizontal and vertical ranges are incorrect, you can click the Restore original values button to return to the original suggested settings.

Click Next when you have finished configuring your monitor.

Custom Configuration

Choose the correct color depth and resolution for your X configuration. Click Test Setting to try out this configuration. If you do not like what you see during the test, click No to choose another resolution.

> **NOTE** If you need to exit out of the X configuration test, use the Ctrl-Alt-Backspace key combination. Please note, this will not work in some cases.

Make sure that you test your configuration to make sure the resolution and color settings are usable.

Next, choose whether you want to boot your system into a graphical or text environment after the installation is complete. Unless you have special needs, booting into a graphical environment (similar to a Windows environment) is recommended. If you choose to boot into a text environment, you will be presented with a command prompt (similar to an MS-DOS environment).

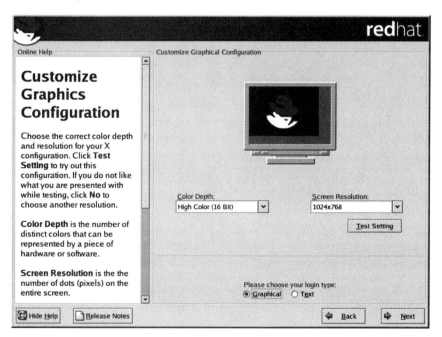

Figure 2-34. X Customization

> **TIP** To change your X configuration after you have completed the installation, use the X Configuration tool. Type the `redhat-config-xfree86` command in a shell prompt to launch the X Configuration Tool. If you are not logged in as root, Linux will prompt you for the root password to continue.

> **TIP** To change from the graphical login to a text login or vice versa after installation, as root you can edit the `/etc/inittab` file and change the line `id:5:initdefault:`. 5 stands for the graphical login and 3 stands for the text login.

Installation Complete!

Congratulations! Your Red Hat Linux 8.0 installation is now complete!

The installation program will prompt you to prepare your system for reboot.

> **NOTE** Remove any installation media (diskette in the diskette drive or CD in the CD-ROM drive) if they are not ejected automatically upon reboot.

If you do not have a boot loader installed and configured, you will need to use the boot disk you created during the installation now.

After your computer's normal power-up sequence has completed, you should see the graphical boot loader prompt, at which you can do any of the following things:

- ◆ *Press Enter* — Causes the default boot entry to be booted.
- ◆ *Select a boot label and press Enter* — Causes the boot loader to boot the operating system corresponding to the boot label. (Press ? or Tab at LILO's text mode boot loader prompt for a list of valid boot labels.)
- ◆ *Do nothing* — After the boot loader's timeout period (by default, five seconds), the boot loader will automatically boot the default OS entry.

Do whatever is appropriate to boot Red Hat Linux. You should see one or more screens of messages scroll by. Eventually, you should see a `login:` prompt or a GUI login screen (if you installed the X Window System and chose to start X automatically).

> **TIP** If you are not sure what to do next, see Part II, which covers topics relating to the basics of your system and introduces you to using Red Hat Linux.

If you are a more experienced user looking for information on administration topics or system configuration, you may find the *Official Red Hat Linux Administrator's Guide* (also from Red Hat Press) a worthwhile companion to this book.

The first time your system boots, the Setup Agent will appear and walk you through the initial configuration of your system. See Chapter 4 for more information on the Setup Agent.

Chapter 3

Upgrading Your Current System

If you have an older installation of Red Hat Linux on your system (Red Hat Linux 6.2 or higher), you may want to upgrade to Red Hat Linux 8.0 rather than installing from scratch so that you can save any files that are currently on your system. This chapter walks you through a typical Red Hat Linux 8.0 upgrade. (You should review the beginning of Chapter 2, up through the point where you choose the Upgrade installation, before reading this chapter.)

> **NOTE** You must have Red Hat Linux 6.2 or later installed on your machine to perform an upgrade.

What It Means to Upgrade

Red Hat Linux 8.0 allows you to upgrade from prior versions of Red Hat Linux — but only if you have version 6.2 and later installed. Upgrading your system installs the modular 2.4.x kernel as well as updated versions of the packages that are currently installed on your system. If you choose to upgrade, keep in mind that the Upgrade installation can take a great deal longer than the regular installation because the Upgrade installation has to perform a lot more disk access to ensure the continued integrity of the existing data.

The upgrade process preserves existing configuration files by renaming them with an `.rpmsave` extension (for example, `sendmail.cf.rpmsave`). The upgrade process also creates a log of its actions in `/root/upgrade.log`.

> **NOTE** As software evolves, configuration file formats can change, so you should carefully compare your original configuration files to the new files before integrating your changes.

Some upgraded packages may require the installation of other packages for proper operation. If you choose to customize your packages to upgrade, you may be required to resolve dependency problems. Otherwise, the upgrade procedure takes care of these dependencies, but it may need to install additional packages that are not installed on your system.

> **NOTE** If the upgrade program does not detect a swap file that equals twice your RAM, it will ask you if you would like to add a new swap file. If your system does not have a lot of RAM (less than 32MB), you should probably add this swap file.

Upgrading Your System

To upgrade your system, you should choose Upgrade as your preferred installation type.

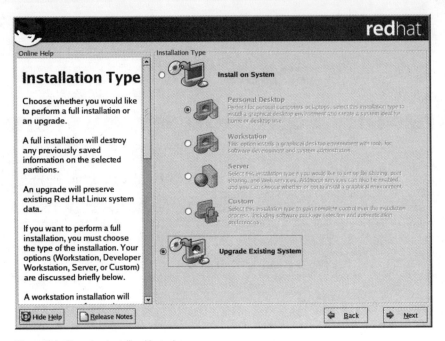

Figure 3-1. Choosing Install or Upgrade

Upgrading Your File System

NOTE This section only pertains to users performing an upgrade from Red Hat Linux version 7.1 or earlier or from a Red Hat Linux 7.2 or 7.3 installation where ext2 was chosen as the file system.

If the installation program detects the ext2 file system on your Red Hat Linux system, you can choose to retain your current ext2 file system or migrate to the ext3 file system.

TIP Unless you have a good reason not to, migrate to the ext3 file system.

The following list describes the ext2 and ext3 file systems and how they can be utilized:

♦ *ext2* — An ext2 file system supports standard Unix file types (regular files, directories, symbolic links, etc) and provides the ability to assign long file names (up to 255 characters). Versions prior to Red Hat Linux 8.0 used ext2 file systems by default.

♦ *ext3* — The ext3 file system is based on the ext2 file system and has one main advantage over ext2 — journaling. A journaling file system reduces time spent recovering a file system after a crash because there is no need to fsck the file system.

NOTE If you choose to migrate to the ext3 file system, your existing system data will not be modified.

Customizing Your Upgrade

Do you want to choose the packages to be upgraded or let the installation program perform an automated upgrade?

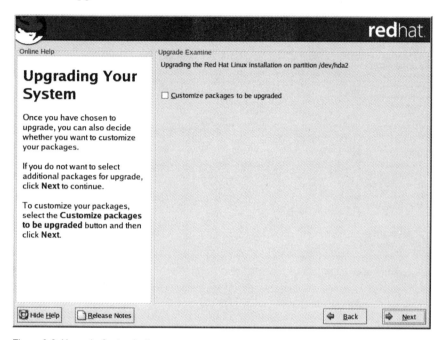

Figure 3-2. Upgrade Customization

To perform an automated upgrade, click Next.

To customize your packages for this upgrade, select the Customize packages to be upgraded option and click Next.

Boot Loader Configuration

A software boot loader is used to start Red Hat Linux on your computer. It can also start other operating systems, such as Windows. If you are using a Red Hat Linux software boot loader (GRUB or LILO), the boot loader will be detected automatically.

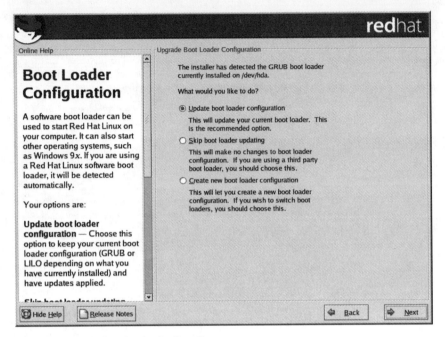

Figure 3-3. Upgrade Boot Loader Configuration

On the Boot Loader Configuration Screen, your options are:

♦ *Update boot loader configuration* — Choose this option to keep your current boot loader configuration (GRUB or LILO depending on what you have currently installed) and have updates applied.

♦ *Skip boot loader updating* — Choose this option if you do not want to make any changes to your current boot loader configuration. If you are using a third-party boot loader, you should skip updating your boot loader.

♦ *Create new boot loader configuration* — Choose this option if you want to create a new boot loader for your system. If you currently have LILO and want to switch to GRUB, or if you have been using boot diskettes to boot your Red Hat Linux system and want to use a software boot loader such as GRUB or LILO, you will want to create a new boot loader configuration (see the "Creating a New Boot Loader Configuration" section later in this chapter for more information).

After making your selection, click Next to continue.

Creating a New Boot Loader Configuration

To boot your system without a boot diskette, you usually need to install a boot loader. A *boot loader* is the first software program that runs when a computer starts; it is responsible for loading and transferring control to the operating system kernel software. The kernel in turn initializes the rest of the operating system.

The installation program provides two boot loaders for you to choose from, GRUB and LILO:

♦ GRUB (GRand Unified Bootloader), which is installed by default, is a very powerful boot loader that can load a variety of free operating systems, as well as proprietary operating systems with chain-loading (the mechanism for loading unsupported operating systems by loading another boot loader, such as DOS or Windows).

♦ LILO (LInux LOader) is a versatile boot loader for Linux. It does not depend on a specific file system, can boot Linux kernel images from floppy diskettes and hard disks, and can even boot other operating systems.

If you do not want to install GRUB as your boot loader, click Change boot loader. You can then choose to install LILO or choose not to install a boot loader at all.

If you already have a boot loader that can boot Linux and do not want to overwrite your current boot loader, or if you plan to boot the system using boot diskettes, choose Do not install a boot loader by clicking on the Change boot loader button.

> **CAUTION** If you choose not to install GRUB or LILO for any reason, you will not be able to boot the system directly, and you will need to use another boot method (such as a boot diskette). Use this option only if you are sure you have another way of booting the system!

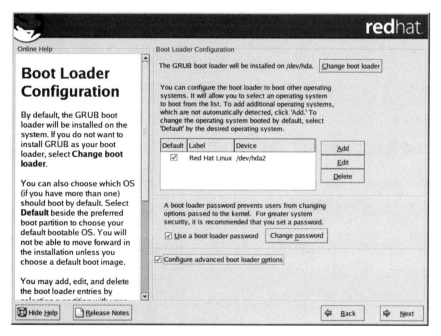

Figure 3-4. Boot Loader Configuration

Every bootable partition is listed, including partitions used by other operating systems. The partition holding your the system's root file system will have a label of Red Hat Linux (for

GRUB) or `linux` (for LILO). Other partitions may also have boot labels. If you would like to add or change the boot label for other partitions that have been detected by the installation program, click once on the partition to select it. Once selected, you can change the boot label by clicking the Edit button.

Select Default beside the preferred boot partition to choose your default bootable OS. You will not be able to move forward in the installation unless you choose a default boot image.

> **NOTE** The Label column lists what you must enter at the boot prompt, in non-graphical boot loaders, in order to boot the desired operating system. After you have loaded the GRUB boot screen, use the arrow keys to choose a boot label or type e for edit. You will be presented with a list of items in the configuration file for the boot label you have selected. At the graphical LILO screen, press Ctrl-x to exit to the boot: prompt. If you forget the boot labels defined on your system, you can always press Tab at the prompt to display a list of defined boot labels.

Boot loader passwords provide a security mechanism in an environment where physical access to your server is available.

If you are installing a boot loader, you should create a password to protect your system. Without a boot loader password, users with access to your system can pass options to the kernel, which can compromise your system security. With a boot loader password in place, the password must first be entered in order to select any non-standard boot options.

If you choose to use a boot loader password to enhance your system security, be sure to select the checkbox labeled Use a boot loader password. Once selected, enter a password and confirm it.

To configure more advance boot loader options, such as changing the drive order or passing options to the kernel, be sure Configure advanced boot loader options is selected before clicking Next.

Advanced Boot Loader Configuration

Now that you have chosen which boot loader to install, you can also determine where you want the boot loader to be installed. You may install the boot loader in one of two places:

- ◆ *The master boot record (MBR)* — This is the recommended place to install a boot loader, unless the MBR already starts another operating system loader, such as System Commander. The MBR is a special area on your hard drive that is automatically loaded by your computer's BIOS, and is the earliest point at which the boot loader can take control of the boot process. If you install it in the MBR, when your machine boots, GRUB (or LILO) will present a boot prompt. You can then boot Red Hat Linux or any other operating system that you have configured the boot loader to boot.

- ◆ *The first sector of your boot partition* — This is recommended if you are already using another boot loader on your system (Windows NT/2000/XP include boot loaders). In this case, your other boot loader will take control first. You can then configure that boot loader to start GRUB (or LILO), which will then boot Red Hat Linux.

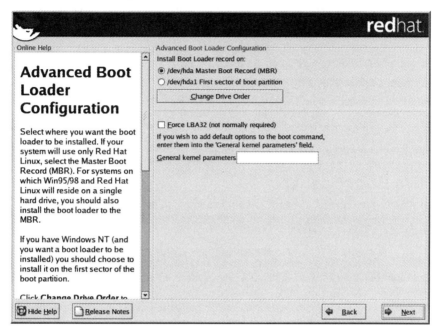

Figure 3-5. Boot Loader Installation

If your system will use only Red Hat Linux, you should choose the MBR. For systems with Windows 95/98, you should also install the boot loader to the MBR so that it can boot both operating systems.

Click the Change Drive Order button if you would like to rearrange the drive order. Changing the drive order may be useful if you have multiple SCSI adapters or both SCSI and IDE adapters and want to boot from the SCSI device.

The Force LBA32 (not normally required) option allows you to exceed the 1024 cylinder limit for the /boot partition. If you have a system that supports the LBA32 extension for booting operating systems above the 1024 cylinder limit and you want to place your /boot partition above cylinder 1024, you should select this option.

If you wish to add default options to the boot command, enter them into the Kernel parameters field.

Any options you enter will be passed to the Linux kernel every time it boots.

Rescue Mode

If you need to use rescue mode, there are several options available to you:

♦ Using the CD-ROM to boot, type **linux rescue** at the boot: prompt.

♦ Booting your system from an installation boot diskette made from the `boot.img` image. This method requires that the Red Hat Linux CD-ROM #1 be inserted as the rescue image or that the rescue image be on the hard drive as an ISO image. After you have booted using this diskette, type `linux rescue` at the `boot:` prompt.

♦ Booting from a network diskette made from the `bootnet.img` or PCMCIA boot diskette made from `pcmcia.img`. After you have booted using this diskette, type `linux rescue` at the `boot:` prompt. You can only do this if your network connection is working. You will need to identify the network host and transfer type.

For more information on Rescue Mode, see Appendix A.

Alternative Boot Loaders

If you do not wish to use the GRUB or LILO boot loaders, you have several alternatives:

♦ *Boot diskette* — You can use the boot diskette created by the installation program (if you create one).

♦ *LOADLIN* — You can load Linux from MS-DOS. Unfortunately, this requires a copy of the Linux kernel (and an initial RAM disk, if you have a SCSI adapter) to be available on an MS-DOS partition. The only way to accomplish this is to boot your Red Hat Linux system using some other method (for example, from a boot diskette) and then copy the kernel to an MS-DOS partition. LOADLIN is available from

```
ftp://metalab.unc.edu/pub/Linux/system/boot/dualboot/
```

and associated mirror sites.

♦ *SYSLINUX* — SYSLINUX is an MS-DOS program very similar to LOADLIN. It is available from

```
ftp://metalab.unc.edu/pub/Linux/system/boot/loaders/
```

and associated mirror sites.

♦ *Commercial boot loaders* — You can load Linux using commercial boot loaders. For example, System Commander and Partition Magic are able to boot Linux (but still require GRUB or LILO to be installed in your Linux root partition).

NOTE Boot loaders such as LOADLIN and System Commander are considered to be third-party boot loaders and are not supported by Red Hat.

Selecting Packages to Upgrade

On this screen, you can choose which packages you would like to upgrade (see Figure 3-6).

You can choose to view the individual packages in Tree View or Flat View. *Tree View* allows you to see the packages grouped by application type. Using Tree View, you see a listing of package groups. When you expand this list (by double-clicking on the folder arrow beside a package group name) and pick one group, the list of packages in that group appears in the panel on the right. *Flat View* allows you to see all of the packages in an alphabetical listing on the right of the screen.

To sort packages alphabetically, click on the Package tab. To sort packages by size, click on the Size (MB) tab.

To select an individual package, click the checkbox beside the package name. A check mark in the box means that a package has been selected.

For more information about a specific package, click on the individual package name. The package information will appear at the bottom of the screen.

You can also select or deselect all packages listed within a particular group by clicking on the Select all in group or Unselect all in group buttons.

> **NOTE** Certain packages (for example, the kernel and certain libraries) are required for every Red Hat Linux system and are not available to select or deselect. These base packages are selected by default.

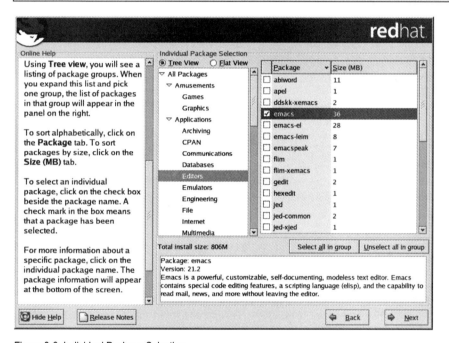

Figure 3-6. Individual Package Selection

Unresolved Dependencies

If any package requires another package that you have not selected to install, the program presents a list of these unresolved dependencies and gives you the opportunity to resolve them.

The Unresolved Dependencies screen appears only if you are missing packages that are needed by your customized package selection.

At the bottom of the screen, under the list of missing packages, an Install packages to satisfy dependencies radio button is selected by default. If you leave this checked, the installation program will resolve package dependencies automatically by adding all required packages to the list of selected packages.

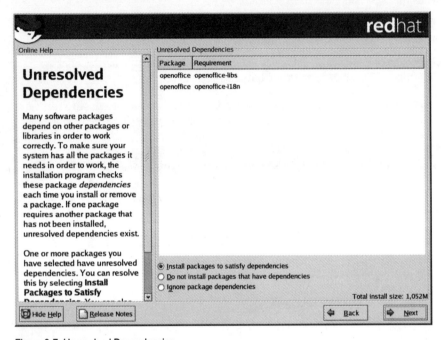

Figure 3-7. Unresolved Dependencies

If you do not wish to install packages that require other packages, select Do not install packages that have dependencies. To install only the packages you have selected and leave the dependencies unresolved, select Ignore package dependencies.

> **TIP** To install or remove packages after you have completed the installation, click System Settings Packages (or type the `redhat-config-packages` command from a shell prompt) to launch the Package Management Tool. If you are not root, Linux will prompt you for the root password to continue.

> **TIP** To change from the graphical login to a text login or vice versa after installation, as root you can edit the `/etc/inittab` file and change the line `id:5:initdefault:`. 5 stands for the graphical login and 3 stands for the text login.

Upgrading Packages

At this point there is nothing left for you to do until all the packages have been upgraded or installed.

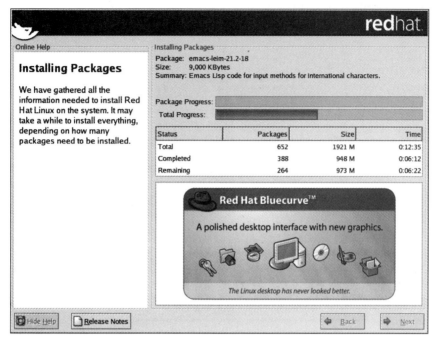

Figure 3-8. Installing Packages

Boot Diskette Creation

To create a boot diskette, insert a blank, formatted diskette into your diskette drive (see Figure 3-9) and click Next.

> **NOTE** We highly recommend that you create a boot diskette. If for some reason your system is not able to boot properly using GRUB, LILO, or a third-party boot loader, a boot diskette enables you to properly boot your Red Hat Linux system.

After a short delay, your boot diskette will be created; remove it from your diskette drive and label it clearly. Note that if you would like to create a boot diskette after the installation, you will be able to do so. For more information, please see the mkbootdisk man page by typing **man mkbootdisk** at the shell prompt.

If you do not want to create a boot diskette, make sure to select the appropriate option before you click Next.

If you boot your system with the boot diskette (instead of GRUB or LILO), make sure you create a new boot diskette whenever you make any changes to your kernel (including the installation of a new kernel).

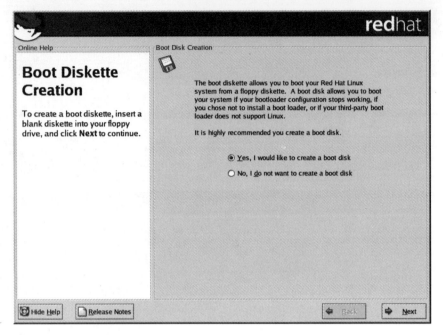

Figure 3-9. Boot Diskette Creation

Upgrade Complete

Congratulations! Your Red Hat Linux 8.0 upgrade is now complete!

You will now be prompted to prepare your system for reboot. Do not forget to remove any diskette in the floppy drive or CD in the CD-ROM drive if they are not ejected automatically upon reboot. If you do not have a boot loader installed and configured, you will need to use your boot diskette now.

> **TIP** For a review of some of the basic Linux concepts, see Part II.

Chapter 4

After Installation . . .

After installing Red Hat Linux, you will run through the Setup Agent to configure your system for use. Also, at some point you may need to troubleshoot your installation or remove Red Hat Linux from your system altogether. This chapter shows you how to perform all of these post-installation tasks.

Setup Agent

The first time you start your Red Hat Linux system, you will be presented with the Setup Agent, which guides you through the initial Red Hat Linux configuration. Using this tool, you can set your system time and date, install software, register your machine with the Red Hat Network, and more.

Setting the Date and Time

Setup Agent lets you set your machine's date and time, or lets you synchronize your date and time with an network time server — a machine that sends date and time information to your machine through a network connection.

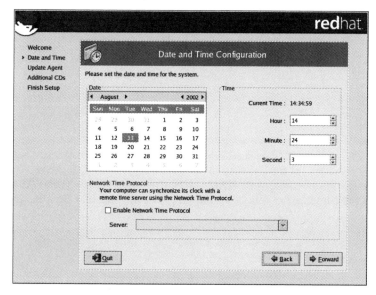

Figure 4-1. Date and Time Configuration

You can set the day, month, and year using the calendar tool and set your time in hours, minutes, and seconds using provided text boxes. After setting your time and date, click Forward to continue.

If you wish to register your system with the Red Hat Network and receive automatic updates of your Red Hat Linux system, choose Yes, I would like to register with Red Hat Network. This will start the Red Hat Update Agent — a utility that guides you step-by-step through the registration of your machine with the Red Hat Network. Selecting No, I do not want to register my machine skips the registration. For more information about Red Hat Network and registering your machine, refer to the Red Hat Network documentation at the following URL:

```
http://www.redhat.com/docs/manuals/RHNetwork/
```

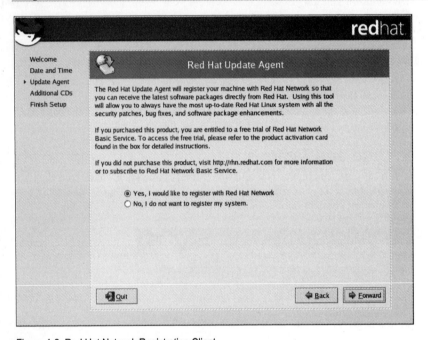

Figure 4-2. Red Hat Network Registration Client

If you want to install Red Hat Linux RPM packages that you did not install during installation, software from third-party providers, or documentation from the Official Red Hat Linux Documentation CD, you can do so at the Install Additional Software screen. Insert the CD containing the software or documentation you want to install, click the Install . . . button, and follow the instructions.

> **NOTE** If you are installing a package from the Red Hat Linux installation CDs, you must insert CD #1, click the Install... button, choose the package(s) or component you want to install, and change the CD *if prompted.*

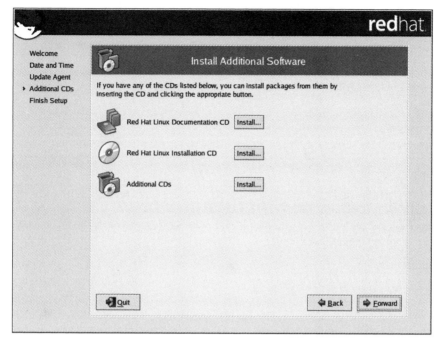

Figure 4-3. Installing Additional Software

Now your system is configured. You are ready to log in and start using Red Hat Linux. See Part II for information on using Red Hat Linux.

Troubleshooting Your Installation of Red Hat Linux

This section discusses some common installation problems and their solutions.

You Are Unable to Boot Red Hat Linux

If you're unable to boot Red Hat Linux, the following sections help you troubleshoot the problem.

Are You Unable to Boot from the CD-ROM?

If you cannot boot from your Red Hat Linux CD-ROM, you have two options:

♦ Change your BIOS so that booting from the CD-ROM is recognized first in the boot order

♦ Boot using a boot disk you have created

> **NOTE** There are a few cases where the system BIOS will not allow the Red Hat Linux CD-ROM to boot because of the size of the boot image on the CD-ROM itself. In cases such as these, a boot disk should be made to boot Red Hat Linux. Once booted, the CD-ROMs will work properly for the installation.

To change your BIOS, refer to your system manual for the correct keyboard combination that allows you to access your BIOS, or you can read the key sequence needed while the system begins to boot.

To create a boot disk, follow the instructions in Chapter 2.

To boot Red Hat Linux using a boot disk, insert the diskette you have created into your floppy drive and then boot/reboot your computer. Make sure that your BIOS is set to use the floppy or removable disk (A:) to boot.

Are You Unable to Boot from the Local Boot Disk?

If you are experiencing difficulties in getting a local boot disk to boot your system correctly, you may need an updated boot disk.

Check the online errata at

```
http://www.redhat.com/support/errata
```

for updated diskette images (if available) and follow the instructions in Chapter 2 to create an updated boot disk for your system.

Are You Unable to Boot from PCMCIA Boot Disks?

If you are experiencing difficulties in getting the PCMCIA boot disks you made to boot your system correctly, you may need an updated boot disk.

Check the online errata at

```
http://www.redhat.com/support/errata
```

for updated diskette images (if available) and follow the instructions provided to make an updated boot disk for your system.

Is Your System Displaying Signal 11 Errors?

If you receive a fatal signal 11 error during your installation, it is probably due to a hardware error in memory on your system's bus. A hardware error in memory can be caused by problems in executables or with the system's hardware. Like other operating systems, Red Hat Linux places its own demands on your system's hardware. Some of this hardware may not be able to meet those demands, even if they work properly under another OS.

Check to see if you have the latest installation and supplemental boot diskettes from Red Hat. Review the online errata at

```
http://www.redhat.com/support/errata
```

to see if newer versions are available. If the latest images still fail, it may be due to a problem with your hardware. Commonly, these errors are in your memory or CPU-cache. A possible solution for this error is turning off the CPU-cache in the BIOS. You could also try to swap your memory around in the motherboard slots to see if the problem is either slot- or memory-related.

For more information concerning signal 11 errors, refer to the following URL:

```
http://www.bitwizard.nl/sig11/
```

Are You Unable to Boot from a Network Boot Disk?

If you are experiencing difficulties in getting the network boot disk you made to boot your system correctly, you may need an updated boot disk.

Check the online errata at

```
http://www.redhat.com/support/errata
```

for updated diskette images (if available) and follow the instructions provided to make an updated boot disk for your system.

Trouble Beginning the Installation

If you're unable to properly begin installing Red Hat Linux, the following sections help you troubleshoot the problem.

Trouble Using PCMCIA Boot Disks?

If you booted using PCMCIA boot disks and want to install via FTP (or NFS or HTTP), but do not see these installation options, you may have a problem with your network card.

If the network card is not initialized during the boot process, the Red Hat Linux installation program will not enable you to configure your system for networking, either during or after the installation itself.

Check the hardware compatibility list at

```
http://hardware.redhat.com/hcl/
```

to see if your network card is compatible and/or supported. If your card is not listed, it may not be compatible with Red Hat Linux.

Is Your Mouse Not Detected?

If the Mouse Not Detected screen appears, then the installation program was not able to identify your mouse correctly.

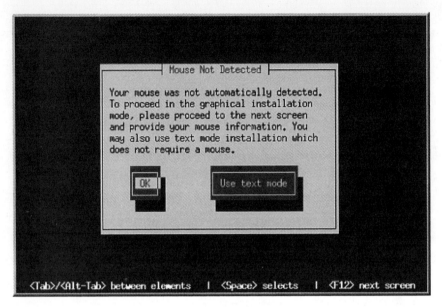

Figure 4-4. Mouse Not Detected

You can choose to continue with the GUI installation or use the text mode installation, which does not require using a mouse. If you choose to continue with the GUI installation, you will need to provide the installation program with your mouse configuration information (see Chapter 2).

Problems Booting into the Graphical Installation

There are some video cards that will not work properly with the Red Hat Linux installation program. The end result will be a problem booting into the graphical installation program. If the installation program will not run using its default settings, it will try to run in a lower resolution mode. If that still fails, the installation program will run in text mode.

Users who have video cards that will not run at 800 x 600 resolution should type **lowres** at the boot: prompt to run the installation program in 640 x 480 resolution.

Trouble During the Installation

If have trouble during the Red Hat Linux installation, the following sections help you troubleshoot the problem.

Partition Creation Problems

If you are having trouble creating a partition, for example, a / (root) partition, make sure you are setting its partition type to Linux Native.

Unless your BIOS supports otherwise, make sure /boot does not exceed the 1023 cylinder head. If you do not, the installation program will not allow you to create a /boot or / (root) partition. Some new systems allow you to exceed the 1023 limit (with GRUB and the newer LILO versions that are available), but most machines with older BIOS will not.

Problems Using Remaining Space

You have a swap and a / (root) partition created, and you have selected the root partition to use the remaining space, but it does not fill the hard drive.

If your hard drive is more than 1024 cylinders, you must create a /boot partition if you want the / (root) partition to use all of the remaining space on your hard drive.

Other Partitioning Problems

If you are using Disk Druid to create partitions, but cannot move to the next screen, you probably have not created all the partitions necessary for Disk Druid's dependencies to be satisfied.

You must have the following partitions as a bare minimum:

♦ A /boot partition of type Linux native

♦ A / (root) partition of type Linux native

♦ A swap partition of type Linux swap

> **TIP** When defining a partition's type as Linux swap, you do not have to assign it a mount point. Disk Druid automatically assigns the mount point for you.

Are You Seeing Python Errors?

During some upgrades or installations of Red Hat Linux, the installation program (also known as Anaconda) may fail with a Python or traceback error. This error may occur after the selection of individual packages or while trying to save the upgrade log in /tmp. The error may look similar to the following:

```
Traceback (innermost last):
    File "/var/tmp/anaconda-7.1//usr/lib/anaconda/iw/progress_gui.py",
line 20, in run
     rc = self.todo.doInstall ()
   File "/var/tmp/anaconda-7.1//usr/lib/anaconda/todo.py", line 1468, in
doInstall
     self.fstab.savePartitions ()
   File "fstab.py", line 221, in savePartitions
     sys.exit(0)
SystemExit: 0

Local variables in innermost frame:
self: <fstab.GuiFstab instance at 8446fe0>
sys: <module 'sys' (built-in)>
ToDo object:
(itodo
ToDo
p1
```

```
(dp2
S'method'
p3
(iimage
CdromInstallMethod
p4
(dp5
S'progressWindow'
p6

<failed>
```

This error occurs in some systems where links to `/tmp` are symbolic to other locations or have been changed since creation. These symbolic or changed links are invalid during the installation process, so the installation program cannot write information and fails.

If you experience such an error, first try to download any available errata for Anaconda. Errata can be found at:

```
http://www.redhat.com/support/errata
```

You can also search for bug reports related to this problem. To search Red Hat's bug tracking system, go to:

```
http://bugzilla.redhat.com/bugzilla
```

Problems After Installation

If have problems after installing Red Hat Linux, the following sections help you troubleshoot the problem.

Trouble with the Graphical GRUB Screen?

If for some reason you need to disable the graphical boot screen, you can do so, as root, by editing the `/boot/grub/grub.conf` file and then rebooting your system.

To do this, comment out the line that begins with `splashimage` in the `grub.conf` file. (To comment out a line, insert the `;` character at the beginning of the line.)

Once you reboot, the `grub.conf` file will be reread and your changes will take place.

Once you've fixed the problem, you may re-enable the graphical boot screen by uncommenting (or adding) the above line back into the `grub.conf` file and rebooting.

Trouble with the Graphical LILO Screen?

If for some reason you need to disable the graphical boot screen, you can do so, as root, by editing the `/etc/lilo.conf` file and then rerunning LILO.

First, as root, comment out (or delete) the line which reads `message=/boot/message` in the `/etc/lilo.conf` file. To comment out a line, insert the `;` character at the beginning of the line.

Next, rerun LILO by typing **/sbin/lilo -v**. The next time you boot, you will see the text `LILO:` prompt that was used in previous Red Hat Linux releases.

You may re-enable the graphical boot screen by adding (or uncommenting) the above line back into the `lilo.conf` file and rerunning LILO.

Booting into a Graphical Environment

If you have installed the X Window System, but are not seeing a graphical desktop environment once you log into your Red Hat Linux system, you can easily start the X Window System graphical interface using the command `startx` after you log in.

Once you enter this command and press Enter, you will be able to log into the Red Hat Linux graphical desktop.

> **TIP** To change from the graphical login to a text login or vice versa after installation, as root you can edit the /etc/inittab file and change the line `id:5:initdefault:`. 5 stands for the graphical login and 3 stands for the text login.

Problems with Server Installations and X

If you performed a server installation and you are having trouble getting X to start, you may not have installed the X Window System during your installation.

If you want the X Window System, you can perform an upgrade to install X. During the upgrade, select the X Window System packages, and choose GNOME, KDE, or both.

Problems When You Try to Log In

If you did not create a user account during the installation, you will need to log in as root and use the password you assigned to root. If you cannot remember your root password, you will need to boot your system as `linux single`.

If you are using GRUB, after you have loaded the GRUB boot screen, type **e** for edit. You will be presented with a list of items in the configuration file for the boot label you have selected. Choose the line that starts with `kernel` and type **e** to edit this boot entry as follows:

At the end of the `kernel` line, add:

```
linux single
```

Press Enter to exit edit mode.

After the GRUB screen has returned, type **b** to boot into single user mode.

If you are using LILO, press Ctrl-x to exit the graphical LILO screen and gain access to the LILO `boot:` prompt.

Next, enter **linux single** at the LILO `boot:` prompt.

After you have booted into single user mode using either GRUB or LILO and have access to the # prompt, you will need to type **passwd root**, which will allow you to enter a new password for root.

At this point you can type **shutdown -r now** and the system will reboot with your new password.

If you cannot remember your user account password, you must become root. To become root, type **su -** and enter your root password when prompted. Then, type **passwd** *username*. This allows you to enter a new password for the specified user account.

If you selected either the custom or workstation installation and do not see the graphical login screen, check your hardware for compatibility issues. The Hardware Compatibility List can be found at the following URL:

```
http://hardware.redhat.com/hcl/
```

Is Your RAM Not Being Recognized?

Sometimes, the kernel does not recognize all of your memory (RAM). You can check this with the following command:

```
cat /proc/meminfo
```

Find out if the displayed quantity is the same as the known amount of RAM in your system. If they are not equal, add the following line to the /boot/grub/grub.conf:

```
mem=XXM
```

Or, if you used LILO, add the following line to the /etc/lilo.conf file:

```
append="mem=XXM"
```

Replace *xx* with the amount of RAM you have in megabytes. Remember that per-image append lines completely overwrite the global append line. It might be worth adding this to the per-image descriptions, as shown in the following example:

```
mem=128M
append="mem=128M"
```

In /boot/grub/grub.conf, the above example would look similar to the following:

```
#NOTICE: You have a /boot partition. This means that
#        all kernel paths are relative to /boot/
default=0
timeout=30
splashimage=(hd0,0)/grub/splash.xpm.gz
title Red Hat Linux (2.4.6-2)
        root (hd0,0)
        kernel /vmlinuz-2.2.6-2 ro root=/dev/hda3 mem=128M
```

After you reboot, the changes made to grub.conf will be reflected on your system.

In /etc/lilo.conf, the above example would look similar to the following:

```
boot=/dev/sda
        map=/boot/map
        install=/boot/boot.b
```

```
prompt
timeout=50

image=/boot/vmlinuz-2.2.12-20
        label=linux
        root=/dev/sda1
        initrd=/boot/initrd-2.2.12-20.img
        read-only
        append="mem=128M"
```

Remember to run `/sbin/lilo -v` after changing `/etc/lilo.conf`.

Note that you can also produce the same effect by actually passing this option when you are specifying the label/image to use in GRUB or LILO.

After you have loaded the GRUB boot screen, type **e** for edit. You will be presented with a list of items in the configuration file for the boot label you have selected.

Choose the line that starts with `kernel` and type **e** to edit this boot entry.

At the end of the `kernel` line, add

`mem=XXM`

where *xx* equals the amount of RAM in your system.

Press Enter to exit edit mode.

After the GRUB screen has returned, type **b** to boot with your new RAM specifications.

At the graphical LILO screen, press Ctrl-x to exit to the `boot:` prompt. Next, enter the following at the `boot:` prompt:

`linux mem=XXM`

Remember to replace *xx* with the amount of RAM in your system. Press Enter to boot.

Your Printer Will Not Work

If you are not sure how to set up your printer or are having trouble getting it to work properly, try using the Printer Configuration Tool.

From the Main Menu, choose System Tools ⇨ Printing (or type the `redhat-config-printer` command from a shell prompt) to launch the Red Hat Printer Config tool. If you are not root, Linux will prompt you for the root password to continue.

Problems with Sound Configuration

If you do not have sound after your installation, you may need to run one of the sound configuration utilities.

From the Main Menu, choose System Settings ⇨ Sound Card Detection (or type the `redhat-config-soundcard` command from a shell prompt) to run the graphical sound configuration tool.

To run the text-based configuration tool, as root, type **sndconfig** in a terminal window.

> **Note** sndconfig must be run in runlevel 3.

If the sound card configuration tools do not help, you may need to select the Enable sound server startup option under Sound in the Control Center. To do this, click on Preferences ⇨ Control Center to launch the Preferences window. In the Preferences window, double click the Sound icon and then select Enable sound server startup on the General tab and click OK.

Apache-Based httpd Service/Sendmail Hangs During Startup

If you are having trouble with the Apache-based httpd service or Sendmail hanging at startup, make sure the following line is in the /etc/hosts file:

```
127.0.0.1 localhost.localdomain localhost
```

Removing Red Hat Linux

To uninstall Red Hat Linux from your system, you will need to remove the GRUB or LILO information from your master boot record (MBR).

In MS-DOS, Windows 95/98/Me you can use fdisk to create a new MBR with the *undocumented* flag /mbr. This will *only* rewrite the MBR to boot the primary DOS partition. The command should look like the following:

```
fdisk /mbr
```

If you need to remove Linux from a hard drive, and have attempted to do this with the default MS-DOS fdisk, you will experience the *Partitions exist but they do not exist* problem. The best way to remove non-MS-DOS partitions is with a tool that understands partitions other than MS-DOS (such as Windows NT/2000/XP, which are not based on MS-DOS).

You can do this with the installation media by typing **linux expert** at the boot: prompt.

Select install (versus upgrade) and at the point when you should partition the drive, choose fdisk.

In fdisk, type **p** to print out the partition numbers and then remove the Linux partitions with the **d** command. When you are satisfied with the changes you have made, you can quit with a **w** and the changes will be saved to disk. If you deleted too much, type **q** and no changes will be made.

After you have removed the Linux partitions, you can reboot your computer using Control-Alt-Delete instead of continuing with the install.

Part II

The Basics

Red Hat Linux 8.0 is a powerful, reliable operating system — but you need to know how to use it before you can truly get the most benefit from the system.

This part shows you the basics of how to use your Red Hat Linux system. It shows you how to use the graphical desktop environment if you installed it, as well as how to use the system prompt (or command-line interface) if you prefer working in that mode. This part also shows you how to manage users and groups, files and directories, and how to deal with disks and CD-ROMs.

Chapter 5: Getting Started

Chapter 6: Using the Graphical Desktop

Chapter 7: Diskettes and CD-ROMs

Chapter 8: Shell Prompt Basics

Chapter 9: Managing Files and Directories

Chapter 10: Managing Users and Groups

Chapter 5
Getting Started

From booting up to shutting down, whether you are working or playing, Red Hat Linux provides tools and applications to help you get the most out of your computing environment. This chapter guides you through some basic tasks that you will commonly perform day-to-day on your Red Hat Linux machine.

Introductory Terms

When you learn about a new operating system, you also need to learn new terminology. Here are a few basic terms you should learn to use Red Hat Linux. You will see these terms often throughout this book:

♦ *Shell prompt* — A command line interface (similar to an MS-DOS screen) between the user and the operating system (Figure 5-1). The shell interprets commands entered by the user and passes them on to the operating system.

```
File   Edit   View   Terminal   Go   Help
[john@dhcp59-229 john]$ ls -l
total 152
-rw-rw-r--    1 john     john          2584 Aug 12 15:11 borderonly-docs-NEW.tar.
gz
-rw-------    1 john     john         45301 Aug 12 15:15 docs-cd.png
-rw-------    1 john     john         55215 Aug 12 15:04 file-roller.png
drwxrwxr-x   78 root     root          4096 Aug 12  2002 mnt
drwxr-xr-x   25 root     root          4096 Aug 12 16:00 nfs
-rw-------    1 john     john         32593 Aug 12 10:40 userconfig.png
[john@dhcp59-229 john]$ ls
borderonly-docs-NEW.tar.gz  file-roller.png  nfs
docs-cd.png                 mnt              userconfig.png
[john@dhcp59-229 john]$
```

Figure 5-1. A Shell Prompt

- *Command line* — The place in the shell prompt where commands are typed.

- *Command* — An instruction given to the computer, most often with the keyboard or mouse.

- *Graphical User Interface (GUI)* — A screen with icons, menus, and panels for the user to click on to initiate actions such as starting applications and opening files.

- *Icons* — Small images representing an application, folder, *shortcut*, or system resource (such as a floppy drive). *Launcher icons* usually refer to application shortcuts.

- *Graphical Desktop Environment* — The most visible area of a GUI. The desktop is where your user Home and Start Here launcher icons are located. You can configure the desktop to have special backgrounds colors and pictures to add a personal touch to your desktop.

- *Panel* — A desktop toolbar, usually located across the bottom of the screen. The Panel contains the GNOME Menu button and shortcut icons to start commonly used programs. It can be customized by the user.

Figure 5-2. The Desktop Panel

- *Root* — The root user account is created during installation and has complete access to the system. You must be logged in as root to accomplish certain system administration tasks. User accounts are created so that typical user tasks can be done without using the root account. This reduces the chance of damaging your Red Hat Linux installation or its applications permanently.

- *su* and *su -* — The su command gives you access to the root account or other accounts on your system. When you type su to switch to your root account while still inside your user account shell, you have access to important system files that you can change — or damage — permanently. Logging in with the su - command makes you root within the root account shell. Use caution when you are logged in as root.

- *Man page* and *info page* — Man (short for manual) and info pages give detailed information about a command or file (man pages tend to be brief and provide less explanation than info pages). To read the man page for the su command, for example, type **man su** at a shell prompt (or type **info su** for the info page). To close one of these pages, press **q**.

- *X* or *X Window System* — These terms refer to the graphical user interface environments. If you are "in X" or "running X" you are working in a GUI rather than a console environment.

- *RPM* — RPM stands for RPM Package manager and is how Red Hat builds and delivers its software files. An RPM is a software package file you can install on your Red Hat Linux computer.

> **NOTE** Although the emphasis throughout this book will be on navigation and productivity using the graphical desktop environment, it will cover both the graphical and shell prompt methods of logging in and using your Red Hat Linux system.

Logging In

The next step to using your Red Hat Linux system is to log in. When you log in, you are introducing yourself to the system (also called *authentication*). If you type the wrong user name or password, you will not be allowed access to your system until you provide the proper user name or password.

Unlike some other operating systems, your Red Hat Linux system uses accounts to manage privileges, maintain security, and more. Not all accounts are created equal; some accounts have fewer rights to access files or services than others.

> **NOTE** Like Unix, Linux is case sensitive. This means that typing **root** refers to a different account than if you typed **Root**. By default, `root` refers to the root user (also known as the *superuser*) or system administrator.

If you did not create a user account during installation, you must log in as root. After you create a user account, it is highly recommended that you log in as that user instead of root to prevent accidental deletion of files or damage to your Red Hat Linux installation. If you have not already created and logged into a user account, see the "Creating a User Account" section later in this chapter.

> **CAUTION** Because your Red Hat Linux system creates the root account during installation, some new users are tempted to use only this account for all of their activities. This is a dangerous idea, because the root account is allowed to do anything on the system. You can easily damage your system by accidentally deleting or modifying sensitive system files.

Graphical Login

During installation, if you selected graphical as the login type, you will see a graphical login screen. Again, unless you have chosen to give your machine its own hostname, which is primarily used in a network setting, your machine will probably be called `localhost`.

Figure 5-3. The Graphical Login Screen

To log in as root from the graphical login screen, type **root** at the login prompt, press Enter, type the root password that you chose during installation at the password prompt, and press Enter again. To log in as a regular user, type your username at the login prompt, type the password that you selected when creating the user at the password prompt, and press Enter.

Logging in from the graphical login screen automatically starts the graphical desktop for you.

Virtual Console Login

During installation, if you selected text as the login type, you will see a login prompt similar to the following after booting your system:

```
Red Hat Linux release 8.0
Kernel 2.4.18-14 on an i686

localhost login:
```

Unless you have chosen to give your machine its own hostname, which is primarily used in a network setting, your machine will probably be called `localhost.localdomain`.

To log in as root from the console, type **root** at the login prompt, press Enter, type the root password that you chose during installation at the password prompt, and press Enter again. To log in as a regular user, type your username at the login prompt, press Enter, type your password that you selected when creating the user at the password prompt, and press Enter again. After logging in, you can type the command **startx** to start the graphical desktop.

Graphical Interface

When you installed Red Hat Linux, you had the opportunity to install a graphical environment. After you start the X Window System, you will find a graphical interface known as a *desktop*.

Figure 5-4. The Graphical Desktop

Opening or Closing a Shell Prompt

The graphical desktop offers access to a *shell prompt,* an application that allows you to type commands to control your interface instead of using a graphical interface for all computing needs. While this book focuses on performing tasks using the graphical interface and graphical tools, it is sometimes useful and faster to perform tasks from a shell prompt. Refer to Chapter 8 for more details.

You can open a shell prompt by clicking the Main Menu button and choosing System Tools ➪ Terminal. You can also start a shell prompt by double-clicking the Start Here icon, then Applications, then System Tools, and finally Terminal.

To exit a terminal window, do one of the following:

♦ Click the X button on the upper-right corner of the window.

♦ Type **exit** at the prompt.

♦ Press Ctrl-D at the prompt.

Creating a User Account

When you installed Red Hat Linux you were given the opportunity to create one or more user accounts. If you did not create at least one (not including the root account), you should do so now.

> **NOTE** We cannot stress this point enough: You should avoid working in the root account unless you absolutely have to.

There are two ways to create new and/or additional user accounts: by using the Red Hat User Manager or from a shell prompt.

To create a user account graphically using the User Manager:

1. Click the Main Menu button and choose System Settings ➪ Users and Groups. If you prefer, you can instead double-click the Start Here icon on the panel at the bottom of your desktop. In the new window that opens, click the System Settings icon, and then click the Users & Groups icon.If you prefer to use the shell prompt, you can start the User Manager by typing `redhat-config-users` at a shell prompt.

2. If you are not logged in as root, you will be prompted for your root password.

3. The window shown in Figure 5-5 will appear. Click Add User.

4. In the Create New User dialog box, enter a username (this can be an abbreviation or nickname), the full name of the user for whom this account is being created, and a password (which you will enter a second time for verification). The name of this user's home directory and the name of the login shell should appear by default. For most users, you can accept the defaults for the other configuration options. See Chapter 10 for details about additional options.

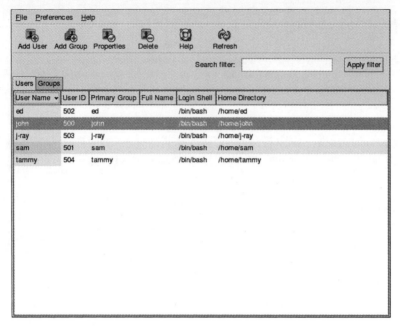

Figure 5-5. The Red Hat User Manager

5. Click OK. The new user will appear in the user list.

To create a user account from a shell prompt, follow these steps:

1. Open a shell prompt.

2. If you are not logged in as root, type the command **su -** and enter the root password.

3. Type **useradd** followed by a space and the username for the new account you are creating at the command line (for example, **useradd jsmith**) and press Enter. Often, usernames are variations on the user's name, such as jsmith for John Smith. User account names can be anything from the user's name, initials, or birthplace to something more creative.

4. Type **passwd** followed by a space and the username again (for example, **passwd jsmith**).

5. At the New password: prompt, enter a password for the new user and press Enter.

6. At the Retype new password: prompt, enter the same password to confirm your selection.

> **IMPORTANT** You can be fancy or plain when you pick a user account name, but take precautions when you choose a password. The password is the key to your account, so it should be both unique and easy for you to remember. Your password should be at least six characters. You can use both uppercase and lowercase letters, as well as numbers and characters. Avoid easily guessed selections such as qwerty or password. If you want to pick an easy-to-remember but somewhat unique password, consider a variation of a word that substitutes numbers and/or symbols for some of the letters, such as a!rPl8nE for airplane.

Logging Out

The following sections discuss how to log out of Red Hat Linux via either the graphical desktop or the virtual console.

Graphical Logout

To log out of your graphical desktop session, click the Main Menu button and choose Log Out.

When the confirmation dialog appears, select the Log Out option and click the Yes button.

> **TIP** If you want to save the configuration of your desktop, as well as any programs which are running, check the Save Current Setup option.

Figure 5-6. Logout Confirmation

Virtual Console Logout

If you are not using the X Window System and are logged in at the console, type **exit** or press Ctrl-D to log out of the console session.

Shutting Down your Computer

Before turning off your computer, it is important to shut down Red Hat Linux.

> **CAUTION** *Never* turn off your computer without shutting down first, as you may lose unsaved data or damage your system if you do.

Graphical Shutdown

If you are in the graphical desktop, log out of your session as described in the "Logging Out" section earlier in this chapter. From the graphical desktop logout screen shown in Figure 5-6, select Shut Down and click OK to confirm.

> **NOTE** You can also shut down from the graphical login screen by clicking Session, selecting the Shut down the computer option, and clicking OK.

Some computers automatically turn the power off after shutting down Red Hat Linux. If your computer does not, you can turn off the power to your computer after you see the following message:

```
Power down.
```

Virtual Console Shutdown

If you are logged in to a console, type the following command to shut down your computer:

```
halt
```

> **NOTE** While you can also use the `shutdown` command, `shutdown` must be performed as root whereas `halt` can be executed by any user.

Some computers automatically power down after shutting down Red Hat Linux. If your computer does not, you can turn off the power to your computer after you see the following message:

```
System halted.
```

Chapter 6

Using the Graphical Desktop

Red Hat Linux includes a powerful graphical desktop environment where you can easily access your applications, files, and system resources. Both new and experienced users will be able to take full advantage of the Red Hat Linux system using the graphical desktop.

This chapter covers the fundamentals of the Red Hat desktop (which is based on the GNOME graphical user interface) and how you can customize it for your needs.

Introducing the Red Hat Desktop

Your first view of the graphical desktop will look something like Figure 6-1.

Figure 6-1. The Graphical Desktop

The graphical desktop gives you access to the applications and system settings on your computer. You will notice that it offers three main tools to make use of the applications on your system: Panel icons, desktop icons, and menus.

The long bar across the bottom of the desktop is called the *Panel*. The Panel contains application launchers, status indicators, and small applications called *applets* that enable you to control sound volume, switch workspaces, and monitor the status of your system.

The icons elsewhere on the desktop can be file folders, application launchers, and removable devices such as CD-ROM and diskettes when they have been mounted. To open a folder or launch an application, double-click on its icon.

The menu systems can be found by clicking on the Main Menu button. They can also be found by clicking on the Start Here icon located on the desktop and then double-clicking the Applications icon.

The desktop works in the manner you might expect it to when working with other operating systems, such as Windows or Mac OS. You can drag and drop files and application icons to areas that are easily accessible. You can add new icons for files and applications to the desktop, panel, and file manager. You can change the appearance of most of the tools and applications, as well as change system settings by using the provided configuration tools.

Introducing the Panel

The desktop Panel is the bar that stretches across the bottom of the screen and holds icons and small applications that make using your system easier. The Panel also holds the Main Menu, which contains menu items for all of your applications. Applets allow you to run specific tasks or monitor your system or services, like the Red Hat Network, while remaining out of your way.

Figure 6-2. The Panel at the Bottom of the Desktop

Using the Main Menu

You can click on the Panel's Main Menu button (the big red hat icon on the left of the Panel) to expand it into a large set of menus that enable you to access the applications on your system. From here, you can start most applications included in Red Hat Linux. Notice that in addition to the recommended applications, you can also access additional applications under the Extras entry. These submenus give you access to a full range of applications on your system. From the Main Menu, you can also do the following:

- ◆ Log out
- ◆ Run applications from a command line
- ◆ Find files
- ◆ Lock your screen (which runs a password-protected screen saver).

Introducing Applets

Applets are small applications that run on the Panel. Applets usually let you monitor things on your system or the Internet. Some have more specific tasks while others are designed to be entertaining.

There are a few applets that run on your Panel by default. These applets are fairly important and are covered in the following sections.

Workspace Switcher

The Workspace Switcher (see Figure 6-3) is a simple applet that allows you to see what applications you have open on your workspace (a *workspace* is also called a *desktop*). The graphical desktop gives you the ability to use multiple workspaces so you do not have to have all your running applications crowding one viewable desktop area. The Workspace Switcher represents each workspace in small squares and shows the applications running on them. You may click on one of the squares with your mouse to move to that workspace.

You can also use the keyboard shortcut Ctrl-Alt-Right Arrow or Ctrl-Alt-Left Arrow to switch between workspaces.

Figure 6-3. The Workspace Switcher

The Taskbar

Next to the Workspace Switcher is the Taskbar. The Taskbar is an applet that shows you the titles of running applications on any desktop. This is very helpful if you decide to minimize an application, as it will seem to disappear from the desktop. After it disappears, you can bring it back by clicking on its title in the Taskbar.

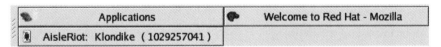

Figure 6-4. The Taskbar

Working with Icons

An icon is a picture (usually small, although you can resize icons as discussed later in this chapter) that represents a file or directory, or even devices and application launchers. Double-clicking an icon enables access to the target of the icon. To access the file or directory that an icon represents, either double-click the icon or right-click it and choose Open (or Open With . . . if you want to choose the application with which to open the file). In Figure 6-1, you can see three icons on the desktop, as well as several icons on the Panel (also called *applets*).

Using the Notification Area

As part of the Panel Notification Area, the Red Hat Network Notification Tool provides you with an easy way to make sure your system is up to date with current errata and bug fixes from Red Hat. The applet shows you different images that indicate whether your system is up to date or needs upgrades. If you click on the applet, a list of available updates will be displayed. To update your system, click the button to launch the Red Hat Update Agent. If you are not registered with Red Hat Network, it will launch the registration application. Right-click on the applet icon and select Help for details.

Figure 6-5. The Red Hat Network Notification Tool

One icon that is sometimes displayed in the Notification Area is a security notification that alerts you whenever you have gained root authentication for your system. It disappears when the authentication times out.

Figure 6-6. The Authentication Icon

Using Nautilus

The graphical desktop includes a file manager called Nautilus that gives you a graphical display of your system and personal files. Nautilus is designed to be much more than a visual listing of files, however; it also allows you to

♦ Configure your desktop

♦ Configure your Red Hat Linux system

♦ Play digital music and video files

♦ Browse photos

♦ Access your network resources

You can do all this and more from one integrated interface. In essence, Nautilus becomes a navigation tool for your entire desktop experience.

Working in Nautilus is efficient and provides an alternative to searching through the various submenus connected to the Main Menu or using a shell prompt to navigate the file system.

To start Nautilus as a file manager, double-click on your home directory icon. Once Nautilus appears, you can navigate through your home directory or the rest of the file system.

To return to your home directory, click the Home button.

When you navigate through your file system, you can always see where you are by looking at the frame on the left that shows you the current directory.

The main frame contains folders and files that you can drag with your mouse to move and copy into new locations. If you prefer, you may click on the Tree tab on the bottom left to display a hierarchical view of your complete file system that may make moving and copying easier for you.

If the Tree tab does not appear on the bottom left, you can make the tab available by right-clicking in the tab area and choosing Tree from the menu.

If you do not want to use the tree view, you can open another Nautilus window by selecting File ⇨ New Window. After you have another Nautilus window, you can drag and drop files to different directories.

> **NOTE** By default, dragging a file from one directory to another will move the file. If you wish to copy the file to another directory, press the Ctrl key while dragging and dropping the file.

By default, text-based files and images in your home directory will be seen as *thumbnails*. For text files, this means you will see a portion of the actual text in the icon. For images, you will see a scaled down (or *thumbnail*) version of the image. To turn off this feature, select Edit ⇨ Preferences. Select Performance from the menu on the left and then select Never for the visual enhancements that you want to disable. Disabling these features will increase the speed of Nautilus.

Start Here

The Start Here window was designed to hold all of the tools and applications you need to access when using your system. From your favorite applications to system and configuration tools, the Start Here window provides a central location for using and customizing your system.

You may access Start Here at any time by double-clicking on the desktop icon labeled Start Here.

The Start Here screen includes icons that allow you to access your favorite applications, desktop preferences, Main Menu items, server configuration tools, and system settings.

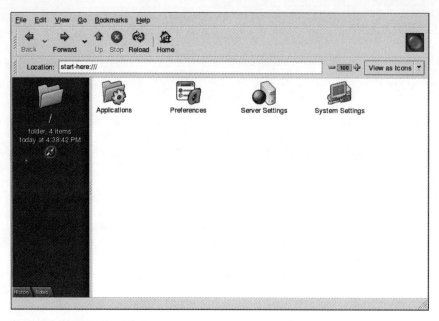

Figure 6-7. The Start Here Window

TIP You can add your own favorite applications to the Bookmarks section of the Start Here window. To add an application to the Bookmarks section, navigate to the location you want to bookmark and then choose Bookmarks ⇨ Add Bookmark. You will see an icon for the application in the Bookmarks menu immediately.

The Home Icon

The Home icon opens Nautilus and takes you to your home directory, which is either under the /home directory or /root if you are logged in as root. If your user name is john, for example, your home directory would be /home/john. Additionally, this icon is named after the user; so, in our example, the Home icon would be called john's Home (refer to Figure 6-1).

NOTE The root user's home directory is under /root.

Your home directory is the default location for all of a user's files. Whenever you create a new file of any type in an application (such as OpenOffice.org Writer) and click Save, the Save dialog that appears will show your home directory as the default directory to save in.

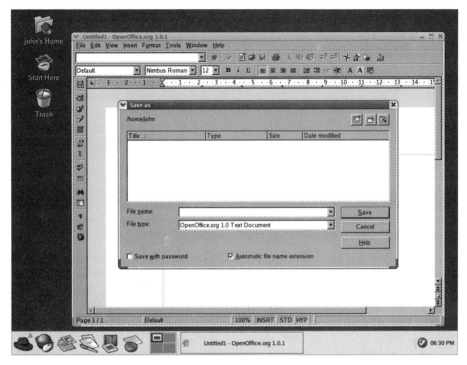

Figure 6-8. Your Default Save Directory — Home

> **TIP** You can save yourself a lot of time browsing through directories by saving your files in your home directory (or its subdirectories).

Of course, saving all of your files within your home directory itself is a bad idea — that is what subdirectories are for. To create a subdirectory within your home folder, you can do one of the following:

- ◆ From the Nautilus file manager, choose File ➪ New Folder.
- ◆ Right-click on the desktop or in a folder window (such as Nautilus) and choose New Folder.

Regardless of which method you prefer to use, the new folder appears with its default name (untitled folder) selected; type in a name for your new folder and then either press Enter or click another part of the interface to accept the new name.

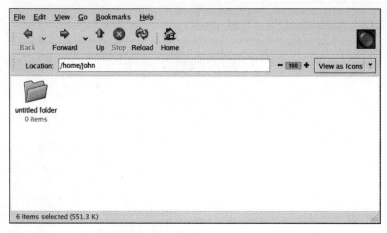

Figure 6-9. Creating a New Folder

Deleting Files with the Trash Icon

The Trash icon on your Red Hat Linux desktop is one of the most obvious methods of deleting files. If you want to delete a file on your desktop or from a window onscreen, click on the file and drag it onto the Trash icon and then release the mouse button. When the Trash has something in it, you will see its icon change from being empty (see Figure 6-1) to being full of paper.

Figure 6-10. A Full Trash Can

> **TIP** Every time you right-click a file in the Red Hat Linux interface (such as in the Nautilus file manager), there will be a Move to Trash item on the menu that appears. You can choose this menu item to instantly move the file to the Trash.

Recovering Files from the Trash

The nice thing about the Trash is that you have a chance to salvage the file — just like you could take a piece of paper out of a trash can after throwing it away. To recover a file that you have thrown in the Trash, double-click the Trash icon on your desktop, find the file you want to recover, and drag it out of the trash onto your desktop or wherever else you want to put it.

> **CAUTION** Keep in mind that you cannot recover a file from the Trash after you have emptied the trash or deleted the file from the Trash (as discussed in the next section).

Emptying the Trash

The trash can is just like a real trash can — it does not empty itself; you have to empty it.

WARNING After you empty the Trash, all files in it are gone forever.

To empty the Trash, do one of the following:

♦ Double-click the Trash icon on your desktop and choose File ⇨ Empty Trash.

♦ Right-click the Trash icon on your desktop and choose Empty Trash.

Note If you only want to delete one file from the Trash, not every file, you can open the Trash, click on the file, and choose Edit ⇨ Delete from Trash.

Customizing your System

You can customize nearly every aspect of the brand-new Red Hat Linux 8.0 interface. From adding new Panels and changing the look of your interface, to resizing icons and adding emblems to icons, Red Hat Linux 8.0 makes it easier than ever to customize the desktop interface.

Figure 6-11 shows just how different you can make your desktop look. Compare this figure with Figure 6-1; the two do not even resemble one another.

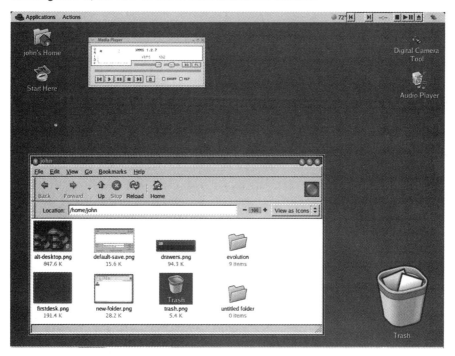

Figure 6-11. Customizing Your Desktop

The following sections show you how to customize your system to suit your needs and preferences.

Setting your Preferences

The central location for customizing your system is from the Preferences menu of the Main Menu. (You can also access Preferences by double-clicking the Start Here icon on your desktop and double-clicking the Preferences icon.) The Preferences menu offers a wide selection of configuration options. The following list discusses these options briefly.

- *About Myself* — From here you can change your login shell, as well as add information about yourself such as your home and office phone numbers.

- *Accessibility* — Here you can make changes to the way Red Hat Linux responds to key presses, mouse clicks, and so on.

- *Background* — You can configure your background with new colors, patterns, or a new image.

- *CD Properties* — From here you can change whether or not CDs are automatically mounted by default, which command is executed when a CD is inserted in the drive, and more.

- *Extras* — A few advanced preferences are under Extras, including an HTML viewer icon that launches the preferences for viewing HTML files in graphical applications, the Desktop Switching tool, and some extra Panel preferences. Also included here is the Preferred Applications utility, which allows you to set your default Web browser, text editor, and terminal.

- *File types and programs* — From here you can add new file types and change the programs that are associated with file types.

- *Font* — Here you can configure which fonts are used for various system elements, such as title bars, terminal windows, the desktop, and applications.

- *Keyboard* — Make decisions about your keyboard, such as the keyboard repeat rates, the cursor blink rate, and whether you want your keyboard to beep at you.

- *Keyboard Shortcuts* — You can configure *shortcuts* (pressing a combination of keystrokes on the keyboard) to perform actions within an application or on your desktop. For example, you can configure a shortcut to move from your current Workspace to Workspace 2 by pressing Ctrl-F2.

- *Menus and Toolbars* — Customize the way your toolbars and menus behave. For example, you can choose not to have icons displayed in menus.

- *Mouse* — Here you can configure your mouse, with options such as allowing for a left-handed mouse, setting your double-click delay, and changing your cursor and the sensitivity of mouse motions.

- *Network Proxy* — Here you can set your HTTP proxy (if you have one) as well as any username and password the proxy might require.

- *Password* — This tool allows you to change your user password; you have to enter your existing password first.

- *Pilot/Handspring Tool* — If you have a Palm Pilot or Handspring Visor, you can configure it to sync with Red Hat Linux using this tool.

- *Screensaver* — This tool lets you change your default screensaver, configure the settings of a given screen saver, and set the number of minutes your system will wait to bring the screensaver up.

- *Sound* — In this section you can configure the system sounds associated with various functions. For example, if you would like to have a sound play when you log in to your desktop, you can configure that here.

- *Theme* — This utility allows you to change your theme or window border as well as install new ones.

- *Window Focus* — This tool enables you to change the way you give a window focus (which means to bring it to front). The default setting is that you have to click somewhere on the window to give it focus, but you can also configure your settings so that you can merely point to a window to give it focus and bring it to the front.

Customizing the Desktop

The Start Here screen in Nautilus contains additional configuration tools that help you with your new Red Hat Linux system and the server applications included. The System Settings icon includes tools that help you set up your system for personal everyday use. Below you will find a list of some of the tools included in System Settings and what you can do with them.

- *Date & Time* — This tool allows you to set the date and time of your machine. You will be able to set your time zone information as well. See Chapter 19 for more information on time and date configuration.

- Soundcard Detection — The Soundcard Detection tool probes your machine for available sound devices. See Chapter 14 for more details on configuring your sound hardware.

- *Users & Groups* — The Users & Groups tool allows you to add and remove users from your system. See Chapter 10 for details.

- *Printing* — The Printer Configuration Tool allows you to add a new printer to your system. The printer may be connected to your machine or available on a network. See Chapter 16 for details.

As mentioned before, you will also find server configuration tools in the Start Here area. These tools help you configure services and applications you are using on the local machine to serve other machines. The server configuration tools are found by clicking on the Server Settings icon. A couple of examples of the tools found in this area are the tools for the Apache Web Server and a DNS/Bind tool. You must have those server applications installed before these tools appear in this section. Refer to the *Official Red Hat Linux Administrator's Guide* (Red Hat Press/Wiley, 2003) for details.

Customizing the Panel

You can hide the Panel automatically or manually, place it on any edge of your desktop, change its size and color, and change the way it behaves. To alter the default Panel settings, right-click in an unused area of the panel and select Properties. You can set the size of the Panel, its position on the desktop, and whether you want the Panel to be automatically hidden (Autohide) when not in use. If you choose to Autohide the Panel, it will not appear on the desktop until you move your mouse pointer towards it.

Adding Icons and Applets to the Panel

To make the panel fit your needs, you may want to add more applets and launcher icons. To add an applet to the Panel, right-click in an unused area on the Panel, select Add to Panel, and choose from the menu of applets. When you select an applet, it will appear on your Panel, as that is the only place it will run.

To add a launcher icon to the panel, right-click in an unused area on the Panel and select Add to Panel ⇨ Launcher. This will launch a dialog box that allows you to enter the name of the application, the location and name of the command that starts the application (such as /usr/bin/foo), and even choose an icon for the application. Click OK and the new launcher icon will appear on the Panel.

> **TIP** Another quick and easy way to add a launcher to the Panel is to right-click on an unused area of the Panel and choose Add to Panel ⇨ Launcher from menu. Then select an application that appears in the menu. This will automatically add a launcher icon based on the properties of the item in the Main Menu.

Autohiding the Panel

Autohiding the Panel makes the Panel disappear altogether until you drag your mouse to the bottom of the screen (or whichever edge of the screen your Panel is located). To autohide the Panel, right-click an empty spot on the Panel and select Properties, check the Autohide checkbox, and click Close. The Panel in Figure 6-11 is not visible because we chose to autohide it.

Adding Drawers to the Panel

A drawer is really like a Panel within a Panel. A drawer can be collapsed to just an icon (a drawer) or extended into an entirely new Panel. Drawers are quite useful for organizing applications on a Panel. For example, you might want to have a drawer on your Panel that includes all of your Internet software and another drawer that contains all of your Office Productivity software to avoid having a cluttered Panel.

To add a drawer to the Panel, right-click an empty spot on the Panel and choose Add to Panel ⇨ Drawer from the menu that appears.

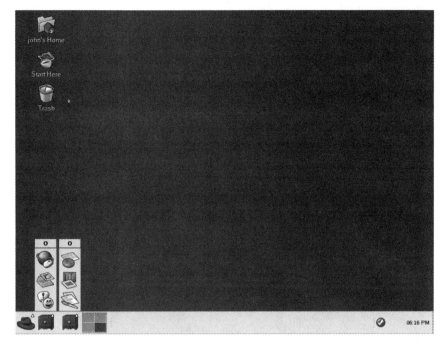

Figure 6-12. Adding a Drawer to the Panel

Moving the Panel

To move a Panel, right-click an empty spot on the Panel and choose Properties. Then click the desired Position for your Panel. The Position options will be different depending on the type of Panel you are dealing with.

Resizing the Panel

To resize a Panel, right-click an empty spot on the Panel and choose Properties. Then pull down the Size: drop-down list and choose a new size for your Panel. The size for the default Panel is Medium (48 pixels).

Adding Panels

To add a Panel, right-click any spot on an empty spot on the Panel and choose New Panel ⇨ Panel Type, and select from among the following types of Panels:

- ♦ *Corner Panel* — A Panel that sits in the corner.
- ♦ *Edge Panel* — A Panel that sits along one edge of the screen.

> **NOTE** The original Panel is an edge Panel.

♦ *Floating Panel* — A floating Panel can be moved anywhere on the screen.

♦ *Sliding Panel* — A sliding Panel can be moved along any edge of the screen, but not out into the middle of the screen.

♦ *Menu Panel* —The menu Panel sits at the top of the screen and is smaller than the original Panel by about one-half. There is an Applications menu button and an Actions menu that, between the two of them, pretty much replace the original Main Menu.

Figure 6-13 shows the desktop with one of each of the five types of Panels (the original Panel at the bottom represents the edge Panel type).

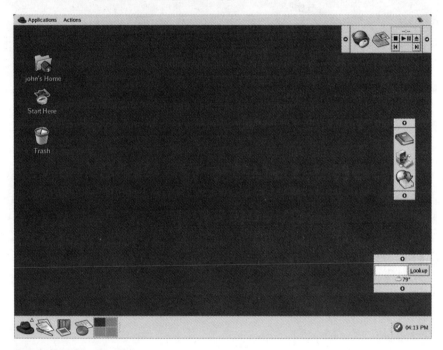

Figure 6-13. Adding New Panels

Deleting a Panel

To delete a Panel, right-click the Panel you want to delete and choose Delete this Panel from the menu that appears. All of the configuration settings of that Panel will be lost.

> **WARNING** You can delete the original Panel, but all of the settings will be lost.

Customizing Workspaces

Workspaces are the equivalent of extra desktops on your system. By default, Red Hat Linux comes with four workspaces that you can work with, but you are by no means limited to four. The following sections show you how to add and remove workspaces, drag applications across workspaces, and make a single application appear on all of your workspaces.

Adding or Removing Workspaces

Depending on your needs, you may want more or fewer than the four default workspaces. To add or remove workspaces from your panel, right-click the Workspace Switcher Panel applet (refer to Figure 6-3) and choose Preferences. The Workspace Switcher Preferences window appears. From this window you can change the number of workspaces, choose to show only the first workspace (if you do not want any additional workspaces), or change the number of rows that your workspaces are displayed in.

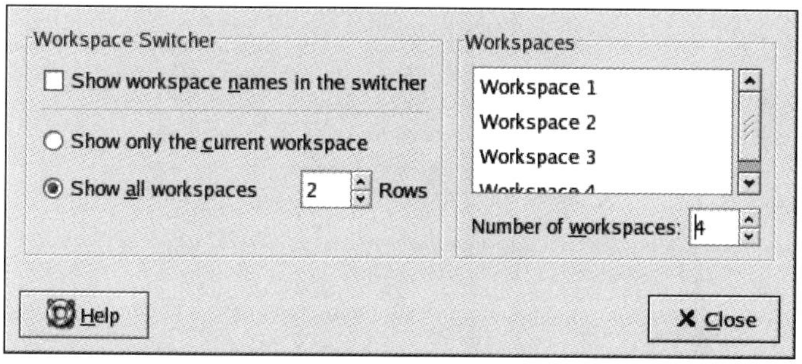

Figure 6-14. The Workspace Switcher Preferences Window

Dragging Applications Across Workspaces

Workspaces can be useful if you find you have a lot of applications open at the same time and do not want all of them cluttering up a single workspace. Using workspaces, you could group applications of a certain type on different workspaces. For example, if you are working with several Internet applications, several OpenOffice.org applications, and several graphics applications, you could have all of the Internet applications on one workspace, all of the OpenOffice.org applications on a second workspace, and all of the graphics applications on another workspace.

Moving an application across workspaces is easy; click the icon for an open window in one workspace on the Workspace Switcher Panel applet (refer to Figure 6-3) and then drag it to a different workspace on the applet.

TIP The current workspace is easily identified because it is the dark box among the rest of the workspaces, which are of a lighter color.

After dragging the application to a different workspace, you can access the application by clicking on that workspace on the Workspace Switcher Panel applet and then clicking on the application.

Making One Window Appear on All Workspaces

You may find that when working with workspaces you have applications that you want to be accessible on all workspaces. For example, if you are waiting on an important email but do not want to have to keep switching workspaces to check your email, making one window appear on all workspaces would allow you to keep your eye on your email client no matter what workspace you are using. To make one window appear on all desktops, click the down arrow in the upper left corner of the window. In the menu displayed, select Put on All Workspaces.

Changing Your System's Appearance

Some customization features do not really change the way you work with your system, but just change the look of your system. For example, your desktop background does not affect the way you work with your system, but it does change the appearance of your desktop.

The following sections show you how to change your system's appearance.

Changing Themes

Themes are becoming more and more popular in modern software; a theme is basically a different interface for your windows and graphical user interface.

> **TIP** Even Mozilla 1.0 supports its own themes (choose View ➪ Apply Theme from the Mozilla browser window).

To change your theme, click the Main Menu button and choose Preferences ➪ Theme, choose a new theme from the Installed themes list, and click Close.

Figure 6-15. The Theme Preferences Window

Red Hat Linux comes with the following choice of themes:

♦ *Bluecurve* — This is the default theme for Red Hat Linux 8.0.

♦ *Raleigh* — This theme is named after the city in North Carolina that Red Hat is based in looks a great deal like Red Hat Linux 7.*x* and earlier.

♦ *Redmond 95* — This theme is named after the city in Washington that Microsoft is based in, and looks quite reminiscent of Windows 95.

♦ *Metal* — This theme looks similar to the default theme (called Bluecurve), but is colored differently and includes some more metallic textures.

New themes can be installed by dragging them from their location in a folder (or desktop) onto the Theme Preferences window.

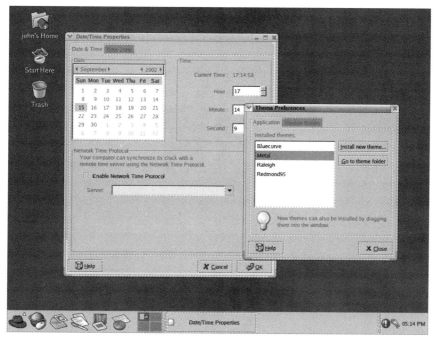

Figure 6-16. The Metal Theme

You can change your interface even more drastically by clicking the Window Borders tab and trying out some of the various window borders.

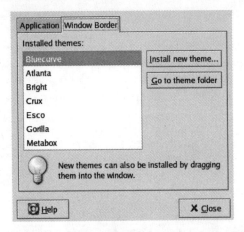

Figure 6-17. Theme Preferences — Window Border Tab

There are several window border styles listed here, some of which are very different from the original, such as the Gorilla window border style.

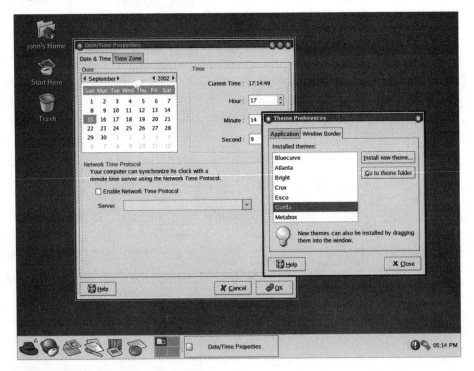

Figure 6-18. The Gorilla Window Border Style

Changing Desktop Backgrounds

To change your desktop background, click the Main Menu button and choose Preferences ⇨ Background. The Background Preferences window appears, from which you can change the background pattern or even drag a picture onto the window to make that picture your background.

Figure 6-19. Changing Your Desktop Background

Changing Window or Desktop Patterns

This feature allows you to change the pattern for a window background or the desktop. To do so, from the Nautilus window choose Edit ⇨ Backgrounds and Emblems and then click the Patterns button on the left. By default, the Patterns customization features are in front. On the Patterns window are different patterns that you can use to change the look of the Nautilus window or even your desktop. Find a pattern that you like, click it, and then drag it to either the Nautilus window or to the desktop and watch Nautilus (or the desktop) change to that pattern. Drag the Reset box onto the item to reset it to its original state.

> **NOTE** As you are dragging a pattern across the screen, you can tell whether or not the item underneath it can be changed by looking at the shape of the cursor. If the cursor shows a plus symbol, you can change the item underneath the pattern; if the cursor shows no plus symbol, dropping the pattern there will do nothing.

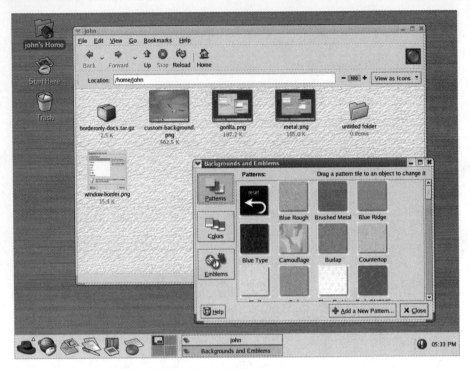

Figure 6-20. Changing Your Desktop and Window Patterns

Changing Window or Desktop Colors

Just like changing a pattern, changing a color is easy. To do so, from the Nautilus window choose Edit ➪ Backgrounds and Emblems and then click the Colors button at left. Then you can click the desired color and, while holding the mouse button down, drag the color onto the desired item and drop it there. Drag the Reset box onto the item to reset it to its original state.

> **NOTE** As you are dragging a color across the screen, you can tell whether or not the item underneath it can be changed by whatever you are dragging by the shape of the cursor. If the cursor shows a plus, you can change the item underneath the color; if the cursor shows no plus symbol, dropping the color there will do nothing.

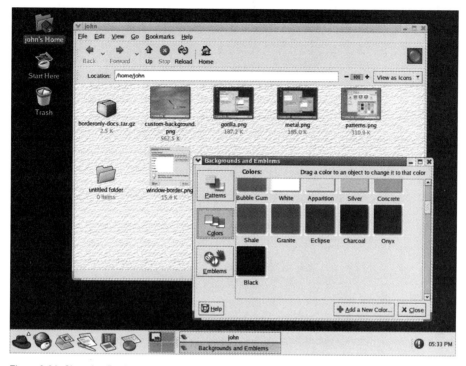

Figure 6-21. Changing Desktop and Window Colors

Adding Emblems to Icons

This feature allows you to add little emblems to icons to help you better distinguish similar icons from one another. For example, one of the emblems says "Draft"; if you have several documents in a folder and want to be able to visually tell the drafts from the final versions, you can add the "Draft" emblem to all the draft versions in the folder so that you can tell them apart.

To add an emblem to an icon, follow these steps:

1. From the Nautilus window choose Edit ⇨ Backgrounds and Emblems. The Backgrounds and Emblems window appears.

2. Click the Emblems button at the left of the window.

3. Find the emblem you want and drag it onto the icon.

NOTE You can also right-click an icon, choose Properties from the context menu, and then add or remove icons from the Emblems tab of the icon's Properties window.

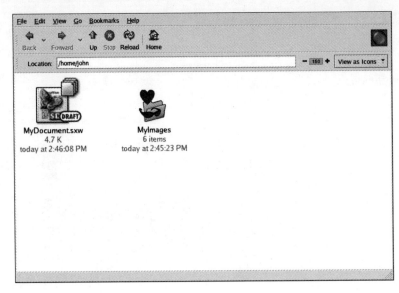

Figure 6-22. Adding Emblems to Icons

Resizing Icons

Red Hat Linux now includes the ability to resize icons to suit your tastes or needs.

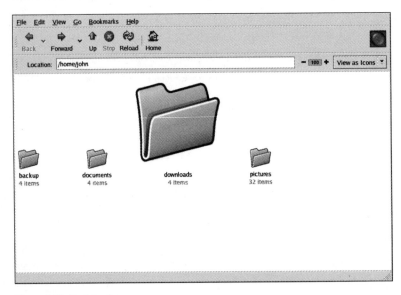

Figure 6-23. Resizing Icons

If you are working with many files and folders in a given folder and want one folder to be very easy to spot compared to the others, right-click the icon and choose Stretch Icon from the menu. Little handles will appear at the icon's corners; you can then stretch the icon by clicking on one of the handles and dragging it away from the center of the icon to make it larger or towards the center of the icon to make it smaller.

To reset the icon to its original size, right-click the icon and choose Restore Icon's Original Size.

Changing Your Screensaver

Red Hat Linux 8.0 comes with some impressive screensavers.

Figure 6-24. Screensavers in Red Hat Linux

To change your screensaver, click the Main Menu button and choose Preferences ⇨ Screensaver. The Screensaver Preferences window appears, from which you can change your screensaver, modify the settings of a screensaver, and preview a screensaver.

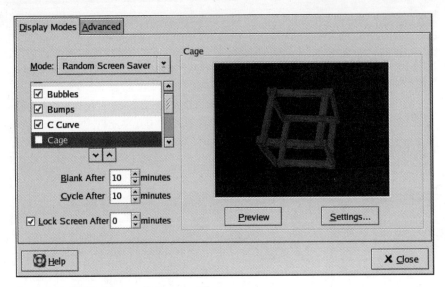

Figure 6-25. The Screensaver Preferences Window

Logging Out

When you have finished working and want to quit the graphical desktop, you are presented with the choice of logging out of the graphical desktop (leaving the system running), restarting the machine, or halting the system completely.

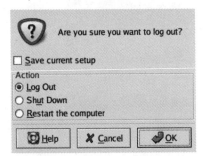

Figure 6-26. The Desktop Log Out Confirmation

To quit the graphical desktop, select the Log Out menu item from the Main Menu. This will bring up a dialog that presents you with the options listed above.

Chapter 7

Diskettes and CD-ROMs

Using diskettes and CD-ROMs with Red Hat Linux requires some understanding about removable media. This chapter discusses how to read and write files to and from diskettes, how to format diskettes, and how to read and copy data from a CD-ROM. This chapter also covers using CD-writable and CD-rewritable drives.

NOTE The term *disk* typically refers to disks such as hard drives; the term *diskette* usually refers specifically to floppy disks; and the term *disc* refers to optical media such as CD-ROMs and DVDs.

Using Diskettes

Diskettes are one of the oldest removable media solutions available for the PC. Diskettes are ideal as a portable storage solution for files that need to be physically moved around. For example, if two PCs are not on the same network, diskettes are a great solution to transfer files from one computer to the other.

Mounting and Unmounting a Diskette

A diskette must be mounted first before it can be used. Insert a diskette into the diskette drive and type **mount /mnt/floppy/** at a shell prompt.

The diskette drive activity light should blink as the diskette's file system is mounted to the `/mnt/floppy` directory.

You can access the contents of the diskette by changing into that directory with the `cd /mnt/floppy/` command.

Alternatively, you can also mount a diskette by right-clicking on the desktop and choosing Disks ⇨ Floppy. This mounts the diskette and adds a desktop icon that you can double-click to explore the diskette contents.

Now that the diskette has been mounted it is available to be copied from or written to. You can open, save, and copy files to or from the diskette as you would normally do to your hard drive. You can even explore the diskette's contents in Nautilus or Konqueror.

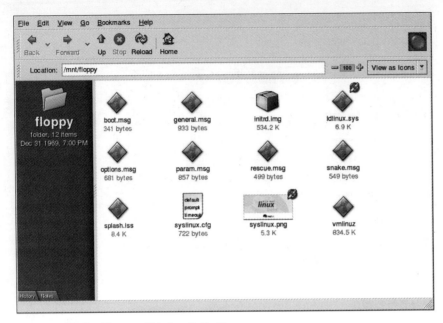

Figure 7-1. Viewing Files on a Diskette with Nautilus

When you are finished using the diskette, you should unmount it before ejecting it from the drive. To do this, close any applications that may be using files on the diskette or exploring the diskette's contents (such as Nautilus or Konqueror), and at a shell prompt type the following command:

```
umount /mnt/floppy/
```

You can now safely eject the diskette from the drive.

> **TIP** If you are using the default Red Hat desktop environment, you can unmount the diskette by right-clicking on the icon and choosing Unmount Volume from the menu that appears.

Reading MS-DOS Formatted Diskettes

If you have an MS-DOS formatted diskette, you can access the files on it by using the mtools utility. mtools offers a wide range of options for working with diskettes, including copying, moving, deleting, and formatting. (To read more about mtools, type **man mtools** at a shell prompt.)

For example, to copy a file called file.txt from an MS-DOS formatted diskette (such as one from a Windows system), type the following command at a shell prompt:

```
mcopy a:file.txt
file.txt
```

`file.txt` will then be copied from the diskette drive (assuming that the disk is in drive A:) to the directory you were in when you issued the `mcopy` command. If you are in your home directory, you will find `file.txt` located there.

If you want to view the contents of an MS-DOS formatted diskette, type **mdir** at the prompt. You will be shown the contents of the diskette. The directory listing will look familiar to some MS-DOS or Windows users, as it is styled in the MS-DOS `dir` listing format. For example:

```
[joe@localhost joe]$ mdir a:
Volume in drive A has no label
Volume Serial Number is 0000-0000
Directory for A:/
FOOBAR TXT 6004 01-01-1999 1:01
ZZTOP COM 1533 01-01-1999 1:01
TAXES99 XLS 26469 01-01-1999 1:01
THISFILE TXT 277 01-01-1999 1:01
COMMAND COM 93890 01-01-1999 1:01
5 files 128 173 bytes
1 271 827 bytes free
```

To change to a subdirectory on the diskette, type the following command at a shell prompt:

```
mcd a:subdir
```

In the above command, replace *subdir* with the name of the subdirectory you want to access.

Putting Linux Files on an MS-DOS Diskette

To copy files from a Linux machine to an MS-DOS formatted diskette so that a Windows machine can read it, you should format your disk with an MS-DOS (FAT) file system, which can be done with a Windows OS or with `gfloppy` (see the "Using gfloppy" section later in this chapter). Then mount it in Linux as described in the preceding section. Copy files using the following command (substituting *filename* with the name of the file you wish to copy):

```
cp filename /mnt/floppy
```

You can then unmount the floppy and eject it from the drive. The new file on the diskette should now be accessible from your Windows machine.

> **NOTE** The file will not be copied until *after* the `umount` command has been successfully executed.

Formatting a Diskette

To use a diskette specifically with Red Hat Linux, you need to format the disk using the ext2 file system. ext2 is one of the file systems supported by Red Hat Linux, and is the default method used for formatting diskettes.

> **WARNING** Formatting a diskette will erase all of its contents. Be sure to back up any files that you need before performing any of the following operations on your diskettes.

After you have created an ext2 file system on the diskette, you can manipulate its contents in the same ways that you manipulate directories and files on your hard drive.

> **NOTE** If you're wondering why a floppy should be formatted with ext2 rather than ext3, it's because the only real difference between ext2 and ext3 is journaling, which increases the size of the file system. Because diskettes are so small, they don't require journaling features (or the increased size of the file system), so ext2 should be used instead of ext3 for diskettes.

Using gfloppy

To start gfloppy, click the Main Menu button and choose System Tools ⇨ Floppy Formatter (or, from a shell prompt, you can type **/usr/bin/gfloppy**). As shown in Figure 7-2, the gfloppy interface is small and has few options.

The default settings are sufficient for most users and needs; however, you can format your diskette with an MS-DOS file system type if you desire. You can also choose the density of your floppy disk (if you are not using the usual high density 3.5" 1.44MB diskette). You can also elect to *quick format* the diskette if it was previously formatted as ext2.

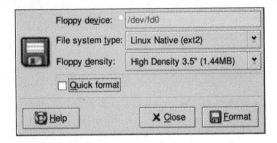

Figure 7-2. gfloppy

Insert a diskette and change the settings to suit your needs; then click Format. The status box will appear on top of the main window, showing you the status of formatting and verifying (see Figure 7-3). When it is complete, you can eject the disk and close gfloppy.

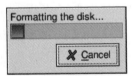

Figure 7-3. gfloppy Status Box

Using KFloppy

Another way to format a diskette for either ext2 or MS-DOS is to use KFloppy. To start the utility, open a shell prompt and type the command **kfloppy**. You will be presented with a graphical interface, as shown in Figure 7-4.

Insert a diskette that you wish to format and choose whether you want a Quick Format or Full Format by choosing the appropriate radio button. To check for bad sectors or blocks on the diskette while formatting, choose Verify Integrity in the associated check box.

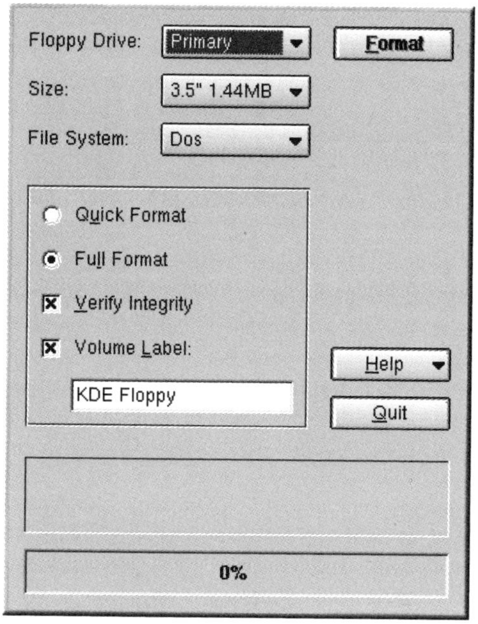

Figure 7-4. KDE Floppy Formatter

To begin formatting, click the Format button. A window will pop up asking if you wish to format the diskette. Click Continue to dismiss this window and begin formatting. A status bar will appear at the bottom of the window showing the status of the format. After the diskette has been formatted, a final window will appear to inform you of a successful format. Click OK, remove the diskette, and click Quit to close the application.

Using mke2fs

The mke2fs command is used to create a Linux ext2 file system on a device such as a hard drive partition or (in this case) a floppy diskette. mke2fs essentially formats the device and creates an empty, Linux-compatible device that can then be used for storing files and data.

Insert your diskette into the drive and issue the following command at a shell prompt:

```
/sbin/mke2fs /dev/fd0
```

On Linux systems, /dev/fd0 refers to the first diskette drive. If your computer has more than one floppy disk drive, your primary floppy drive will be /dev/fd0, your second floppy drive will be designated /dev/fd1, and so on.

The mke2fs utility has a number of options. The -c option makes the mke2fs command check the device for bad blocks before creating the file system. The other options are covered in the mke2fs man page.

Once you have created an ext2 file system on the diskette, it is ready to be used with your Red Hat Linux system.

Using CD-ROMs

The CD-ROM format is a popular way to deliver large software applications and multimedia presentations. Most of the software that can be purchased from retail outlets comes on CD-ROMs. This section shows you how to use CD-ROMs on your Red Hat Linux system.

By default, Red Hat Linux automatically detects a CD-ROM when it is inserted in the CD-ROM device. The disc will then be mounted and your file manager will open a window with the disc drive's contents for you to explore.

Using CD-ROMs with Your File Manager

By default, CDs are automatically mounted and the default file manager opens for you to explore the contents of the CD. Figure 7-5 shows the contents of a CD-ROM within the Nautilus file manager.

Figure 7-5. Contents of a CD-ROM in Nautilus

A CD desktop icon will also appear, which you can use to unmount and eject your CD-ROM after use. Right-click on the icon to view all of the available choices. For example, to unmount and eject the CD-ROM, right-click the icon and choose Eject from the menu.

Using CD-ROMs from a Shell Prompt

You can also manually mount and unmount your CD-ROMs from a shell prompt. Insert a CD into your CD-ROM drive, open a shell prompt, and type the following command:

```
mount /mnt/cdrom
```

The CD-ROM should now be mounted and available for use with your file manager. For example, if you are using Konqueror, you can access your CD-ROM by clicking the icon on the desktop and typing **/mnt/cdrom** in the location bar. Figure 7-6 shows the contents of a CD-ROM displayed in the Konqueror file manager.

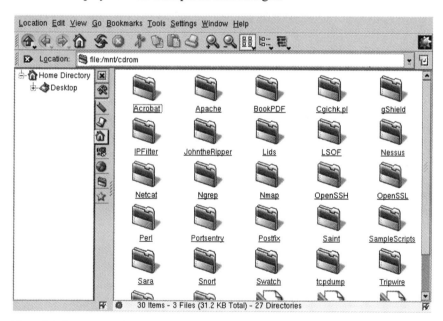

Figure 7-6. Contents of a CD-ROM in Konqueror

After working with your CD, you must unmount it before you eject it from your CD-ROM drive.

Close any applications or file managers that are using the CD-ROM and type the following at a shell prompt:

```
umount /mnt/cdrom
```

You can now safely press the eject button on your CD-ROM drive (or by using the `eject` command) to retrieve your CD.

CD-Rs and CD-RWs

CD-writable (CD-R) drives have grown in popularity as an inexpensive way to back up and archive data, including applications, personal files, and even multimedia (audio/video and still image) presentations. Red Hat Linux includes several tools for using CD-Rs and CD-rewritable (CD-RW) drives.

Using X-CD-Roast

X-CD-Roast is a graphical application for duplicating and creating (mastering) CD-ROMs. X-CD-Roast automates the process of burning CD-Rs and CD-RWs and is highly configurable to many CD mastering or duplicating needs.

To start X-CD-Roast, choose Main Menu ⇨ System Tools ⇨ CD Writer. To start it at a shell prompt, type **/usr/bin/xcdroast**. X-CD-Roast will first scan your device busses and find your CD-R(W) drive. It will then allow you to configure settings for CD-writer, CD-ROM drive, and more.

Figure 7-7 illustrates the Setup screen and its configuration options. Note that your CD-R(W) drive brand may be different from the drive shown.

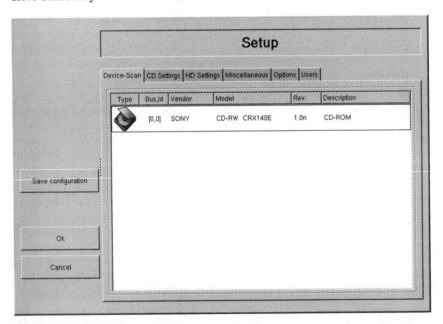

Figure 7-7. X-CD-Roast Setup Screen

Check your CD-R(W) manufacturer documentation to set some of the CD Settings options, such as CD Writer Speed and CD Writer FIFO-Buffer Size. All CD image (.iso or .img) files need to be stored in a central location accessible to X-CD-Roast. You will have to specify a path on your hard drive's file system that has at least 700MB of free space available. You can configure the path where you wish to store CD images in the HD Settings tab under Path.

X-CD-Roast is well documented within the interface itself, as several of the options have long, descriptive pop-up tips that inform you of the associated function in detail. You can access these *tooltips* by leaving your mouse pointer on a button or drop-down menu for at least two seconds.

Using X-CD-Roast to Duplicate CD-ROMs

To duplicate an existing CD-ROM for backup purposes, click the Duplicate CD button in the main panel. You can read all of the *tracks* on a CD — all CD-ROM information, including data and audio, is stored on tracks — by clicking Read CD. You can set the speed at which you read a CD-ROM as well as find out some information about the CD-ROM track such as its type and size. If you are copying tracks from an audio CD, you can preview each track with Play Audio-Tracks. Because X-CD-Roast reads all tracks of a CD-ROM by default, you can delete unwanted tracks with Delete Tracks.

Finally, to burn your tracks onto CD-R(W) media, choose Write CD. Figure 7-8 shows the Write CD dialog box where you can configure the speed at which you read and write the tracks to CD-R as well as whether you wish to copy the CD-ROM *on-the-fly* or create an image file first before burning, which is recommended to prevent write or read errors from occurring during the duplication process.

Click the Write CD button to start the burning process.

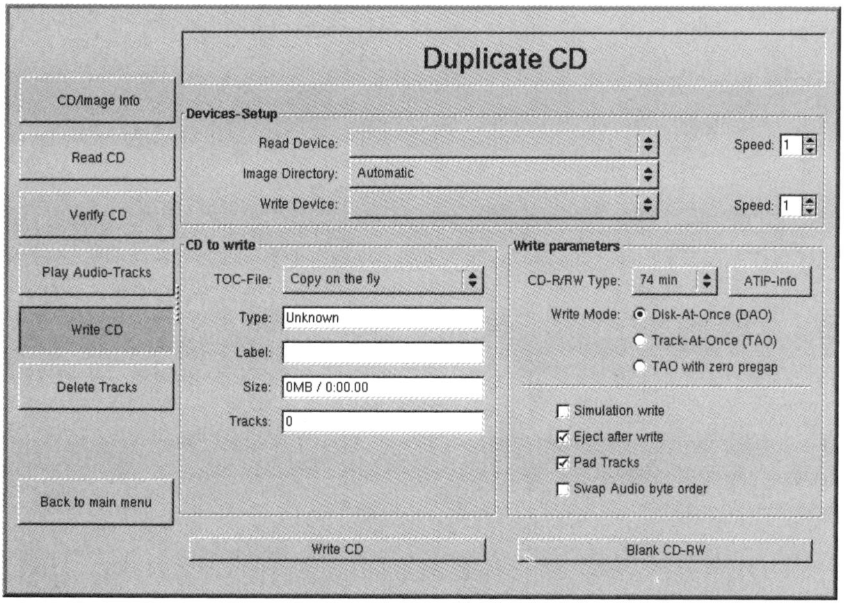

Figure 7-8. Using X-CD-Roast to Duplicate CDs

Using X-CD-Roast to Create a CD

You should always back up personal data and information often in case of hardware failure or file system corruption. X-CD-Roast allows you to backup files on your hard drive partition using Create CD. This facility allows you to add files and directories into a CD *session* using Master Tracks.

There are other options within the Master Tracks dialog that allows you to configure advanced settings; however, the defaults are set correctly to create data CD-ROMs, so no further configuration is necessary. Figure 7-9 shows a session that is preparing the entire /home directory for backup.

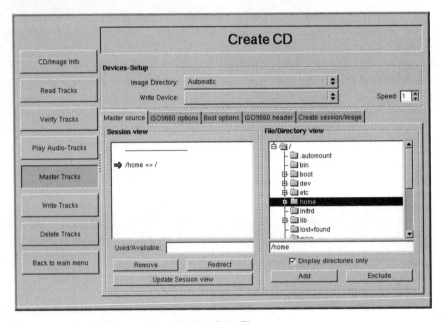

Figure 7-9. Using X-CD-Roast to Back Up Hard Drive Files

Highlight the files and directories that you wish to add to the session and click Add. After you have added all the files and directories you want to write to the CD-R(W), click the Create session/image tab to create the .img file. You must first click Calculate size and then Master to image file to create the image.

To write your tracks to the CD-R(W), click Write Tracks from the panel on the left. In the Layout Tracks tab, highlight the image file you created in the box on the right, and click Add. The image will be displayed in the Tracks to write box on the left side. Click Accept track layout, and click the Write Tracks tab to return to the main writing dialog. Click Write tracks to write the image to the CD-R(W).

Writing ISOs with X-CD-Roast

Large files that end in .iso are known as ISO9660 (or ISO) image files. For example, Red Hat Linux is freely available as ISO images that you can download and write to the CD-R(W). There are other ISO image files available on FTP and websites. There are other file types that can be burned as images, such as .img and .raw, but ISO images are the most common CD image format.

To write an ISO image file to a CD-R(W) with X-CD-Roast, move the ISO file to the path specified during setup and then click Create CD. In the Layout tracks tab, highlight the ISO image file you wish to burn and click Add, then Accept track layout. This will automatically load the Write Tracks tab where you can click Write Tracks to burn the image to the CD-R(W).

Using CD-Rs and CD-RWs with Command Line Tools

If you want to use a shell prompt to write images to CD-R or CD-RWs, there are two utilities available: mkisofs and cdrecord. These two utilities have several advanced options that are beyond the scope of this guide; however, for basic image creation and writing, these tools save some time over the graphical alternatives such as X-CD-Roast, and so we discuss them briefly in the following sections.

Using mkisofs

The mkisofs utility creates ISO9660 image files that can be written to a CD-R(RW). The images that mkisofs creates can be made up of all types of files. It is most useful for archival and file backup purposes.

Suppose you wish to backup a directory called /home/joeuser/, but you wish to exclude the subdirectory /home/joeuser/junk/ because it contains unnecessary files. You want to create an ISO image called backup.iso and write it to CD-R so that you can use it on your Red Hat Linux PC at work and your Windows laptop for trips. This can be done with mkisofs by running the following command:

```
mkisofs -o backup.iso -x /home/jouser/junk/ -J -R -A -V -v /home/joeuser/
```

The image will be created in the directory you were in when you ran the command. Table 7-1 explains each command-line option. For more information on using mkisofs, refer to the additional resources in the "Additional Resources" section later in this chapter.

You can now use the ISO image file with either X-CD-Roast as described in the "Using X-CD-Roast" section earlier in this chapter, or by using cdrecord, the command-line-based CD recording utility. For more information about using cdrecord, see the next section.

Table 7-1: mkisofs Options

Option	Function
-o	Specify an output filename of the ISO image.
-J	Generate Joliet naming records; useful if the CD will be used in Windows environments.
-R	Generate Rock Ridge (RR) naming records to preserve filename length and casing, especially for UNIX/Linux environments.
-A	Set an Application ID — a text string that will be written into the volume header of the image that can be useful to determine what applications are on the CD.
-V	Set a Volume ID — a name that will be assigned to it if the image is burned and the disc is mounted in Solaris and Windows environments.
-v	Set verbose execution, which is useful for viewing the status of the image as it is being made.
-x	Exclude any directory immediately following this option; this option can be repeated (for example, ... -x /home/joe/trash -x /home/joe/delete ...).

Using cdrecord

The cdrecord utility writes audio, data, and *mixed-mode* (a combination of audio, video, and/or data) CD-ROMs using options to configure several aspects of the write process, including speed, device, and data settings.

To use cdrecord, you must first establish the device address of your CD-R(W) device by running the following command as root at a shell prompt:

```
cdrecord -scanbus
```

This command will show all CD-R(W) devices on your computer. Remember the device address of the device you will use to write your CD. The following is an example output from running cdrecord:

```
-scanbus.
Cdrecord 1.8 (i686-pc-linux-gnu) Copyright (C) 1995-2000 Jorg Schilling
Using libscg version 'schily-0.1'
scsibus0:
    0,0,0     0) *
    0,1,0     1) *
    0,2,0     2) *
    0,3,0     3) 'HP ' 'CD-Writer+ 9200 ' '1.0c' Removable CD-ROM
    0,4,0     4) *
    0,5,0     5) *
```

```
0,6,0     6) *
0,7,0     7) *
```

To write the backup file image created with mkisofs in the previous section, switch to the root user and type the following at a shell prompt:

```
cdrecord -v -eject speed=4 dev=0,3,0 backup.iso
```

The command above sets the write speed at 4, the device address as 0,3,0, and sets write output to verbose (-v), which is useful for tracking the status of the write process. The -eject argument ejects the CD-ROM after the write process is complete. The same command can also be used for burning ISO image files downloaded from the Internet, such as Red Hat Linux ISO images.

You can use cdrecord to erase CD-RW discs for reuse by typing the following:

```
cdrecord --dev=0,3,0 --blank=fast
```

Additional Resources

This chapter covers several applications briefly. Refer to the following resources for more information about the applications in this chapter.

Installed Documentation

- ♦ cdrecord *man page* — Discusses how to burn data, audio, and mixed-mode CD-ROMs. Offers all options and commands in detail, including some example commands for common CD-R(W) burning tasks.

- ♦ /usr/share/doc/cdrecord-*version* (where version is the version of cdrecord installed on your system) — Several documentation files are included with general usage and licensing information.

- ♦ mkisofs *man page* — Comprehensive detail of the utility, including some warnings about creating certain types of ISO images. Offers all options and commands in detail, including some example commands for creating common ISO image files.

- ♦ /usr/share/doc/mkisofs-*version* (where version is the version of mkisofs installed on your system) — Several documentation files are included with general usage and licensing information.

- ♦ /usr/share/doc/xcdroast-*version* (where version is the version of X-CD-Roast installed on your system) — Contains useful command-line options and usage information for this graphical CD-R(W) mastering application.

- ♦ /usr/share/doc/dvdrecord-*version* (where version is the version of dvdrecord installed on your system) — For users who have DVD-R(+W) devices, this set of documentation helps you get started mastering DVD-ROMs for data backup and multimedia presentation.

Useful Websites

♦ `http://www.xcdroast.org/` — The official website of the X-CD-Roast project.

♦ `http://freshmeat.net/projects/cdrecord/` — The `cdrecord` project page on Freshmeat is regularly updated with the newest releases, news, and user commentary.

♦ `http://www.freesoftware.fsf.org/dvdrtools/` — The official website of the `dvdrtools` project, which includes the `dvdrecord` utility for writing DVD-R(+W) discs.

Chapter 8

Shell Prompt Basics

The shell prompt (also known as the command line interface, or CLI) is a text-only interface to your Red Hat system. Just about any administration task (such as managing files, users, and groups) can be performed from the shell prompt.

> **NOTE** By default, Red Hat Linux uses the bash shell prompt, although you can change to another shell if you prefer by typing the name of the shell at the command prompt.

This chapter shows you the basics of how to interact with Red Hat Linux from a shell prompt.

Why Use a Shell Prompt?

Graphical environments for Linux have come a long way in the past few years. You can be perfectly productive in the X Window System and only have to open a shell prompt to complete a few tasks. However, many Red Hat Linux functions can be completed faster from the shell prompt than from a GUI. In less time than it might take you to open a file manager, locate a directory, and then create, delete, or modify files from a GUI, you could have finished your work with just a few commands at a shell prompt.

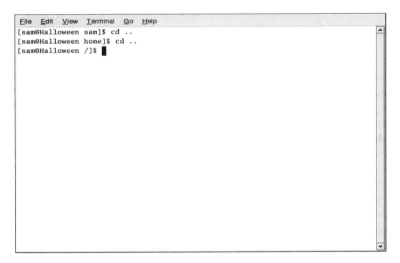

Figure 8-1. A Shell Prompt

A shell prompt looks similar to other command-line interfaces you might be familiar with, such as MS-DOS. When you enter commands at a shell prompt, the shell interprets these commands and then tells the Linux operating system (OS) what to do. Experienced users can write shell scripts to expand their capabilities even further.

The following sections explain how to navigate, manipulate files, perform simple administration tasks, and other shell prompt basics.

Determining Your Current Directory with pwd

Once you start looking through directories, it is easy to get lost or forget the name of your current directory. By default, the bash shell shows only your current directory, not the entire path.

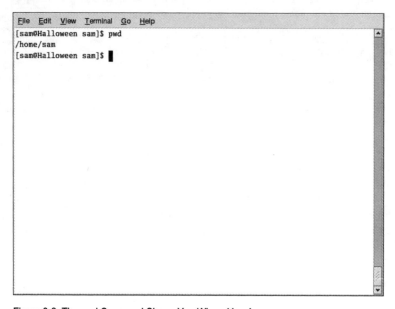

File   Edit   View   Terminal   Go   Help
```
[sam@Halloween sam]$ pwd
/home/sam
[sam@Halloween sam]$ ▌
```

Figure 8-2. The pwd Command Shows You Where You Are

To determine the exact location of your current directory within the file system, go to a shell prompt, type the command **pwd**, and press Enter.

You should see something like:

```
/home/sam
```

This tells you that you are in the user sam's directory, which is located in the /home directory.

The pwd command stands for *print working directory*. When you enter the pwd command, you're basically asking Linux to display your current location within the file system. Linux responds by printing the name of the current directory at the shell prompt, also known as the *standard output*.

You will find that using pwd is very helpful as you learn to navigate Red Hat Linux.

Changing Directories with cd

Changing directories is easy as long as you know your current directory and how that location relates to where you want to go.

To change directories, use the cd command. Typing this command by itself will always return you to your home directory; moving to any other directory requires a pathname.

You can use *absolute* or *relative* pathnames. Absolute paths start at the top with / (referred to as the root directory) and then look down through the file system from there for the requested directory; relative paths look in your current directory and then down from there. The following directory tree illustrates how cd operates.

```
/
/directory1
/directory1/directory2
/directory1/directory2/directory3
```

If you are currently in directory3 and you want to switch to directory1, you need to move up in the directory tree.

Executing the command

```
cd directory1
```

while you are in directory3 will thus present you with an error message explaining that there is no such directory. This is because there is no directory1 within directory3.

To move up to directory1 you'll have to type the absolute pathname, as follows:

```
cd /directory1
```

This is an example of an absolute path; it tells Linux to start at the top (/) and look down until it finds directory1. A path is absolute if the first character is a /. Otherwise, it is a relative path.

Absolute paths will take you to any directory from any directory. Relative paths will only take you to directories below your current one.

Use the following exercise to test what you have learned so far regarding absolute and relative paths.

From your home directory, type the relative path:

```
cd ../../etc/X11
```

After using the full command in the example, you should be in the directory X11, which is where you will find configuration files and directories related to the X Window System.

Take a look at your last cd command. You told your system to:

1. Go up one level to your login directory's parent directory (probably /home).
2. Then go up to that directory's parent (which is the root, or /, directory).
3. Then go down to the etc directory.
4. Finally, go to the X11 directory.

Conversely, using an absolute path would get you to the /etc/X11 directory more quickly. For example:

```
cd /etc/X11
```

Absolute paths start from the root directory (/) and move down to the directory you specify.

> **NOTE** Always make sure you know which working directory you are in before you state the relative path to the directory or file you want to get to. You do not have to worry about your position in the file system, though, when you state the absolute path to another directory or file. If you are not sure, type pwd and your current working directory will be displayed.

Table 8-1: cd Options

Command	Function
cd	Returns you to your home directory.
cd ~	Also returns you to your home directory
cd /	Takes you to the system's root directory.
cd /root	Takes you to the home directory of the root, or superuser, account created at installation; you must be the root user to access this directory.
cd /home	Takes you to the home directory, where user login directories are usually stored.
cd ..	Moves you up one directory.
cd ~otheruser	Takes you to *otheruser's* login directory, if *otheruser* has granted you permission to do so.
cd /dir1/subdirfoo	Regardless of which directory you are in, this absolute path would take you straight to subdirfoo, a subdirectory of dir1.
cd ../../dir3/X11	This relative path would take you up two directories to the root directory, then to dir3, then to the X11 directory.

Now that you are starting to understand how to change directories, see what happens when you change to root's login directory (the superuser account). Type:

```
cd /root
```

If you are not logged in as root, you are denied permission to access that directory. Denying access to the root and other users' accounts (or login directories) is one way your Linux system prevents accidental or malicious tampering. See the "Ownership and Permissions" section later in this chapter.

To change to the root login and root directory, use the su command. For example:

```
[sam@halloween sam]$su
Password:your_root_password
[root@halloween sam]#cd /root
[root@halloween /root]#
```

> **TIP** The su command means *switch users* and allows you to temporarily log in as another user. When you type **su** by itself, you become root (also called the superuser) while still inside your login shell (your user's home directory). Typing **su -** makes you become root with root's login shell as if you had logged in as root originally.

As soon as you give the root password, you will see the changes in your command prompt to show your new, superuser status, the root account designation at the front of the prompt and "#" at the end (as shown in the prior example).

When you are done working as root, type **exit** at the prompt and you will return to your user account.

```
[root@halloween /root]#exit
exit
[sam@halloween sam]$
```

View Directory Contents with ls

Now that you know how to change directories, it is time to learn how to view the contents of these directories. Using the ls command, you can display the contents of your current directory.

Many options are available with the ls command. The ls command by itself will not show you all the files in your directory. Some files are hidden files (also called *dot files* because their filenames start with a dot) and can only be seen by using the -a option with the ls command.

> **TIP** To see all the options of the ls command, you can read the man page for the ls command by typing **man ls** at a shell prompt. If you want to print the man page, at the prompt type **man ls | col -b | lpr**.

```
File  Edit  View  Terminal  Go  Help
[sam@Halloween sam]$ ls -a
.    .bash_history  .bash_profile  .canna   .gtkrc    .kde          sneakers.txt
..   .bash_logout   .bashrc        .emacs   home.txt  saturday.txt  .xauth3rSVvU
[sam@Halloween sam]$
```

Figure 8-3. ls with the -a Option

> **NOTE** Hidden files are mostly configuration files that set preferences in programs, window managers, shells, and more. The reason they are hidden is to help prevent any accidental tampering by the user.

When you are searching for something in a directory, you are not usually looking for these configuration files, so keep them hidden to help avoid some screen clutter when viewing directories at the shell prompt.

Viewing all the files using the ls -a command can give you plenty of detail, but you can view still more information by adding the -1 option.

Adding the -i option to the ls command shows you information such as the size of a file or directory, the file creation date, size, ownership, permissions, and more.

You do not have to be in the directory whose contents you want to view to use the ls command. For example, to see what is in the /etc directory from your home directory, type:

```
ls -al /etc
```

```
 File   Edit   View   Terminal   Go   Help
drwxr-xr-x    2 root     root         4096 Aug 29 15:38 smrsh
drwxr-xr-x    2 root     root         4096 Sep  6 17:43 snmp
drwxr-xr-x    3 root     root         4096 Aug 27 17:30 sound
drwxr-xr-x    2 root     root         4096 Sep  6 22:26 ssh
-r--r-----    1 root     root          580 Jun 27 19:57 sudoers
drwxr-xr-x    7 root     root         4096 Sep  6 22:27 sysconfig
-rw-r--r--    1 root     root          526 Sep  4 13:23 sysctl.conf
-rw-r--r--    1 root     root          693 Jun 23 20:29 syslog.conf
-rw-r--r--    1 root     root       737535 Jun 23 20:38 termcap
-rw-r--r--    1 root     root          140 Jun 23 20:22 updatedb.conf
-rw-r--r--    1 root     root           35 Sep  3 03:29 updfstab.conf
-rw-r--r--    1 root     root          772 Sep  3 03:29 updfstab.conf.default
lrwxrwxrwx    1 root     root           34 Sep  6 17:46 vfontcap -> ../usr/share
/VFlib/2.25.6/vfontcap
drwxr-xr-x    3 root     root         4096 Sep  6 17:52 vfs
-rw-r--r--    1 root     root          864 Aug  7 21:47 warnquota.conf
-rw-r--r--    1 root     root         4022 Jul 24 19:23 wgetrc
drwxr-xr-x   17 root     root         4096 Sep  6 18:24 X11
-rw-r--r--    1 root     root          289 Aug 15 16:54 xinetd.conf
drwxr-xr-x    2 root     root         4096 Sep  6 17:43 xinetd.d
drwxr-xr-x    2 root     root         4096 Sep  6 17:46 xml
-rw-r--r--    1 root     root         4941 Aug 26 18:09 xpdfrc
-rw-r--r--    1 root     root          361 Sep  6 18:23 yp.conf
[sam@halloween sam]$ █
```

Figure 8-4. Sample ls Output for the /etc Directory

Table 8-2 shows some options commonly used with ls. Remember, you can view the full list by reading the ls man page (man ls).

Table 8-2: Options for ls

Option	What It Does
-a	Lists all the files in the directory, including the hidden files (.filename). The .. and . at the top of your list refer to the parent directory and the current directory, respectively.
-l	Lists details about contents, including permissions (modes), owner, group, size, creation date, whether the file is a link to somewhere else on the system, and where its link points.
-F	Adds a symbol to the end of each listing. These symbols include / to indicate a directory; @ to indicate a symbolic link to another file; and * to indicate an executable file.
-r	Lists the contents of the directory from back to front.
-R	This option lists the contents of all directories below the current directory recursively.
-S	Sorts files by their size.

Locating Files and Directories

There will be times when you know a file or directory exists but you will not know where to find it. Searching for a file or directory can be easier with the `locate` command.

With `locate`, you will see every file or directory whose name contains the search criterion. For example, if you want to search for all files with the word `finger` in the name, type:

```
locate finger
```

The `locate` command uses a database to locate files and directories that have the word `finger` in the file or directory name. The search results could include a file called `finger.txt`, a file called `pointerfinger.txt`, a directory named `fingerthumbnails`, and so on. To learn more about `locate`, read the `locate` man page (type `man locate` at a shell prompt).

The `locate` command works very quickly, as long as the database is up to date. That database is automatically updated on a nightly basis through a `cron` job. `cron` is a small program that runs in the background, performing various tasks (such as updating the `locate` database) at regularly scheduled intervals.

> **TIP** `cron` is a daemon that executes tasks at regularly scheduled intervals. To read the `cron` man page, type **man cron** at the shell prompt.

`cron` periodically updates the `slocate` database, which is used to catalog file locations used by the `locate` command. Switching between operating systems and shutting down your machine at the end of the day can interfere with the automatic database update run by `cron`.

To update the database manually, log in as root (type **su** at a shell prompt and then enter your root password) and type the command **updatedb**.

After a few minutes, the `slocate` database that is used by the `locate` command will be current.

> **NOTE** You can run `anacron` to have your system execute commands periodically, with a frequency specified in days. Unlike `cron`, `anacron` does not assume that the machine is running continuously. Hence, it can be used on machines that are not running 24 hours a day to control daily, weekly, and monthly jobs that are usually controlled by `cron`.

Refer to the man page on `anacron` (type **man anacron** at the command line) for more information.

Printing from the Command Line

Printing is not an involved process, whether you click on a button in a GUI or type commands from the command line. This section explains how to print, cancel, and view print jobs from the command line, assuming you have a properly configured printer connected to your system. Refer to Chapter 16 for more information about setting up your printer.

The `lpr` command, followed by a filename, sends that specified file to the print queue. For example, `lpr foo.txt` prints the `foo.txt` file.

To view the jobs waiting in the print queue, type **lpq** at the command line and you will see information similar to the following:

```
active root 389 foo.txt
```

In this example, `389` is the job number.

You can cancel jobs in the queue by typing **lprm** followed by the print job number displayed when you use the `lpq` command. To cancel the `foo.txt` print job, for example, you would type **lprm 389** and press Enter.

Clearing and Resetting the Terminal

After even one `ls` command in a shell prompt, the terminal window you are working in can begin to look crowded. You can always exit from the terminal window and open a new one, but there is a quicker and easier way to clear the contents displayed in the terminal: clearing the terminal.

To clear the terminal, type the command `clear` at the shell prompt. The command then clears the terminal window.

Sometimes, you may accidentally open a program file or some other non-text file in a terminal window. After closing the file, you could find that the text you are typing does not match the output on the monitor.

In such cases, type `reset` to return the terminal window to its default values.

Manipulating Files with cat

Red Hat Linux has a utility that can help you keep short lists, gather lists together, and even show you information about your system. The utility is called `cat`, short for *concatenate*, which means to combine files.

The `cat` command will also display the contents of an entire file on the screen (for example, type **cat** *filename***.txt**). If the file is fairly long, it will quickly scroll past you on the screen. To prevent this, use the `cat filename.txt | less` command.

Using the pipe (`|`) and `less` command together displays the file one page at a time. You can then use the up and down arrow keys to move backward and forward through the pages. For more on using pipes to combine two separate functions, see the "Pipes and Pagers" section later in this chapter.

Using Redirection

Redirection means causing the shell to change what it considers to be standard input or where the standard output should be going.

To redirect standard output, use the > symbol. Placing > after the cat command (or after any utility or application that writes to standard output) will direct its output to the filename following the symbol.

For example, using cat by itself simply outputs whatever you input to the screen as if it were repeating the line you just typed. The following example shows cat repeating every line that is entered:

```
[sam@halloween sam]$cat
buy some sneakers
buy some sneakers
then go to the coffee shop
then go to the coffee shop
then buy some coffee
then buy some coffee
```

To redirect cat output to a file, type the following at a shell prompt (pressing the Enter key takes you to the next blank line):

```
[sam@halloween sam]$cat > sneakers.txt
buy some sneakers
then go to the coffee shop
then buy some coffee
```

Press Enter to go to an empty line and use the Ctrl-D keys to quit cat.

Note that in Figure 8-5 there are no repeated entries. That is because the standard output from cat was redirected. That redirection was to a brand new file you made called sneakers.txt. You can find the file in the directory you were in when you started cat (type **ls** if you want to see it listed).

As you learned earlier, you can then use cat to read the file. At the prompt, type:

```
cat sneakers.txt
```

CAUTION Be careful when you redirect the output to a file, because you can easily overwrite an existing file! Make sure the name of the file you are creating does not match the name of a pre-existing file, unless you want to replace it.

Use output redirection again for another file and call it home.txt. For this example, type the following:

```
[sam@halloween sam]$cat > home.txt
bring the coffee home
take off shoes
put on sneakers
make some coffee
relax!
```

Now, on an empty line, use the Ctrl-D key combination again to quit cat. Next, use cat to join home.txt with sneakers.txt and redirect the output of both files to a brand new file called saturday.txt (you will find an example in Figure 8-5). Type the following:

```
[sam@halloween sam]$cat sneakers.txt home.txt > saturday.txt
```

```
File  Edit  View  Terminal  Go  Help
[sam@Halloween sam]$ cat sneakers.txt home.txt > saturday.txt
[sam@Halloween sam]$ cat saturday.txt
buy some sneakers
then go to the coffee shop
then buy some coffee
bring the coffee home
take off shoes
put on sneakers
make some coffee
relax!
[sam@Halloween sam]$ ▉
```

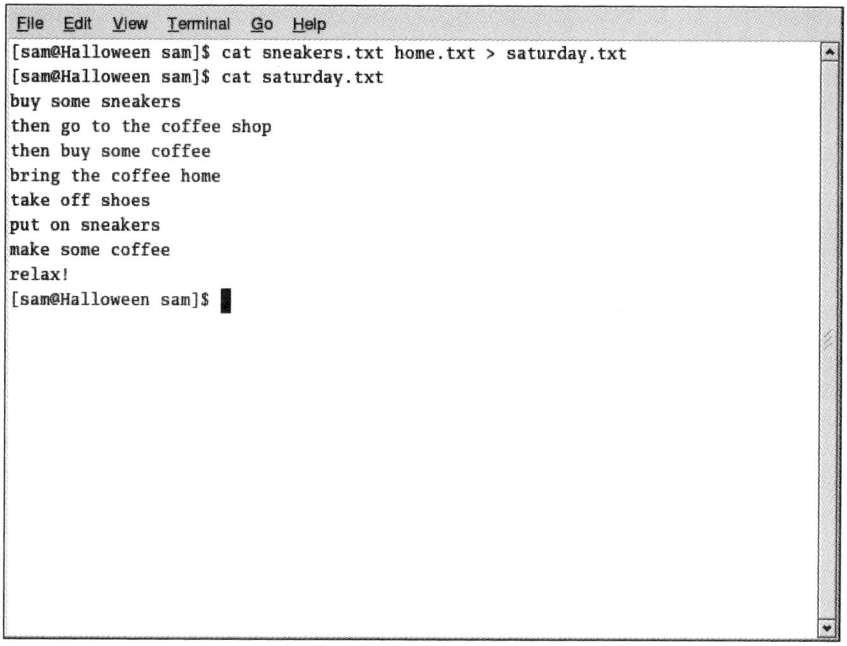

Figure 8-5. Joining Files and Redirecting Output

You can see that cat has added home.txt where sneakers.txt ended.

Appending Standard Output

You can use output redirection to add new information to the end of an existing file. Similar to when you used the > symbol, you tell your shell to send the information somewhere other than standard output.

However, when you use >>, you are adding information to a file, rather than replacing the contents of a file entirely.

The best explanation is a demonstration. Take two files which have already been created in previous examples (sneakers.txt and home.txt) and join them by using the append output symbol (>>). You want to add the information in home.txt to the information already in sneakers.txt, so type the following:

```
cat home.txt >> sneakers.txt
```

Now check the file using the command cat sneakers.txt. The final output shows the contents of home.txt at the end of the file.

```
[sam@halloween sam]$cat sneakers.txt
buy some sneakers
```

```
then go to the coffee shop
then buy some coffee
bring the coffee home
take off shoes
put on sneakers
make some coffee
relax!
[sam@halloween sam] $
```

The command you typed told the system to append the output from the file home.txt to the file sneakers.txt.

By appending the output, you save yourself time (and a bit of disk clutter) by using existing files instead of creating a new file.

Compare the results of the files sneakers.txt and saturday.txt now, and you will see that they are identical. To make your comparison, type the following:

```
cat sneakers.txt; cat saturday.txt
```

The contents of both files will be displayed — first sneakers.txt, then saturday.txt.

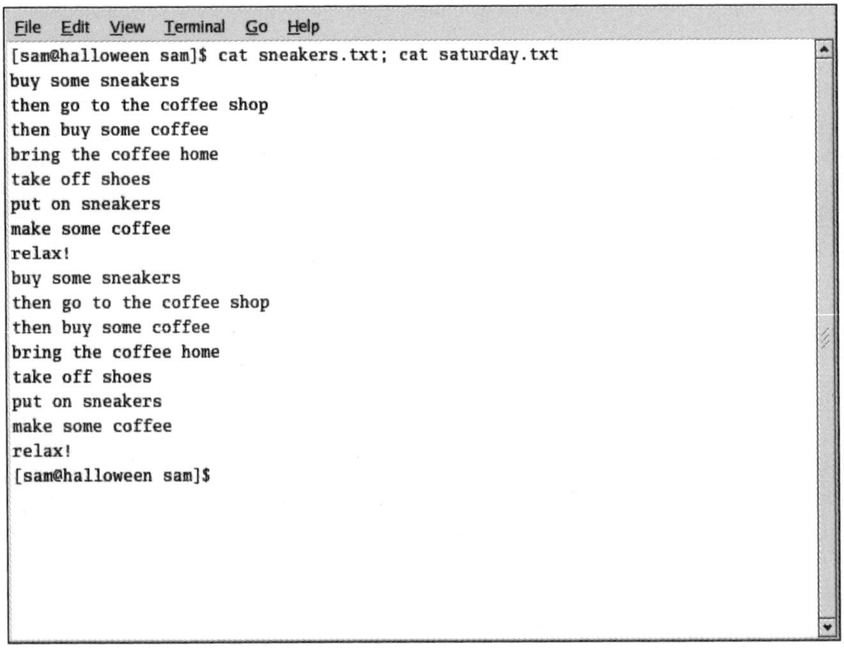

```
File  Edit  View  Terminal  Go  Help
[sam@halloween sam]$ cat sneakers.txt; cat saturday.txt
buy some sneakers
then go to the coffee shop
then buy some coffee
bring the coffee home
take off shoes
put on sneakers
make some coffee
relax!
buy some sneakers
then go to the coffee shop
then buy some coffee
bring the coffee home
take off shoes
put on sneakers
make some coffee
relax!
[sam@halloween sam]$
```

Figure 8-6. Stringing Commands and Comparing Files

Redirecting Standard Input

Not only can you redirect standard output, you can perform the same type of redirection with standard input.

When you use the redirect standard input symbol < , you are telling the shell that you want a file to be read as input for a command.

Use a file you have already created to demonstrate this idea. Just type the following:

```
cat < sneakers.txt
```

Because you used the less-than symbol (<) to separate the cat command from the file, the output of sneakers.txt was read by cat.

Pipes and Pagers

A pipe is the | symbol located on the same key as the backslash on your keyboard. In Linux, pipes connect the standard output of one command to the standard input of another command. Consider the ls command that was discussed earlier in this chapter. There are plenty of options available with ls, but what if the contents of a directory scroll by too quickly for you to view them?

As an example, view the contents of the /etc directory.

```
ls -al /etc
```

How do you get a closer look at the output before it moves off the screen?

One way is to pipe the output to a utility called less. less is a pager utility that allows you to view information one page (or screen) at a time.

```
ls -al /etc | less
```

Now you can view the contents of /etc one screen at a time. To move forward a screen, press the spacebar; to move back a screen, press b; to quit, press q. Alternatively, you can use the arrow keys to navigate with less.

> **Tip** To read startup messages more closely, at a shell prompt, type **dmesg | less**. You will be able to read the file one screen at a time. Use the arrow keys to navigate the file.

Pipes can also be used to print only certain lines from a file. Type the following:

```
grep coffee sneakers.txt | lpr
```

This will print every line in the sneakers.txt file that mentions the word "coffee" (read more about grep in the "The grep Command" section later in this chapter).

The more Command

The main difference between more and less is that less lets you move backward and
forward using the arrow keys, while more uses the spacebar and the b key for forward and
backward navigation.

List the contents of the /etc directory using ls and more.

```
ls -al /etc | more
```

```
 File   Edit   View   Terminal   Go   Help
[sam@halloween sam]$ ls -al /etc | more
total 1840
drwxr-xr-x   56 root       root        4096 Sep  8 23:35 .
drwxr-xr-x   21 root       root        4096 Sep  8 21:22 ..
-rw-r--r--    1 root       root       15228 Aug  5 06:14 a2ps.cfg
-rw-r--r--    1 root       root        2562 Aug  5 06:14 a2ps-site.cfg
-rw-r--r--    1 root       root          46 Sep  8 19:58 adjtime
drwxr-xr-x    4 root       root        4096 Sep  6 17:51 alchemist
-rw-r--r--    1 root       root        1295 Aug 29 15:38 aliases
-rw-r-----    1 root       smmsp      12288 Sep  8 21:22 aliases.db
drwxr-xr-x    2 root       root        4096 Sep  6 18:07 alternatives
-rw-r--r--    1 root       root         317 Aug 28 06:33 anacrontab
-rw-------    1 root       root           1 Jul 24 22:45 at.deny
-rw-r--r--    1 root       root         145 Sep  8 19:58 .aumixrc
-rw-r--r--    1 root       root         212 Aug 27 00:49 auto.master
-rw-r--r--    1 root       root         575 Aug 27 00:49 auto.misc
-rw-r--r--    1 root       root        1497 Aug 29 20:37 bashrc
drwxr-xr-x    2 root       root        4096 Sep  6 17:41 bonobo-activation
-rw-r--r--    1 root       root         756 Jun 23 10:31 cdrecord.conf
drwxr-xr-x    3 root       root        4096 Sep  6 17:57 CORBA
drwxr-xr-x    2 root       root        4096 Jul 19 18:51 cron.d
drwxr-xr-x    2 root       root        4096 Sep  6 17:45 cron.daily
drwxr-xr-x    2 root       root        4096 Jun 23 10:34 cron.hourly
--More--
```

Figure 8-7. Piping Output of ls to more

Use the spacebar to move forward through the pages. Press q to exit.

More Commands for Reading Text Files

You have already been introduced to several basic shell prompt commands for reading files in
text editors. The following sections describe a few more.

The head Command

You can use the head command to look at the beginning of a file. The command syntax is
head *filename*.

head can be a useful command, but because it is limited to the first several lines, you will not
see how long the file actually is. By default, you can only read the first ten lines of a file. You

can change the number of lines displayed by specifying a number option, as shown in the following command:

```
head -20 filename
```

The tail Command

The reverse of `head` is `tail`. Using `tail`, you can view the last ten lines of a file.

The grep Command

The `grep` command is useful for finding specific character strings in a file. For example, if you want to find every reference made to "coffee" in the file `sneakers.txt`, you would type:

```
grep coffee sneakers.txt
```

You would see every line in that file where the word "coffee" is found.

> **TIP** Unless otherwise specified, `grep` searches are case sensitive. That means that searching for "Coffee" is different than searching for "coffee." So, among `grep`'s options is `-i`, which allows you to make a case-insensitive search through a file. Read the `grep` man page for more about this command.

I/O Redirection and Pipes

You can use pipes and output redirection when you want to store and/or print information to read at a later time.

You can, for example, use `grep` to search for particular contents of a file and then have those results either saved as a file or sent to a printer.

To print the information about references to "coffee" in `sneakers.txt`, for example, just type the following:

```
grep coffee sneakers.txt | lpr
```

Wildcards and Regular Expressions

What if you forget the name of the file you are looking for? Using wildcards or regular expressions, you can perform actions on a file or files without knowing the complete filename. Just fill out what you know, then substitute the remainder with a *wildcard*. Wildcards are special symbols that you can substitute for letters, numbers, and symbols that make finding particular directories and files easier than examining long directory listings to find what you are searching for.

> **TIP** To read more about wildcards and regular expressions, take a look at the `bash` man page (man `bash`).

Remember that you can save the file to a text file by typing **man bash | col –b > bash.txt**. Then, you can open and read the file with `less` or `pico` (`pico bash.txt`). If you want to print the file, be aware that it is quite long.

We know the file starts with sneak, as in sneak*something*.txt, so type:

```
ls sneak*.txt
```

and find the name of the file:

```
sneakers.txt
```

You will probably use the asterisk (*) most frequently when you are searching. The asterisk will search out everything that matches the pattern you are looking for. So, even by typing:

```
ls *.txt
```

or:

```
ls sn*
```

You would find sneakers.txt and any other files whose names begin with sn or ends with .txt. It helps to narrow your search as much as possible.

One way to narrow a search is to use the question mark symbol (?). Like the asterisk, using ? can help locate a file matching a search pattern.

In this case, though, ? is useful for matching a single character, so if you were searching for sneaker?.txt, you would get sneakers.txt as a result, and/or sneakerz.txt, if there were a file with that name.

Regular expressions are more complex than the straightforward asterisk or question mark.

When an asterisk, for example, just happens to be part of a filename, as might be the case if the file sneakers.txt was called sneak*.txt, that is when regular expressions can be useful.

Using the backslash (\), you can specify that you do not want to search out *everything* by using the asterisk, but you are instead looking for a file with an asterisk in the name. This is called *escaping* the wildcard.

For example, if the file is called sneak*.txt, type:

```
sneak\*.txt
```

Table 8-3 shows a brief list of wildcards and regular expressions.

Table 8-3: Wildcards and Regular Expressions

Character	*What It Matches*
*	All characters
?	One character in a string (such as sneaker?.txt)
*	The * character
\?	The ? character
\)	The) character

Command History and Tab Completion

It does not take long before the thought of typing the same command over and over becomes unappealing.

One minor typing error can ruin lines of a command. One solution is to use the command line history. By scrolling with the up arrow and down arrow keys, you can find plenty of your previously typed commands.

Try it by taking a look again at `sneakers.txt` (created in earlier examples in this chapter). The first time, however, at the shell prompt, type:

```
cat sneakrs.txt
```

Nothing happens, of course, because there is no `sneakrs.txt` file. No problem. We will just use the up arrow key to bring back the command and then use the left arrow key to get to the point where we missed the "e." Insert the letter and press Enter again.

We now see the contents of `sneakers.txt`.

By default, up to 500 commands can be stored in the bash command-line history file.

> **TIP** By typing the `env` command at a shell prompt, we can see the environment variable that controls the size of the command-line history. The line that reads `HISTFILESIZE=500` shows the number of commands that bash will store.

The command-line history is actually kept in a file called `.bash_history` in your home directory. You can read it in a number of ways: by using `pico` (or `emacs` or `vi`), `cat`, `less`, `more`, and others.

Be aware that the `.bash_history` file can be quite long. To read it with the `more` command, from your home directory type:

```
more .bash_history
```

To move forward a screen, press the spacebar; to move back a screen, press b; to quit, press q.

To find a command in your history file without having to keep hitting the arrow keys or page through the history file, use `grep`, a powerful search utility (see the "The grep Command" section earlier in this chapter for more details). Say you are searching for a previously used command that is similar to `cat sneaksomething`.

Say you have used the command fairly recently and you think it might be in your history file. At the shell prompt, type:

```
history | grep sneak
```

Another timesaving tool is known as command completion. If you type part of a file, command, or pathname and then press the Tab key, `bash` will present you with either the remaining portion of the file/path, or a beep (if the beep sound is enabled on your system). If you get a beep, just press Tab again to obtain a list of the files/paths that match what has been typed so far.

For example, if you forget the command `updatedb`, but remember a portion of the command, you can `su` to root and then type **up** at the shell prompt, press the Tab key twice, and you will see a list of possible completions including `updatedb`. By typing the partial command `upd` and pressing Tab again, your command is completed for you.

Using Multiple Commands

Linux allows you to enter multiple commands at one time. The only requirement is that you separate the commands with a semicolon.

Want to see how long you have been online and open your Web browser at the same time? Just combine the date command with Mozilla's command.

```
date; mozilla; date
```

Remember that commands are case sensitive, so the command to start Mozilla must be in lowercase to start the browser.

```
[sam@halloween sam]$date; mozilla; date
Mon Feb 7 13:26:27 EST 2000
Mon Feb 7 14:28:32 EST 2000
[sam@halloween sam]$
```

Running the combination of commands prints out the time and date, starts Mozilla, and then prints the time and date again after you close Mozilla. The discrepancy between the two results from the `date` command shows that you were using Mozilla for just over an hour.

Ownership and Permissions

Earlier in this chapter, when you tried to `cd` to root's login directory, you received the following message:

```
[sam@halloween sam]$cd /root
bash: /root: Permission denied
[sam@halloween sam]$
```

That was one demonstration of Linux's security features. Linux, like UNIX, is a multiuser system, and file permissions are one way the system protects against accidental or malicious tampering.

One way to gain entry when you are denied permission is to `su` to root, as you learned earlier. This is because whoever knows the root password has complete access to the system.

```
[sam@halloween sam]$su
Password: your_root_password
[root@localhost sam]#cd /root
[root@localhost /root]#
```

But switching to the root user is not always convenient or recommended, because it is easy to make mistakes and alter important configuration files as root.

All files and directories are "owned" by the person who created them. If, for example, you created the file sneakers.txt in your login directory, then sneakers.txt belongs to you.

That means you can specify who is allowed to read the file, write to the file, or (if it is an application instead of a text file) who can execute the file.

Reading, writing, and executing are the three main settings in permissions. Because users are placed into a group when their accounts are created, you can also specify whether certain groups can read, write to, or execute a file.

Take a closer look at sneakers.txt with the ls command using the -l (long) option (see Figure 8-8).

```
[sam@halloween sam]$ls -l sneakers.txt
-rw-rw-r--    1 sam sam      150 Mar 19 08:08 sneakers.txt
```

There is a lot of detail provided here. You can see who can read (r) and write to (w) the file, as well as who created the file (sam), and to which group the owner belongs (sam). Remember that, by default, the name of your group is the same as your login name.

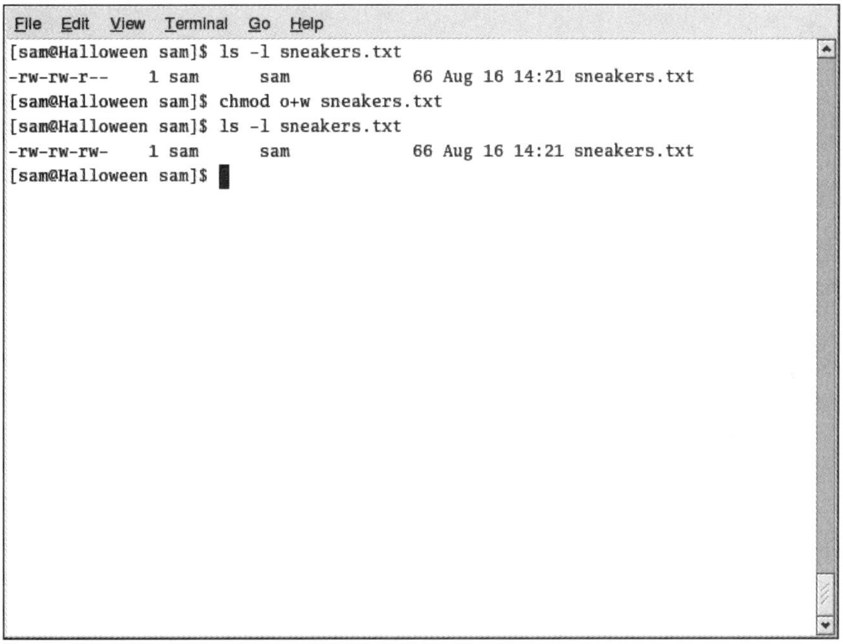

```
File  Edit  View  Terminal  Go  Help
[sam@Halloween sam]$ ls -l sneakers.txt
-rw-rw-r--    1 sam        sam           66 Aug 16 14:21 sneakers.txt
[sam@Halloween sam]$ chmod o+w sneakers.txt
[sam@Halloween sam]$ ls -l sneakers.txt
-rw-rw-rw-    1 sam        sam           66 Aug 16 14:21 sneakers.txt
[sam@Halloween sam]$ █
```

Figure 8-8. Permissions for sneakers.txt

Other information to the right of the group includes file size, date and time of file creation, and file name. The first column shows current permissions; it has ten slots. The first slot represents the type of file. The remaining nine slots are actually three sets of permissions for three different categories of users.

```
-rw-rw-r--
```

Those three sets are: the owner of the file, the group in which the file belongs, and "others," meaning users and groups not yet specified.

```
-       (rw-)   (rw-)   (r--) 1 sam sam
|        |       |       |
type   owner   group   others
```

The first item, which specifies the file type, can show one of the following:

- ♦ d — A directory
- ♦ - (dash) — A regular file (rather than directory or link)
- ♦ l — A symbolic link to another program or file elsewhere on the system

Beyond the first item, in the following three sets, you will see one of the following:

- ♦ r — File can be read
- ♦ w — File can be written to
- ♦ x — File can be executed (if it is a program)

When you see a dash in owner, group, or others, it means that particular permission has not been granted. Look again at the first column of sneakers.txt and identify its permissions.

```
[sam@halloween sam]$ls -l sneakers.txt
-rw-rw-r--    1 sam sam      150 Mar 19 08:08 sneakers.txt
[sam@halloween sam]$
```

The file's owner (in this case, sam) has permission to read and write to the file. The group, also called sam, has permission to read and write to sneakers.txt as well. It is not a program, so neither the owner or the group has permission to execute it because it simply cannot be executed. People not in the sam group can only read the file. They cannot write to it or execute it.

The chmod Command

Use the chmod command to change permissions easily. This example shows how to change the permissions on sneakers.txt with the chmod command.

The original file looks like this, with its initial permissions settings:

```
-rw-rw-r--    1 sam sam      150 Mar 19 08:08 sneakers.txt
```

If you are the owner of the file or are logged into the root account you can change any permissions for the owner, group, and others.

Right now, the owner and group can read and write to the file (rw-). Anyone outside of the group can only read the file (r--).

> **CAUTION** Remember that file permissions are a security feature. Whenever you allow anyone else to read, write to, and execute files, you are increasing the risk of files being tampered with, altered, or deleted. As a rule, you should only grant read and write permissions to those who truly need them.

In the following example, you want to allow everyone to write to the file, so they can read it, write notes in it, and save it. That means you will have to change the "others" section of the file permissions.

Take a look at the file first. At the shell prompt, type:

```
ls -l sneakers.txt
```

The command displays this file information:

```
-rw-rw-r--    1 sam sam      150 Mar 19 08:08 sneakers.txt
```

Now, type the following:

```
chmod o+w sneakers.txt
```

The `chmod o+w` command tells the system you want to give others write permission to the file `sneakers.txt`. To check the results, list the file's details again. Now, the file looks like this:

```
-rw-rw-rw-    1 sam sam      150 Mar 19 08:08 sneakers.txt
```

Now, everyone can read and write to the file.

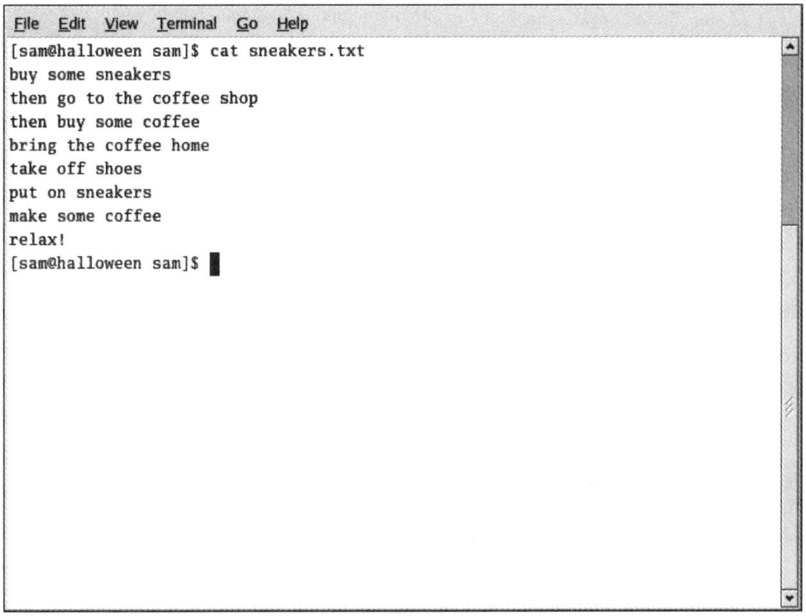

```
File  Edit  View  Terminal  Go  Help
[sam@halloween sam]$ cat sneakers.txt
buy some sneakers
then go to the coffee shop
then buy some coffee
bring the coffee home
take off shoes
put on sneakers
make some coffee
relax!
[sam@halloween sam]$ █
```

Figure 8-9. Changing Permissions for sneakers.txt

To remove read and write permissions from `sneakers.txt` use the `chmod` command to take away both the read and write permissions.

```
chmod go-rw sneakers.txt
```

By typing **chmod go-rw**, you are telling the system to remove read and write permissions for the group and for others from the file `sneakers.txt`.

The result will look like this:

```
-rw-------    1 sam sam     150 Mar 19 08:08 sneakers.txt
```

Think of these settings as a kind of shorthand when you want to change permissions with `chmod`, because all you really have to do is remember a few symbols and letters with the `chmod` command.

Here is a list of what the shorthand represents:

- ♦ Identities:
  - u — The user who owns the file (that is, the owner)
  - g — The group to which the user belongs
  - o — Others (not the owner or the owner's group)
  - a — Everyone or all (u, g, and o)
- ♦ Permissions:
  - r — Read access
  - w — Write access
  - x — Execute access
- ♦ Actions:
  - + — Adds the permission
  - - — Removes the permission
  - = — Makes it the only permission

Want to test your permissions skills? Remove all permissions from `sneakers.txt` — for everyone.

```
chmod a-rwx sneakers.txt
```

Now, see if you can read the file:

```
[sam@halloween sam]$ cat sneakers.txt
cat: sneakers.txt: Permission denied
[sam@halloween sam]$
```

Removing all permissions, including your own, successfully locked the file. But because the file belongs to you, you can always change its permissions back (refer to Figure 8-9).

```
[sam@halloween sam]$ chmod u+rw sneakers.txt
```

```
[sam@halloween sam]$ cat sneakers.txt
buy some sneakers
then go to the coffee shop
then buy some coffee
bring the coffee home
take off shoes
put on sneakers
make some coffee
relax!
[sam@halloween sam]$
```

Here are some common examples of settings that can be used with chmod:

- g+w — Adds write access for the group
- o-rwx — Removes all permissions for others
- u+x — Allows the file owner to execute the file
- a+rw — Allows everyone to read and write to the file
- ug+r — Allows the owner and group to read the file
- g=rx — Lets the group only read and execute (not write)

By adding the -R option, you can change permissions for entire directory trees.

Because you cannot really "execute" a directory as you would an application, when you add or remove execute permission for a directory, you are really allowing (or denying) permission to search through that directory.

To allow everyone read and write access to every file in the example directory tigger, type

```
chmod -R a+rw tigger
```

If you do not allow others to have execute permission to tigger, it will not matter who has read or write access: no one will be able to get into the directory unless they know the exact filename they want.

For example, type

```
chmod a-x tigger
```

to remove everyone's execute permissions.

Here is what happens now when you try to cd into tigger:

```
[sam@halloween sam]$cd tigger
bash: tigger: Permission denied
[sam@halloween sam]$
```

Next, restore your own and your group's access.

```
chmod ug+x tigger
```

Now, if you check your work with `ls -dl` you will see that only others will be denied access to the `tigger` directory.

Changing Permissions with Numbers

Remember the reference to the shorthand method of `chmod`? Here is another way to change permissions, although it may seem a little complex at first.

Go back to the original permissions for `sneakers.txt` (type **ls -l sneakers.txt**).

```
-rw-rw-r--    1 sam sam     150 Mar 19 08:08 sneakers.txt
```

Each permission setting can be represented by a numerical value:

♦ r = 4

♦ w = 2

♦ x = 1

♦ - = 0

When these values are added together, the total is used to set specific permissions. For example, if you want read and write permissions, you would have a value of 6; that is, 4 (read) + 2 (write) = 6.

For `sneakers.txt`, here are the numerical permissions settings:

```
-   (rw-)    (rw-)   (r--)
     |        |       |
   4+2+0    4+2+0   4+0+0
```

The total for the user is six, the total for the group is six, and the total for others is four. The permissions setting is read as 664.

If you want to change `sneakers.txt` so those in your group will not have write access but can still read the file, remove the access by subtracting two (2) from that set of numbers.

The numerical values, then, would become six, four, and four (644).

To implement these new settings, type:

```
chmod 644 sneakers.txt
```

Now verify the changes by listing the file. Type:

```
ls -l
sneakers.txt
```

The output should be:

```
-rw-r--r--    1 sam sam     150 Mar 19 08:08 sneakers.txt
```

Now, neither the group nor others have write permission to `sneakers.txt`. To return the group's write access for the file, add the value of w (2) to the second set of permissions.

```
chmod 664 sneakers.txt
```

WARNING Setting permissions to 666 will allow everyone to read and write to a file or directory. Setting permissions to 777 allows everyone read, write, and execute permission. These permissions could allow tampering with sensitive files, so in general, it is not a good idea to use these settings.

Table 8-4 shows a list of some common settings, numerical values, and their meanings.

Table 8-4: Example Permission Settings

Permissions	What It Means
-rw------- (600)	Only the owner has read and write permissions.
-rw-r--r-- (644)	Only the owner has read and write permissions; the group and others have read only permissions.
-rwx------ (700)	Only the owner has read, write, and execute permissions.
-rwxr-xr-x (755)	The owner has read, write, and execute permissions; the group and others have only read and execute permissions.
-rwx--x--x (711)	The owner has read, write, and execute permissions; the group and others have only execute.
-rw-rw-rw- (666)	Everyone can read and write to the file. (Be careful with these permissions.)
-rwxrwxrwx (777)	Everyone can read, write, and execute. (Again, this permissions setting can be hazardous.)
drwx------ (700)	Only the user can read or write in this directory.
drwxr-xr-x (755)	Everyone can read the directory, but its contents can only be changed by the user.

Chapter 9
Managing Files and Directories

Your desktop file manager is a powerful and important tool for managing files and directories using a graphical interface. This chapter discusses various shell prompt commands that can be used to manage files and directories on your Red Hat Linux system. This chapter also discusses compression tools to create archives of your files for backups or to send to others conveniently.

> **NOTE** Due to system security, unless you are root, you will not be able to gain access to all system-level files and directories. If you do not have the permission to open, delete, or execute a file, you will receive an error message saying your access is denied. This is normal behavior and is used to prevent non-privileged users from deleting or altering important system files.

A Larger Picture of the File System

Every operating system has a method of storing data in files and directories so that it can keep track of additions, modifications, and other changes.

In Linux, every file is stored in a directory. Directories can also contain directories; these *subdirectories* can also contain files and other subdirectories.

You might think of the file system as a tree-like structure, in which directories *branch off*. These directories may contain, or be the "parent" of, other directories that may hold files and directories of their own.

There would not be a tree without a root, and the same is true for the Linux file system. No matter how far away the directories branch, everything is connected to the root directory, which is represented as a single forward slash (/).

> **TIP** Red Hat Linux uses the term *root* in several different ways, which might be confusing to new users. There is the root account (also called the superuser), who has permission to do anything, the root account's home directory (/root), and the root directory for the entire file system (/). When you are speaking to someone and using the term *root*, be sure you know which root you are talking about.

Unless you are a system administrator or have root (superuser) access, you probably do not have permission to write to the files and directories outside of your home directory. Certain directories are reserved for specific purposes. For example, /home is the default location for non-root users' home directories.

Users who are not system administrators might find the following directories useful for finding their home directories, reading documentation, or storing temporary files:

- ◆ /home — The default location for non-root users' home directories. For example, a user with the username foo has the home directory /home/foo.

- ◆ /usr/share/doc — Location of documentation for installed packages. For example, the documentation for the dateconfig software package is located in /usr/share/doc/dateconfig-*version-number*.

- ◆ /tmp — The reserved directory for all users to store temporary files. Files stored here are not permanent. A system process removes old files from this directory on a periodic basis. Do not write any files or directories that you want to keep here.

Your Red Hat Linux system is compatible with many other Linux distributions because of the Filesystem Hierarchy Standard (FHS). The FHS guidelines help to standardize the way system programs and files are stored on all Linux systems.

To learn more about the FHS, see Chapter 25.

You can also visit the FHS website at http://www.pathname.com/fhs.

Identifying and Working with File Types

If you are new to Linux, you may see files with extensions you do not recognize. A file's extension is the last part of a file's name after the final dot (in the file sneakers.txt, "txt" is that file's extension).

Table 9-1 shows the major file extensions and their meanings.

Table 9-1: File Types and Extensions

Compressed and Archived Files*	
Extension	*File Type*
.bz2	A file compressed with bzip2
.gz	A file compressed with gzip
.tar	A file archived with tar (short for *tape archive*), also known as a tar file
.tbz	A tarred and bzipped file
.tgz	A tarred and gzipped file
File Formats	
Extension	*File Type*
.au	An audio file
.gif	A GIF image file

.html/.htm	An HTML file
.jpg	A JPEG image file
.pdf	An electronic image of a document (PDF stands for Portable Document Format)
.png	A PNG image file (PNG stands for Portable Network Graphic)
.ps	A PostScript file; formatted for printing
.txt	A plain ASCII text file
.wav	An audio file
.xpm	An image file
System Files	
Extension	**File Type**
.conf	A configuration file
.lock	A lock file; determines whether a program or device is in use
.rpm	A Red Hat Package Manager file used to install software
Programming and Scripting Files	
Extension	**File Type**
.c	A C program language source code file
.cpp	A C++ program language source code file
.h	A C or C++ program language header file
.o	A program object file
.pl	A Perl script
.so	A library file
.tcl	A TCL script

* For information on working with bzip2, gzip, and tar files, refer to the "Compressing Files from the Shell Prompt" section later in this chapter.

But file extensions are not always used, or used consistently. So what happens when a file does not have an extension, or the file does not seem to be what the extension says it is supposed to be?

That is when the file command can be helpful.

For instance, you find a file called saturday without an extension. Using the file command, you can tell what type of file it is by typing

```
file saturday
```

In the example, the command output display tells you the file is an ASCII text file.

Any file that is designated as a text file should be readable using the cat, more, or less commands, or using a text editor.

> **TIP** To learn more about file, read the man page by typing **man file**. For more information on helpful commands for reading files, see Chapter 8.

File Compression and Archiving

Sometimes it is useful to store a group of files in one file so that they can be backed up, easily transferred to another directory, or even transferred to a different computer. It is also sometimes useful to compress files into one file so that they use less disk space and download faster.

It is important to understand the distinction between an *archive file* and a *compressed file*. An archive file is a collection of files and directories that are stored in one file. The archive file is not compressed — it uses the same amount of disk space as all the individual files and directories combined. A compressed file is a collection of files and directories that are stored in one file *and* stored in a way that uses less disk space than all the individual files and directories combined. If you do not have enough disk space on your computer, you can compress files that you do not use very often or files that you want to save but do not use anymore. You can even create an archive file and then compress *that* to save even more disk space.

> **NOTE** An archive file is not compressed, but a compressed file can be an archive file.

Using File Roller

Red Hat Linux includes a graphical utility called File Roller that can compress, decompress, and archive files and directories. File Roller supports common Unix and Linux file compression and archiving formats, and has a simple interface and extensive help documentation if you need it. It also has the advantage of being integrated into the graphical desktop environment and graphical file manager.

To start File Roller, click Main Menu ⇨ Accessories ⇨ Archive Manager. You can also start File Roller from a shell prompt by typing **file-roller**. Figure 9-1 shows File Roller in action.

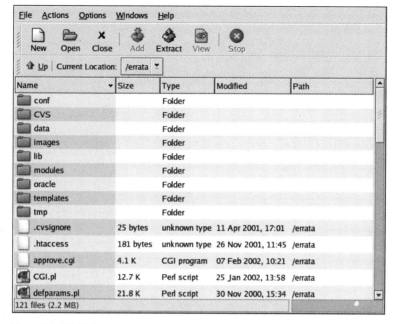

Figure 9-1: File Roller

> **TIP** If you using a file manager (such as Nautilus), you can simply double-click the file you wish to unarchive or decompress to start File Roller. The File Roller browser window will appear with the decompressed/unarchived file in a folder for you to extract or browse.

Decompressing and Unarchiving with File Roller

To decompress and/or unarchive a file, click the Open toolbar button. A file menu will pop up, allowing you to choose the archive you wish to work with. For example, if you have a file called `foo.tar.gz` located in your home directory, highlight the file and click OK. The file will appear in the main File Roller browser window as a folder, which you can navigate by double-clicking the folder icon. File Roller preserves all directory and subdirectory hierarchies, which is convenient if you are looking for a particular file in the archive. You can extract individual files or entire archives by clicking the Extract button, choosing the directory where you would like to save the unarchived files, and clicking OK.

Creating Archives with File Roller

If you need to free some hard drive space, or send multiple files or a directory of files to another user over email, File Roller allows you to create archives of your files and directories. To create a new archive, click New on the toolbar. A file browser will pop up, allowing you to specify an archive name and the compression technique (you can usually leave this set as Automatic and simply type in the file archive name and file name extension in the provided text box). Click OK, and your new archive is now ready to be filled with files and directories. To add files to your new archive, click Add, which will pop up a browser window (see Figure

9-2) that you can navigate to find the file or directory you want to be in the archive. Click OK when you are finished and then click Close to close the archive.

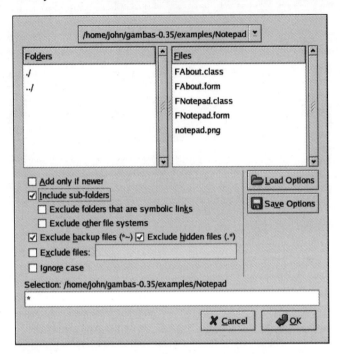

Figure 9-2: Adding Files to an Archive

TIP There is much more you can do with File Roller than is explained here. Refer to the File Roller manual (available by clicking Help ⇨ Manual) for more information.

Compressing Files from the Shell Prompt

Compressed files use less disk space and download faster than large, uncompressed files. While File Roller is a useful utility for the graphical interface, you can also use the shell prompt to compress files. In Red Hat Linux you can compress files from the shell prompt with the compression tools gzip, bzip2, or zip.

The bzip2 compression tool is recommended because it provides the most compression and is found on most Unix-like operating systems. The gzip compression tool can also be found on most Unix-like operating systems. If you need to transfer files between Linux and other operating system such as Microsoft's Windows, you should use zip because it is more commonly used on those other operating systems.

Table 9-2: Shell Prompt Compression Tools

Compression Tool	File Extension	Uncompression Tool
gzip	.gz	gunzip
bzip2	.bz2	bunzip2
Zip	.zip	unzip

bzip2 and bunzip2

To use `bzip2` to compress a file, type the following command at a shell prompt:

```
bzip2 filename
```

The file will be compressed and saved as *filename*.bz2.

To expand the compressed file, type the following command:

```
bunzip2 filename.bz2
```

The *filename*.bz2 file is replaced with `filename`.

You can use `bzip2` to compress multiple files and directories into a single archive by listing them with a space between each one:

```
bzip2 filename.bz2 file1 file2 file3 /usr/work/school
```

The above command compresses `file1`, `file2`, `file3`, and the contents of the `/usr/work/school` directory (assuming this directory exists) and places them in a file named `filename.bz2`.

> **TIP** For more information, type **man bzip2** and **man bunzip2** at a shell prompt to read the man pages for `bzip2` and `bunzip2`.

gzip and gunzip

To use `gzip` to compress a file, type the following command at a shell prompt:

```
gzip filename
```

The file will be compressed and saved as *filename*.gz.

To expand the compressed file, type the following command:

```
gunzip filename.gz
```

The `filename.gz` is replaced with `filename`.

You can use `gzip` to compress multiple files and directories at the same time by listing them with a space between each one:

```
gzip -r filename.gz file1 file2 file3 /usr/work/school
```

The above command compresses `file1`, `file2`, `file3`, and the contents of the `/usr/work/school` directory (assuming this directory exists) and places them in a file named `filename.gz`.

> **TIP** For more information, type **man gzip** and **man gunzip** at a shell prompt to read the man pages for `gzip` and `gunzip`.

zip and unzip

To compress a file with `zip`, type the following command:

```
zip -r filename.zip filesdir
```

In this example, `filename.zip` represents the file you are creating, and `filesdir` represents the directory you want to put in the new `zip` file. The `-r` option specifies that you want to include all files contained in the `filesdir` directory recursively.

To extract the contents of a `zip` file, type the following command:

```
unzip filename.zip
```

You can use `zip` to compress multiple files and directories at the same time by listing them with a space between each one:

```
zip -r filename.zip file1 file2 file3 /usr/work/school
```

The above command compresses `file1`, `file2`, `file3`, and the contents of the `/usr/work/school` directory (assuming this directory exists) and places them in a file named `filename.zip`.

> **TIP** For more information, type **man zip** and **man unzip** at a shell prompt to read the man pages for `zip` and `unzip`.

Archiving Files at the Shell Prompt

A `tar` (tar stands for *tape archive*, a term which hails back to a time when the only storage media around were tapes) file is a collection of several files and/or directories in one file. This is a good way to create backups and archives.

Some of the options used with `tar` are listed in Table 9-3.

Table 9-3: tar Options

Option	What It Does
-c	Create a new archive.
-f	When used with the -c option, use the filename specified for the creation of the tar file; when used with the -x option, unarchive the specified file.
-t	Show the list of files in the tar file.

-v	Show the progress of the files being archived.
-x	Extract files from an archive.
-z	Compress the tar file with gzip.
-j	Compress the tar file with bzip2.

To create a tar file, type

```
tar -cvf filename.tar files/directories
```

In this example, *filename.tar* represents the file you are creating, and *files/directories* represents the files or directories you want to put in the archived file.

You can tar multiple files and directories at the same time by listing them with a space between each one:

```
tar -cvf filename.tar /home/mine/work /home/mine/school
```

The above command places all the files in the work and the school subdirectories of the home directory for user mine in a new file called *filename*.tar in the current directory.

To list the contents of a tar file, type

```
tar -tvf filename.tar
```

To extract the contents of a tar file, type

```
tar -xvf filename.tar
```

This command does not remove the tar file, but places copies of its contents in the current working directory.

Remember, the tar command does not compress the files by default. To create a tarred and bzipped compressed file, use the -j option as follows:

```
tar -cjvf filename.tbz
```

tar files compressed with bzip2 are conventionally given the extension .tbz.

This command creates an archive file and then compresses it as the file *filename.tbz*. If you uncompress the *filename.tbz* file with the bunzip2 command, the *filename.tbz* file is removed and replaced with *filename.tar*.

You can also expand and unarchive a bzip tar file in one command:

```
tar -xjvf filename.tbz
```

To create a tarred and gzipped compressed file, use the -z option:

```
tar -czvf filename.tgz
```

tar files compressed with gzip are conventionally given the extension .tgz.

This command creates the archive file *filename*.tar and then compresses it as the file *filename*.tgz. (The file *filename*.tar is not saved.) If you uncompress the *filename*.tgz file with the gunzip command, the *filename*.tgz file is removed and replaced with *filename*.tar.

You can expand a gzip tar file in one command:

```
tar -xzvf filename.tgz
```

> **TIP** Type the command **man tar** for more information about the tar command.

Manipulating Files at the Shell Prompt

Files can be manipulated quite easily using one of the graphical file managers such as Nautilus or Konqueror. They can also be manipulated using a shell prompt, which is often faster. This section explains how to manipulate files at the shell prompt.

Creating Files

You can create new files either with applications (such as text editors) or by using the command touch, which will create an empty file that you can use to add text or data. To create a file with touch, type the following at a shell prompt:

```
touch filename
```

Replace *filename* with the name you wish to give the new file. If you run a directory listing after executing the touch command, you'll see that the file contains zero (0) bytes of information because it is an empty file.

```
ls -l newfile
-rw-rw-r--    1 sam sam     0 Apr 10 17:09 newfile
```

Copying Files

Like so many other Linux features, there are a variety of ways to manipulate files and directories. You can also use wildcards, as explained in Chapter 8, to make the process of copying, moving, or deleting multiple files and directories faster.

To copy a file, type the following command:

```
cp source destination
```

Replace *source* with the name of the file you want to copy, and *destination* with the name of the directory where you want the file to go.

So, to copy the file sneakers.txt to the directory tigger/ in your home directory, move to your home directory and type:

```
cp sneakers.txt tigger/
```

You can use both relative and absolute pathnames with cp.

Read the `cp` man page (type **man cp** at the shell prompt) for a full list of the options available with `cp`. Among the options you can use with `cp` are the following:

- ♦ `-i` (interactive) — Prompts you to confirm if the file is going to overwrite a file in your destination. This is a handy option because it can help prevent you from making mistakes.

- ♦ -r (recursive) — Rather than just copying all the specified files and directories, this will copy the whole directory tree, subdirectories and all.

- ♦ -v (verbose) — Shows the progress of the files as they are being copied.

Now that you have the file `sneakers.txt` in the tigger directory, use `cp -i` to copy the file again to the same location.

```
cp -i sneakers.txt tigger
cp: overwrite 'tigger/sneakers.txt'?
```

To overwrite the file that is already there, press Y and then Enter. If you do not want to overwrite the file, press N and Enter.

Moving Files

To move files, use the `mv` command. For more about `mv`, see the `mv` man page (type **man mv**).

Common options for `mv` include the following:

- ♦ `-i` (interactive) —This will prompt you if the file you have selected will overwrite an existing file in the destination directory. This is a good option, because like the `-i` option for `cp`, you will be given the chance to make sure you want to replace an existing file.

- ♦ `-f` (force) —Overrides the interactive mode and moves the file without prompting. Unless you know what you are doing, this option is dangerous; be very careful about using it.

- ♦ -v (verbose) —Shows the progress of the files as they are being moved.

If you want to move a file out of your home directory and into another existing directory, type the following (you will need to be in your home directory):

```
mv sneakers.txt tigger
```

Alternatively, the same command using absolute pathnames looks like

```
mv sneakers.txt /home/newuser /home/newuser/tigger
```

Deleting Files and Directories

Earlier in the chapter we showed you how to create files with the `touch` command.

Now we show you how to delete files and directories. Deleting files and directories with the `rm` command is a straightforward process (see the `rm` man page for more information). Options for removing files and directories include:

- ♦ -i (interactive) — Prompts you to confirm the deletion. This option can stop you from deleting a file by mistake.
- ♦ -f (force) — Overrides interactive mode and removes the file(s) without prompting. This might not be a good idea, unless you know exactly what you are doing.
- ♦ -v (verbose) — Shows the progress of the files as they are being removed.
- ♦ -r (recursive) — Deletes a directory and all files and subdirectories it contains.

To delete the file piglet.txt with the rm command, type:

```
rm piglet.txt
```

WARNING After a file or directory is removed with the rm command, it is gone permanently and cannot be retrieved.

Use the -i (interactive) option to give you a second chance to think about whether or not you really want to delete the file.

```
rm -i piglet.txt
rm: remove 'piglet.txt'?
```

You can also delete files using the wildcard *, but be careful — you can easily delete files you did not intend to throw away.

To remove a file using a wildcard, you would type:

```
rm pig*
```

The above command will remove all files in the directory that start with the letters *pig*.

You can also remove multiple files using the rm command. For example:

```
rm piglet.txt sneakers.txt
```

You can use rmdir to remove a directory (rmdir foo, for example), but only if the directory is empty. To remove directories with rm, you must specify the -r option.

For example, if you want to recursively remove the directory tigger, you would type:

```
rm -r tigger
```

If you want to combine options, such as forcing a recursive deletion, you can type:

```
rm -rf tigger
```

A safer alternative to using rm for removing directories is the rmdir command. With this command, you will not be allowed to use recursive deletions, so a directory that has files in it will not be deleted.

WARNING The rm command can delete your entire file system! If you are logged in as root and you type the simple command rm -rf /, the command will recursively remove everything on your system!

Read the rmdir man page (man rmdir) to find out more about this command.

Chapter 10

Managing Users and Groups

Users can be either people, meaning accounts tied to physical users, or logical users, meaning accounts that exist for specific applications to use. *Groups* are logical expressions of organization. Groups tie users together, giving them permissions to read, write, or execute files.

When a file is created, it is assigned a user and group. It is also assigned separate read, write, and execute permissions for the file's owner, group, and everyone else. The user and group of a particular file, as well as the access permissions on the file, can be changed by root or, in most cases, by the creator of the file. (See Chapter 8 for more information on permissions.)

This chapter shows you how to manage users and groups with the User Manager tool in Red Hat Linux and describes the importance of shadow passwords.

Managing Users

Managing users and groups can be a tedious task, but Red Hat Linux provides a few tools and conventions to make management easier.

You can use tools like `useradd` or `groupadd` to create new users and groups from the shell prompt. But an easier way to manage users and groups is through the graphical application, User Manager. For more information on `useradd` and `groupadd`, refer to the *Official Red Hat Linux Administrator's Guide* (Red Hat Press/Wiley, 2003).

User and Group Configuration

User Manager allows you to view, modify, add, and delete local users and groups. To use User Manager, you must be running the X Window System, have root privileges, and have the `redhat-config-users` RPM package installed. To start User Manager from the desktop, click the Main Menu Button and choose System Settings ⇨ Users & Groups (or type the command `redhat-config-users` at a shell prompt.

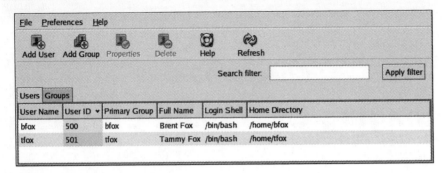

Figure 10-1. User Manager — Users Tab

To view a list of all local users on the system, click the Users tab. To view a list of all local groups on the system, click the Groups tab.

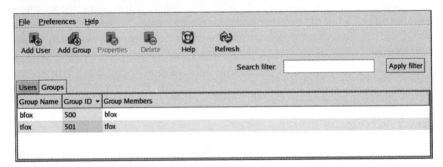

Figure 10-2: User Manager — Groups Tab

If you need to find a specific user or group, type the first few letters of the name in the Filter by field. Press Enter or click the Apply filter button. The filtered list will be displayed.

To sort the users or groups, click on the column name. The users or groups will be sorted by the value of that column.

Red Hat Linux reserves user IDs above 500 for system users. By default, User Manager does not display system users. To view all users, including the system users, uncheck Preferences ⇨ Filter system users and groups from the pull-down menu.

For more information on users and groups, refer to the *Official Red Hat Linux Administrator's Guide*.

Adding a New User

To add a new user, click the New User button. A window as shown in Figure 10-3 will appear. Type the username and full name for the new user in the appropriate fields. Type the user's password in the Password and Confirm Password fields. The password must be at least six characters.

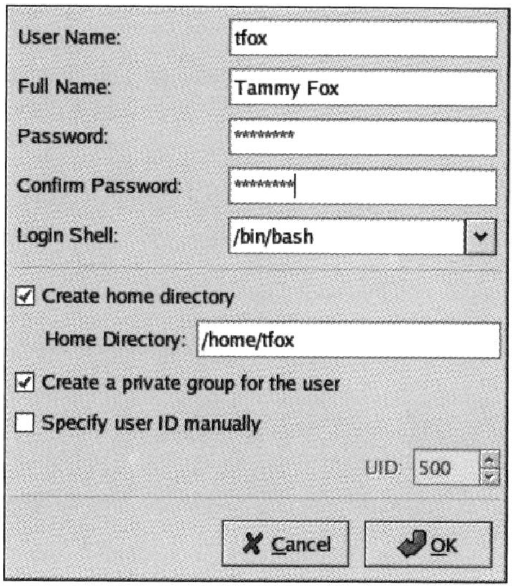

User Name:	tfox
Full Name:	Tammy Fox
Password:	********
Confirm Password:	********|
Login Shell:	/bin/bash ⌄

☑ Create home directory

Home Directory: /home/tfox

☑ Create a private group for the user

☐ Specify user ID manually

UID: 500 ⬍

✗ Cancel   ✔ OK

Figure 10-3: Adding a New User

Tip The longer the user's password, the more difficult it is for someone else to guess it and log in to the user's account without permission. It is also recommended that the password not be based on a word and that the password be a combination of letters, numbers, and special characters.

Select a login shell. If you are not sure which shell to select, accept the default value of /bin/bash.

The default home directory is /home/username. You can change the home directory that is created for the user or you can choose not to create the home directory by unselecting Create home directory.

Whenever you create a new user, by default a unique group with the same name as the user is created. If you do not want to create this group, unselect Create a private group for the user.

To specify a user ID for the user, select Specify user ID manually. If the option is not selected, the next available user ID starting with number 500 will be assigned to the new user. Red Hat Linux reserves user IDs below 500 for system users. Click OK to create the user.

To configure more advanced user properties such as password expiration, modify the user's properties after adding the user. (Refer to the next section for more information.)

To add the user to more user groups, click on the User tab, select the user, and click Properties. In the User Properties window, select the Groups tab. Select the groups that you want the user to be a member of, select the primary group for the user, and click OK.

Modifying User Properties

To view the properties of an existing user, click on the Users tab, select the user from the user list, and click Properties from the button menu (or choose File ⇨ Properties from the pull-down menu). A window similar to Figure 10-4 will appear.

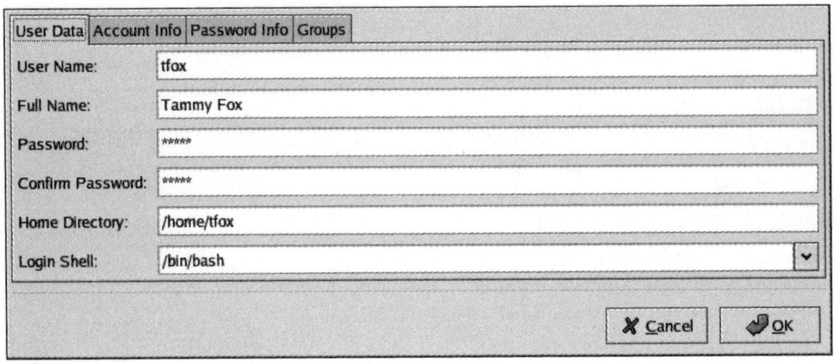

Figure 10-4. User Properties

The User Properties window is divided into tabbed pages:

♦ *User Data* — Basic user information that is configured when you add the user. Use this tab to change the user's full name, password, home directory, or login shell.

♦ *Account Info* — Select Enable account expiration if you want the account to expire on a certain date. Enter the date in the provided fields. Select User account is locked to lock the user account so that the user cannot log in to the system.

♦ *Password Info* — This tab shows the date that the user last changed his password. To force the user to change his password after a certain number of days, select Enable password expiration. You can also set the number of days before the user is allowed to change his password, the number of days before the user is warned to change his password, and days before the account become inactive.

♦ *Groups* — Select the groups that you want the user to be a member of and the user's primary group.

Adding a New Group

To add a new user group, click the New Group button. A window similar to Figure 10-5 will appear. Type the name of the new group to create. To specify a group ID for the new group, select Specify group ID manually and select the GID. Red Hat Linux reserves group IDs lower than 500 for system groups. Click OK to create the group. The new group will appear in the group list.

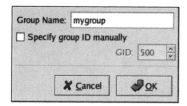

Figure 10-5. New Group

To add users to the group, refer to the "Adding a New User" section earlier in this chapter.

Modifying Group Properties

To view the properties of an existing group, select the group from the group list and click Properties from the button menu (or choose File ⇨ Properties from the pull-down menu). A window similar to Figure 10-6 will appear.

Figure 10-6. Group Properties

The Group Users tab displays which users are members of the group. Select additional users to add them to the group and unselect users to remove from the group. Click OK or Apply to modify the users in the group.

Shadow Utilities

If you are in a multiuser environment and not using a networked authentication scheme such as Kerberos, you should consider using *shadow passwords* for the enhanced protection offered for your system's authentication files. During the installation of Red Hat Linux, shadow password protection for your system is enabled by default, as are *MD5 passwords* (an alternative and arguably more secure method of encrypting passwords for storage on your system, MD5 passwords are beyond the scope of this book).

Shadow passwords offer a few distinct advantages over the previous standard of storing passwords on UNIX and Linux systems, including

♦ Improved system security by moving the encrypted passwords (normally found in /etc/passwd) to /etc/shadow which is readable only by root.

♦ Information concerning password aging (how long it has been since a password was last changed).

♦ Control over how long a password can remain unchanged before the user is required to change it.

♦ The ability to use the /etc/login.defs file to enforce a security policy, especially concerning password aging.

The shadow-utils package contains a number of utilities that support the following features:

♦ Conversion from normal to shadow passwords and back (pwconv, pwunconv).

♦ Verification of the password, group, and associated shadow files (pwck, grpck).

♦ Industry-standard methods of adding, deleting, and modifying user accounts (useradd, usermod, and userdel).

♦ Industry-standard methods of adding, deleting, and modifying user groups (groupadd, groupmod, and groupdel).

♦ Industry-standard method of administering the /etc/group file using gpasswd.

There are some additional points of interest concerning these utilities:

♦ The utilities will work properly whether shadowing is enabled or not.

♦ The utilities have been slightly modified to support Red Hat's user private group scheme. For a description of the modifications, see the useradd man page. For more information on user private groups, see the *Official Red Hat Linux Administrator's Guide*.

♦ The adduser script has been replaced with a symbolic link to /usr/sbin/useradd.

♦ The tools in the shadow-utils package are not Kerberos-, NIS-, hesiod-, or LDAP-enabled. New users will be local only. For more information on Kerberos and LDAP, see the *Official Red Hat Linux Administrator's Guide*.

Part III

Getting the Most from Your Red Hat Linux System

Red Hat Linux 8 includes a wealth of applications. This part explains some of the common tasks that desktop users want to perform, such as using the OpenOffice.org suite (which includes word processor, spreadsheet, presentation, and drawing applications), playing multimedia files, and configuring an Internet connection.

Chapter 11

Working with Documents

Red Hat Linux includes several tools for managing all of your documents. Whether you are preparing for a business or school presentation, writing a formal letter, or opening a document from an email attachment, Red Hat Linux has a tool that suits your needs.

This chapter shows you how to get up and running with the OpenOffice.org suite of applications, a new addition to Red Hat Linux in version 8.0, and shows you how to view PDF documents.

The OpenOffice.org Suite

Office productivity suites are collections of applications designed to save time and assist users at the office, at school, and at home. Usually, productivity suites are graphical and include such applications as word processors, spreadsheets, and presentation utilities. The applications that comprise a productivity suite are integrated — meaning that you can, for example, write a document with an embedded chart created by the spreadsheet application as well as a slide from a graphical presentation application.

Integration of the software that makes up a productivity suite helps you to give impact to your presentations, lectures, or printed material.

Red Hat Linux includes a powerful business productivity suite called OpenOffice.org, which incorporates several complementary applications into one integrated package. Using OpenOffice.org is much faster and easier than learning complex tags and code to format your documents and presentations.

The OpenOffice.org suite allows you complete control over the layout and content of your documents and lets you see the results as you edit it. This real-time, visual form of document formatting is called *what you see is what you get* (or WYSIWYG — pronounced "wizzywig") editing.

OpenOffice.org Features

The OpenOffice.org suite contains several applications for creating and editing documents, spreadsheets, business presentations, and artwork. It includes templates, forms, and wizards for creating basic professional documents and presentations quickly. The OpenOffice.org suite is able to read, edit, and create files in several formats, including files that are commonly associated with Microsoft Office, such as .doc (for Microsoft Word files), .xls (for Microsoft Excel files), and .ppt (for Microsoft PowerPoint files).

Table 11-1 shows the many different types of files you can use and tasks you can accomplish with the OpenOffice.org suite.

Table 11-1: OpenOffice.org Features

Application	File Compatibility	Document Types
OpenOffice.org Writer	`.sxw, .sdw, .doc, .rtf, .txt, .htm/.html`	Formal letters, business forms, school papers, resumes, newsletters, reports
OpenOffice.org Calc	`.sxc, .dbf, .xls, .sdc, .slk, .csv, .htm/.html`	Spreadsheets, charts, tables, graphs, directories, address books, receipts and bills, budgets, small databases
OpenOffice.org Impress	`.sxi, .ppt, .sxd, .sdd`	Business and academic presentations, Web presentations, lectures, slide shows
OpenOffice.org Draw	`.sxd, .sda;` export files to several image formats, including `.jpg, .bmp, .gif,` and `.png`	Illustrations, line drawings, clip art, organizational charts

As you can see, the OpenOffice.org suite has many file compatibility features, and allows you to accomplish several tasks for academic, business, or home use. The following sections will show you how to use the OpenOffice.org suite.

OpenOffice.org Writer

Writing documents using OpenOffice.org is similar to other word processing applications you may have used before, such as Microsoft Word, WordPerfect, and so on. A word processor is like a text editor but has several additional features that allow you to format, design, and print your documents without the need to memorize complex formatting tags or codes. OpenOffice.org Writer is a powerful word processor that features WYSIWYG formatting — what you see in the OpenOffice.org Writer window is exactly what you will get if you print the document or if you give the document file to someone else for them to view. Figure 11-1 shows OpenOffice.org Writer in action.

To start OpenOffice.org Writer from your desktop panel, choose Main Menu ⇨ Office ⇨ OpenOffice.org Writer (to start Writer from a shell prompt, type **oowriter**).

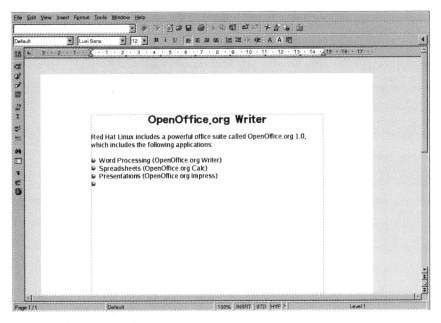

Figure 11-1. OpenOffice.org Writer

The main interface is the document editing area (the white space in the middle of the window where you can type your text). At the top of the window are various functions collected into toolbars that control fonts, letter sizes, justification (to align the text of your document to the left, center, or right margins), and other text formatting buttons. There is also a text box that enables you to type in the exact location of a document on your machine and load the document into the editing area. There are buttons for opening, saving, and printing documents, as well as buttons for creating new documents (which will open up a new window with a blank document for you to add content).

Along the left side of the window there is a toolbar with buttons for checking your spelling, automatic highlighting of misspelled words, word and phrase searching, and other convenient editing functions.

If you hover over a toolbar button, a pop-up tip (often called a *tooltip*) will display a brief explanation of the button's functionality. You can display more detailed tips by clicking the Help menu and checking Extended Tips.

You can immediately begin typing text into the document editing area at any time using the default settings.

While OpenOffice.org Writer is useful for general document editing, you can also add objects such as images, illustrations, charts, and tables to your document to complement your text or give impact to your documents. To add an image, click Insert ⇨ Graphics ⇨ From File, and choose the image from the pop-up file browser. The image will appear where you placed your cursor and can be sized larger or smaller to fit your needs. Figure 11-2 shows an image added to a document.

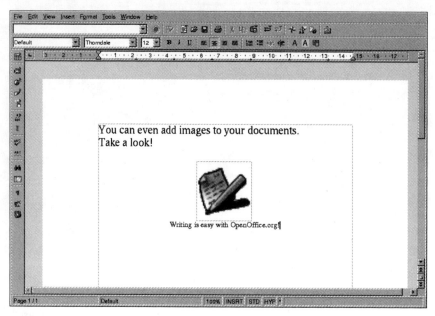

Figure 11-2. Adding an Image to Your Document

After you have created your document, you can save it in any format that you wish. To save your text, click the Save button (it looks like a little floppy disk). You can choose the file format from the File type drop-down menu. The default file type is appropriate for files that you are working on exclusively with OpenOffice.org applications. However, for files that you need to distribute to Microsoft Office users, or if you are editing a file that was sent as an email attachment with the .doc extension, you can save the file as a Microsoft Word file type that others will be able to open in Microsoft Word. Please consult Table 11-1 for available file formats.

OpenOffice.org Calc

From large enterprises to home offices, professionals in every industry use spreadsheets for keeping records, creating business charts, and manipulating data. OpenOffice.org Calc is a software spreadsheet application that allows you to enter and manipulate data in cells organized into columns and rows.

You can perform calculations on groups of cells (such as adding or subtracting a column of cells) or create charts based on cell groupings. You can even incorporate spreadsheet data into your documents for a professional touch.

To start OpenOffice.org Calc from the desktop panel, select Main Menu ⇨ Office ⇨ OpenOffice.org Calc (to start OpenOffice.org Calc from a shell prompt, type **oocalc**).

Figure 11-3 shows OpenOffice.org Calc in action.

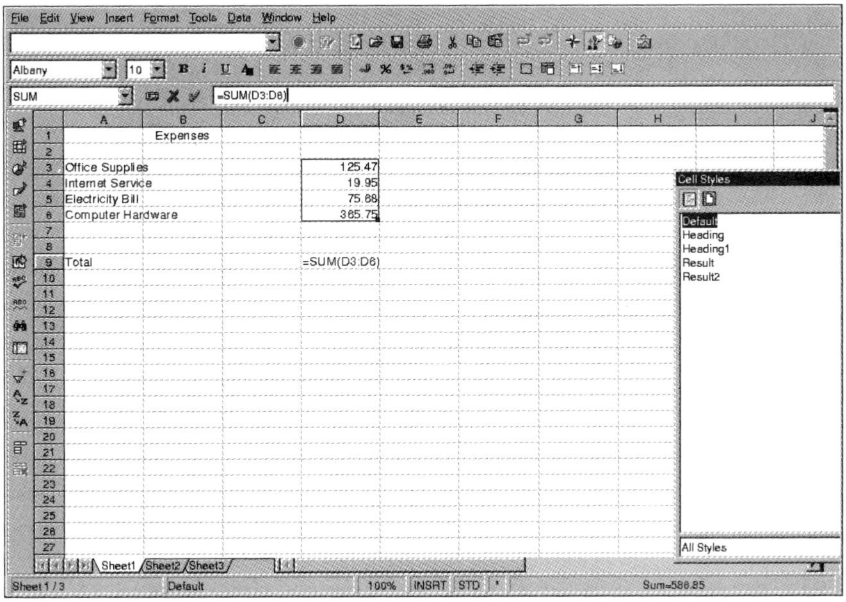

Figure 11-3. OpenOffice.org Calc

OpenOffice.org Calc allows you to enter and manipulate personal or business data. For example, you can create a personal budget by entering data descriptions (such as rent, groceries, and utilities) into column A and the quantities of those data descriptions in column B.

OpenOffice.org Calc allows you to enter the data either in the cell itself by double-clicking the cell and typing your information or by using the Input Line (the text box on the toolbar). Then you can run arithmetic commands on column B to come up with a total.

OpenOffice.org Calc has several preset functions and calculations (such as =SUM() for addition/multiplication, =quotient() for division, and =subtotal() for preparing receipts). For detailed information about creating functions for calculating your numerical data in OpenOffice.org Calc, refer to the OpenOffice.org Calc documentation by selecting Help ⇨ Contents.

If you need to create charts or graphs for class or business presentations, OpenOffice.org has several chart and graph templates available to choose from. Highlight the areas you would like to chart, then click Insert ⇨ Chart . . . . In the Chart window, the data ranges you chose will be shown in the text box for you to customize further if you desire. Click Next to display the many different charts and graphs you can create using your data. Choose the style you want, and click Create. The graph will be displayed anchored within the spreadsheet window. You can move it anywhere on the screen for printing, or you can save the graph as an object that you can then embed in OpenOffice.org Writer documents or OpenOffice.org Impress presentations.

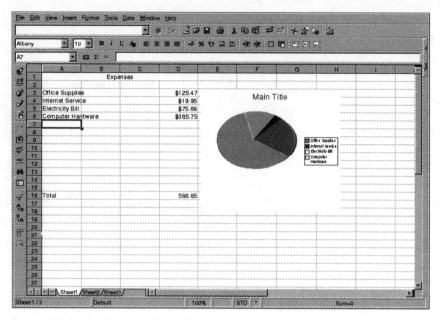

Figure 11-4. Creating Charts with OpenOffice.org Calc

OpenOffice.org Impress

Visual aids can give your presentations an added impact that catches your audience's attention and keeps them interested. OpenOffice.org Impress is a graphical tool that can help you make a more convincing presentation.

To start OpenOffice.org Impress from the desktop, select Main Menu ⇨ Office ⇨ OpenOffice.org Impress (to start OpenOffice.org Impress from a shell prompt, type **ooimpress**).

OpenOffice.org Impress features several AutoPilot features that allow you to create presentations from a collection of style templates. You can make slides with itemized lists, outlines, or images. You can even import charts and graphs from OpenOffice.org Calc into a slide.

Figure 11-5 shows OpenOffice.org Impress in action.

Figure 11-5. OpenOffice.org Impress

When you first start OpenOffice.org Impress, you will be presented with a presentation setup screen, which will prompt you for basic information about what type of presentation you want to make. You can choose the style of your slides, the medium with which you will present your slides (plain paper, transparent paper for overhead projectors, slides, or a display monitor), and any visual effects you want to apply to the slides during presentations from your computer.

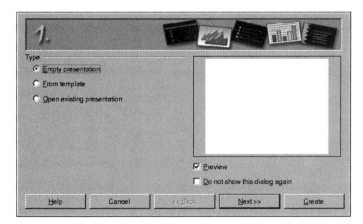

Figure 11-6. OpenOffice.org Impress AutoPilot Wizard

After you have chosen your preferences with AutoPilot tool, you can choose the type of slide you want to create. You can select a pre-formatted slide from the list or start with a blank slide and customize the layout yourself. To create new slides for your presentation, click Insert

Slide . . . in the floating toolbar, and a pop-up window will appear allowing you to choose the layout of the new slide. You can have as many slides in your presentation as you need.

You can also preview your presentation at any point by selecting Slide Show ➪ Slide Show from the pull-down menu. The presentation will be in full screen, which you can exit by cycling through every slide until you reach the end or by pressing the Esc key at any point in the slide show.

Your presentation can be saved in several file formats. You can save in the native OpenOffice.org Impress format (.sxi), the Microsoft PowerPoint format (.ppt), or StarImpress format (.sdd). You can also print your presentation to plain or transparent paper formats by clicking File ➪ Print from the file menu. Refer to Table 11-1 for the complete list of compatible image file formats.

To learn more about OpenOffice.org Impress, click Help ➪ Contents from the File menu to access the help browser.

OpenOffice.org Draw

If you would like to create graphics to include in your documents and presentations, you can use OpenOffice.org Draw. Using your mouse as you would a pen or a paintbrush, OpenOffice.org Draw allows you to make illustrations and save them in several formats that you can add to printed documents, place on websites, or attach to an email.

To start OpenOffice.org Draw from the desktop, click the Main Menu button and choose Office ➪ OpenOffice.org Draw (to start OpenOffice.org Draw from a shell prompt, type **oodraw**). Figure 11-7 Shows OpenOffice.org Draw in action.

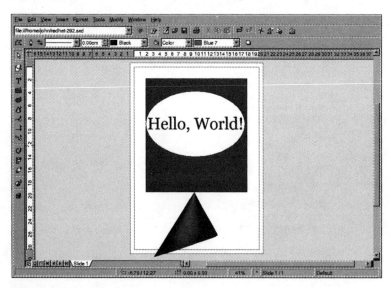

Figure 11-7. OpenOffice.org Draw

If you are familiar with illustration and graphics applications such as The GIMP (refer to Chapter 15 for more information), you will find that OpenOffice.org Draw has some of the same basic functions with the added benefit of being integrated with the rest of the OpenOffice.org suite.

There are toolbars for creating straight and curved lines, basic shapes such as squares and circles, 3-D objects such as cones and cubes, and more. You can create images and fill them with the color of your choice using the Area Style/Filling drop-down menu on the main toolbar. You can additionally insert text into your illustrations. OpenOffice.org Draw also allows you to open and import images and modify them with the tools provided.

When you complete your illustration or image modifications, you can save the file in one of several native file formats or export your work to a universal format such as `.jpg` or `.png`. Refer to Table 11-1 for the complete list of compatible image file formats.

Viewing PDFs

A PDF (Portable Document Format) file is an electronic image of a document. PDF captures formatting information from a variety of desktop publishing applications, making it possible to send formatted documents and have them appear on the recipient's monitor or printer as they were intended. To view a PDF you must have a PDF reader.

Figure 11-8: The xpdf PDF Viewer

An open source application called `xpdf` is included with Red Hat Linux.

To view a PDF with `xpdf`:

1. In your desktop environment, click the Main Menu button and choose Graphics ⇨ xpdf (to launch xpdf from a shell prompt, type **xpdf**).

2. Right-click in the xpdf screen to display a list of options.

3. Select Open to display a list of files.

4. Select the PDF file you want to view and click Open.

To see a list of menu options, right-click inside the screen. The toolbar at the bottom has navigational tools that let you move backward and forward through the document, as well as standard zoom, print, and find tools. The xpdf man page provides useful information on the xpdf options. To view the xpdf man page, at a shell prompt type **man xpdf**.

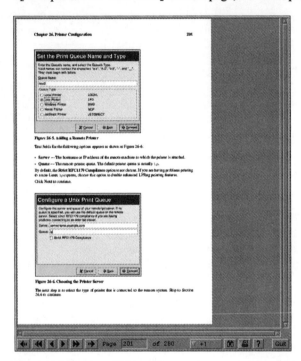

Figure 11-9: Viewing a PDF in xpdf

Another popular PDF viewer is Adobe Acrobat Reader. While it is not included with Red Hat Linux, you can download it free at http://www.adobe.com/.

Chapter 12

Getting Online

There are many types of Internet connections, the most common of which include

♦ Modems

♦ xDSL modems

♦ Cable modems

♦ Wireless devices

While this is by no means an exhaustive list of connection types, these are by far the most common methods of connecting to the Internet today. Other connection types, such as ISDN and token ring, are pretty much exclusively the domain of business-class networks and as such are beyond the scope of this book. For more information on these more advanced connection types, see the *Official Red Hat Linux Administrator's Guide* (Red Hat Press/Wiley, 2003).

Network Configuration

To communicate with other computers, your computer needs a network connection. Computers connect to networks by having the operating system recognize a network interface adapter (such as Ethernet) or other hardware (such as a dial-up modem).

The Network Administration Tool comes with Red Hat Linux and can be used to configure your network interface. To use the Network Administration Tool, you must be running the X Window System and have root privileges. To start the application, click the Main Menu Button and choose System Settings ⇨ Network (or type the command **redhat-config-network** at a shell prompt).

If you prefer modifying the configuration files directly, refer to the *Official Red Hat Linux Administrator's Guide* for information on their location and contents.

TIP Visit the Red Hat Hardware Compatibility List at `http://hardware.redhat.com/hcl/` to determine if Red Hat Linux supports your hardware device.

Overview of Configuring a Network Connection

To configure a network connection with the Network Administration Tool, perform the following steps:

1. Add the physical hardware device to the hardware list.

2. Add a network device associated with the physical hardware device.

3. Configure any hosts that cannot be looked up through DNS.

4. Configure the hostname and DNS settings.

This chapter will discuss each of these steps for each of the following types of network connections:

♦ *Modem Connection* — A modem connection uses a modem to establish a connection to the Internet. Digital data is modulated into analog signals and sent over phone lines. To configure this type of connection, see the "Establishing a Modem Connection" section later in this chapter for more information.

♦ *xDSL Connection* — An xDSL (Digital Subscriber Line) connection uses high-speed transmissions through telephone lines. There are different types of DSL such as ADSL, IDSL, and SDSL. The term xDSL means any type of DSL connection. See the "Establishing an xDSL Connection" later in this chapter for more information.

♦ *Cable Modem Connection* — A cable modem connection uses the same coaxial cable that your TV cable travels on to transmit data. Most cable Internet providers require you to install an Ethernet card (or other Ethernet adapter, such as a USB adapter) in your computer that connects to the cable modem. Then, the cable modem connects to the coaxial cable and to your Ethernet card. The Ethernet card is usually required to be configured for DHCP. See the "Establishing an Ethernet Connection" section for more information on setting up your Ethernet card.

♦ *Wireless Connection* — If you are connecting your Red Hat Linux computer to a wireless access point (WAP) or peer-to- peer (also called ad-hoc) network with a wireless (802.11x) network card, then you will need to configure your wireless device. See the "Establishing a Wireless Connection" section later in this chapter for more information.

Establishing an Ethernet Connection

To establish an Ethernet connection (such as for a cable modem or DSL connections), you need a network interface card (NIC), a network cable (usually a CAT5 cable), and a network to connect to. There are different speeds to networks; make sure your NIC is compatible with the network to which you want to connect.

To add an Ethernet connection, start the Network Administration Tool and follow these steps:

1. Click the Devices tab.

2. Click the Add button.

3. Select Ethernet connection from the Device Type list, and click Forward.

4. If you have already added the network interface card to the hardware list, select it from the Ethernet card list. Otherwise, select Other Ethernet Card to add the hardware device.

> **Note** The installation program usually detects supported Ethernet devices and prompts you to configure them. If you configured any Ethernet devices during the installation, they will already appear in the hardware list on the Hardware tab.

5. If you selected Other Ethernet Card, the Select Ethernet Adapter window appears. Select the manufacturer and model of the Ethernet card. Select the device name. If this is the system's first Ethernet card, select eth0 as the device name, if this is the second Ethernet card, select eth1, and so on. The Network Administration Tool also allows you to configure the resources for the NIC. Click Forward to continue.

6. On the Configure Network Settings page (shown in Figure 12-1), choose between DHCP and a static IP address. If the device receives a different IP address each time the network is started, do not specify a hostname. Click Forward to continue.

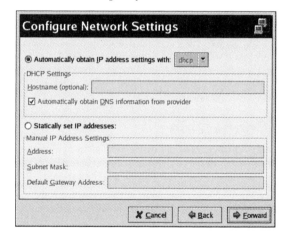

Figure 12-1. Ethernet Settings

7. Click Apply on the Create Ethernet Device page to save the changes.

After configuring the Ethernet device, it appears in the device list.

Figure 12-2. Ethernet Device

After adding the Ethernet device, you can edit its configuration by selecting the device from the device list and clicking Edit. For example, when the device is added, it is configured to start at boot time by default. You can edit its configuration to modify this setting.

When the device is added, it is not activated, as seen by its Inactive status. To activate the device, select it from the device list and click the Activate button.

Establishing a Modem Connection

A modem can be used to configure a dial-up Internet connection over an active phone line. An Internet Service Provider (ISP) account (also called a *dial-up account*) is required. To add a modem connection, start the Network Administration Tool and follow these steps:

1. Click the Devices tab.
2. Click the Add button.
3. Select Modem connection from the Device Type list and click Forward.
4. If there is a modem already configured in the hardware list (on the Hardware tab), the Network Administration Tool assumes you want to use it to establish a modem connection. If there is not a modem already configured, it tries to detect any modems in the system. This probe might take a while. After probing, the window shown in Figure 12-3 appears.

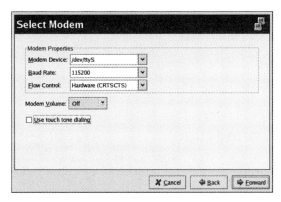

Figure 12-3. Modem Settings

5. Configure the baud rate, flow control, and modem volume. If you do not know these values, accept the defaults. If you do not have touch tone dialing, uncheck the corresponding checkbox.

6. Click Forward.

7. If your ISP is in the pre-configured list, select it. Otherwise, enter the required information about your ISP account. If you do not know the values, contact your ISP.

8. Click Forward.

9. On the Create Dialup Connection page, click Apply to save the changes.

After configuring the modem device, it appears in the device list as shown in Figure 12-4.

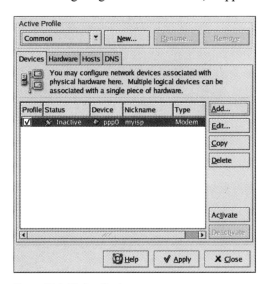

Figure 12-4. Modem Device

After adding the modem device, you can edit its configuration by selecting the device from the device list and clicking Edit. For example, when the device is added, it is configured not to start at boot time by default. Edit its configuration to modify this setting. Compression, PPP options, login name, password, and more can also be changed.

When the device is added, it is not activated, as seen by its Inactive status. To activate the device, select it from the device list, and click the Activate button.

Establishing an xDSL Connection

DSL stands for Digital Subscriber Lines. There are different types of DSL such as ADSL, IDSL, and SDSL. The Network Administration Tool uses the term xDSL to mean all types of DSL connections.

Some DSL providers require you to configure your system to obtain an IP address through DHCP with an Ethernet card. If you are required to use DHCP, refer to the "Establishing an Ethernet Connection" section earlier in this chapter to configure your Ethernet card.

Some DSL providers require you to configure a PPPoE (Point-to-Point Protocol over Ethernet) connection with an Ethernet card. If you must supply a username and password to connect, you are probably using PPPoE. Ask your DSL provider which method to use.

If you are required to use PPPoE, start the Network Administration Tool and follow these steps:

1. Click the Devices tab.
2. Click the Add button.
3. Select xDSL connection from the Device Type list and click Forward.
4. If your Ethernet card is already in the hardware list, select the Ethernet Device from the pull-down menu on the page shown in Figure 12-5. Otherwise, the Select Ethernet Adapter window appears.

> **NOTE** The installation program usually detects supported Ethernet devices and prompts you to configure them. If you configured any Ethernet devices during the installation, they will already appear in the hardware list on the Hardware tab.

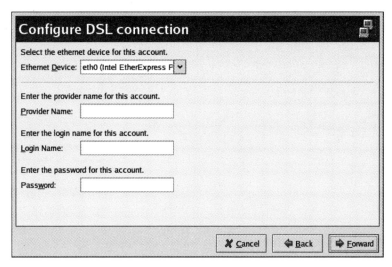

Figure 12-5. Configuring a DSL Connection

5. If the Select Ethernet Adapter window appears, select the manufacturer and model of the Ethernet card. Select the device name. If this is the system's first Ethernet card, select eth0 as the device name, if this is the second Ethernet card, select eth1, and so on. The Network Administration Tool also allows you to configure the resources for the NIC. Click Forward to continue.

6. Enter the Provider Name, Login Name, and Password.

7. Click Forward.

8. On the Create DSL Connection page, click Apply to save your changes.

After configuring the DSL connect, it appears in the device list, as shown in Figure 12-6.

After adding the xDSL connection, you can edit its configuration by selecting the device from the device list and clicking Edit. For example, when the device is added, it is configured not to start at boot time by default. Edit its configuration to modify this setting.

When the device is added, it is not activated, as seen by its Inactive status. To activate the device, select it from the device list, and click the Activate button.

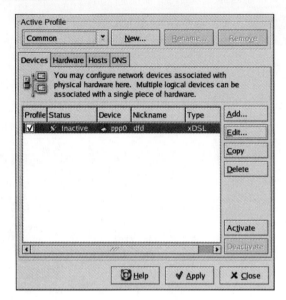

Figure 12-6. Viewing a New xDSL Device

Establishing a Wireless Connection

Wireless Ethernet devices are becoming increasingly popular, especially with broadband connections such as xDSL and cable modems. The configuration for a wireless connection is similar to the Ethernet configuration except that it allows you to configure SSID, mode, frequency, channel, transmit rate, and key for your wireless device.

To add a wireless Ethernet connection, start the Network Administration Tool and follow these steps:

1. Click the Devices tab.

2. Click the Add button.

3. Select Wireless connection from the Device Type list and click Forward.

4. If you have already added the wireless network interface card to the hardware list, select it from the Ethernet card list. Otherwise, select Other Ethernet Card to add the hardware device.

Note The installation program usually detects supported wireless Ethernet devices and prompts you to configure them. If you configured them during the installation program, they will already appear in the hardware list on the Hardware tab.

5. If you selected Other Ethernet Card, the Select Ethernet Adapter window appears. Select the manufacturer and model of the Ethernet card and the device. If this is the first Ethernet card for the system, select eth0, if this is the second Ethernet card for the system, select eth1, and so on. The Network Administration Tool also allows the user to

configure the resources for the wireless network interface card. Click Forward to continue.

6. On the Configure Wireless Connection page, configure the ESSID, mode, frequency, channel, transmit rate, and key for your wireless device.

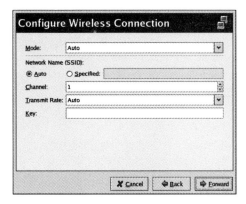

Figure 12-7. Wireless Settings

7. On the Configure Network Settings page, choose between DHCP and static IP address. You may specify a hostname for the device. If the device receives a dynamic IP address each time the network is started, do not specify a hostname. Click Forward to continue.

8. Click Apply on the Create Wireless Device page to save your changes.

After configuring the wireless device, it appears in the device list as shown in Figure 12-8.

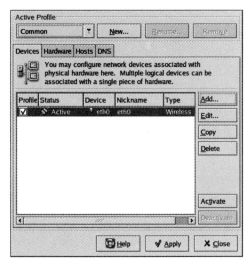

Figure 12-8. Wireless Device

After adding the wireless device, you can edit its configuration by selecting the device from the device list and clicking Edit. For example, you can configure the device to activate at boot time.

When the device is added, it is not activated, as seen by its Inactive status. To activate the device, select it from the device list, and click the Activate button.

Chapter 13

Choosing Your Internet Software

In version 8.0, Red Hat Linux offers a wealth of choices of Web browsing and email software for the Internet aficionado. This chapter describes the major applications that you can choose from in Red Hat Linux 8.0 for your Web browsing and email needs.

Web Browsing

After you have configured your Internet connection (see Chapter 12), you are ready to get online and start surfing. Red Hat Linux comes with several open source browsers for you to choose from. This chapter briefly explains how to surf the Web using the following browsers:

- ◆ Mozilla
- ◆ Nautilus
- ◆ Konqueror
- ◆ Galeon

Mozilla

Mozilla functions like any other Web browser. Mozilla has fairly standard navigation toolbars, buttons, and menus.

If you have previously been using Netscape as your Web browser and performed an upgrade of Red Hat Linux, the first time that you start Mozilla you will not see the main Mozilla browser (shown in Figure 13-5). Instead, you will first see Mozilla asking to convert your Netscape profile.

Figure 13-1. Mozilla Profile Creation

If you click Convert Profile, your prior Netscape bookmarks and preferences will be converted to a Mozilla profile for you. When you next launch Mozilla, either from the panel or by clicking the Main Menu button and choosing Internet ⇨ Web Browser, you will see that your previous bookmarks are now available in Mozilla.

If you click Manage Profiles, you will have the opportunity to create one or more profiles, or user accounts, for Mozilla.

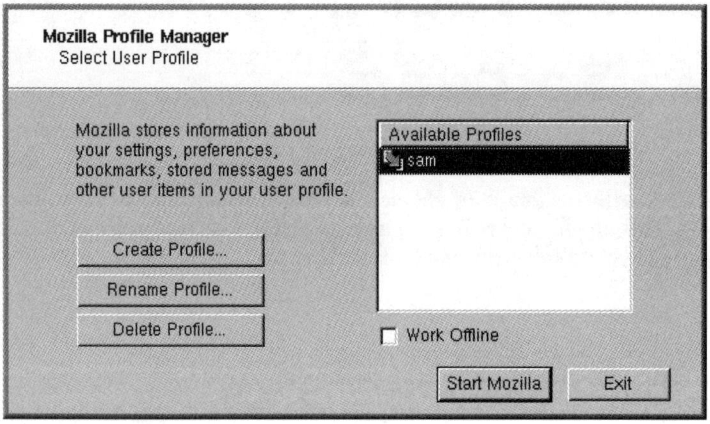

Figure 13-2. Mozilla Profile Manager

Here you can choose to create a new profile or to create a profile based on your existing user account. This feature helps you stay organized by creating separate user accounts for business use, personal use, etc.

Clicking Create Profile will take you to an information screen explaining what this process entails. To continue, click Next.

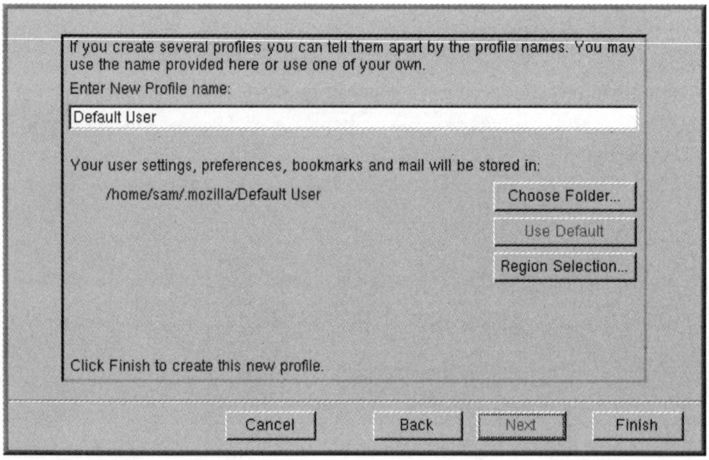

Figure 13-3. Profile Configuration

Next, choose a name to use for this new profile. If you do not enter a name, the profile will be called Default User.

You can also click Choose Folder to select where your Mozilla settings and preferences will be stored. By default, these settings are stored in the following directory:

```
/home/youraccountname/.mozilla/Default User
```

When you click Finish, your new profile will be added.

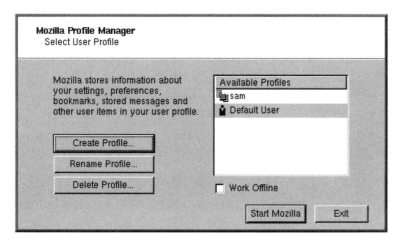

Figure 13-4. Profile Screen with New Profile Added

Now that you have created a user profile, click on Start Mozilla to launch the application or click on Exit to close it.

To add new profiles or delete existing profiles later on, you will need to run the Mozilla Profile Manager again. To launch the Mozilla Profile Manager, at the shell prompt type the following command:

```
mozilla --ProfileManager
```

Mozilla Web Browser

After you have configured your user profile, you are ready to use the browser. To access Mozilla, click the Web browser launcher on the panel or click the Main Menu button and choose Internet ⇨ Web Browser.

The Mozilla screen has all of the standard Web browser functions that other browsers have. There is a main menu at the top of the screen and a navigation bar below it. There is a sidebar on the left that contains additional options. And in the bottom left corner, there are four small icons: Navigator, Mail, Composer, and Address Book.

Figure 13-5. Mozilla Main Browser Window

To browse the Internet, click on Search and enter a topic in the search engine that opens, type a website URL in the location bar, click on and create bookmarks, or check the What's Related sidebar tab to see pages related to the one you are viewing currently.

> **TIP** Mozilla allows you to browse multiple websites within one browser window using navigational tabs. Instead of using two separate windows to read Web pages, you can open a tab by clicking File ➪ New ➪ Navigation Tab or by pressing Ctrl-t. This will open a new tab and allow you to switch between tabs by clicking on them. To close a tab, click the X button at the right of the tab toolbar.

For additional information on using Mozilla, choose Help ➪ Help Content.

Mozilla Composer

You can use Mozilla Composer to create Web pages. You do not need to know HTML to use this tool, as Composer is a WYSIWYG (what you see is what you get) HTML editor.

To open Composer, go to Tasks ➪ Composer on the Mozilla main menu, or click on the Composer icon in the lower left part of the screen.

The Mozilla help files provide information on creating Web pages with Composer. To access help files for Composer, choose Help ➪ Help Contents. When the help screen opens, click on the Contents tab and expand the Creating Web pages menu by clicking on the arrow next to it. A list of topics will appear and clicking on any of these will provide you with information for creating and editing Web pages using Mozilla Composer.

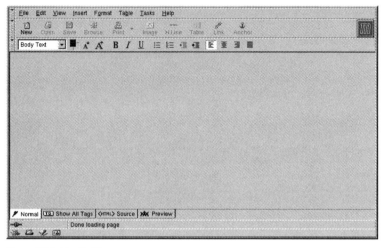

Figure 13-6. Mozilla Composer

Nautilus

Nautilus is a core component of the GNOME desktop environment and provides an easy way to view, manage, and customize your files and folders, as well as browse the Web.

Nautilus integrates your access to files, applications, media, Internet-based resources, and the Web, making it convenient for you to locate and use all the resources that are available.

If you are using Nautilus, browsing the Web is always just one mouse click away. Click Web Search in the toolbar to launch the Nautilus Web browser feature.

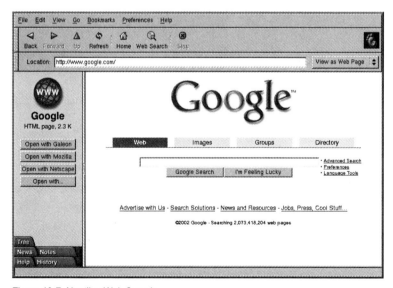

Figure 13-7. Nautilus Web Search

You can also use the Location: bar to enter path names, URLs, or other types of addresses.

When you are viewing a Web page, Nautilus gives you additional browser choices in case you want to use a full-featured Web browser. To select a different browser, click one of the buttons in the sidebar.

For additional information on using Nautilus, choose Help ⇨ Nautilus User Manual or Help ⇨ Nautilus Quick Reference.

Konqueror

Konqueror not only allows you to browse your local and network file system, but with component technology used throughout KDE, Konqueror is also a full featured Web browser that you can use to explore the Internet.

To launch Konqueror, click the Main Menu button and choose Extras ⇨ Internet ⇨ Konqueror Web Browser.

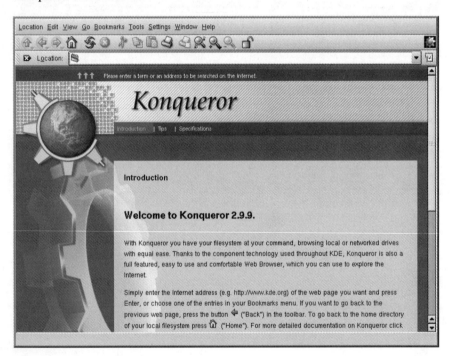

Figure 13-8. Welcome to Konqueror

When you first launch Konqueror, you will be presented with an Introduction screen. This screen offers basic instructions for browsing a Web page or your local file system.

If you click Continue, you will be presented with the Tips screen. This screen shows you basic tips for using Konqueror so that you can begin to take advantage of the features.

By clicking Continue from the Tips screen, you will see the Specifications screen. This screen displays information on supported standards (such as Cascading Stylesheets, plug-ins, and OpenSSL), featured protocols, and more.

To begin your first Web search, enter a URL in the Location: field.

For additional information on using Konqueror, choose Help ➪ Konqueror Handbook.

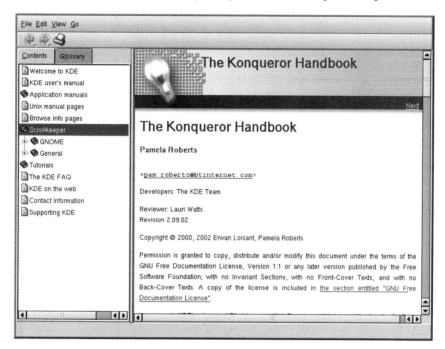

Figure 13-9. The Konqueror Handbook

Galeon

Galeon is a GNOME browser based on Mozilla. Unlike Mozilla, which is a full-featured suite of Web applications, Galeon is *only* a Web browser; it does not feature email, newsgroups, or anything other than Web browsing and searching.

To use Galeon, a working installation of Mozilla is required. Galeon uses Mozilla's rendering engine to display content. If you cannot run Mozilla, it is doubtful that you will be able to run Galeon.

To launch Galeon, click the Main Menu button and choose Extras ⇨ Internet ⇨ Galeon. The first time you launch Galeon, it will take you through the configuration process.

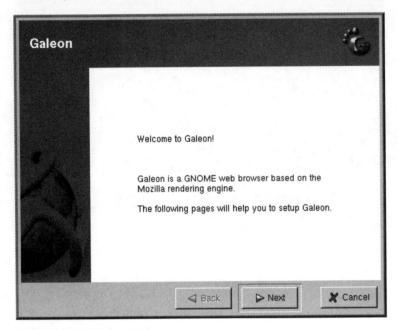

Figure 13-10. Configuring Galeon

During the initial configuration, you have the option of importing bookmarks from Netscape or Mozilla, as well as some preferences from Netscape if you have been using it as your previous Web browser.

After you have finished your configuration of Galeon, the main browser will appear.

> **TIP** Like Mozilla, Galeon also has a navigational tab feature that can help you avoid having your desktop cluttered with browser windows. Multiple pages can be stored in a single Galeon window, and you can switch between them by clicking on each tab. To launch a new Tab, use the Ctrl-T key combination or choose File ⇨ New Tab. The tabbed browsing mode can be configured in the Tabs page of the Preferences Window.

Figure 13-11. Online with Galeon

For additional information or help with Galeon, choose Help ⇨ Galeon FAQ or Help ⇨ Galeon manual.

Email Applications

Email is a very popular way of communicating with others over the Internet. You can use email with an *email client*, an application that understands the various email transmission standards and allows you to send, receive, and read email. Red Hat Linux includes several email applications, including graphical email clients like Evolution and Mozilla Mail, as well as text-based clients like Pine and Mutt.

All of the email client applications are designed to suit certain types of users; so, you can choose one with the features that best suits your particular needs.

The purpose of this section is to demonstrate how to use some of the popular email applications included in Red Hat Linux. Because all email clients perform the same basic tasks (send and receive email), choose the one that is most convenient and easy to use.

The following sections briefly discuss the following email clients:

- ◆ Evolution
- ◆ KMail

♦ Mozilla Mail

♦ Text-based email clients (Pine and Mutt)

Before you launch an email client, you should have some information from your Internet Service Provider (ISP) handy so that you can configure the client properly. The following lists a few important things you may need to know:

♦ *Your email address* — The email address you will use to send and receive mail. This is usually in the form of *yourname@yourisp.net*.

♦ *Server type for receiving email (POP or IMAP)* — In order to receive mail, you must know what type of server your network administrator or ISP is using. This POP or IMAP address is usually in the form of *mail.someisp.net*.

   • POP, short for *Post Office Protocol*, is used to send email from a mail server to your email client's *inbox*, the place where incoming email is stored. Most ISP email servers use the POP protocol, although some can use the newer IMAP

   • IMAP, short for *Internet Message Access Protocol*, is a protocol for retrieving email messages from your ISP's email server. IMAP differs from POP in that email from IMAP servers are stored on the server and stays there even as you download and read your mail, whereas POP mail is downloaded to your computer directly and *does not* stay on the server.

♦ *Server type for sending email (SMTP)* — The Simple Mail Transfer Protocol (SMTP) is a protocol for sending email messages between servers. Most email systems that send mail over the Internet use SMTP to send messages from one server to another; the messages can then be retrieved with an email client using either POP or IMAP. SMTP is also used to send messages from a mail client to a mail server. This is why you need to specify both the POP or IMAP server and the SMTP server when you configure your email application.

If you have any questions regarding what information you need, contact your ISP or network administrator.

NOTE Unless properly configured, you will not be able to make full use of the email clients discussed in this chapter.

Evolution

Evolution is more than just an email client: it provides all of the standard email client features, including powerful mailbox management, user-defined filters, and quick searches. It additionally features a flexible calendar/scheduler that allows users to create and confirm group meetings and special events online. Evolution is a full-featured personal and workgroup information management tool for Linux and Unix-based systems, and is the default email client for Red Hat Linux.

To launch Evolution from the desktop panel, click the Main Menu button and choose Internet ⇨ Email.

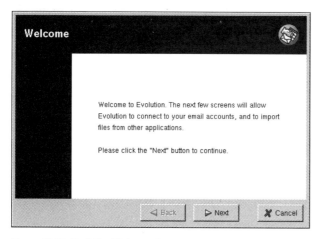

Figure 13-12. Evolution Welcome Screen

The first time you start Evolution you will be presented with the Welcome Screen, which allows you to configure your email connection. Follow the on-screen instructions and fill in the information you collected from your ISP or administrator in the text boxes provided. When you are done, click Finish, and you will be presented with the Main Screen.

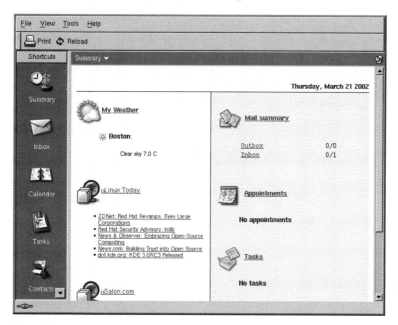

Figure 13-13. Evolution Main Screen

To see what is in your inbox or to send an email, click on the Inbox icon.

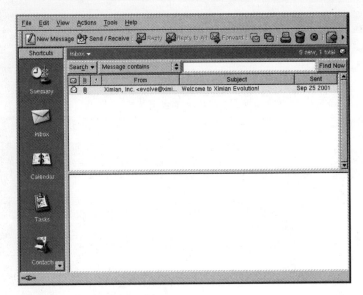

Figure 13-14. Evolution Inbox Screen

To compose an email, click the New Message icon on the toolbar.

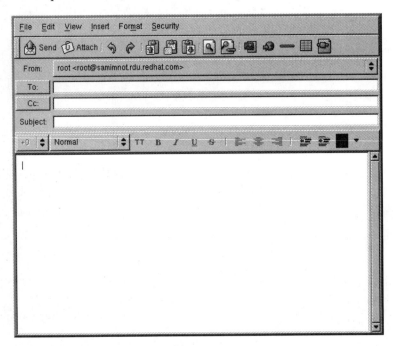

Figure 13-15. Evolution New Email Message Screen

After you have composed a message and entered an email address to send the email to, click Send on the toolbar.

While Evolution does much more than read and send email, this chapter focuses exclusively on its email capabilities. If you would like to learn more about using some of the other features of Evolution, like calendaring/scheduling and group messaging, choose Help ⇨ *component*, choosing the Evolution component you want to learn more about.

Mozilla Mail

This section briefly covers the basic steps for sending and receiving email with Mozilla. If you need further information about using Mozilla Mail, the Mozilla Help contents are located under the Help menu at the top of the Mozilla window.

To start Mozilla Mail, click the Main Menu button and choose Internet ⇨ Mozilla Mail.

To open Mozilla Mail while in any other Mozilla window (such as the browser or Composer), click on the mail icon near the lower left corner of the Mozilla screen.

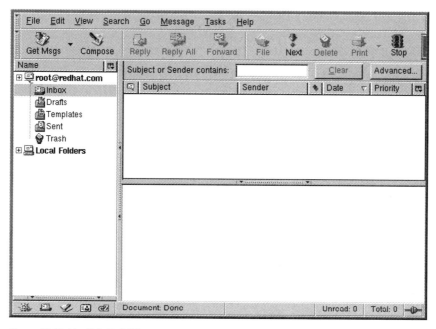

Figure 13-16. Mozilla's Mail Client

To send an addressed and composed email, click the Send button or go to File ⇨ Send Now or Send Later; if you choose to send later, you can go back to the main mail screen and go to File ⇨ Send unsent messages.

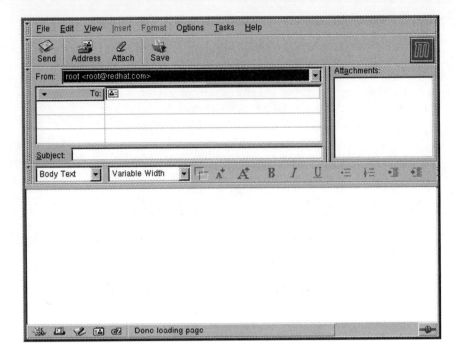

Figure 13-17. Mozilla Mail New Email Message Screen

To read email, click on the mail folder you created for yourself to see a list of messages waiting for you. Then, click on the message you want to read.

After you read a message, you can delete it, save it to a separate folder, and more.

Mozilla and Newsgroups

Newsgroups are Internet discussion groups with specific topics. The discussions are in threaded format (which means all topics and responses to the topic are sorted and organized for convenient reading), and subscribing to a group is very easy. You do not have to post messages if you do not want to; you can just *lurk*, which is a newsgroup term for reading messages without posting your own. There are a great many newsgroups on the Web with topics ranging from politics to computer games to random strange thoughts. You can even post and download pictures and files to newsgroups (although your ISP may restrict newsgroups to text-based postings only).

To join a newsgroup, you first need to set up a newsgroup account. Click on your mail account name in the sidebar and select Create a new account from the options that appear on the right of the screen.

The New Account Setup screen will appear. Select Newsgroup account and then click Next.

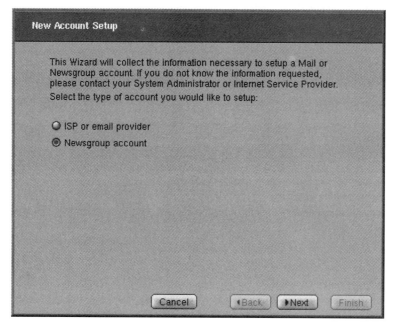

Figure 13-18. Newsgroup Account Setup

Enter your name and email address on the next screen and click Next. On the following screen, enter the name of your news server (if you do not know the name of your news server, contact your Internet service provider or network administrator for this information). On the last few screens, you can determine the name that this account will be referred to and review your settings.

The newsgroup account you created will appear in the sidebar of the Mozilla mail screen. Right-click on this account name and select Subscribe. A dialog box appears, listing all the newsgroups available.

Select the groups you are interested in reading and click Subscribe. When you are done, click OK.

Now, click the arrow next to the newsgroup account name, and the list of groups you are subscribed to will appear beneath. Select the newsgroup you want to access, and a dialog box appears with information about downloading and reading existing messages. Posting to a newsgroup is just like writing an email, except that the newsgroup name appears in the To field rather than an email address. To unsubscribe from a newsgroup, right-click on the group name and select Unsubscribe.

KMail

If you chose a custom installation of Red Hat Linux, your system may have the KMail email client.

KMail is an email tool for KDE, the K Desktop Environment. It has an intuitive graphical interface similar to Evolution that makes sending and receiving email simple. To open KMail, click on the Main Menu button and choose Extras ⇨ Internet ⇨ KMail.

Before you can use KMail, you must configure it so it can send and receive mail. To run the configuration tool, from the KMail toolbar choose Settings ⇨ Configure KMail.

The Configure Mail Client window consists of seven sections: Identity, Network, Appearance, Composer, Mime Headers, Security, and Miscellaneous. To begin sending and receiving messages, you will only have to change the settings in the Identity and Network tabs. Have your email information from your ISP or administrator handy so that you can fill in the required information to begin using KMail. For additional information, refer to the KMail user manual (Help ⇨ Contents) or visit KMail's homepage at http://kmail.kde.org.

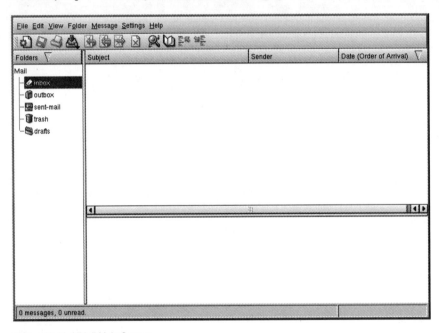

Figure 13-19. KMail Main Screen

After you have your email settings configured, you can begin sending and receiving email. The folders on the left side of the KMail screen allow you to view emails you have received, emails ready to be sent, emails you have sent, and more.

To compose an email, click on the new message icon in the toolbar.

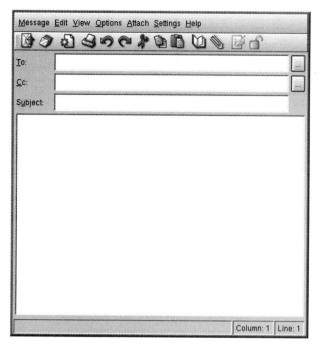

Figure 13-20. KMail New Email Message Screen

After you have composed a message and entered an email address to send the email to, click Send in the toolbar.

Plain Text Email Clients

Most modern email clients allow the user to select whether they want to send their emails in *plain text* or in HTML. The advantage of HTML-formatted email is that they can contain graphics and interactive links to websites. The particular font can be specified; the layout is very controllable; textures, pictures, or backgrounds can be added; all this makes for a visually appealing message when it gets to the recipient.

On the other hand, plain text email is just that — plain text. There is nothing fancy, no pictures embedded in the email, and no special fonts. Plain text emails are simple.

The term *plain text* refers to textual data in ASCII format. Plain text is the most portable format because it is supported by nearly every email application on various types of machines.

This chapter will discuss two plain text email clients, Pine and Mutt.

Using Pine

Pine is a character-based email client for Unix systems.

To launch Pine, type **pine** at a shell prompt, and the Main Menu screen appears.

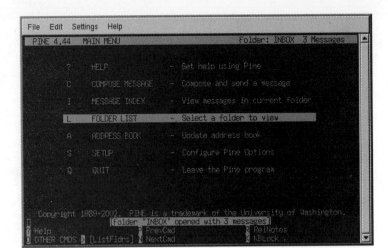

Figure 13-21. Pine Main Menu Screen

Each Pine screen has a similar layout: the top line tells you the screen name and additional useful information, below that is the work area (on the Main Menu screen, the work area is a menu of options), then the message/prompt line, and finally the menu of commands.

From the Main Menu you can choose to read online help, compose and send a message, look at an index of your mail messages, open or maintain your mail folders, update your address book, configure Pine, and quit Pine. There are additional options listed at the bottom of the screen as well.

To write a message, press c (short for Compose). The Compose Message screen will then appear.

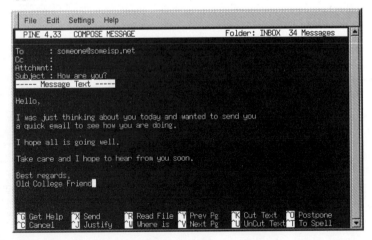

Figure 13-22. Pine Compose Message Screen

Different commands are available to you when your cursor is in different fields on this screen. To see additional commands available when your cursor is in the Message Text field, type Ctrl-g (for Get Help). For example, to move around, use the arrow keys or Ctrl-n (for Next line) and Ctrl-p (for Previous line); to correct typing errors, use Backspace or Delete.

In the command menu shown in Figure 13-22, the ^ character is used to indicate the Control key. This character means you must hold down the Control (Ctrl) key while you press the letter for each command.

When you want to leave Pine, press q (for Quit).

To view a message in the Message Index screen, use the arrow keys to highlight the message you want to view. Press v (ViewMsg) or press Enter to read a selected message. To see the next message, press n (NextMsg). To see the previous message, press p (PrevMsg) To return from your message to the Message Index, press i (Index).

For addition help with Pine, refer to the Pine man page. To view this man page, type the command **man pine** at a shell prompt.

Using Mutt

Mutt is a small but very powerful text-based mail client for Unix operating systems.

Mutt's configuration file, ~/.muttrc, gives Mutt its flexibility and configurability. It is also this file that might give new users problems. The number of options that Mutt has available to it are truly astounding. Mutt allows the user to control nearly all of the functions that Mutt uses to send, receive, and read your mail. As is true with all powerful software, it takes time to understand the features and what they can do for you.

Most of the options are invoked using the set or unset commands, with either Boolean or string values, e.g. set folder = ~/Mail.

All configuration options can be changed at any time by typing : (colon) followed by the relevant command.

For example, :unset help turns off the handy keyboard command hints at the top of the screen. To turn those hints back on, type :set help.

If you cannot remember the command you want to use, there is always tab-completion to help you.

You do not have to type all your preferred configuration commands each time you run Mutt; you can save them in a file that is loaded every time the program starts up. This configuration file must exist in your home directory; it has to be named either ~/.muttrc or ~/.mutt/muttrc.

When you launch Mutt, the first thing you see is a screen with a list of email messages. This initial menu is called the index.

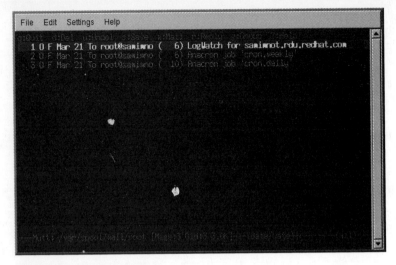

Figure 13-23. Mutt Main Screen

These messages are in a default mail folder, often called the *mailspool*, that you can think of as your inbox. Use the K and J keys on your keyboard to move the highlighted cursor up and down the list of messages.

In the index or pager views, use the R key to reply to a message or the M key to create a new one. Mutt will prompt for the To: address and the Subject: line. A text editor (defined by your $EDITOR environmental variable in the configuration file) will then launch, allowing you to compose your message. Type your message, save your file, and exit the editor.

After editing your email, Mutt displays the compose menu where you can customize your message headers, change the encoding, add file attachments, or simply press y to send your email on its way.

To learn more about Mutt, refer to the man pages for muttrc and Mutt (type **man muttrc** or **man mutt** at the shell prompt). You may also find the Mutt manual to be very helpful. The Mutt manual is installed in /usr/share/doc/mutt-1.2.x, where *x* is the version number of Mutt installed on your system.

Chapter 14

Audio, Video, and General Amusement

This chapter presents you with the lighter side of Red Hat Linux. From games and toys to audio and video applications, Red Hat Linux provides many packages to let you have some fun with your computer.

Playing CDs

To play an audio CD, place the CD in your CD-ROM drive and click Main Menu ⇨ Sound & Video ⇨ CD Player to open the CD Player application.

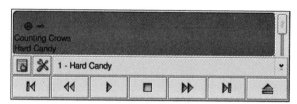

Figure 14-1. CD Player Interface

The CD Player interface acts like a standard CD player, with play, pause, and stop functions. There is also a sliding bar that allows you to adjust the volume. You can press the Next track and Previous track buttons to skip forward or backward one track; you may also use the Track List drop-down menu to choose a track from the available menu.

You can edit the track listings for your CDs by clicking the Open track editor button. You can also change the way the utility functions by clicking on the Open Preferences button. Here you can set themes for the player as well as set the behavior of the CD-ROM drive when you open or quit the CD Player application.

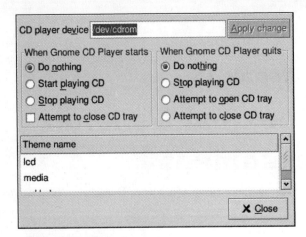

Figure 14-2. CD Player Preferences

Playing Digital Music Files

Digital audio has become very popular in recent years. Users enjoy the technology because the sound quality is excellent compared to analog tape or records, and the files are compact, so an audio file can easily be transferred across the Internet.

To allow you to take advantage of this technology, Red Hat Linux includes the powerful *X Multimedia System* (XMMS), a cross-platform multimedia player that allows you to play several digital music file formats.

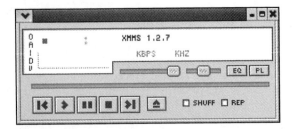

Figure 14-3. XMMS Interface

XMMS can be used for more than just playing digital audio files. By default XMMS can play Ogg Vorbis, RIFF wave, and most module formats. XMMS can be extended through plugins to play a number of other digital multimedia formats.

To launch XMMS, click the Main Menu button and choose Sound & Video ➪ XMMS (or type the command **xmms** to launch XMMS from a shell prompt).

To learn more about XMMS, refer to the XMMS man page by typing **man xmms** at a shell prompt.

Playing Digital Videos

It has become more and more popular to play digital movie files, such as Video Compact Discs (VCDs), Digital Versatile (or Video) disks (DVDs), and streaming video from the Web. Red Hat Linux offers a tool called Xine that can play several digital video file formats on your graphical desktop.

Xine uses a panel that lets you open files and media, control volume, create playlists, take screenshots of the video stills, and more. Figure 14-4 shows the Xine panel playing a file.

Figure 14-4. The Xine Panel

To start Xine, click the Main Menu button and choose Extras ⇨ Sound & Video ⇨ Video Player (or type **xine** to start it from a shell prompt).

To play a movie on disc, choose either VCD or DVD on the bottom of the panel. This should automatically mount and load your video disk for viewing by pressing the Play button.

To play a video file that you have downloaded from the Internet, choose the MRL browser on the left side of the panel. This will pop up a file browser that allows you to choose the video from a listing of your home directory. Choose the file and press the Play button. You can close the MRL browser by clicking Dismiss.

By default, Xine will play a file in a window on your desktop. To play a file full screen (where the video fills your desktop screen), click the Fullscreen/Window Mode button next to the Quit button at the top-right side of the panel. Right-click anywhere on the screen to hide the panel. When you are finished viewing the video, right-click again to show the panel and press the Quit button to quit Xine.

For more information on Xine, type **man xine** at a shell prompt or visit the Xine home page at the following URL:

```
http://xine.sourceforge.net
```

Troubleshooting Your Sound or Video Card

Although Red Hat Linux is good about configuring sound and video hardware, there are times when the configuration either doesn't happen properly or becomes corrupted. The following sections show you how to troubleshoot your sound and video cards.

Troubleshooting Your Sound Card

If, for some reason, you do not hear sound and know that you do have a sound card installed, you can run the Sound Card Configuration Tool utility.

To use the Sound Card Configuration Tool, click the Main Menu button and choose System Settings ⇨ Soundcard Detection. A small text box will pop up prompting you for your root password.

> **NOTE** Most sound cards are supported by Red Hat Linux, but there are some sound cards that are not completely compatible or may not work at all. If you are having trouble configuring your sound card, check the Hardware Compatibility List at `http://hardware.redhat.com/` to see if your card is supported.

The Sound Card Configuration Tool utility probes your system for sound cards. If the utility detects a plug and play sound card, it will automatically try to configure the correct settings for your card. You can then click the Play test sound button to play a sound sample. If you can hear the sample, select OK and your sound card configuration is complete.

Figure 14-5. Sound Card Configuration Tool

If the Sound Card Configuration Tool does not work (if the sample does not play and you still do not have audio sounds), there are alternatives, although they are not quite as simple as running the Sound Card Configuration Tool. You can edit your `modules.conf` file as discussed below (this strategy is not recommended for most new users), or refer to the documentation that came with your sound card for more information.

If your sound card is not a plug and play card, you can manually edit your `/etc/modules.conf` file to include the sound card module that it should use, for example:

```
alias sound sb
alias midi opl3
options opl3 io=0x388
options sb io=0x220 irq=7 dma=0,1 mpu_io=0x300
```

Troubleshooting Your Video Card

Video card configuration is handled during the Red Hat Linux installation (see Chapter 2). However, if you did not choose to configure a video card at that time, or if you need to reconfigure your settings, you can use the X Configuration Tool utility. You will want to do this, for example, if you install a new video card.

> **NOTE** The X Configuration Tool will backup your system's original video configuration file to `/etc/X11/XF86Config.backup` in case you need it to switch back.

To run the X Configuration Tool, click the Main Menu button and choose System Settings ➪ Display. A pop-up window will prompt you for your root password. You can also start from a shell prompt by typing the command **redhat-config-xfree86**, which will then prompt you to input your root password. If you are working from a shell prompt and X is not working, the redhat-config-xfree86 command will attempt to start a minimal X session to allow you to continue your configuration. Follow the instructions that appear on the screen. X Configuration Tool will attempt to automatically configure your video card and monitor settings for you. Figure 14-6 shows the Advanced tab for configuring your video devices manually.

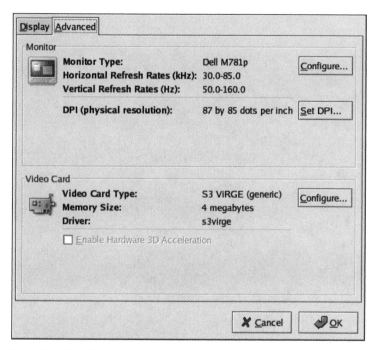

Figure 14-6. X Configuration Tool

To configure your monitor manually, click the Advanced tab, then click the Configure . . . button next to the Monitor Type entry. A pop-up window will display a list of monitor models. Choose your model and click OK. You can also let X Configuration Tool probe your monitor for the correct model and vertical/horizontal frequency settings.

To configure your video card manually, click the Advanced tab and then click the Configure... button next to the Video Card entry. A pop-up window will display a list of video card models. Choose your model and click OK. You can also let X Configuration Tool probe your video card for the correct model and settings by clicking the Probe Videocard button.

When you have finished reconfiguring your video card and monitor, you should be able to start an X session and enjoy your graphical desktop environment.

Games

The games included in Red Hat Linux appeal to quite a large number of video game enthusiasts. Whether you enjoy card games like Aisle Riot (a solitaire card game), arcade games like Tux Racer, board games like Chess, or space shooting games like Chromium and Maelstrom, you can find it in Red Hat Linux.

To start a game, click the Main Menu button and choose a game from the Games menu. Figure 14-7 shows a fun game for kids of all ages called Same Gnome. In this game you point your mouse at matching marbles until they start to spin; then, you can click them to make them disappear. Try to make all the marbles disappear.

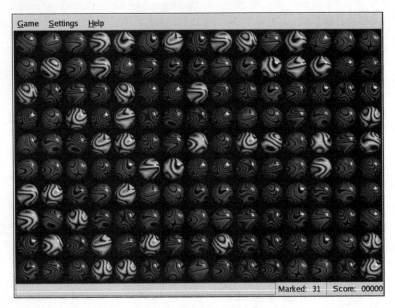

Figure 14-7. Same Gnome — Match the Marbles Game

There are many more games available within Red Hat Linux and online. For more information, here are a few suggestions:

- `http://www.evil3d.net/` — A 3-D gaming site that covers 3-D Linux games in depth.
- `http://www.tuxgames.com` — A store where you can buy games just for Linux.
- `http://www.linuxgames.com/` — A Linux gaming news site.
- `http://happypenguin.org/` — A Linux gaming repository.

> **TIP** You can also browse the Internet for Linux games using a search engine, such as `http://www.google.com`.

Chapter 15

Working with Images

There are several types of image files. Some images are created using sophisticated software packages, while others are made from digital cameras and scanners. You may have downloaded some of these image files from the Internet or received them in an email. You may also want to create your own images to send to others. You can view and manipulate the most common types of image files using the many applications included in Red Hat Linux.

This chapter shows you how to work with images using the major image-capable software in Red Hat Linux.

> **NOTE** One of the major applications that you can use for image files — OpenOffice.org Draw — is covered in Chapter 11.

Viewing Images

This section discusses some of the common tools for viewing image files. Certain tools available are specialized applications with several functions that enhance your image viewing experience, while others are general-purpose browsers that have some image viewing functionality.

Viewing Images with Nautilus

Nautilus is a general-purpose file manager and browser for your desktop environment. Nautilus has many functions beyond simple image viewing; however, for this section, we will focus on showing you how to use it for basic image browsing. For more information about Nautilus, see chapters 6 and 13.

Nautilus is known for its ease-of-use, and it handles images with the same ease as it does for other file types. To begin browsing your image collection with Nautilus, double-click on your home desktop icon.

You will be presented with a view of all the files and folders within your home directory. Double-click an image (or folder containing the image), and Nautilus will open the new file or folder within its browser window. Figure 15-1 shows that Nautilus automatically creates thumbnails of any images in your folders.

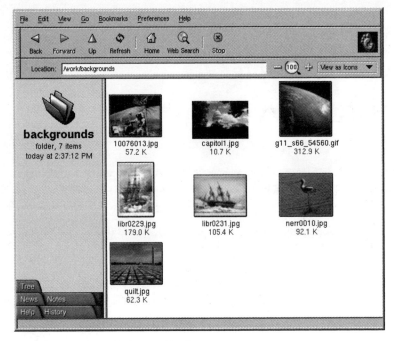

Figure 15-1. Contents of a Folder in Nautilus

Double-click on any thumbnail icon to view the image in its native size. The image will load within the browser window, along with a thumbnail view and detailed file information along the left panel.

Below the file information are advanced options for working with the file. By default, Nautilus offers you the option of opening the file with Eye of Gnome, a robust image viewer with more advanced imaging features than Nautilus.

To increase and decrease the size of the viewed image in Nautilus, click on the magnifying glass icon on the location bar.

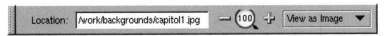

Figure 15-2. The Zoom Function in Nautilus

Click the plus (+) icon to increase the size of the image or minus (-) to decrease it.

Viewing Images with GQview

GQview is a powerful image viewer for GNOME desktop users that supports several image file formats, including the following:

   ♦ JPG/JPEG

- ◆ GIF
- ◆ PGM
- ◆ XPM
- ◆ PNG
- ◆ PCX
- ◆ TIF/TIFF
- ◆ PPM
- ◆ BMP

GQview is useful for viewing individual image files as well as browsing collections of files in folders. It supports zoom in and zoom out functions, as well as thumbnail views of all image files within a directory. It also supports several advanced options not found in the simple image viewers such as Nautilus and Konquerer.

GQview can be started from your desktop by clicking the Main Menu button and choosing Graphics ⇨ GQview (to start GQview from a shell or terminal prompt, type **gqview**).

Upon start-up, GQview will browse your user home directory by default. If you have any images in this directory, the gallery panel will automatically generate thumbnails for you to highlight and view in the main display area.

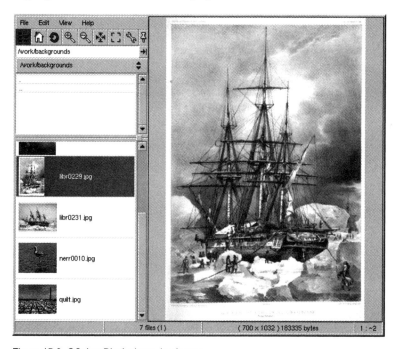

Figure 15-3. GQview Displaying a .jpg Image

The interface of GQview is straightforward. The toolbar allows you to fit the image to the display window, zoom in and out, and toggle between thumbnail view and text-only browser panels. It also has a text field for you to enter a particular path to your image directories. Right-clicking on an image in the display area opens a pop-up menu of image size and other file options such as renaming, moving, copying. You can also hide and unhide the thumbnail file panel and toggle window and full-screen modes within the pop-up menu.

You can also combine functions within GQview and create a dynamic presentation effect for groups of images within a directory. In the text field below the toolbar, type the path to the directory where your images are located and highlight the first image in the thumbnail file list panel on the left. Now press v then s, and you will start a full-screen slideshow where GQview displays images against a black background over your entire desktop. By default, each image in the slideshow is presented for 15 seconds. You can stop and resume the slideshow at any time by pressing s. When the slideshow ends, press v to exit full-screen mode.

GQview can also be used to change your desktop wallpaper quickly and easily. Right-click on the image and choose Edit ⇨ Set as wallpaper. From the Edit menu, you can also choose to open the file with a number of image editing utilities, including The GIMP, Xview, and Xpaint.

GQview also allows you to customize several settings by clicking the Configure button. The configuration pop-up menu allows advanced users to configure several options. You can customize a directory on startup, change thumbnail sizes, and even change the default image editors to manipulate the file if you would like to use one that is not listed.

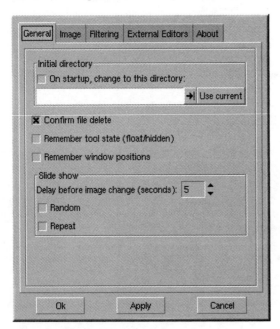

Figure 15-4. The GQview Options Dialog Box

Manipulating Images with The GIMP

The GNU Image Manipulation Program (GIMP) is a powerful tool that can be used to create, alter, manipulate, and enhance digital image files — photographs, scanned images, computer-generated images, and more. This section offers a quick overview of The GIMP and refers you to comprehensive references for learning more about it.

GIMP Basics

To use The GIMP, you will need to know some of the basics. Start The GIMP from the desktop by clicking the Main Menu button and choosing Graphics ⇨ The GIMP (from the shell prompt, you can start GIMP by typing **gimp**).

Figure 15-5 shows a typical GIMP session.

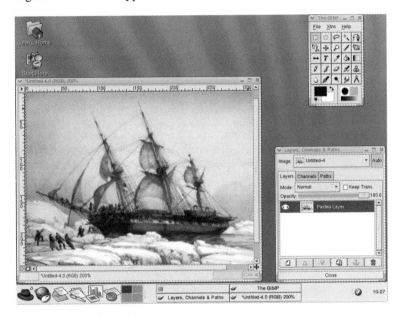

Figure 15-5. The GIMP in Action

Loading a File

To load an existing file, choose File ⇨ Open. You will see the Load Image dialog, as shown in Figure 15-6.

The Load Image dialog displays your working directory — the directory you were in when The GIMP was launched. You can navigate up and down the file system tree by double-clicking on the Directories list on the left, then selecting a file to open from the Files list on the right.

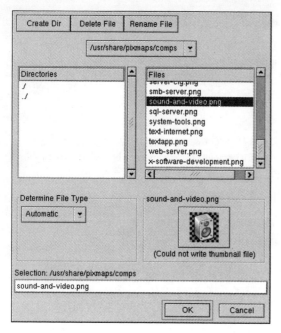

Figure 15-6. The Load Image Dialog

File name completion is supported by The GIMP. If you type the first letter (or more) of a file name into the Selection field and press the Tab key, the view will change to only those subdirectories and/or files beginning with that letter or letters.

The file you select will appear in the Selection field near the bottom of the dialog. A thumbnail preview will be displayed on the dialog; alternatively, you will see a Generate Preview button. If you want to see a thumbnail of the image, click the Generate Preview button.

After you have selected a file, click the OK button to open it. You can also double-click a file name to open it.

Saving a File

To save an image file, right-click on the image and choose File ⇨ Save (or Save as).

> **NOTE** You will see the Save Image dialog if you choose Save as or if you choose Save and the file has not been saved before.

The Save Image dialog looks almost exactly like the Load Image dialog and navigation of the file system tree and choosing files works in the same way.

When you are saving an image, you will need to choose an image format. The GIMP supports a wide variety of image formats, including .gif, .png, .jpg, and .bmp.

GIMP Options

Like many applications, The GIMP provides more than one method to accomplish tasks. The easiest way to work with images is to right-click on the image, which will display a set of menus containing most of The GIMP's many capabilities, including image sizing, rotation, and filter application.

For example, imagine you have a picture that you would like to modify to make it look as if it were clipped from a newspaper. To do this, right-click on the image and select Filters ⇨ Distorts ⇨ Newsprint . . . . Select the quantity of lines per inch using the sliders. When you reach a desired quantity and are ready to render the image, click OK. The GIMP will then render the image with the new effect applied. Figure 15-7 shows an example of an image after the Newsprint filter has been applied.

Figure 15-7. An Image Modified with a GIMP Filter

The Toolbox (Figure 15-8) also has several easily accessible functions. Using the Toolbox you can add text to images, erase regions of an image, or even fill selected regions with the color of your choice.

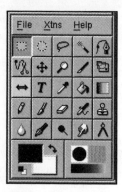

Figure 15-8. The GIMP Toolbox

For example, if you wish to add text to a file, select the Text button and click on your image. This will load the Text Tool dialog box, where you can choose a font and type some text in the provided text box. Click OK and your text will be displayed as a floating section on the image. You can then move the text to the position you wish using the Move Layers tool. Figure 15-9 shows a photo with exciting new text.

Figure 15-9. Using the Text Tool on an Image

TIP As you can see, The GIMP is a powerful imaging tool, and it takes some time to master all of the functions. Try exploring some of the options yourself. If you make a mistake, don't worry. You can always undo your mistakes by right-clicking on the image and choosing Edit ⇨ Undo.

Additional Resources

While this chapter covers several applications briefly, there is so much more you can do with them. Refer to the following resources if you are interested in learning more about the applications in this chapter.

Useful Websites

The Web has several sites of interest if you are looking for more detailed information about an application covered in this chapter:

♦ `http://gqview.sourceforge.net` — The official GQview home page.

♦ `http://www.gimp.org/` — The official GIMP website.

♦ `http://www.rru.com/~meo/gimp/faq-user.html` — A Frequently Asked Questions (FAQ) list for questions commonly asked about The GIMP by GIMP users (as opposed to developers).

♦ `http://manual.gimp.org/manual/` — The GIMP User Manual website.

♦ `http://gimp-savvy.com/` — The companion website to the book *Grokking the GIMP* by Carey Bunks (New Riders Publishing). The entire book is also available on the site for download!

♦ `http://tigert.gimp.org/gimp/` — The GIMP website of tigert (Tuomas Kuosmanen).

Related Documentation

Some applications discussed have online documentation included with the package, accessible right from your PC.

♦ For more information about using GQview, refer to the documentation in `/usr/share/doc/gqview-version-number/README` (where *version-number* is the version of GQview installed on your system).

♦ The GIMP manual page contains some of the more advanced command-line options and environment variables associated with it. You can read the manual page by typing **man gimp** at a shell prompt.

Books about The GIMP

If you need in-depth information about the many capabilities of The GIMP, try your favorite bookstore. The following books were available at the time of this writing:

♦ *GIMP for Linux Bible* by Stephanie Cottrell Bryant, et al (John Wiley and Sons Publishing)

♦ *Grokking the GIMP* by Carey Bunks (New Riders Publishing)

♦ *The Artists' Guide to the GIMP* by Michael J. Hammel; Frank Kasper and Associates, Inc.

Part IV

Configuring Your Red Hat Linux System

One of the major benefits to Linux is the ability to customize nearly every aspect of the operating system, from simple tasks such as setting your system's time and date, configuring a printer, and setting up a firewall to protect your data and privacy.

This part shows you how to configure your Red Hat Linux system to meet your needs.

Chapter 16: Printer Configuration

Chapter 17: Basic Firewall Configuration

Chapter 18: Time and Date Configuration

Printer Configuration

Red Hat Linux includes the Printer Configuration Tool to allow users to configure a printer. The Printer Configuration Tool helps maintain the /etc/printcap configuration file, print spool directories, and print filters.

This chapter provides information on configuring, testing, and modifying a local printer with the Printer Configuration Tool.

> **NOTE** For information on configuring various types of printers, configuring a printer without the Printer Configuration Tool, and more, refer to the *Official Red Hat Linux Administrator's Guide* (Red Hat Press/Wiley, 2003) or click on the Help button once you open the Printer Configuration Tool.

Introducing the Printer Configuration Tool

To use the Printer Configuration Tool, you must have root privileges. To start the Printer Configuration Tool, use one of the following methods:

- In a graphical desktop environment, click the Main Menu button and choose System Settings ⇨ Printing.
- Type the command **redhat-config-printer** at a shell prompt to start the graphical version.
- You can also run Printer Configuration Tool as a text-based application if you do not have the X Window System installed, or if you just prefer the text-based interface. To do so, type the command **redhat-config-printer-tui** from a shell prompt, which will prompt your for the root password before it continues.

> **IMPORTANT** Do not edit the /etc/printcap file. Each time the printer daemon (lpd) is started or restarted, a new /etc/printcap file is dynamically created.

If you want to add a printer without using the Printer Configuration Tool, edit the /etc/printcap.local file. The entries in /etc/printcap.local are not displayed in the Printer Configuration Tool but are read by the printer daemon. If you upgrade your system from a previous version of Red Hat Linux, your existing configuration file is converted to the new format used by the Printer Configuration Tool. Each time a new configuration file is generated by the Printer Configuration Tool, the old file is saved as /etc/printcap.old.

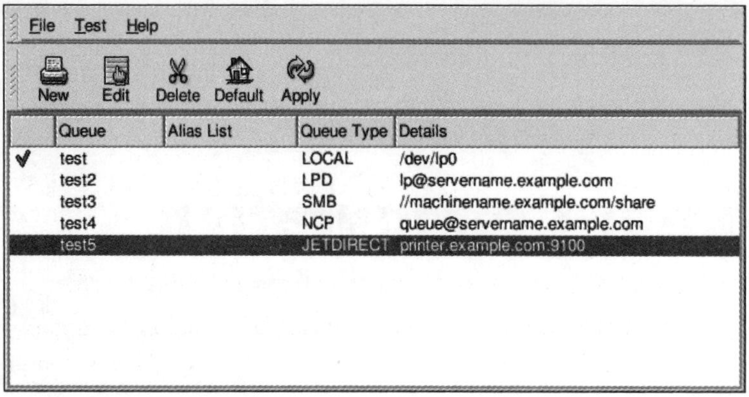

Figure 16-1. Printer Configuration Tool

> **NOTE** Starting with version 8.0, Red Hat Linux ships with two printer systems. Printer Configuration Tool configures the printing system called LPRng. LPRng is also the default printing system. This chapter focuses on using Printer Configuration Tool to configure LPRng. It is recommended that new users use the default printing system as described in this chapter. For information on the CUPS printing system, refer to the *Official Red Hat Linux Administrator's Guide.*

Print Queue Types

This chapter explains local printer configuration only, but a total of five types of print queues can be configured with the Printer Configuration tool:

♦ *Local Printer* — A printer attached directly to your computer through a parallel or USB port. In the main printer list (shown in Figure 16-1), the Queue Type for a local printer is set to LOCAL.

♦ *Unix Printer (lpd Spool)* — A printer attached to a different Unix system that can be accessed over a TCP/IP network (for example, a printer attached to another Red Hat Linux system on your network). In the main printer list the Queue Type for a remote Unix printer is set to LPD.

♦ *Windows Printer (SMB)* — A printer attached to a different system that is sharing a printer over an SMB network (for example, a printer attached to a Microsoft Windows machine). In the main printer list the Queue Type for a remote Windows printer is set to SMB.

♦ *Novell Printer (NCP Queue)* — A printer attached to a different system that uses Novell's NetWare network technology. In the main printer list the Queue Type for a remote Novell printer is set to NCP.

♦ *JetDirect Printer* — A printer connected directly to the network instead of to a computer. In the main printer list the Queue Type for a JetDirect printer is set to JETDIRECT.

See the *Official Red Hat Linux Administrator's Guide* or click on the Printer Configuration Tool Help button for information on configuring printers other than local printers.

> **IMPORTANT** If you add a new print queue or modify an existing one, you need to restart the printer daemon (lpd) for the changes to take effect.

Clicking the Apply button saves any changes that you have made and restarts the printer daemon. The changes are not written to the /etc/printcap configuration file until the printer daemon (lpd) is restarted. Alternatively, you can choose File ⇨ Save Changes and then choose File ⇨ Restart lpd to save your changes and then restart the printer daemon.

If a printer appears in the main printer list with the queue type set to INVALID, the printer configuration is missing options that are required for the printer to function properly. To remove this printer from the list, select it from the list and click the Delete button.

Adding a Local Printer

To add a local printer such as one attached to the parallel port or USB port of your computer, click the New button in the main Printer Configuration Tool window. The window shown in Figure 16-2 will appear. Click Forward to proceed.

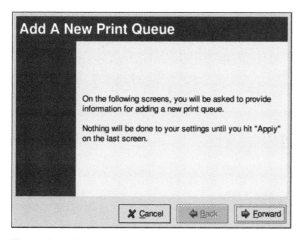

Figure 16-2. Adding a Printer

You will then see the screen shown in Figure 16-3. Enter a unique name for the printer in the Queue Name text field. This can be any descriptive name for your printer. The printer name cannot contain spaces and must begin with a letter a through z (or A through Z). The valid characters are a through z, A through Z, 0 through 9, -, and _. Select Local Printer from the Queue Type menu and click Forward.

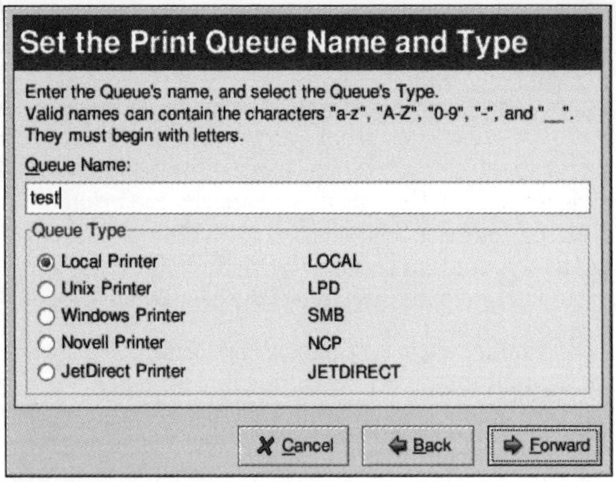

Set the Print Queue Name and Type

Enter the Queue's name, and select the Queue's Type.
Valid names can contain the characters "a-z", "A-Z", "0-9", "-", and "_".
They must begin with letters.

Queue Name:

test

Queue Type

◉ Local Printer   LOCAL
○ Unix Printer   LPD
○ Windows Printer   SMB
○ Novell Printer   NCP
○ JetDirect Printer   JETDIRECT

✗ Cancel   ⬅ Back   ➡ Forward

Figure 16-3. Adding a Local Printer

The Printer Configuration Tool attempts to detect your printer device and display it, as shown in Figure 16-4. If the Printer Configuration Tool detected your printer model, it will display the recommended print driver.

If your printer device is not shown, click Custom Device. Type the name of your printer device and click OK to add it to the printer device list. A printer device attached to the parallel port is usually referred to as `/dev/lp0`. A printer device attached to the USB port is usually referred to as `/dev/usblp0`. If your printer model does not appear, you will be given the opportunity to select it in the next step. Click Next to continue. After selecting your printer device, click Forward.

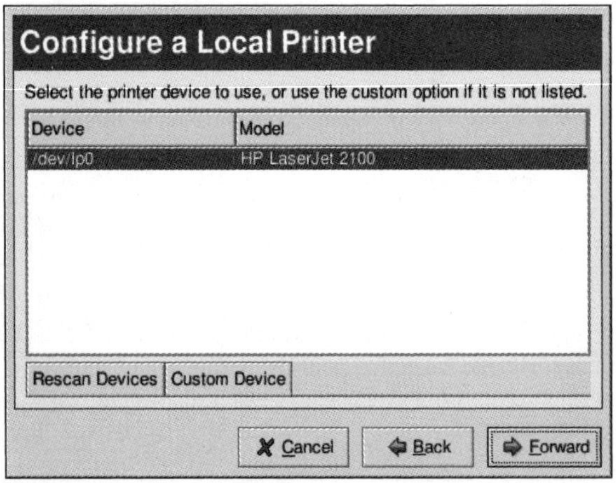

Configure a Local Printer

Select the printer device to use, or use the custom option if it is not listed.

Device	Model
/dev/lp0	HP LaserJet 2100

Rescan Devices | Custom Device

✗ Cancel   ⬅ Back   ➡ Forward

Figure 16-4. Choosing a Printer Device

Next, the Printer Configuration Tool will try to detect which printer is attached to the printer device you selected. If you are configuring a local printer and the model was auto-detected, the recommended driver is automatically selected and marked with an asterisk (*). If the tool detects the wrong printer or does not detect any printer, you can manually select one. The printers are organized by manufacturer. Click the arrow beside the manufacturer for your printer. Find your printer from the expanded list and click the arrow beside the printer name. A list of drivers for your printer will appear. Select one. If you do not know which one to use, select the first one in the list. If you are having problems using that driver, edit the printer in the Printer Configuration tool and select a different driver. By using this process of elimination, you should be able to select a driver that works with your printer. If not, contact your printer's manufacturer and ask them about Unix/Linux drivers.

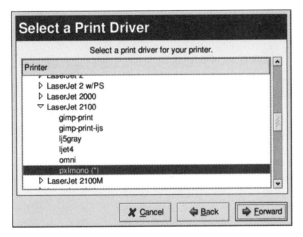

Figure 16-5. Choosing a Printer Driver

Confirming Your Printer

The last step is to confirm your printer. Click Apply if this is the printer that you want to add. Click Back to modify your printer configuration.

The new printer will appear in the printer list in the main window. Click the Apply button in the main window to save your changes to the `/etc/printcap` configuration file and restart the printer daemon (`lpd`). After applying the changes, print a test page to ensure the configuration is correct (see the next section for details).

Printing a Test Page

After you have configured your printer, you should print a test page to make sure the printer is functioning properly. Also, if you change the print driver or modify the driver options, you should print a test page to test the different configuration.

To print a test page, select the printer that you want to test from the printer list and choose Test ⇨ Print US Letter Postscript Test Page, Print A4 Postscript Test Page, or Print ASCII Test

Page from the pull-down menu. If your printer does not support PostScript printing, choose to print the ASCII test page.

Modifying Existing Printers

After adding your printer(s), you can edit settings by selecting the printer from the printer list and clicking the Edit button. The tabbed window shown in Figure 16-6 will appear. This window contains the current values for the printer that you selected to edit. Make any changes and click OK. Click Apply in the main Printer Configuration Tool window to save the changes and restart the printer daemon.

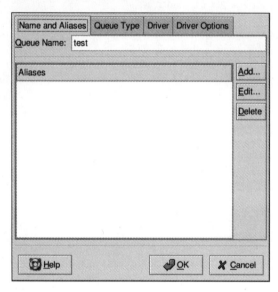

Figure 16-6. Editing a Printer

Deleting a Printer

To delete an existing printer, select the printer and click the Delete button on the toolbar. The printer will be removed from the printer list. Click Apply to save the changes and restart the printer daemon.

Setting the Default Printer

To set the default printer, select the printer from the printer list and click the Default button on the toolbar. The default printer icon (which looks like a checkmark) appears in the first column of the printer list beside the default printer.

Renaming a Printer

If you want to rename a printer, change the value of Queue Name in the Names and Aliases tab. Click OK to return to the main window. The name of the printer should change in the printer list. Click Apply to save the change and restart the printer daemon.

Changing a Printer's Queue Type

The Queue Type tab shows the queue type that you selected when adding the printer and its settings. You can change the queue type of the printer or just change the settings. After making modifications, click OK to return to the main window. Click Apply to save the change and restart the printer daemon.

Depending on which queue type you choose, you will see different options. Refer to the "Print Queue Type" section earlier in this chapter for a description of the options.

Changing a Printer's Driver

The Driver tab shows the print driver that is currently being used. This is the same list that you used when adding the printer. If you change the print driver, click OK to return to the main window. Click Apply to save the change and restart the printer daemon.

> **TIP** If you are having problems printing, try selecting a different driver from this list and printing a test page. Some drivers might work better than others for your printer.

Changing a Printer's Driver Options

The Driver Options tab displays advanced printer options. Options vary for each print driver. Common options include:

- *Send Form-Feed (FF)* — This option should be selected if the last page of your print job is not ejected from the printer (for example, the form feed light flashes). If this does not work, try selecting Send End-of-Transmission (EOT) instead. Some printers require both Send Form-Feed (FF) and Send End-of-Transmission (EOT) to eject the last page.

- *Send End-of-Transmission (EOT)* — This option should be selected if sending a form-feed does not work. Refer to Send FF above.

- *Assume Unknown Data is Text* — This option should be selected if your print driver does not recognize some of the data sent to it. Only select this option if you are having problems printing. If this option is selected, the print driver will assume that any data that it cannot recognize is text and try to print that data as text. If you select this option and the Convert Text to Postscript option, the print driver will assume the unknown data is text and then convert it to PostScript.

- *Prerender Postscript* — This option should be selected if you are printing characters beyond the basic ASCII set (such as Japanese characters) but they are not printing correctly. This option will prerender non-standard PostScript fonts so that they are printed correctly. If your printer does not support the fonts you are trying to print, try selecting this option. For example, you should select this option if you are printing Japanese fonts to a non-Japanese printer. Extra time is required to perform this action.

Do not choose it unless you are having problems printing the correct fonts. You should also select this option if your printer cannot handle PostScript level 3. This option converts it to PostScript level 1.

♦ *Convert Text to Postscript* — This option is selected by default. If your printer can print plain text, try unselecting this when printing plain text documents to decrease the time it takes to print.

♦ *Page Size* — This option allows you to select the paper size for your printer, such as US Letter, US Legal, A3, and A4.

♦ *Effective Filter Locale* — This option defaults to C. If you are printing Japanese characters, select ja_JP. Otherwise, accept the default of C.

♦ *Media Source* — This option defaults to Printer default. Change this option to use paper from a different tray.

If you modify the driver options, click OK to return to the main window. Click Apply to save the change and restart the printer daemon.

Managing Your Print Jobs

When you send a print job to the printer daemon such as printing files from OpenOffice.org applications or printing an image from The GIMP, the print job is added to the print spool queue.

The *print spool queue* is a list of print jobs that have been sent to the printer and information about each print request, such as:

♦ The status of the request

♦ The username of the person who sent the request

♦ The hostname of the system that sent the request

♦ The job number

Viewing Print Jobs

To view the list of print jobs in the print spool, open a shell prompt and type the command **lpq**. The last few lines will look similar to the following:

```
Rank    Owner/ID               Class   Job Files       Size Time
active  user@localhost+902      A       902 sample.txt   2050 01:20:46
```

Canceling a Print Job

If you want to cancel a print job, find the job number of the request with the command lpq (see the previous section) and then use the command lprm *job_number*. For example, typing the command **lprm 902** would cancel the print job shown in the example in the previous section.

> **NOTE** You must have proper permissions to cancel a print job. You cannot cancel print jobs that were started by other users unless you are logged in as root on the machine to which the printer is attached.

Printing from a Shell Prompt

You can also print a file directly from a shell prompt. For example, the command `lpr sample.txt` will print the text file `sample.txt`. The print filter determines what type of file it is and converts it to a format the printer can understand.

Additional Resources

To learn more about printing on Red Hat Linux, go to the GNU/Linux Printing site at `http://www.linuxprinting.org`, whichcontains a large amount information about printing in Linux. Also, the following documentation on your Red Hat Linux machine can be very helpful:

♦ `man printcap` — The manual page for the `/etc/printcap` printer configuration file.

♦ `map lpr` — The manual page for the `lpr` command, which allows you to print files from the command line.

♦ `man lpd` — The manual page for the LPRng printer daemon (`lpd`).

♦ `man lprm` — The manual page for the command line utility that allows you to remove print jobs from the LPRng spool queue.

♦ `man mpage` — The manual page for the command line utility that allows you to print multiple pages on one sheet of paper.

Chapter 17

Basic Firewall Configuration

Just as a firewall in a building or automobile attempts to prevent a fire from spreading, a computer firewall attempts to prevent computer viruses from spreading to your computer and to prevent unauthorized users from accessing your computer. A firewall exists between your computer and the network. It determines which services on your computer remote users on the network can access. A properly configured firewall can greatly increase the security of your system. It is recommended that you configure a firewall for any Red Hat Linux system with an Internet connection.

Security Level Configuration Tool

In the Firewall Configuration screen of the Red Hat Linux installation (see Chapter 2), you were given the option to choose a high, medium, or no security level as well as the choice to allow specific devices, incoming services, and ports.

After installation, you can change the security level of your system by using the Security Level Configuration Tool. (If you prefer a wizard-based application, see the "GNOME Lokkit" section later in this chapter.)

Figure 17-1. Security Level Configuration Tool

To start the Security Level Configuration Tool, click the Main Menu button and choose System Settings ⇨ Security Level (or type the command **redhat-config-securitylevel** from a shell prompt).

Select the desired security level from the pull-down menu. There are three levels: High, Medium, and No Firewall. The following sections discuss these levels in more detail.

High

If you choose High for your security level, your system will not accept connections (other than the default settings) that are not explicitly defined by you. By default, only the following connections are allowed in a High security level setting:

- ◆ DNS replies
- ◆ DHCP — So any network interfaces that use DHCP can be properly configured

If you choose High for your security level, your firewall will not allow the following:

- Active mode FTP (passive-mode FTP, used by default in most clients, should still work)
- IRC DCC file transfers
- RealAudio
- Remote X Window System clients

If you are connecting your system to the Internet but do not plan to run a server, this is the safest choice. If additional services are needed, you can choose Customize to allow specific services through the firewall.

NOTE If you select a medium or high firewall, network authentication methods (NIS and LDAP) will not work.

Medium

If you choose Medium for your security level, your firewall will not allow remote machines to have access to certain resources on your system. By default, access to the following resources are not allowed:

- ◆ Ports lower than 1023 — The standard reserved ports, used by most system services, such as FTP, SSH, Telnet, HTTP, and NIS.
- ◆ The NFS server port (2049) — NFS is disabled for both remote severs and local clients.
- ◆ The local X Window System display for remote X clients.
- ◆ The X Font server port (by default, `xfs` does not listen on the network; it is disabled in the font server).

If you want to allow resources such as RealAudio while still blocking access to normal system services, choose Medium. Select Customize to allow specific services through the firewall.

> **NOTE** If you select a medium or high firewall, network authentication methods (NIS and LDAP) will not work.

No Firewall

No firewall provides complete access to your system and does no security checking. *Security checking* involves the disabling of access to certain services. This setting should only be selected if you are running on a trusted network (not the Internet) or plan to do more firewall configuration later.

Choose Customize to add trusted devices or to allow additional incoming services.

Trusted Devices

Selecting any of the Trusted Devices allows access to your system for all traffic from that device; it is excluded from the firewall rules. For example, if you are running a local network, but are connected to the Internet via a PPP dialup, you can check eth0 and any traffic coming from your local network will be allowed. Selecting eth0 as trusted means that all traffic over the Ethernet is allowed but the ppp0 interface is still protected by a firewall. If you want to restrict traffic on an interface, leave it unchecked.

> **WARNING** It is not recommended that you make any device that is connected to public networks, such as the Internet, a Trusted Device.

Allow Incoming

Enabling these options allows the specified services to pass through the firewall. Note, during a workstation installation, the majority of these services are *not* installed on the system.

- ◆ *DHCP* — If you allow incoming DHCP queries and replies, you allow any network interface that uses DHCP to determine its IP address. DHCP is normally enabled. If DHCP is not enabled, your computer can no longer get an IP address.

- ◆ *SSH* — *S*ecure *SH*ell (SSH) is a suite of tools for logging into and executing commands on a remote machine. If you plan to use SSH tools to access your machine through a firewall, enable this option. You need to have the openssh-server package installed in order to access your machine remotely using SSH tools.

- ◆ Telnet — Telnet is a protocol for logging into remote machines. Telnet communications are unencrypted and provide no security from network snooping. Allowing incoming Telnet access is not recommended. If you do want to allow inbound Telnet access, you will need to install the telnet-server package.

- ◆ *WWW (HTTP)* — The HTTP protocol is used by Apache (and by other Web servers) to serve Web pages. If you plan on making your Web server publicly available, enable this option. This option is not required for viewing pages locally or for developing Web pages. You will need to install the apache package if you want to serve Web pages.

> **NOTE** Enabling WWW (HTTP) will not open a port for HTTPS. To enable HTTPS, specify it in the Other ports field.

- ◆ *Mail (SMTP)* — If you want to allow incoming mail delivery through your firewall so that remote hosts can connect directly to your machine to deliver mail, enable this option. You do not need to enable this if you collect your mail from your ISP's server using POP3 or IMAP, or if you use a tool such as `fetchmail`. Note that an improperly configured SMTP server can allow remote machines to use your server to send spam.

- ◆ *FTP* — The FTP protocol is used to transfer files between machines on a network. If you plan on making your FTP server publicly available, enable this option. You need to install the `wuftpd` (and possibly the `anonftp`) package for this option to be useful.

- ◆ *Other ports* — You can allow access to ports that are not listed here by listing them in the Other ports field. Use the following format: `port:protocol`. For example, if you want to allow IMAP access through your firewall, you can specify `imap:tcp`. You can also explicitly specify numeric ports. For example, to allow UDP packets on port 1234 through the firewall, enter **1234:udp**.

> **TIP** To specify multiple ports, separate them with commas.

You must have the iptables service enabled and running to activate the security level. See the "Activating the iptables Service" section later in this chapter for details.

GNOME Lokkit

GNOME Lokkit allows you to configure firewall settings for an average user by constructing basic `iptables` networking rules. Instead of having to write the rules, this program asks you a series of questions about how you use your system and then writes the rules for you in the `/etc/sysconfig/iptables` file.

> **NOTE** You should not try to use GNOME Lokkit to generate complex firewall rules. GNOME Lokkit is intended for average users who want to protect themselves while using a dial-up modem, cable modem, or DSL Internet connection.

To configure specific firewall rules or to disable specific services and deny specific hosts and users, see the *Official Red Hat Linux Administrator's Guide* (Red Hat Press/Wiley 2003).

To start GNOME Lokkit, type the command **gnome-lokkit** at a shell prompt as root. If you do not have the X Window System installed or if you prefer a text-based program, use the command **lokkit** to start the text-mode version of GNOME Lokkit.

GNOME Lokkit Configuration

After starting the program, choose the appropriate security level for your system:

♦ *High Security* — This option disables almost all network connects except DNS replies and DHCP so that network interfaces can be activated. IRC, ICQ, and other instant messaging services as well as RealAudio will not work without a proxy.

♦ *Low Security* — This option will not allow remote connections to the system, including NFS connections and remote X Window System sessions. Services that run below port 1023 will not accept connections, including FTP, SSH, Telnet, and HTTP.

♦ *Disable Firewall* — This option does not create any security rules. This option should only be chosen if the system is on a trusted network (*not* the Internet), if the system is behind a larger firewall, or if you write your own custom firewall rules. If you choose this option and click Next, proceed to the "Activating the iptables Service" section later in this chapter. The security of your system will not be changed.

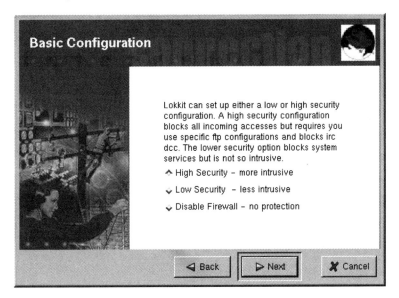

Figure 17-2. Basic Configuration

Local Hosts

If there are Ethernet devices on the system, the Local Hosts page allows you to configure whether the firewall rules apply to connection requests sent to each device. If the device connects the system to a local area network behind a firewall and does not connect directly to the Internet, select Yes. If the Ethernet card connects the system to a cable or DSL modem, it is recommended that you select No.

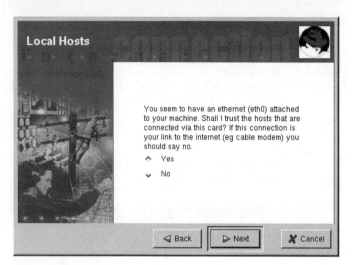

Figure 17-3. Local Hosts

DHCP

If you are using DHCP to activate any Ethernet interfaces on the system, you must say Yes to the DHCP question. If you say no, you will not be able to establish a connect using the Ethernet interface.

Many cable and DSL Internet providers require you to use DHCP to establish an Internet connection.

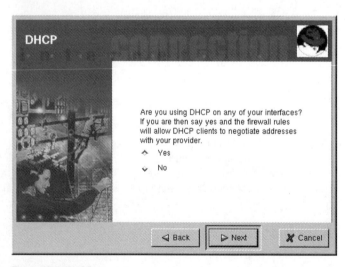

Figure 17-4. DHCP

Configuring Services

GNOME Lokkit also allows you to turn common services on and off. If you answer Yes to configuring services, you are prompted about the following services:

- *Web Server* — Choose this option if you want people to connect to a Web server such as Apache running on your system. You do not need to choose this option if you only want to view pages on your own system or on other servers on the network.

- *Incoming Mail* — Choose this option if your system needs to accept incoming mail. You do not need this option if you retrieve email using IMAP, POP3, or `fetchmail`.

- *Secure Shell* — Secure Shell, or SSH, is a suite of tools for logging into and executing commands on a remote machine over an encrypted connection. If you need to access your machine remotely through SSH, select this option.

- *Telnet* — Telnet allows you to log into your machine remotely; however, it is not secure. Telnet sends plain text (including passwords) over the network. It is recommended that you use SSH to log into your machine remotely if you need to. If you are required to have Telnet access to your system, select this option.

To disable other services that you do not need, see the *Official Red Hat Linux Administrator's Guide*.

Activating the Firewall

Clicking Finish will write the firewall rules to `/etc/sysconfig/iptables` and start the firewall by starting the `iptables` service.

It is highly recommended that you run GNOME Lokkit from the machine, not from a remote X session. If you disable remote access to your system, you will no longer be able to access it or disable the firewall rules.

Click Cancel if you do not want to write the firewall rules.

Mail Relay

A *mail relay* is a system that allows other systems to send email through it. If your system is a mail relay, someone can possibly use it to spam others from your machine.

If you chose to enable mail services, after you click Finish on the Activate the Firewall page, you will be prompted to check for mail relay. If you choose Yes to check for mail relay, GNOME Lokkit will attempt to connect to the Mail Abuse Prevention System website at `http://www.mail-abuse.org/` and run a mail relay test program. The results of the test will be displayed when it is finished. If your system is open to mail relay, it is highly recommended that you configure `Sendmail` to prevent it.

You must have the `iptables` service enabled and running to activate the firewall. See the next section for details.

Activating the iptables Service

The firewall rules will only be active if the iptables service is running. To manually start the service, use the following command:

```
/sbin/service iptables restart
```

To ensure that `iptables` is started when the system is booted, issue the following command:

```
/sbin/chkconfig --level 345 iptables on
```

You can also use the Service Configuration Tool to activate `iptables`. To do so, see the *Official Red Hat Linux Administrator's Guide*.

You cannot run the `ipchains` service along with the `iptables` service. To make sure the `ipchains` service is disabled, execute the following command:

```
/sbin/chkconfig --level 345 ipchains off
```

Chapter 18

Time and Date Configuration

The Time and Date Properties tool allows you to change the system date and time, to configure the time zone used by the system, and to setup the Network Time Protocol (NTP) daemon to synchronize the system clock with a time server.

You must be running the X Window System and have root privileges. To start the application from the desktop, click the Main Menu Button and choose ⇨ System Settings ⇨ Date & Time, or type the command **redhat-config-date** at a shell prompt.

Time and Date Properties

The first tabbed window that appears after starting the Time and Date Properties tool is for configuring the system date and time and the NTP daemon (ntpd).

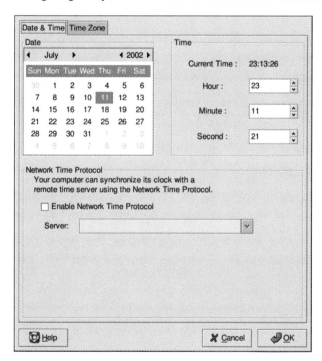

Figure 18-1. Time and Date Properties

To change the date, use the arrows to the left and right of the month to change the month. Use the arrows to the left and right of the year to change the year, and click on the day of the week to change the day of the week. Changes will not take place until you click the OK button.

To change the time, use the up and down arrow buttons beside the Hour, Minute, and Second in the Time section. Changes will not take place until you click the OK button.

> **NOTE** Changing the date and time will change the system clock as well as the hardware clock. Clicking Apply or OK is equivalent to executing the `date` and `hwclock` commands with the selected date and time.

The Network Time Protocol (`ntpd`) daemon synchronizes the system clock with a remote time server or time source (such as a satellite). The application allows you to configure a NTP daemon to synchronize your system clock with a remote server. To enable this feature, click the Enable Network Time Protocol button. This will enable the Server pull-down menu. You can then choose one of the predefined servers or type a server name in the pull-down menu. Your system will not start synchronizing with the NTP server until you click Apply. After you click Apply, the configuration will be saved and the NTP daemon will be started (or restarted if it is already running). If you want this daemon to start automatically at boot time, you need to execute the command `/sbin/chkconfig --level 345 ntpd on` to enable `ntpd` for runlevels 3, 4, and 5.

For more information on NTP, read the NTP documentation available in the `/usr/share /doc/ntp-version` directory.

The NTP server is written to the `/etc/ntp.conf` and `/etc/ntp/step-tickers` files.

Clicking the OK button will apply any changes that you have made to the date and time, the NTP daemon settings, and the time zone settings and then exit the program.

> **WARNING** If you configured a medium or high security level during installation or with the Security Level Configuration Tool, the firewall rules will block the connection to the NTP port. To allow NTP to work, run the Security Level Configuration Tool, select Customize, and add `udp:ntp` to the other ports.

Time Zone Configuration

To configure the system time zone, click the Time Zone tab. The time zone can be changed by either using the interactive map or by choosing the desired time zone from the list below the map. To use the map, click on the city that represents the desired time zone. A red X will appear, and the time zone selection will change in the list below the map. Click Apply to save the changes.

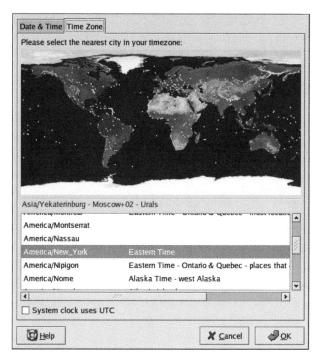

Figure 18-2. The Time Zone Tab

If your system clock is set to use UTC, select the System clock uses UTC option. UTC stands for the universal time zone, also known as Greenwich Mean Time (GMT). Other time zones are determined by adding or subtracting from the UTC time.

Part V

Updating and Adding Packages to Red Hat Linux

Linux installs new applications with files called *packages*. Packages are similar to executables in Windows — installing a new package typically involves a new application on your Linux system. Using RPM files, you can install new applications simply by double-clicking the RPM file in a graphical environment. If you're more comfortable using the command-line interface, or system prompt, you can use the rpm command from the system prompt.

This part shows you how to install and/or update packages using either of these methods.

Chapter 19: Package Management
Chapter 20: Package Management with RPM

Chapter 19

Package Management

Red Hat Linux consists of various software applications and utilities, known as RPM packages. A package is just a file that contains a software program (identical in concept to .exe files in Windows).

This chapter explains four ways to update your system: using the Package Management Tool, the Red Hat Network, the online Errata List, or the Red Hat Linux Installation CD-ROMs.

Updating with the Package Management Tool

During installation, users select an installation type such as Workstation or Server. Software packages are installed based on this selection. Because people use their computers differently, users might want to install or remove packages after installation. The Package Management Tool allows users to perform these actions.

To start the application, click the Main Menu button and choose System Settings ⇨ Packages (or type the command **redhat-config-packages** at the shell prompt).

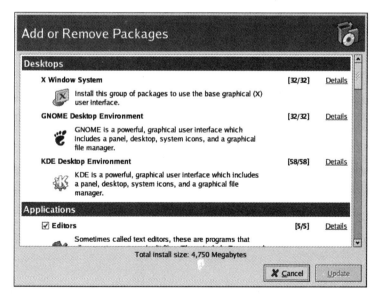

Figure 19-1. Package Management Tool

The interface for the Package Management tool is similar to the one used during the package management stage of installation (see Chapter 2). Packages are divided into package groups, which contain a list of *standard packages* and *extra packages* that share common functionality. For example, the Graphical Internet group contains a Web browser, email client, and other graphical programs that are used to connect to the Internet. The standard packages cannot be selected for removal unless the entire package group is removed. The extra packages are optional packages that can be selected for installation or removal as long as the package group is selected.

The main window shows a list of package groups. If the package group has a checkmark in the checkbox beside it, packages from that group are currently installed. To view the individual packages list for a group, click the Details button beside it. The individual packages with a checkmark beside them are currently installed.

Installing Packages

To install the standard packages in a package group that is not currently installed, check the checkbox beside it. To customize the packages to be installed within the group, click the Details button beside it.

The list of standard and extra packages is displayed. Clicking on the package name displays the disk space required to install the package at the bottom of the window. Checking the checkbox beside the package name marks it for installation.

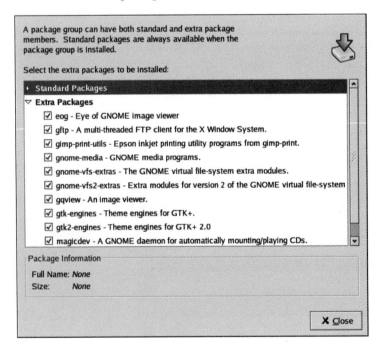

Figure 19-2. Individual Package Selection

You can also select individual packages from already installed package groups by clicking the Details button and checking any of the extra packages not already installed.

After selecting package groups and individual packages to install, click the Update button on the main window. The application will then compute the amount of disk space required to install the packages as well as any package dependencies and then display a summary window. If there are package dependencies, they will be automatically added to the list of packages to be installed. Click the Show Details button to view the complete list of packages to be installed.

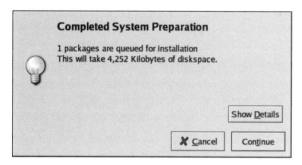

Completed System Preparation

1 packages are queued for installation
This will take 4,252 Kilobytes of diskspace.

Show Details

✖ Cancel   Continue

Figure 19-3. Package Installation Summary

Click Continue to start the installation process. When it is finished, an Update Complete message will appear.

> **TIP** If you use Nautilus to browse the files and directories on your computer, you can also use it to install packages. In Nautilus, go to the directory that contains an RPM package (they usually end in .rpm), and double-click on the RPM icon to start installing the package.

Removing Packages

To remove all the packages installed within a package group, uncheck the checkbox beside it. To remove individual packages, click the Details button beside the package group and uncheck the individual packages.

When you are finished selecting packages to remove, click the Update button in the main window.

Package Manager computes the amount of disk space that will be freed up as well as the software package dependencies. If other packages depend on the packages you selected to remove, they will be automatically added to the list of packages to be removed. Click the Show Details button to view the list of packages to be removed.

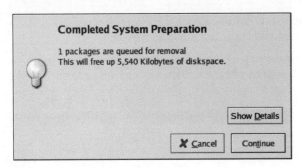

Completed System Preparation

1 packages are queued for removal
This will free up 5,540 Kilobytes of diskspace.

Show Details

✗ Cancel   Continue

Figure 19-4. Package Removal Summary

Click Continue to start the removal process. When it is finished, an Update Complete message will appear.

> **TIP** You can combine the installation and removal of packages by selecting package groups/packages to be installed or removed and then by clicking Update. The Completed System Preparation window will display the number of packages to be installed and removed.

Updating Packages with the Red Hat Network

Red Hat Network is an Internet solution for managing one or more Red Hat Linux systems. All Security Alerts, Bug Fix Alerts, and Enhancement Alerts (collectively known as *Errata Alerts*) can be downloaded directly from Red Hat using the Red Hat Update Agent standalone application or through the RHN Web interface available at `http://rhn.redhat.com/`.

> **NOTE** Everyone receives a free Red Hat Network account for one system. Additional accounts must be purchased.

What You Get with Red Hat Network

Red Hat Network saves users time because they receive an email when updated packages are released. Thus, users do not have to search the Web for updated packages or security alerts. By default, the Red Hat Network installs the packages as well. Users do not have to learn how to use RPM or worry about resolving software package dependencies; RHN does it all.

Each Red Hat Network account comes with:

- *Errata Alerts* — Learn when Security Alerts, Bug Fix Alerts, and Enhancement Alerts are issued for all the systems in your network through the Basic interface.
- *Automatic email notifications* — Receive an email notification when an Errata Alert is issued for your system.
- *Scheduled Errata Updates* — Schedule delivery of Errata Updates (with optional automatic installation).
- *Package installation* — Schedule package installation on one or more systems with the click of a button.

♦ *Red Hat Update Agent* — Use the Red Hat Update Agent to download the latest software packages for your system (with optional package installation).

♦ *Red Hat Network website* — Manage multiple systems, download individual packages, and schedule actions such as Errata Updates through a secure Web browser connection from any computer.

Start Using the Red Hat Network

To start using Red Hat Network, follow these steps:

1. Create a System Profile using one of the following methods:

    • Register the system with the Red Hat Network during the Setup Agent the first time your system boots after installation.

    • Click the Main Menu button and choose System Tools ➪ Red Hat Network on your desktop.

    • Execute the up2date command from a shell prompt.

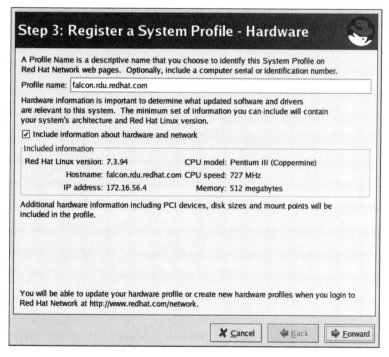

Figure 19-5. Registering with Red Hat Network

2. Log in to RHN at http://rhn.redhat.com/ and entitle the system to a service offering. (Everyone receives a free Red Hat Network account for one system; additional accounts must be purchased.)

3. Start scheduling updates through the RHN website or download and install Errata Updates using the Red Hat Update Agent.

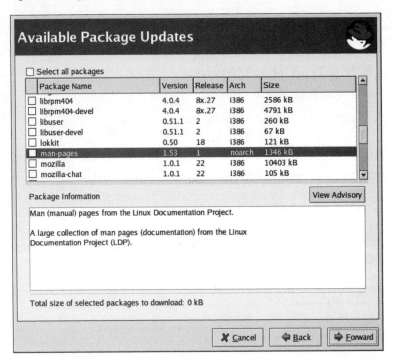

Figure 19-6. Applying Errata with the Update Agent

For more detailed instructions, read the Red Hat Network User Reference Guide available at the following URL:

```
http://www.redhat.com/docs/manuals/RHNetwork/
```

> **TIP** Red Hat Linux includes the Red Hat Network Alert Notification tool, a convenient Panel applet that displays visible alerts when there is an update for your Red Hat Linux system. Refer to `http://rhn.redhat.com/help/basic/applet.html` for more information about the applet.

Updating Using the Errata List

It is recommended that new users use Red Hat Network (as described in the previous section) to download, install, and upgrade packages. Updating Errata packages from the Red Hat Linux Errata website is recommended only for more experienced Red Hat Linux users. This method also requires users to resolve *software dependencies* manually (a software dependency is the term for a package that is dependent on other package being installed).

All Security Alerts, Bug Fix Alerts, and Enhancement Alerts (collective known as Errata Alerts) can also be downloaded from the Red Hat website at the following URL:

```
http://www.redhat.com/apps/support/errata/
```

Click on the Red Hat Linux version you are using to view a list of all available errata for Red Hat Linux.

Click on the name of the Errata Alert that you want to apply to your system. Instructions for updating the packages can be found on the individual Errata pages.

> **NOTE** Red Hat tests and approves the RPMs posted on this site. RPMs downloaded from other sites are not supported.

Updating Using the Installation CD-ROMs

After installation, you can install software from the Red Hat Linux CD-ROMs by inserting CD-ROM #1 into your computer. You will be prompted for the root password. After entering the password successfully, the Package Management Tool interface will appear and allow you to select package groups to be installed as well as individual packages within the groups. Refer to the "Updating with the Package Management Tool" section earlier in this chapter for details.

Chapter 20

Package Management with RPM

The RPM Package Manager (RPM) is an open packaging system that runs on Red Hat Linux as well as other Linux and Unix systems. Red Hat encourages other vendors to use RPM for their own products, and some (such as Mandrake Linux, which is based on Red Hat Linux) do use RPM. This chapter describes how to install and manage packages using RPM.

> **NOTE** If you're new to Red Hat Linux or you just prefer a graphical interface, you can use the Package Management Tool to manage RPM packages. See Chapter 19 for details.

Introducing RPM

For the end user, RPM makes system updates easy. Installing, uninstalling, and upgrading RPM packages can be accomplished with short commands. RPM maintains a database of installed packages and their files, so you can invoke powerful queries and verifications on your system.

During upgrades, RPM handles configuration files carefully so that you never lose your customizations — something that you will not accomplish with regular .tar.gz files.

> **Note** Because RPM makes changes to your system, you must be logged in as root to install, remove, or upgrade an RPM package.

RPM Design Goals

To understand how to use RPM, it can be helpful to understand RPM's design goals:

- *Upgradability* — Using RPM, you can upgrade individual components of your system without completely reinstalling. When you get a new release of an operating system based on RPM (such as Red Hat Linux), you don't need to reinstall on your machine (as you do with operating systems based on other packaging systems). RPM allows intelligent, fully-automated, in-place upgrades of your system. Configuration files in packages are preserved across upgrades, so you won't lose your customizations. No special upgrade files are needed to upgrade a package because the same RPM file is used to install and upgrade the package on your system.

- *Powerful Querying* — RPM is designed to provide powerful querying options. You can search through your entire database for packages or just for certain files. You can also easily find out what package a file belongs to and from where the package came. The files an RPM package contains are in a compressed archive, with a custom binary header containing useful information about the package and its contents, allowing you to query individual packages quickly and easily.

♦ *System Verification* — Another powerful feature is the ability to verify packages. If you are worried that you deleted an important file for some package, simply verify the package. You will be notified of any anomalies. At that point, you can reinstall the package if necessary. Any configuration files that you modified are preserved during reinstallation.

♦ *Pristine Sources* — A crucial design goal was to allow the use of pristine software sources, as distributed by the original authors of the software. With RPM, you have the pristine sources along with any patches that were used, plus complete build instructions. This is an important advantage for several reasons.

For instance, if a new version of a program comes out, you do not necessarily have to start from scratch to get it to compile. You can look at the patch to see what you *might* need to do. All the compiled-in defaults, and all of the changes that were made to get the software to build properly are easily visible using this technique.

The goal of keeping sources pristine may only seem important for developers, but it results in higher quality software for end users, too.

Using RPM

RPM has five basic modes of operation (not counting package building): installing, uninstalling, upgrading, querying, and verifying. The following sections contain an overview of each mode. For complete details and options try `rpm --help`, or see the "Additional Resources" section later in this chapter for more sources of information on RPM.

Finding RPM Packages

Before using an RPM, you must know where to find them. An Internet search will return many RPM repositories, but if you are looking for RPM packages built by Red Hat, you can find them at the following locations:

♦ The official Red Hat Linux CD-ROMs

♦ The Red Hat Errata Page available at the following URL:

```
http://www.redhat.com/apps/support/errata/
```

♦ A Red Hat FTP mirror site; many of these mirror sites are available at the following URL:

```
http://www.redhat.com/download/mirror.html
```

♦ The Red Hat Network. See Chapter 19 for more information on the Red Hat Network

Installing a Package

RPM packages typically have file names like `foo-1.0-1.i386.rpm`. The file name includes the package name (`foo`), the package version (`1.0`), the release (`1`), and the architecture for which the package was intended (i386). Installing this example package is as simple as logging in as root and typing the following command at a shell prompt:

```
rpm -Uvh foo-1.0-1.i386.rpm
```

The -Uvh options that follow the command specify that you want to install or upgrade the package, that you want to see verbose messages, and that you want to see hash marks (#) while the package is installing.

If installation is successful, you will see the following:

```
Preparing...                 ######################################### [100%]
   1:foo                      ######################################### [100%]
```

As you can see, RPM prints out the name of the package and then prints a succession of hash marks as the package is installed as a progress meter.

The signature of a package is checked when installing or upgrading a package. If verifying the signature fails, you will see an error message such as:

```
error: V3 DSA signature: BAD, key ID 0352860f
```

If is it a new, header-only signature, you will see an error message such as:

```
error: Header V3 DSA signature: BAD, key ID 0352860f
```

If you do not have the appropriate key installed to verify the signature, the message will contain NOKEY such as:

```
warning: V3 DSA signature: NOKEY, key ID 0352860f
```

See the "Checking a Package's Signature" section later in this chapter for more information on checking a package's signature.

Installing packages is designed to be simple, but you may sometimes see errors. The following sections describe the most common package installation errors.

Package Already Installed

If the package of the same version is already installed, you will see the following error:

```
Preparing...                 ######################################### [100%]
package foo-1.0-1 is already installed
```

If you want to install the package anyway and the same version you are trying to install is already installed, you can use the --replacepkgs option, which tells RPM to ignore the error. The installation command would then look as follows:

```
rpm -ivh --replacepkgs foo-1.0-1.i386.rpm
```

This option is helpful if files installed from the RPM were deleted or if you want the original configuration files from the RPM to be installed.

Conflicting Files

If you attempt to install a package containing a file that has already been installed by another package or an earlier version of the same package, you will see the following error:

```
Preparing...                 ######################################### [100%]
file /usr/bin/foo from install of foo-1.0-1 conflicts with file from package bar-2.0.20
```

To make RPM ignore this error, use the `--replacefiles` option as follows:

```
rpm -ivh --replacefiles foo-1.0-1.i386.rpm
```

Unresolved Dependency

RPM packages can depend on other packages, which means that they require other packages to be installed in order to run properly. If you try to install a package that has an unresolved dependency, you will see the following error:

```
Preparing...                 ######################################### [100%]
error: Failed dependencies:
        bar.so.2 is needed by foo-1.0-1
    Suggested resolutions:
        bar-2.0.20-3.i386.rpm
```

If you are installing an official Red Hat package, the system will usually suggest the package(s) needed to resolve the dependency. You can then find this package on the Red Hat Linux CD-ROMs or from the Red Hat FTP site (or mirror), and add it to the command, as follows:

```
rpm -ivh foo-1.0-1.i386.rpm bar-2.0.20-3.i386.rpm
```

If installation of both packages is successful, you will see the following output:

```
Preparing...                 ######################################### [100%]
   1:foo                      ######################################### [ 50%]
   2:bar                      ######################################### [100%]
```

If the system does not suggest a package to resolve the dependency, you can try the `--redhatprovides` option as follows to determine which package contains the required file. You need the `rpmdb-redhat` package installed to use this option.

```
rpm -q --redhatprovides bar.so.2
```

If the package that contains `bar.so.2` is in the installed database from the `rpmdb-redhat` package, the name of the package will be displayed:

```
bar-2.0.20-3.i386.rpm
```

If you want to force the installation anyway (a bad idea since the package probably will not run correctly), use the `--nodeps` option.

Uninstalling a Package

Uninstalling a package is just as simple as installing one. Type the following command at a shell prompt:

```
rpm -e foo-1.0-1.i386.rpm
```

> **NOTE** Make sure to use the actual name of the original package in your uninstall command.

You may encounter a dependency error when uninstalling a package if another installed package depends on the one you are trying to remove. For example:

```
Preparing...                ######################################## [100%]
error: removing these packages would break dependencies:
        foo is needed by bar-2.0.20-3.i386.rpm
```

To cause RPM to ignore this error and uninstall the package anyway (which is also a bad idea because the package that depends on it will probably thereafter fail to work properly), use the --nodeps option.

Upgrading

Upgrading a package is similar to installing one. To upgrade the foo package, for example, you would type the following command at a shell prompt:

```
rpm -Uvh foo-2.0-1.i386.rpm
```

The use of the -U option in the above command makes RPM automatically uninstalls any old versions of the foo package.

> **TIP** You may want to always use -U to install packages;the command will work even when there are no previous versions of the package installed.

Because RPM performs intelligent upgrading of packages with configuration files, you may see a message similar to the following:

```
saving /etc/foo.conf as /etc/foo.conf.rpmsave
```

This message means that your changes to the configuration file may not be forward compatible with the new configuration file in the package, so RPM saved your original file and installed a new one.

You should investigate the differences between the two configuration files and resolve them as rapidly as possible to ensure that your system continues to function properly.

Upgrading is really a combination of uninstalling and installing, so during an RPM upgrade you may encounter uninstalling and installing errors, plus one more. If RPM thinks you are trying to upgrade to a package with an *older* version number, you will see an error message similar to the following:

```
package foo-2.0-1 (which is newer than foo-1.0-1) is already installed
```

To force RPM to "upgrade" anyway, use the --oldpackage option, as follows:

```
rpm -Uvh --oldpackage foo-1.0-1.i386.rpm
```

Freshening a Package

Freshening a package is similar to upgrading one. To freshen the foo package, for example, type the following command at a shell prompt:

```
rpm -Fvh foo-1.2-1.i386.rpm
```

RPM's freshen option checks the versions of the packages specified in the command against the versions of packages that have already been installed on your system. When a newer version of an already-installed package is processed by RPM's freshen option, it will be upgraded to the newer version. However, RPM's freshen option will not install a package if no previously-installed package of the same name exists. This differs from RPM's upgrade option, as an upgrade *will* install packages whether or not an older version of the package was already installed.

RPM's freshen option works for single packages or a group of packages. If you have just downloaded a large number of different packages and you only want to upgrade those packages that are already installed on your system, freshening will do the job. If you use freshening, you will not have to delete any unwanted packages from the group that you downloaded before using RPM.

In this case, you can simply issue the following command:

```
rpm -Fvh *.rpm
```

RPM will automatically upgrade only those packages that are already installed.

Querying a Package

Use the rpm -q command to query the database of installed packages. The rpm -q foo command will print the package name, version, and release number of the installed package foo:

```
foo-2.0-1
```

> **NOTE** Notice that we used the package name foo. To query a package, you will need to replace foo with the actual package name.

Instead of specifying the package name, you can use the following options along with -q to specify the package(s) you want to query. These are called *Package Specification Options*.

♦ -a — Queries all currently installed packages.

♦ -f *file* — Queries the package which owns *file*. When specifying a file, you must specify the full path of the file (for example, /usr/bin/ls).

♦ -pZ *packagefile* — Queries the package *packagefile*.

There are a number of ways to specify what information to display about queried packages. The following options are used to select the type of information for which you are searching. These are called *Information Selection Options*.

- ♦ -i — Displays package information including name, description, release, size, build date, install date, vendor, and other miscellaneous information.

- ♦ -l — Displays the list of files that the package contains.

- ♦ -s — Displays the state of all the files in the package.

- ♦ -d — Displays a list of files marked as documentation (man pages, info pages, READMEs, etc.).

- ♦ -c — Displays a list of files marked as configuration files. These are the files you change after installation to adapt the package to your system (for example, sendmail.cf, passwd, inittab, etc.).

> **TIP** For options that display lists of files, you can add -v to the command to display the lists in a familiar ls -l format.

Verifying a Package

Verifying a package compares information about files installed from a package with the same information from the original package. Among other things, verifying compares the size, MD5 sum, permissions, type, owner, and group of each file.

The command rpm -V verifies a package. You can use any of the Package Selection Options listed for querying to specify the packages you wish to verify. A simple use of verifying is rpm -V foo (where foo is the package you're verifying), which verifies that all the files in the foo package are as they were when they were originally installed.

For example:

- ♦ To verify a package containing a particular file (in this case, the vi file), use the following command:

```
rpm -Vf /bin/vi
```

- ♦ To verify ALL installed packages, use the following command:

```
rpm -Va
```

- ♦ To verify an installed package against an RPM package file, use the following command:

```
rpm -Vp foo-1.0-1.i386.rpm
```

This command can be useful if you suspect that your RPM databases are corrupt.

If everything verified properly, there will be no output. If there are any discrepancies, they will be displayed. The format of the output is a string of eight characters (a c denotes a configuration file) and then the file name. Each of the eight characters denotes the result of a comparison of one attribute of the file to the value of that attribute recorded in the RPM database. A single . (a period) means the test passed. The characters listed in Table 20-1 denote failure of certain tests.

Table 20-1: Error Code Characters

Error Character	What Failed
5	MD5 checksum
S	File size
L	Symbolic link
T	File modification time
D	Device
U	User
G	Group
M	Mode (includes permissions and file type)
?	Unreadable file

If you see any output, use your best judgment to determine whether you should remove or reinstall the package or fix the problem in another way.

Checking a Package's Signature

If you wish to verify that a package has not been corrupted or tampered with, examine only the md5sum by typing the following command at a shell prompt (replace *rpm-file* with the filename of the RPM package):

```
rpm -K --nogpg rpm-file
```

You will see the following message

```
rpm-file : md5 OK
```

This brief message means that the file was not corrupted by the download.

> **TIP** To see a more verbose message, replace -K with -Kvv in the command.

On the other hand, how trustworthy is the developer who created the package? If the package is signed with the developer's GnuPG *key*, you will know that the developer really is who he says he is.

An RPM package can be signed using the Gnu Privacy Guard (or GnuPG), to help you make certain your downloaded package is trustworthy.

GnuPG is a tool for secure communication; it is a complete and free replacement for the encryption technology of PGP, an electronic privacy program. With GnuPG, you can authenticate the validity of documents and encrypt/decrypt data to and from other recipients. GnuPG is capable of decrypting and verifying PGP 5.*x* files as well.

During the installation of Red Hat Linux, GnuPG is installed by default. That way you can immediately start using GnuPG to verify any packages that you receive from Red Hat. First, you will need to import Red Hat's public key.

Importing Keys

To verify official Red Hat packages, you must import the Red Hat GPG key. To do so, execute the following command at a shell prompt:

```
rpm --import /usr/share/rhn/RPM-GPG-KEY
```

To display a list of all keys installed for RPM verification, execute the command:

```
rpm -qa gpg-pubkey*
```

For the Red Hat key, the output will include:

```
gpg-pubkey-db42a60e-37ea5438
```

To display details about a specific key, use `rpm -qi` followed by the output from the previous command, as follows:

```
rpm -qi gpg-pubkey-db42a60e-37ea5438
```

Verifying the Signature of Packages

To check the GnuPG signature of an RPM file after importing the builder's GnuPG key, use the following command (replace *rpm-file* with filename of the RPM package):

```
rpm -K rpm-file
```

If all goes well, you will see the message: md5 gpg OK. That means that the signature of the package has been verified and that it is not corrupt.

Impressing Your Friends with RPM

RPM is a useful tool for both managing your system and diagnosing and fixing problems. The best way to make sense of all of its options is to look at some examples.

♦ Perhaps you have deleted some files by accident, but you are not sure what you deleted. If you want to verify your entire system and see what might be missing, you could try the following command:

```
rpm -Va
```

If some files are missing or appear to have been corrupted, you should probably either re-install the package or uninstall and then reinstall the package.

♦ At some point, you might see a file that you do not recognize. To find out which package owns it, you would enter the following command:

```
rpm -qf /usr/X11R6/bin/ghostview
```

The output would look like the following:

```
gv-3.5.8-18
```

♦ We can combine the previous two examples in the following scenario. Say you are having problems with /usr/bin/paste and would like to verify the package that owns that program, but you do not know which package owns paste. In that case, simply enter the following command:

```
rpm -Vf /usr/bin/paste
```

and the appropriate package will be verified.

♦ Do you want to find out more information about a particular program? You can try the following command to locate the documentation which came with the package that owns that program:

```
rpm -qdf /usr/bin/md5sum
```

The output will look like the following:

```
/usr/share/doc/textutils-2.0a/NEWS
/usr/share/doc/textutils-2.0a/README
/usr/info/textutils.info.gz
/usr/man/man1/cat.1.gz
/usr/man/man1/cksum.1.gz
/usr/man/man1/comm.1.gz
/usr/man/man1/csplit.1.gz
/usr/man/man1/cut.1.gz
/usr/man/man1/expand.1.gz
/usr/man/man1/fmt.1.gz
/usr/man/man1/fold.1.gz
/usr/man/man1/head.1.gz
/usr/man/man1/join.1.gz
/usr/man/man1/md5sum.1.gz
/usr/man/man1/nl.1.gz
/usr/man/man1/od.1.gz
/usr/man/man1/paste.1.gz
/usr/man/man1/pr.1.gz
/usr/man/man1/ptx.1.gz
/usr/man/man1/sort.1.gz
/usr/man/man1/split.1.gz
/usr/man/man1/sum.1.gz
/usr/man/man1/tac.1.gz
/usr/man/man1/tail.1.gz
/usr/man/man1/tr.1.gz
/usr/man/man1/tsort.1.gz
/usr/man/man1/unexpand.1.gz
/usr/man/man1/uniq.1.gz
/usr/man/man1/wc.1.gz
```

♦ Say you find a new RPM, but you do not know what it does. To find information about it, use the following command:

```
rpm -qip sndconfig-0.68-3.i386.rpm
```

The output would look like the following:

```
Name        : sndconfig                Relocations: (not relocateable)
Version     : 0.68                            Vendor: Red Hat
Release     : 3                          Build Date: Sun 23 Jun 2002 08:22:52 PM EDT
Install date: Mon 01 Jul 2002 08:40:06 AM EDT      Build Host: perf90.perf.redhat.com
Group       : Applications/Multimedia    Source RPM: sndconfig-0.68-3.src.rpm
Size        : 619097                        License: GPL
Packager    : Red Hat  http://bugzilla.redhat.com/bugzilla
Summary     : The Red Hat Linux sound configuration tool.
Description :
Sndconfig is a text based tool that sets up the configuration files
you will need to use a sound card with a Red Hat Linux system.
Sndconfig can be used to set the proper sound type for programs that
use the /dev/dsp, /dev/audio, and /dev/mixer devices. The sound
settings are saved by the aumix and sysV runlevel scripts.
```

♦ Perhaps you now want to see what files the `sndconfig` RPM installs. You would enter the following:

```
rpm -qlp sndconfig-0.68-3.i386.rpm
```

The output will look like the following:

```
/sbin/sndconfig
/usr/sbin/sndconfig
/usr/share/locale/bs/LC_MESSAGES/sndconfig.mo
/usr/share/locale/cs/LC_MESSAGES/sndconfig.mo
/usr/share/locale/da/LC_MESSAGES/sndconfig.mo
/usr/share/locale/de/LC_MESSAGES/sndconfig.mo
/usr/share/locale/es/LC_MESSAGES/sndconfig.mo
/usr/share/locale/eu_ES/LC_MESSAGES/sndconfig.mo
/usr/share/locale/fi/LC_MESSAGES/sndconfig.mo
/usr/share/locale/fr/LC_MESSAGES/sndconfig.mo
/usr/share/locale/gl/LC_MESSAGES/sndconfig.mo
/usr/share/locale/hu/LC_MESSAGES/sndconfig.mo
/usr/share/locale/id/LC_MESSAGES/sndconfig.mo
/usr/share/locale/is/LC_MESSAGES/sndconfig.mo
/usr/share/locale/it/LC_MESSAGES/sndconfig.mo
/usr/share/locale/ja/LC_MESSAGES/sndconfig.mo
/usr/share/locale/ko/LC_MESSAGES/sndconfig.mo
/usr/share/locale/no/LC_MESSAGES/sndconfig.mo
/usr/share/locale/pl/LC_MESSAGES/sndconfig.mo
/usr/share/locale/pt/LC_MESSAGES/sndconfig.mo
/usr/share/locale/pt_BR/LC_MESSAGES/sndconfig.mo
/usr/share/locale/ro/LC_MESSAGES/sndconfig.mo
```

```
/usr/share/locale/ru/LC_MESSAGES/sndconfig.mo
/usr/share/locale/sk/LC_MESSAGES/sndconfig.mo
/usr/share/locale/sl/LC_MESSAGES/sndconfig.mo
/usr/share/locale/sr/LC_MESSAGES/sndconfig.mo
/usr/share/locale/sv/LC_MESSAGES/sndconfig.mo
/usr/share/locale/tr/LC_MESSAGES/sndconfig.mo
/usr/share/locale/uk/LC_MESSAGES/sndconfig.mo
/usr/share/locale/wa/LC_MESSAGES/sndconfig.mo
/usr/share/locale/zh/LC_MESSAGES/sndconfig.mo
/usr/share/locale/zh_CN.GB2312/LC_MESSAGES/sndconfig.mo
/usr/share/locale/zh_TW.Big5/LC_MESSAGES/sndconfig.mo
/usr/share/locale/zh_TW/LC_MESSAGES/sndconfig.mo
/usr/share/man/man8/sndconfig.8.gz
/usr/share/sndconfig
/usr/share/sndconfig/sample.au
/usr/share/sndconfig/sample.midi
/usr/share/sndconfig/sample2.au
```

These are just a few examples. As you use RPM, you will find many more uses for it.

Additional Resources

RPM is an extremely complex utility with many options and methods for querying, installing, upgrading, and removing packages. Refer to the following resources to learn more about RPM.

Installed Documentation

See the following documentation on your Red Hat Linux system for more information about RPM:

- ◆ `rpm --help` — This command displays a quick reference of RPM parameters.
- ◆ `man rpm` — The RPM man page will give you more detail about RPM parameters than the `rpm --help` command.

Useful Websites

See the following websites for more information about RPM:

- ◆ `http://www.rpm.org/` — The RPM website.
- ◆ `http://www.redhat.com/mailing-lists/rpm-list/` — The RPM mailing list is archived here. To subscribe to the mailing list, send mail to `rpm-list-request@redhat.com` with the word `subscribe` in the subject line.

Related Books

See Maximum RPM by Ed Bailey (Red Hat Press) for more information about RPM. An online version of the book is available at the following URL:

```
http://www.rpm.org/ and http://www.redhat.com/docs/books/
```

Part VI

Additional References

Red Hat Linux 8 has a brand new interface that is user-friendly and extremely customizable. This part gives you tips, tricks, and answers to frequently asked questions about Red Hat Linux. This part also contains chapters on navigating the Red Hat Linux interface with keyboard shortcuts, navigating the Red Hat Linux directory structure, a comparison of similar MS-DOS and Linux commands for readers familiar with the MS-DOS (or Windows) environments, and how to get information about your system's status.

## Chapter 21

Frequently Asked Questions

This chapter answers some of the most common questions about using Red Hat Linux that you may ask as you become more familiar with it. From recovering forgotten passwords to troubleshooting package installation problems, this chapter will ease you step-by-step through some common tasks to help get you on your way.

Localhost Login and Password

Question: *I have installed Red Hat Linux. After rebooting, I get a message telling me it needs a localhost login and password. What do I need to do?*

Unless you specified a host name for your computer or received that information from a network, your Red Hat Linux installation will call your machine `localhost.localdomain` by default.

When you get to that initial prompt, Linux asks you to log in to your system. If you created a user account during installation, you can log in using that username and password. If you didn't create a user account during installation, then you can log in as the root user. The root password is the system password you assigned to root during installation.

> **NOTE** You should create at least one user account during installation. If you did not, you can create a new user after logging in as root with the Red Hat User Manager GUI application or with the `useradd` command-line utility. For more information, refer to Chapter 2.

Error Messages During Installation of RPMs

Question: *How do I install an RPM from a CD or the Internet? I keep getting an error message when I use* rpm.

If you are getting an error message similar to the following

```
failed to open /var/lib/rpm/packages.rpm
```

it is because you do not have proper permission to install RPM files.

When you install software, you are often required to make systemwide changes that only root can make, such as creating new directories outside of your user home directory or making changes to your system configuration. If you are using your normal user account, you will not have permission to make such changes by default.

You need to be the root user in order to install RPM files. At a shell prompt, you can switch to the root user by running the following command:

```
su
```

You should then be able to install the RPM package without further errors.

> **NOTE** For more information about using RPM and Package Management Tool, see Part V of this book.

Starting Applications

Question: I installed an application that I downloaded from the Internet, and everything seemed to go fine, but I still get "command not found" when I type its name. I think I have the right name, so why will it not start?

If you are trying to start an application from the shell prompt and it is not working, try typing out the full directory path before the name of the application's executable (such as /usr/local/bin/myexecutable).

For example, imagine that you have downloaded the setiathome client application and want to try it out. You follow the directions for installing the software, which creates a subdirectory in your home directory called seti/. Now, start the application using the full path to the executable file as shown below:

```
/home/joe/seti/setiathome
```

The reason you may need to use the full pathnames in order to start an application is because the executable wasn't placed in a directory where your user shell environment knew it could be found (such as /usr/local/bin) — that is, the application's starting command is not in your PATH. You can customize your settings so that you won't be required to type the full path to the application each time. To do this, you will have to edit your PATH environment variable, as discussed in the next section.

Editing Your PATH

Question: Why do I always have to specify the full path of the commands for my favorite programs?

If you frequently start programs that are not located in a directory that your user shell has been configured to search, you will have to edit your user shell configuration file to add the directory containing the executable you wish to run. You can do this by adding the directory to your PATH environment variable.

> **CAUTION** These instructions are intended *only* for user accounts. Avoid modifying files such as the root user's .bash_profile because of the potential security risks.

Start a text editor such as pico at a shell prompt. You can open the file called .bash_profile by typing the following:

```
pico .bash_profile
```

You will see a PATH statement similar to the one shown below:

```
PATH=$PATH:$HOME/bin:/usr/local/bin:
```

To the end of this statement, append **$HOME/seti:** as follows:

```
PATH=$PATH:$HOME/bin:/usr/local/bin/:$HOME/seti:
```

Now, press Ctrl-X; you will be asked whether you want to save "the modified buffer" (that's what `pico` calls an updated file); type **y** for "yes." Next, you will see the name the file will be saved as; press the Enter key.

You can then make the changes to `.bash_profile` take effect immediately by typing the following command:

```
source .bash_profile
```

By doing the above, you do not have to manually add **$HOME/seti:** to the beginning of the executable to start an application located in the directory you've added to your PATH.

Accessing a Windows Partition

Question: I have a dual-boot system with Red Hat Linux and Windows 95/98/Me. Is there a way to access my Windows partition while I am running Linux?

You can access another partition on your system (for example, a Windows partition), in two different ways, as discussed in the following sections.

Mounting a Windows Partition Manually

To mount a Windows partition manually (for example, if you only need to access your Windows partition once in a while and don't want to have Windows mounted every time you boot your system), follow these steps:

1. First, assume that your Windows partition is on your first IDE hard drive, in the first partition (`/dev/hda1`).

2. At a shell prompt, log in as root (type **su** and then enter the root password).

3. Create a directory at which the Windows partition will be mounted by typing the following command:

```
mkdir /mnt/windows
```

4. Before you can access the partition, you will need to mount it at the directory you just created. As root, type the following command at a shell prompt:

```
mount -t vfat /dev/hda1 /mnt/windows
```

Mounting a Windows Partition Automatically

To mount a Windows partition upon system boot (for instance, if you want to have access to Windows as though it were another hard drive), follow these steps to modify the `/etc/fstab` file.

1. At a shell prompt, log in as root (type **su** and then enter the root password).

2. Open the `/etc/fstab` in a text editor by typing (for example):

```
pico /etc/fstab
```

3. Add the following on a new line (the `/dev/hda1` may vary, but for most users this is correct):

```
/dev/hda1 /mnt/windows vfat auto,owner,users 0 0
```

4. Press Ctrl-x and then type **y** for yes when prompted to save the changes. The next time the system is rebooted, the `/etc/fstab` file will be read and the Windows partition will be automatically mounted in the `/mnt/windows` directory.

> **NOTE** You do not have to reboot your computer to mount the Windows partition. After this line is in your `/etc/fstab` file, use the command `mount /mnt/windows` to mount it without rebooting.

To access the partition, type **cd /mnt/windows**. To navigate through Windows's embedded spaces in their directories, surround the directory in quotation marks, as in **ls "Program Files"**.

Finding Commands Quickly

Question: I was looking at a man page yesterday, but I can't remember the name of the command I was reading about and I didn't write it down. How do I get the man page back?

The command you used will most likely be stored in a file called `.bash_history`. By default, this file records the last 500 commands you typed at the shell prompt.

You can glimpse the history of your commands by typing **history** at the shell prompt, but the results will scroll by too quickly for you to be able to read every line.

Another way to view `.bash_history` is with a utility such as `less`. Type **less .bash_history** at the shell prompt, and the results will display one page at a time. To move forward a screen, press the spacebar; to move back a screen, press the b key; and to quit, press q.

Paging through `.bash_history` to find a command can be tedious. To save time, you can search through the file for keywords using `grep`, a powerful search utility.

Say you were reading a man page the day before, but cannot recall its name. To search for the command, type:

```
history | grep man
```

You will see a list of all the commands you typed that have the word *man* in them.

There are plenty of ways to use your command history. For other tips and tricks, see the next section.

Tips on Using Command History

Question: What are some other ways I can use command history?

If you type **history**, you will see a numbered list scroll by very quickly, showing you the previous 500 commands you have used.

You probably do not need to see all of the last 500 commands, so the command `history number` might be useful. For example, using the command `history 20` displays only the previous 20 commands you typed (you can use any quantity as an argument of the `history` command).

Here are other command history shortcuts that may be useful to you:

- ♦ *! ! (called "bang bang")* — Executes the last command in the history.
- ♦ *`!number` (as in !302)* — Executes the command that is numbered 302 in the history file.
- ♦ *`!string` (as in !rpm)* — Executes a command with the most recent matching string from the history file.
- ♦ *Up arrow and down arrow* — At the shell or GUI terminal prompt, you can simply press the up arrow to move back through previous commands in your history list (the down arrow will move you forward through the commands) until you find the command you want. Press Enter to execute the command, just as if you had typed it on the command line.

Keep ls Output from Scrolling

Question: Whenever I type **ls** I can barely see the output of the directory because it scrolls by too quickly. How can I actually read the output?

To prevent the output of ls from scrolling by too quickly, pipe the output to a utility such as `less` or `more`. You will then be able to see the output one screen, or *page*, at a time.

To read the contents of `/etc` with `less`, type the following command at the shell prompt:

```
ls -al /etc | less
```

To move forward a screen, press the spacebar; to move back a screen, press the b key; to quit, press q.

> **TIP** You can achieve the same results with `more`, another paging utility.

You can also print directory listings by piping the output to a printer in the same way that you piped the output to your screen. If you have configured a printer, type the following to pipe the output of a command to the printer:

```
ls -al /etc | lpr
```

Forgotten Password

Question: Help! I forgot my root password. How do I log in now?

You can log in using single-user mode and create a new root password.

To enter single-user mode, reboot your computer. If you use the default bootloader, GRUB, you can enter single-user mode by following these steps:

1. At the bootloader menu, type **e** to enter editing mode.

2. You will be presented with a boot entry listing. Look for the line that looks similar to the following:

```
kernel /vmlinuz-2.4.18-0.4 ro root=/dev/hda2
```

   Press the arrow key until this line is highlighted and press e.

3. You can now add the word `single` one space after the end of the text to tell GRUB to boot into single-user Linux mode. Press Enter to make the editing change take effect.

4. You will be brought back to the edit mode screen. From here, press **b** and GRUB will boot single-user Linux mode. After it finishes loading, you will be presented with a shell prompt similar to the following:

```
sh-2.05#
```

5. You can now change the root password by typing

```
bash# passwd root
```

You will be asked to re-type the password for verification. After you are finished, the password will be changed. You can then reboot by typing **reboot** at the prompt; then you can log in to root as you normally would.

Password Maintenance

Question: I forgot or want to change my user account password.

Open a shell prompt and type the following:

```
passwd username
```

Replace *username* with your normal user name.

The `passwd` program will then ask for the new password, which you will need to enter twice. You can now use the new password to log in to your user account.

> **NOTE** You cannot change any password but your own unless you are logged in as the root user.

Changing Login from Console to X at Startup

Question: How do I change my login from the shell prompt to the graphical screen?

Instead of logging in to your system at the console and typing the **startx** command to start the X Window System, you can configure your system so that you can log in directly to X and bypass the shell prompt altogether.

To do this you must edit the /etc/inittab file by changing just one number in the runlevel section. When you are finished, reboot the computer. The next time you log in, you will have a graphical login prompt.

Open a shell prompt. If you're logged in to your user account, su to root by typing

```
su
Password: yourrootpassword
```

Now, type **pico /etc/inittab** to edit the file with pico. The file /etc/inittab will open. On the first screen, you will see the runlevel section of the file, which looks like the following:

```
# Default runlevel. The runlevels used by RHS are:
# 0 - halt (Do NOT set initdefault to this)
# 1 - Single user mode
# 2 - Multiuser, without NFS (The same as 3, if you do not have
networking)
# 3 - Full multiuser mode
# 4 - unused
# 5 - X11
# 6 - reboot (Do NOT set initdefault to this)
#
id:3:initdefault:
```

To change from a system prompt to a graphical login, you should change the number in the following line:

```
id:3:initdefault: from a 3 to a 5.
```

> **WARNING** Change only the number of the default runlevel from 3 to 5.

Your changed line should look like the following:

```
id:5:initdefault:
```

When you are satisfied with your change, save and exit the file using the Ctrl-x keys. You will see a message telling you that the file has been modified, and asking you to confirm your change. Press y for yes.

Now, your next login after reboot will be from the graphical screen.

Chapter 22

Keyboard and Shell Prompt Shortcuts

Red Hat Linux includes various shortcuts to help you more smoothly navigate your interface, be it text or graphical, as well shortcuts to kill applications, switch virtual consoles, and more.

The tables in this chapter describe some of the more useful keyboard shortcuts (Table 22-1) and shell prompt shortcut characters (Table 22-2) that are available in Red Hat Linux.

Many more are available in addition to those listed in this chapter. For more command line and keyboard shortcuts, visit:

`http://sunsite.dk/linux-newbie/lnag_commands.html#shortcuts`

Table 22-1: Red Hat Linux Keyboard Shortcuts

Shortcut	What It Does
Alt-Tab	If you have more than one application open at a time, you can use Alt-Tab to switch among open tasks and applications.
Ctrl-Alt-+	Switches to the next X-server resolution (this works only when X is running and if you have configured more than one resolution for your system).
Ctrl-Alt--	Switches to the previous X-server resolution (this works only when X is running and if you have configured more than one resolution for your system).
Ctrl-Alt-Backspace	Kills your current X session and returns you to the login screen. Use this if the normal exit procedure does not work.
Ctrl-Alt-Delete	Shut down and reboot. Shuts down your current session and reboots the OS. Use only when the normal shutdown procedure does not work.

Shortcut	*What It Does*
Ctrl-Alt-Fn	Switches virtual consoles. Ctrl-Alt - one of the function keys displays a new screen. F1 through F6 are text (console) screens and F7 is a graphical screen. When at a text terminal, Alt-Fn works instead (Ctrl is not needed).
Ctrl-a	Moves the cursor to the beginning of a line. This works in most text editors and in the URL field in Mozilla.
Ctrl-c	Kills the current process (works with some text-mode applications).
Ctrl-d	Log out of a terminal or console instead of having to type **exit** or **logout**.
Ctrl-e	Move the cursor to end of a line. This works in most text editors and in the URL field in Mozilla.
Ctrl-l	Clears the terminal. This shortcut does the same thing as typing **clear** at a command line.
Ctrl-u	Clears the current line. If you are working in a terminal, use this shortcut to clear the current line from the cursor all the way to the end of the line.
Middle Mouse Button	Pastes highlighted text. Use the left mouse button to highlight the text. Point the cursor to the spot where you want it pasted. Click the middle mouse button to paste it. If you do not have a middle mouse button, but selected the Emulate 3 buttons option during the installation, you can emulate a middle mouse button by holding down both mouse buttons at the same time.
Shift-PgUp	Scrolls the terminal output up. Note that you can also use this shortcut to scroll up through your boot messages even if there is not currently any output at the terminal.
Shift-PgDwn	Scrolls the terminal output down (see Shift-PgUp).
Tab	While working in a terminal, type the first few characters of a command and then press Tab. Linux will automatically complete the command or show all the commands that match the characters you typed.
Up and Down arrow	While working in a terminal, press the up or down arrow to scroll through a history of commands you have typed from the current directory. When you see the command you want to use, press Enter.

Table 22-2: System Prompt Shortcut Characters

Character	What It Represents
~ (tilde character)	Stands for the home directory for the currently logged in user. For example, if root is logged in, typing **cd ~** will take you to the /root directory (which is root's home directory).
. (dot)	Stands for the current working directory. For example, typing **./program** attempts to execute the program file in the current working directory.
.. (two dots)	Stands for the parent directory of the current working directory. For example, if you're in the /home/user directory, typing **cd ..** will take you up one directory to the /home directory.
* (asterisk)	Also called a wildcard character, the asterisk allows you to shorten file names in commands. To use the wildcard, you can simply type as much of the file or directory's name needed to distinguish it from the other file and directory names in the current working directory and then type * to represent the rest of the file. For example, if you have two files in a directory named file1111 and file2222, you can simply type **file1*** and Linux will know that you mean file1111.

Chapter 23

System Directories

Getting to know Red Hat Linux is much easier if you know the basic structure of the operating system. This chapter provides you with an overview of the directories that make up the Red Hat Linux file/directory structure, a brief overview of the FHS standard to which the Red Hat Linux structure adheres, and an introduction to the concept of virtual files and the related /proc directory.

Overview of the Red Hat Linux File System

Following is a list of the primary Red Hat Linux system directories. Each directory is described briefly. For additional directory information, refer to the *Official Red Hat Linux Administrator's Guide* (Red Hat Press/Wiley, 2003).

- /bin — Used to store user commands. The directory /usr/bin also stores user commands.

- /sbin — Location of many system commands, such as shutdown. The directory /usr/sbin also contains many system commands.

- /root — The home directory of root, the superuser.

- /mnt — This directory typically contains the mount points for file systems mounted after the system is booted. For example, the default CD-ROM mount point is /mnt/cdrom.

- /boot — Contains the kernel and other files used during system startup.

- /lost+found — Used by fsck to place orphaned files (files without names).

- /lib — Contains many library files used by programs in /bin and /sbin. The directory /usr/lib contains more library files.

- /dev — Stores device files.

- /etc — Contains many configuration files and directories.

- /var — For "variable" files, such as log files and the printer spool.

- /usr — Contains files and directories directly relating to users of the system.

- /proc — A virtual file system (meaning a file system that's not actually stored on the disk) that contains system information used by certain programs.

- /initrd — A directory that is used to mount the initrd.img image file and load necessary device modules during bootup.

> **WARNING** Do *not* delete this directory. You will be unable to boot your computer if you delete it and reboot your Red Hat Linux machine.

- ◆ `/tmp` — A "scratch pad" for users and programs. `/tmp` has global read/write access.
- ◆ `/home` — Typical location of user home directories.

The File System Hierarchy Standard (FHS)

Red Hat is committed to the *Filesystem Hierarchy Standard (FHS)*, a collaborative document that defines the names and locations of many files and directories. The current FHS document is the authoritative reference to any FHS-compliant file system, but the standard leaves many areas undefined or extensible. In this section, we provide an overview of the standard and a description of the parts of the file system not covered by the standard.

The complete standard is available at:

```
http://www.pathname.com/fhs
```

Compliance with the standard means many things, but the two most important are compatibility with other FHS-compliant systems and the ability to mount a `/usr` partition as read-only because it contains common executables and is not meant to be changed by users. Because the `/usr` directory is mounted read-only, it can be mounted from the CD-ROM or from another machine via a read-only NFS mount.

Why Share a Common Structure?

An operating system's file system structure is its most basic level of organization. Almost all of the ways an operating system interacts with its users, applications, and security model are dependent upon the way it stores its files on a storage device. It is crucial for a variety of reasons that users, as well as programs, be able to refer to a common guideline to know where to read and write files.

A file system can be seen in terms of two different logical categories of files:

- ◆ *Shareable vs. unshareable files* — *Shareable* files are those that can be accessed by various hosts; *unshareable* files are not available to any other hosts.

- ◆ *Variable vs. static files* — *Variable* files can change at any time without any intervention; *static* files, such as read-only documentation and binaries, do not change without an action from the system administrator or an agent that the system administrator has placed in motion to accomplish that task.

The reason for looking at files in this way is to help you understand the type of permissions given to the directory that holds them. The way in which the operating system and its users need to use the files determines the directory where those files should be placed, whether the directory is mounted read-only or read-write, and the level of access allowed on each file. The top level of this organization is crucial, as the access to the underlying directories can be restricted or security problems may manifest themselves if the top level is left disorganized or without a widely-used structure.

However, simply having a structure does not mean much unless it is a standard. Competing structures can actually cause more problems than they fix. Because of this, Red Hat has chosen the most widely used file system structure for Unix-like systems (FHS) and has extended it only slightly to accommodate special files used within Red Hat Linux.

FHS Organization

The directories and files noted here are just a small subset of those specified by the FHS document. Check the latest FHS document at `http://www.pathname.com/fhs` for the most complete information.

The /dev Directory

The `/dev` directory contains file system entries that represent devices that are attached to the system. These files are essential for the system to function properly.

The /etc Directory

The `/etc` directory is reserved for configuration files that are local to your machine. No binaries are to be put in `/etc`. Any binaries that were formerly put in `/etc` should now go into `/sbin` or possibly `/bin`.

The `X11` and `skel` directories are subdirectories of the `/etc` directory. The `X11` directory is for X11 configuration files such as `XF86Config`. The `skel` directory is for "skeleton" user files, which are used to populate a home directory when a user is first created.

The /lib Directory

The `/lib` directory should contain only those libraries that are needed to execute the binaries in `/bin` and `/sbin`. These shared library images are particularly important for booting the system and executing commands within the root file system.

The /mnt Directory

The `/mnt` directory is for temporarily mounted file systems, such as CD-ROMs and floppy disks.

The /opt Directory

The `/opt` directory provides an area for large, static application software packages to be stored.

For packages that wish to avoid putting their files throughout the file system, `/opt` provides a logical and predictable organizational system under that package's directory. This gives the system administrator an easy way to determine the role of each file within a particular package.

For example, if `sample` is the name of a particular software package located within `/opt`, then all of its files could be placed within directories inside `/opt/sample`, such as `/opt/sample/bin` for binaries and `/opt/sample/man` for manual pages.

Large packages that encompass many different subpackages, each of which accomplish a particular task, also go within `/opt`, giving that large package a standardized way to organize itself. In this way, our `sample` package may have different tools that each go in their own subdirectories, such as `/opt/sample/tool1` and `/opt/sample/tool2`, each of which can have their own `bin`, `man`, and other similar directories.

The /proc Directory

The `/proc` directory contains special "files" that either extract information from or send information to the kernel. For more information on the great variety of data available within `/proc` and the many ways this directory can be used to communicate with the kernel, see the section "The /proc File System" later in this chapter.

The /sbin Directory

The `/sbin` directory is for executables used only by the root user. The executables in `/sbin` are only used to boot and mount `/usr` and perform system recovery operations.

The /usr Directory

The `/usr` directory is for files that can be shared across a whole site. The `/usr` directory usually has its own partition, and it should be mountable read-only. Table 23-1 briefly describes the major subdirectories of `/usr`.

Table 23-1: Subdirectories of /usr

Subdirectory	*What It Contains*
`/bin`	Executables
`/dict`	Non-FHS compliant documentation pages
`/etc`	System-wide configuration files
`/games`	Games
`/include`	C header files
`/kerberos`	Binaries (and much more) for Kerberos
`/lib`	Object files and libraries that are not designed to be directly utilized by users or shell scripts
`/libexec`	Small helper programs called by other programs
`/sbin`	System administration binaries (those that do not belong in `/sbin`)
`/share`	Files that are not architecture-specific, `src` is for source code
`/X11R6`	Files for the X Window System (XFree86 on Red Hat Linux)

The /usr/local Directory

The `/usr/local` directory is similar in structure to the `/usr` directory.

In Red Hat Linux, the intended use for /usr/local is slightly different from that specified by the FHS. The FHS says that /usr/local should be where you store software that is to remain safe from system software upgrades. Because system upgrades from Red Hat are done safely with the rpm command and graphical Package Manager tool, you do not need to protect files by putting them in /usr/local. Instead, we recommend you use /usr/local for software that is local to your machine.

For instance, say you have mounted /usr via read-only NFS from a host named jake. If there is a package or program you would like to install, but you are not allowed to write to jake, you should install it under /usr/local. Later perhaps, if you have managed to convince the system administrator of jake to install the program on /usr, you can uninstall it from /usr/local.

The /var Directory

Because the FHS requires that you be able to mount /usr read-only, any programs that write log files or need spool or lock directories should write them to the /var directory. System log files such as messages and lastlog go in /var/log. The /var/lib/rpm directory also contains the RPM system databases. Lock files go in /var/lock, usually in directories particular for the program using the file. The /var/spool directory has subdirectories for various systems that need to store data files.

Special File Locations

Red Hat extends the FHS structure slightly to accommodate special files used by Red Hat Linux. The following list describes the major special file locations in Red Hat Linux:

♦ /var/lib/rpm/ — Most files pertaining to the Red Hat Package Manager (RPM) are kept in the directory. See Part V for more information on RPM.

♦ /var/spool/up2date/ — This directory contains files used by Red Hat Update Agent, including RPM header information for the system. This location may also be used to temporarily store RPMs downloaded while updating your system. For more information on Red Hat Network, see the Red Hat Network website at https://rhn.redhat.com/.

♦ /etc/sysconfig/ — This directory stores a variety of configuration information. Many scripts that run at boot time use the files in this directory.

♦ /initrd/ — This directory is empty after the system is booted, but is used as a critical mount point during the boot process.

> **WARNING** Do not remove the /initrd/ directory for any reason. Removing this directory will cause your system to fail to boot with a kernel panic error message.

The /proc File System

The Linux kernel has two primary functions: to control access to physical devices on the computer and to schedule when and how processes interact with these devices. The /proc/

directory contains a hierarchy of special files that represent the current state of the kernel —
allowing applications and users to peer into the kernel's view of the system.

Within the `/proc/` directory, one can find a wealth of information about the system hardware
and any processes currently running. In addition, some of the files within the `/proc/` directory
tree can be manipulated by users and applications to communicate configuration changes to
the kernel.

A Virtual File System

In Linux, all data are stored as files. Most users are familiar with the two primary types of
files: text and binary. But the `/proc/` directory contains another type of file called a *virtual
file*. It is for this reason that `/proc/` is often referred to as a virtual file system.

These virtual files have unique qualities. Most of them are listed as zero bytes in size and yet
when one is viewed, it can contain a large amount of information. In addition, most of the time
and date settings on virtual files reflect the current time and date, indicative of the fact they
constantly changing.

Virtual files such as `interrupts`, `/proc/meminfo`, `/proc/mounts`, and
`/proc/partitions` provide an up-to-the-moment glimpse of the system's hardware. Others,
like `/proc/filesystems` and the `/proc/sys/` directory provide system configuration
information and interfaces.

For organizational purposes, files containing information on a similar topic are grouped into
virtual directories and subdirectories. For instance, `/proc/ide/` contains information for all
physical IDE devices. Likewise, process directories contain information about each running
process on the system.

Viewing Virtual Files

By using the `cat`, `more`, or `less` commands on files within the `/proc/` directory, you can
immediately access an enormous amount of information about the system. For example, if you
want to see what sort of CPU your computer has, type **cat /proc/cpuinfo** and you will see
output similar to the following:

```
processor       : 0
vendor_id       : AuthenticAMD
cpu family      : 5
model           : 9
model name      : AMD-K6(tm) 3D+ Processor
stepping        : 1
cpu MHz         : 400.919
cache size      : 256 KB
fdiv_bug        : no
hlt_bug         : no
f00f_bug        : no
coma_bug        : no
fpu             : yes
fpu_exception   : yes
```

```
cpuid level    : 1
wp             : yes
flags          : fpu vme de pse tsc msr mce cx8 pge mmx syscall 3dnow k6_mtrr
bogomips : 799.53
```

When viewing different virtual files in the /proc/ file system, you will notice some of the information is easily understandable while some is not human-readable. This is in part why utilities exist to pull data from virtual files and display it in a useful way. Some examples of such applications are lspci, apm, free, and top.

> **NOTE** Some of the virtual files in the /proc/ directory are only readable by the root user.

As a general rule, most virtual files within the /proc/ directory are read-only. However, some can be used to adjust settings in the kernel. This is especially true for files in the /proc/sys/ subdirectory.

To change the value of a virtual file, use the echo command and a > symbol to redirect the new value to the file. For instance, to change your hostname on the fly, you can type:

```
echo name.example.com > /proc/sys/kernel/hostname
```

Other files act as binary or boolean switches. For instance, if you type **cat /proc/sys/net/ipv4/ip_forward**, you will see either a 0 or a 1. A 0 indicates the kernel is not forwarding network packets. By using the echo command to change the value of the ip_forward file to 1, you can immediately turn packet forwarding on.

Directories in /proc/

Common groups of information concerning the kernel are grouped into directories and subdirectories within the /proc/ directory.

/proc Directories

Every /proc/ directory contains a number of directories numerical names. A listing of them may start off like this:

```
dr-xr-xr-x   3   root     root       0 Feb 13 01:28 1
dr-xr-xr-x   3   root     root       0 Feb 13 01:28 1010
dr-xr-xr-x   3   xfs      xfs        0 Feb 13 01:28 1087
dr-xr-xr-x   3   daemon   daemon     0 Feb 13 01:28 1123
dr-xr-xr-x   3   root     root       0 Feb 13 01:28 11307
dr-xr-xr-x   3   apache   apache     0 Feb 13 01:28 13660
dr-xr-xr-x   3   rpc      rpc        0 Feb 13 01:28 637
dr-xr-xr-x   3   rpcuser  rpcuser    0 Feb 13 01:28 666
```

These directories are called *process directories* because they are named after a program's process ID and contain information specific to that process. The owner and group of each process directory is set to the user running the process. When the process is terminated, its /proc/ process directory vanishes.

Other than the process's name and ID, the state (such as S (sleeping) or R (running) and user/group ID running the process is available, as well as much more detailed data regarding memory usage.

/proc/self/

The /proc/self/ directory is a link to the currently running process. This allows a process to look at itself without having to know its process ID. Within a shell environment, a listing of the /proc/self/ directory produces the same contents as listing the process directory for that process.

/proc/bus/

This directory contains information specific to the various buses available on the system. So, for example, on a standard system containing ISA, PCI, and USB busses, current data on each of these buses is available in its directory under /proc/bus/.

The contents of the subdirectories and files available vary greatly on the precise configuration of your system. However, each of the directories for each of the bus types has at least one directory for each bus of that type. These individual bus directories, usually signified with numbers such as 00, contain binary files that refer to the various devices available on that bus.

For example, a system with a USB bus but no USB devices connected to it has a /proc/bus/usb/ directory containing several files.

The /proc/bus/usb/ directory contains files that track the various devices on any USB busses, as well as the drivers required to use them. The /proc/bus/usb/001/ directory contains all devices on the first USB bus. By looking at the contents of the devices file, you can identify the USB root hub on the motherboard.

/proc/driver/

This directory contains information for specific drivers in use by the kernel. A common file found here is rtc, which provides output from the driver for the system's Real Time Clock (RTC), the device that keeps the time while the system is switched off. For more information about the RTC, review /usr/src/linux-2.4/Documentation/rtc.txt.

/proc/fs

This directory shows which file systems are exported. If you are running an NFS server, you can type **cat /proc/fs/nfs/exports** to view the file systems being shared and the permissions granted for those file systems.

/proc/ide/

This directory holds information about IDE devices on the system. Each IDE channel is represented as a separate directory, such as /proc/ide/ide0 and /proc/ide/ide1. In addition, a drivers file is also available, providing the version number of the various drivers used on the IDE channels:

```
ide-cdrom version 4.59
```

```
ide-floppy version 0.97
ide-disk version 1.10
```

Many chipsets also provide an informational file in this directory that gives additional data concerning the drives connected through the channels. For example, a generic Intel PIIX4 Ultra 33 chipset produces a `/proc/ide/piix` that tells you whether DMA or UDMA is enabled for the devices on the IDE channels.

The Device Directory

Within each IDE channel directory is a device directory. The name of the device directory corresponds to the drive letter in the `/dev/` directory. For instance, the first IDE drive on ide0 would be hda.

> **Note** There is a symlink to each of these device directories in the `/proc/ide/` directory.

Each device directory contains a collection of information and statistics. The contents of these directories vary according to the type of device connected. Some of the more useful files common to many devices include:

- ♦ cache — The device's cache.
- ♦ capacity — The capacity of the device, in 512 byte blocks.
- ♦ driver — The driver and version used to control the device.
- ♦ geometry — The physical and logical geometry of the device.
- ♦ media — The type of device, such as a disk.
- ♦ model — The model name or number of the device.
- ♦ settings — A collection of current parameters of the device. This file usually contains useful technical information.

/proc/irq/

This directory is used to set IRQ-to-CPU affinity, which allows you to connect a particular IRQ to only one CPU. Alternatively, you can exclude a CPU from handling any IRQs. Each IRQ has its own directory, allowing for individual configuration of each IRQ. The `/proc/irq/prof_cpu_mask` file is a bitmask that contains the default values for the smp_affinity file in the IRQ directory. The values in smp_affinity specify which CPUs handle that particular IRQ. `/usr/src/linux-2.4/Documentation/filesystems/proc.txt` contains more information.

/proc/net/

This directory provides a comprehensive look at various networking parameters and statistics. Each of the files covers a specific range of information related to networking on the system.

/proc/scsi/

This directory is analogous to the `/proc/ide/` directory only it is for connected SCSI devices. The primary file in this directory is `/proc/scsi/scsi`, which contains a list of every recognized SCSI device. From this listing, the type of devices, as well as the model name, vendor, SCSI channel, and ID data is available.

Each SCSI driver used by the system has its own directory in /proc/scsi/, which contains files specific to each SCSI controller using that driver. So, for the Adaptec AIC-7880 Ultra SCSI host adapter, for example, the aic7xxx and megaraid directories are present because those two drivers are being utilized. The files in each of the directories typically contain I/O address range, IRQ, and statistics for the particular SCSI controller using that driver. Each controller can report a different type and amount of information.

/proc/sys/

The /proc/sys/ directory is different from others in /proc/ because it not only provides information about the system but also allows you to make configuration changes to the kernel. This allows the administrator of the machine to immediately enable and disable kernel features. The /proc/sys/ directory contains several subdirectories that control different aspects of a running kernel.

> **WARNING** Use caution when changing settings on a production system using the various files in the /proc/sys/ directory. Changing the wrong setting may render the kernel unstable, requiring a reboot of the system. For this reason, be sure you know the valid options for that file and the expected outcome before attempting to change a value in /proc/sys/.

/proc/sys/dev/

This directory provides parameters for particular devices on the system. Most systems have at least two directories, cdrom and raid, but customized kernels can have others, such as parport, which provides the ability to share one parallel port between multiple device drivers.

The cdrom directory contains a file called info that reveals a number of important CD-ROM parameters. Various files in /proc/sys/dev/cdrom, such as autoclose and checkmedia, can be used to control the system's CD-ROM. Use the echo command to enable or disable to disable these features.

If RAID support is compiled into the kernel, a /proc/sys/dev/raid/ directory will be available with at least two files in it: speed_limit_min and speed_limit_max. These settings determine how much to accelerate the RAID device for particularly I/O-intensive tasks, such as resyncing the disks.

/proc/sys/fs/

This directory contains an array of options and information concerning various aspects of the file system, including quota, file handle, inode, and dentry information. The binfmt_misc directory is used to provide kernel support for miscellaneous binary formats.

/proc/sys/kernel/

This directory contains a variety of different configuration files that directly affect the operation of the kernel.

/proc/sys/net/

This directory contains assorted directories concerning various networking topics. Various configurations at the time of kernel compilation make different directories available here, such as `appletalk`, `ethernet`, `ipv4`, `ipx`, and `ipv6`. Within these directories you can adjust the assorted networking values for that configuration on a running system. Additional information about these directories and the possible values for their configuration files can be found in `/usr/src/linux-2.4/Documentation/filesystems/proc.txt`.

> **CAUTION** An erroneous change to these files may affect your remote connectivity to the system.

/proc/sys/vm/

This directory facilitates the configuration of the Linux kernel's virtual memory (VM) subsystem. The kernel makes extensive and intelligent use of virtual memory, which is commonly called swap space. The `/usr/src/linux-2.4/Documentation/sysctl/vm.txt` file contains additional information on these various files.

/proc/sysvipc/

This directory contains information about System V IPC resources. The files in this directory relate to System V IPC calls for messages (`msg`), semaphores (`sem`), and shared memory (`shm`).

/proc/tty/

This directory contains information about the available and currently used tty devices on the system. Originally called a *teletype device*, any character-based data terminals are called *tty devices*. In Linux, there are three different kinds of tty devices:

♦ *Serial devices* — These tty devices are used with serial connections, such as over a modem or using a serial cable.

♦ *Virtual terminals* — These tty devices create the common console connection, such as the virtual consoles available by pressing Alt-Function key at the system console.

♦ *Pseudo terminals* — These tty devices create a two-way communication that is used by some higher level applications such as X11. The `drivers` file is a list of the current tty devices in use.

Additional /proc Resources

Most of the best `/proc/` documentation is available on your system:

♦ `/usr/src/linux-2.4/Documentation/filesystems/proc.txt` — Contains assorted but limited information about all aspects of the `/proc/` directory.

♦ `/usr/src/linux-2.4/Documentation/sysrq.txt` — An overview of System Request Key options.

♦ `/usr/src/linux-2.4/Documentation/sysctl` — A directory containing a variety of `sysctl` tips, including modifying values that concern the kernel (`kernel.txt`), accessing file systems (`fs.txt`), and virtual memory use (`vm.txt`).

♦ `/usr/src/linux-2.4/Documentation/networking/ip-sysctl.txt` — A look at various IP networking options.

♦ `/usr/src/linux-2.4` — Some of the most authoritative information on `/proc/` can be found by reading the kernel source code. Make sure the kernel-source RPM is installed on your system and look in the `/usr/src/linux-2.4` directory for the source code.

♦ `http://www.linuxhq.com` — This site maintains a complete database of source, patches, and documentation for various versions of the Linux kernel.

Chapter 24

Comparing Common MS-DOS and Linux Commands

Many Linux commands typed at a shell prompt are similar to the commands you would type in MS-DOS. In fact, some commands are identical.

This chapter provides common commands used at the MS-DOS prompt in Windows and their counterparts in Linux. Basic examples of how the commands are used at the Linux shell prompt are also provided. Note that these commands usually have a number of options. To learn more about each command, read its associated man page (for example, type **man ls** at the shell prompt to read about the ls command).

Table 24-1: A Comparison of MS-DOS and Linux Commands

Command's Purpose	MS-DOS	Linux	Linux Example
Copies files	copy	Cp	cp thisfile.txt /home/directory
Moves files	move	Mv	mv thisfile.txt /home/directory
Lists files	dir	ls	ls
Clears screen	cls	clear	clear
Closes prompt window	exit	exit	exit
Displays or sets date	date	date	date
Deletes files	del	rm	rm file.txt
"Echoes" output on the screen	echo	echo	echo message
Edits files with simple text editor	edit	pico	pico file.txt
Compares the contents of files	fc	diff	diff file1 file2

Command's Purpose	MS-DOS	Linux	Linux Example
Finds a string of text in a file	`find`	`grep`	`grep word_or_phrase file.txt`
Formats a diskette	`format a:` (if diskette is in A:)	`mke2fs` or `mformat`	`/sbin/mke2fs /dev/fd0` (`/dev/fd0` is the Linux equivalent of A:)
Displays command help	`command /?`	`man`	`man command`
Creates a directory	`mkdir`	`mkdir`	`mkdir directory`
View a file	`more`	`less`	`less file.txt`
Renames a file	`ren`	`mv`	`mv this_file.txt that_file.txt`
Displays your location in the file system	`chdir`	`pwd`	`pwd`
Changes directories with a specified path (absolute path)	`cd pathname`	`cd pathname`	`cd /directory/directory`
Changes directories with a relative path	`cd ..`	`cd ..`	`cd ..`
Displays the time	`time`	`date`	`date`
Shows amount of RAM and use	`mem`	`free`	`free`

Chapter 25

Gathering System Information

Sometimes you may need to gather essential system information. For example, you should know how to find the amount of free memory, the amount of available hard drive space, how your hard drive is partitioned, and what processes are running. This chapter discusses how to retrieve this type of information from your Red Hat Linux system using simple commands and a few simple programs.

System Processes

The ps ax command displays a list of current system processes, including processes owned by other users. To display the owner of the processes along with the processes themselves, use the command ps aux. This list is a static list; in other words, it is a snapshot of what is running when you invoke the command.

If you want a constantly updated list of running processes, use the top command (as described later in this section).

The ps output can be long. To prevent it from scrolling off the screen, you can pipe it through less:

```
ps aux | less
```

You can use the ps command in combination with the grep command to see if a process is running. For example, to determine if emacs is running, use the following command:

```
ps ax | grep emacs
```

The top command displays currently running processes and important information about them, including their memory and CPU usage. The list is both real-time and interactive. An example of top's output is as follows:

```
  6:14pm up 2 days, 19:29, 5 users, load average: 0.10, 0.06, 0.07
71 processes: 68 sleeping, 2 running, 1 zombie, 0 stopped
CPU states:  2.7% user,  0.5% system,  0.0% nice,  96.6% idle
Mem:   256812K av,  252016K used,   4796K free,  97228K shrd,  43300K buff
Swap:  265032K av,    1328K used,  263704K free                86180K cached

  PID USER     PRI  NI  SIZE  RSS SHARE STAT %CPU %MEM   TIME COMMAND
15775 joe        5   0 11028  10M  3192 S     1.5  4.2   0:46 emacs
14429 root      15   0 63620  62M  3284 R     0.5 24.7  63:33 X
```

```
17372 joe      11   0  1056 1056   840 R    0.5  0.4   0:00 top
17356 joe       2   0  4104 4104  3244 S    0.3  1.5   0:00 gnome-terminal
14461 joe       1   0  3584 3584  2104 S    0.1  1.3   0:17 sawfish
    1 root      0   0   544  544   476 S    0.0  0.2   0:06 init
    2 root      0   0     0    0     0 SW   0.0  0.0   0:00 kflushd
    3 root      1   0     0    0     0 SW   0.0  0.0   0:24 kupdate
    4 root      0   0     0    0     0 SW   0.0  0.0   0:00 kpiod
    5 root      0   0     0    0     0 SW   0.0  0.0   0:29 kswapd
  347 root      0   0   556  556   460 S    0.0  0.2   0:00 syslogd
  357 root      0   0   712  712   360 S    0.0  0.2   0:00 klogd
  372 bin       0   0   692  692   584 S    0.0  0.2   0:00 portmap
  388 root      0   0     0    0     0 SW   0.0  0.0   0:00 lockd
  389 root      0   0     0    0     0 SW   0.0  0.0   0:00 rpciod
  414 root      0   0   436  432   372 S    0.0  0.1   0:00 apmd
  476 root      0   0   592  592   496 S    0.0  0.2   0:00 automount
```

To exit top, press the q key.

Table 25-1 lists some of the more useful interactive commands that you can use with top.

Table 25-1: Interactive top Commands

Command	Description
Spacebar	Immediately refresh the display.
h	Display a help screen.
k	Kill a process. You will be prompted for the process ID and the signal to send to it.
n	Change the number of processes displayed. You will be prompted to enter the number.
u	Sort by user.
M	Sort by memory usage.
P	Sort by CPU usage.

If you prefer a graphical interface for top, you can use the GNOME System Monitor. To start the System Monitor from the desktop, click the Main Menu button and choose System Tools ⇨ System Monitor (or type **gnome-system-monitor** at a shell prompt from within the X Window System). Then select the Process Listing tab.

The GNOME System Monitor allows you to search for processes in the list of running process as well as view all processes, your processes, or active processes.

To learn more about a process, select it and click the More Info button. Details about the process will be displayed at the bottom of the window.

To stop a process, select it and click End Process. This function is useful for processes that have stopped responding to user input.

To sort by the information in a specific column, click on the name of the column. The column that the information is sorted by appears in a darker gray color.

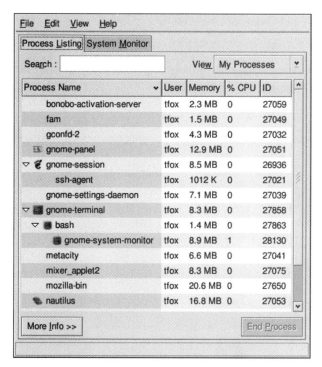

Figure 25-1. GNOME System Monitor — Process Listing Tab

By default, the GNOME System Monitor does not display threads. To change this preference, choose Edit ⇨ Preferences, click the Process Listing tab, and select Show Threads. The preference also allows you to configure the update interval, what type of information to display about each process by default, and the colors of the system monitor graphs.

Memory Usage

The free command displays the total amount of physical memory and swap space for the system as well as the amount of memory that is used, free, shared, in kernel buffers, and cached. Following is a sample output of the free command:

	total	used	free	shared	buffers	cached
Mem:	256812	240668	16144	105176	50520	81848
-/+ buffers/cache:		108300	148512			
Swap:	265032	780	264252			

Using the `free -m` command shows the same information in megabytes, which are easier to read.

	total	used	free	shared	buffers	cached
Mem:	250	235	15	102	49	79
-/+ buffers/cache:		105	145			
Swap:	258	0	258			

If you prefer a graphical interface for `free`, you can use the GNOME System Monitor. To start the System Monitor from the desktop, click the Main Menu button and choose System Tools ➪ System Monitor (or type **gnome-system-monitor** at a shell prompt from within X Window System). Then choose the System Monitor tab.

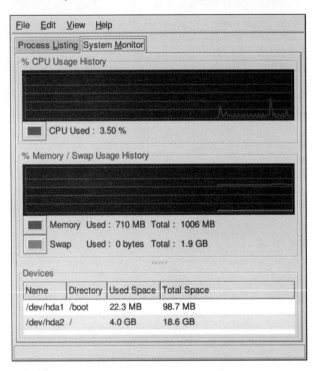

Figure 25-2. GNOME System Monitor — System Monitor Tab

File Systems

The `df` command reports the system's disk space usage. If you type the command `df` at a shell prompt, the output looks similar to the following:

Filesystem	1k-blocks	Used	Available	Use%	Mounted on
/dev/hda2	10325716	2902060	6899140	30%	/
/dev/hda1	15554	8656	6095	59%	/boot
/dev/hda3	20722644	2664256	17005732	14%	/home
none	256796	0	256796	0%	/dev/shm

By default, df shows the partition size in 1 kilobyte blocks and the amount of used and available disk space in kilobytes. To view the information in megabytes and gigabytes, use the -h option with the df command. The -h option stands for *human-readable format*. The output for the df -h command looks similar to the following:

Filesystem	Size	Used	Avail	Use%	Mounted on
/dev/hda2	9.8G	2.8G	6.5G	30%	/
/dev/hda1	15M	8.5M	5.9M	59%	/boot
/dev/hda3	20G	2.6G	16G	14%	/home
none	251M	0	250M	0%	/dev/shm

In the list of partitions (the Mounted on column), you can see an entry for /dev/shm. This entry represents the system's virtual memory file system.

The du command displays the estimated amount of space being used by files in a directory. If you type du at a shell prompt, the disk usage for each of the subdirectories will be displayed in a list. The grand total for the current directory and subdirectories will also be shown as the last line in the list. If you do not want to see the totals for all the subdirectories, use the command du -hs to see only the grand total for the directory in human-readable format.

Use the du --help command to see more options.

To view the system's partitions and disk space usage in a graphical format, use the System Monitor tab (as shown at the bottom of Figure 25-2).

Hardware

If you are having trouble configuring your hardware or just want to know what hardware is in your system, you can use the Hardware Browser application to display the hardware that can be probed.

To start the program from the desktop, click the Main Menu button and choose System Tools ⇨ Hardware Browser (or type **hwbrowser** at a shell prompt) and enter the root password when the system requests it. The Hardware Browser displays your CD-ROM devices, floppy disks, hard drives (and their partitions), network devices, pointing devices, system devices, and video cards. Click on the desired category name in the left menu and the information will be displayed.

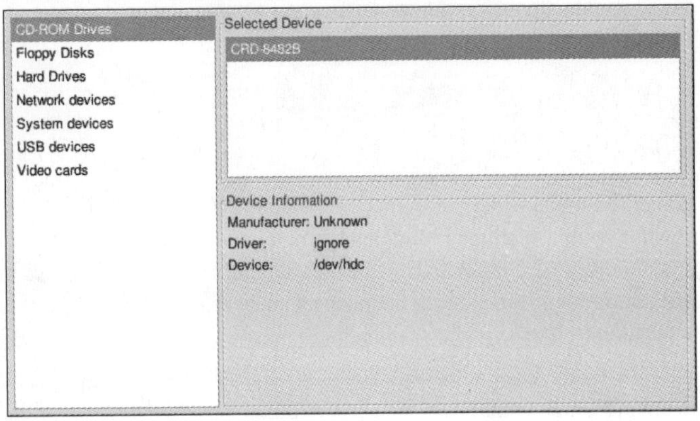

Figure 25-3. Hardware Browser

You can also use the lspci command (but only as the root user) to list all PCI devices.

> **TIP** Use the command lspci -v for more verbose information or lspci -vv for very verbose output.

For example, lspci can be used to determine the manufacturer, model, and memory size of a system's video card, as follows:

```
01:00.0 VGA compatible controller: Matrox Graphics, Inc. MGA G400 AGP (rev 04)   (progif
00 [VGA])
Subsystem: Matrox Graphics, Inc. Millennium G400 Dual Head Max
Flags: medium devsel, IRQ 16
Memory at f4000000 (32-bit, prefetchable) [size=32M]
Memory at fcffc000 (32-bit, non-prefetchable) [size=16K]
Memory at fc000000 (32-bit, non-prefetchable) [size=8M]
Expansion ROM at 80000000 [disabled] [size=64K]
Capabilities: [dc] Power Management version 2
Capabilities: [f0] AGP version 2.0
```

The lspci command is also useful to determine the network card in your system if you do not know the manufacturer or model number.

Additional Resources

To learn more about gathering system information, refer to the following resources:

♦ ps --help — Displays a list of options that can be used with ps.

♦ /proc — The contents of the /proc directory can also be used to gather more detailed system information. See Chapter 23 for more information about the /proc directory.

♦ top *manual page* — Type **man top** at a shell prompt to learn more about top and its many options.

- ◆ free *manual page* — Type **man free** at a shell prompt to learn more about free and its many options.

- ◆ df *manual page* — Type **man df** at a shell prompt to learn more about the df command and its many options.

- ◆ du *manual page* — Type **man du** at a shell prompt to learn more about the du command and its many options.

Part VII

Appendixes

Red Hat Linux comes with many applications, as well as a wealth of resources for helping you get started with Red Hat Linux.

This part helps you rescue your Red Hat Linux installation if you need to, use the KDE as an alternative to the default Red Hat Linux graphical environment, and learn about the CD-ROMs that come with this book. It also contains references to help you perform common tasks such as configuring a dual-boot system, partitioning your hard disk, and working with the X Window System.

Appendix A: Rescue Mode

Appendix B: The KDE Desktop Environment

Appendix C: Configuring a Dual-Boot System

Appendix D: An Introduction to Disk Partitions

Appendix E: The X Window System

Appendix F: About the CD-ROMs

Appendix A

Rescue Mode

When things go wrong, there are ways to fix problems. However, these methods require that you understand the system well. This chapter describes how to boot into rescue mode and single user mode, where you can use your own knowledge to repair the system.

What Is Rescue Mode?

Rescue mode provides the ability to boot a small Linux environment entirely from a diskette, CD-ROM, or using some other method. As the name implies, rescue mode is provided to rescue you from something.

During normal operation, your Red Hat Linux system uses files located on your system's hard drive to do everything — run programs, store your files, and more. However, there may be times when you are unable to get Linux running completely enough to access its files on your system's hard drive. Using rescue mode, you can access the files stored on your system's hard drive even if you cannot actually run Linux from that hard drive.

Normally, you will need to get into rescue mode for one of two reasons:

♦ You are unable to boot Linux.

♦ You are having hardware or software problems and you want to get a few important files off your system's hard drive.

In the following sections we take a closer look at each of these scenarios.

What to Do if You Are Unable to Boot Linux

This problem is often caused by the installation of another operating system — such as Windows — after you have installed Red Hat Linux. Some other operating systems assume that you have no other operating systems on your computer, and they overwrite the Master Boot Record (MBR) that originally contained the GRUB or LILO boot loader. If the boot loader is overwritten in this manner, you will not be able to boot Red Hat Linux unless you can get into rescue mode.

Another common problem occurs when using a partitioning tool to resize a partition or create a new partition from free space after installation and it changes the order of your partitions. If the partition number of your / (root) partition changes, the boot loader will not be able to find it to mount the partition. To fix this problem, boot into rescue mode and modify /boot/grub/grub.conf if you are using GRUB or /etc/lilo.conf if you are using

LILO. See the "Booting Rescue Mode" section later in this chapter for instructions on how to boot into rescue mode.

Hardware/Software Problems

This category includes a wide variety of situations. Two examples include failing hard drives and forgetting to run LILO after building a new kernel (if you are using LILO as your boot loader). If you are using GRUB, you do not have to execute a command to reread the GRUB configuration file. However, if you specify an invalid root device or kernel in the GRUB configuration file, you might not know until you reboot your computer.

In these situations, you may be unable to boot Red Hat Linux. If you can get into rescue mode, you might be able to resolve the problem or at least get copies of your most important files.

Booting Rescue Mode

To boot your system in rescue mode, boot from a Red Hat Linux boot disk or the Red Hat Linux CD-ROM #1 and enter the following command at the installation boot prompt:

```
boot: linux rescue
```

You can get to the installation boot prompt in one of these ways:

- ◆ By booting your system from an installation boot diskette made from the boot.img image. This method requires that the Red Hat Linux CD-ROM #1 be inserted as the rescue image or that the rescue image be on the hard drive as an ISO image.

> **TIP** To create an installation boot diskette, insert a blank floppy disk and use the images/boot.img file on the Red Hat Linux CD-ROM #1 with the command dd if=boot.img of=/dev/fd0.

- ◆ By booting your system from the Red Hat Linux CD-ROM #1.
- ◆ By booting from a network disk made from the bootnet.img or PCMCIA boot disk made from pcmcia.img. You can only do this if your network connection is working. You will need to identify the network host and transfer type. For an explanation of how to specify this information, refer to Chapter 2.

After booting off of a boot disk or Red Hat Linux CD-ROM #1 and providing a valid rescue image, you will see the following message:

```
The rescue environment will now attempt to find your Red Hat
Linux installation and mount it under the directory
/mnt/sysimage. You can then make any changes required to your
system. If you want to proceed with this step choose
'Continue'. You can also choose to mount your filesystem
read-only instead of read-write by choosing 'Read-only'.
If for some reason this process fails you can choose 'Skip'
and this step will be skipped and you will go directly to a
command shell.
```

If you select Continue, Linux will attempt to mount your file system under the directory
`/mnt/sysimage`.

If it fails to mount a partition, it will notify you. If you select Read-Only, it will attempt to
mount your file system in read-only mode. If you select Skip, your file system will not be
mounted. Choose Skip if you think your file system is corrupted.

After Entering Rescue Mode...

After you have your system in rescue mode, a prompt appears on VC (virtual console) 1 and
VC 2 (use the Ctrl-Alt-F1 key combination to access VC 1 and Ctrl-Alt-F2 to access VC 2) as
follows:

```
sh-2.05a#
```

If you selected Continue to mount your partitions automatically and they were mounted
successfully, you are in single-user mode.

To mount a Linux partition manually inside rescue mode, create a directory such as `/foo` and
type the following command:

```
mount -t ext3 /dev/hda5 /foo
```

In the above command, `/foo` is a directory that you have created and `/dev/hda5` is the
partition you want to mount.

> **NOTE** If the partition is of type `ext2`, replace `ext3` with `ext2`.

If you do not know the names of your partitions, use the following command to list them:

```
fdisk -l
```

If your file system is mounted and you want to make your system the root partition, use the
command `chroot /mnt/sysimage`. This is useful if you need to run commands such as `rpm`
that require your root partition to be mounted as `/`. To exit the `chroot` environment, type **exit**
to return to the prompt.

Commands You Can Run in Rescue Mode

From the `bash#` prompt, you can run many useful commands, including the following:

anaconda	gzip	mkfs.ext2	probe
badblocks	head	mknod	ps
bash	hwclock	mkraid	python2.2
cat	ifconfig	mkswap	raidstart
chattr	init	mlabel	raidstop
chmod	insmod	mmd	rcp
chroot	less	mmount	rlogin
clock	ln	mmove	rm
collage	loader	modprobe	rmmod
cp	ls	mount	route

cpio	lsattr	mpartition	rpm
dd	lsmod	mrd	rsh
ddcprobe	mattrib	mread	sed
depmode	mbadblocks	mren	sh
df	mcd	mshowfat	sync
e2fsck	mcopy	mt	tac
fdisk	mdel	mtools	tail
fsck	mdeltree	mtype	tar
fsck.ext2	mdir	mv	touch
fsck.ext3	mdu	mzip	traceroute
ftp	mformat	open	umount
gnome-pty-helper	minfo	parted	uncpio
grep	mkdir	pico	uniq
gunzip	mke2fs	ping	zcat

Booting Single-User Mode

You may be able to boot single-user mode directly. If your system boots but does not allow you to log in when it has completed booting, try single-user mode.

Booting into Single-User Mode in GRUB

If you are using GRUB, use the following steps to boot into single-user mode:

1. If you have a GRUB password configured, type **p** and enter the password.
2. Select Red Hat Linux with the version of the kernel that you wish to boot and type **e** for edit. You will be presented with a list of items in the configuration file for the title you just selected.
3. Select the line that starts with kernel and type **e** to edit the line.
4. Go to the end of the line and type **single** as a separate word (press the spacebar and then type **single**). Press Enter to exit edit mode.
5. Back at the GRUB screen, type **b** to boot into single user mode.

Booting into Single-User Mode in LILO

If you are using LILO, specify one of these options at the LILO boot prompt (if you are using the graphical LILO, you must press Ctrl-x to exit the graphical screen and go to the boot: prompt):

```
boot: linux single
boot: linux emergency
```

In single-user mode, your computer boots to runlevel 1. Your local file systems will be mounted, but your network will not be activated. You will have a usable system maintenance shell.

In emergency mode, you are booted into the most minimal environment possible. The root file system will be mounted read-only, and almost nothing will be set up. The main advantage of emergency mode over single-user mode is that your `init` files are not loaded. If `init` is corrupted or not working, you can still mount file systems to recover data that could be lost during a reinstallation.

Appendix B

The KDE Desktop Environment

KDE, which stands for the *K Desktop Environment*, is a graphical desktop environment that allows you to access your Red Hat Linux system and applications using your mouse and keyboard.

This chapter covers the fundamental aspects of using KDE, including:

◆ System navigation

◆ Working with files and applications

◆ Customizing the desktop to suit your needs

This book focuses more on the default Red Hat desktop environment (which is based on GNOME) that is described in detail in Chapter 6. If you would like to learn more about KDE than this chapter covers, visit the official website at the following URL:

```
http://www.kde.org
```

TIP If you have both KDE and GNOME installed on your system, you can use applications from both environments. For example, you can use the GNOME email and personal information management suite, Evolution, while you are working in KDE, or use K-Mail, the KDE email application, in GNOME.

Setting Up KDE

To use KDE in Red Hat Linux, you either need to have installed KDE during the installation of your Red Hat Linux system (as described in Chapter 2) or you need to add the KDE package to Red Hat Linux after the installation. (See Part V for more information about adding packages to Red Hat Linux.)

The first time you log into KDE (refer to Chapter 5 for more information about logging into your Red Hat Linux machine), a setup wizard will appear that allows you to set up your language and locale settings. Figure B-1 shows the welcome screen of the KDE setup wizard.

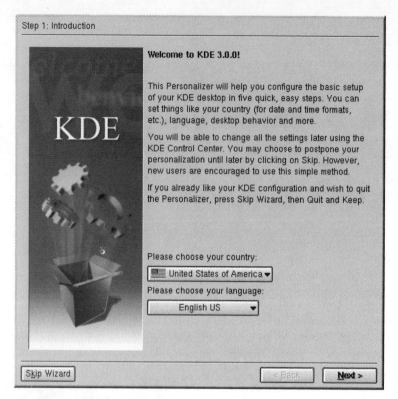

Figure B-1. The KDE Setup Wizard

Using the Desktop

After setting up KDE using the wizard, your default desktop will look similar to Figure B-2.

The KDE desktop displays application launchers, document windows, file folders, and so on. You can also access the Main Menu and configure the desktop to suit your needs.

The long bar across the bottom of the desktop is called the *Panel*. The Panel contains application launchers, status indicators, and the desktop manager. You can have up to 16 desktops running at the same time in KDE. The Panel's taskbar shows your currently running applications.

Icons located on the desktop can be files, folders, device links, or application launchers. Click on an icon to open the associated resource.

Figure B-2. A Typical KDE Desktop

The KDE desktop works similarly to other graphical desktop environments. You can drag and drop files and application icons to any location on the desktop. You can also add new icons for all types of applications and resources to the desktop, Panel, or file manager. The desktop itself is also highly customizable. You can change the appearance of buttons, window and frame decorations, and backgrounds easily. Configuration tools are also available that allow you to customize the way the desktop behaves at events such as single- and double-clicking mouse buttons and combining (also called *chording*) keystrokes to create time-saving shortcuts.

The default KDE desktop displays icons for the trash can, your home directory, the KDE Control Panel, and a link to the Red Hat website. You can access any one of these resources by clicking on the associated icon.

When you right-click on these icons, you will see several options for working with these resources, such as Delete, Rename, Move to Trash, and Copy.

You can drag and drop unwanted items such as files to the Trash icon if you no longer need them. Right-click on the trash can and select Empty Trash Bin to delete the items from your system permanently.

Using the Panel

The Panel stretches across the bottom of the desktop. By default, it contains the Main Menu icon (the big Red Fedora) and quick-launch icons for logging out, opening a terminal window, and other common applications and utilities.

Figure B-3. The KDE Panel

The Panel is highly configurable. You can add and remove buttons that launch applications easily. To do so, right-click on the Panel and choose Panel ⇨ Configuration to open the Panel Settings.

Other tabs in Settings contain options to further customize your Panel. Click Help for more information on these options.

Applications and utilities can be added easily to the Panel. To add an application to the Panel, right-click on the Panel and choose Panel ⇨ Add. Then select Button, Applet, Extension, or Special Button, and make your choice from the corresponding menus.

Using the KDE Main Menu

The Main Menu is the central point for using KDE. Clicking the Main Menu button on the Panel displays a large master menu from which you can perform tasks such as launching applications, finding files, and configuring your desktop. The Main Menu also contains several submenus that organize applications and tools into several categories, including Extras, Graphics, Internet, and Games.

From the Main Menu, you can also lock your screen (which will display a password-protected screensaver), run applications from a command line, and log out of your KDE session.

Using Applets

Applets are small applications that run on the Panel. There are several types of applets that perform functions such as system/network monitoring, launching applications by typing commands in a text box, and even checking the local weather.

There are some applets that run on the Panel by default. The following sections cover those default applets in detail.

Working with Multiple Desktops

By default, KDE provides four desktops (sometimes called *workspaces*) that you can use to display multiple applications without having to crowd all of them onto one desktop. Each desktop can hold icons, open applications, and even have individually customized backgrounds.

For example, while you are writing a message in KMail on Desktop 1, you can have Konqueror browsing the Web on Desktop 2, the KWord word processor open on Desktop 3, and so on.

You can change the number and names of desktops available in KDE by following these steps:

1. Right-click on the desktop; you will see a brief menu of actions you can take.
2. Select Configure Desktop; the KDE Panel configuration tool will open.
3. Click the Number of Desktops tab.

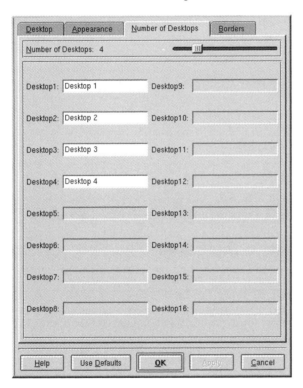

Figure B-4. The Number of Desktops Tab in the Panel Configuration

You can change the names of your desktops (from Desktop 1, Desktop 2, etc.) by deleting the default names and typing a new name in each desktop's corresponding text box. You can also change the number of desktops available to you by adjusting the slider at the top of the Desktops tab. For more desktops, drag the bar to the right; for fewer desktops, drag the bar to the left.

The Desktop, Appearance, and Borders tabs are where you can make various desktop configuration selections, like icon arrangement and font size.

After you make any adjustments to your desktop configuration, click Apply to save the changes and close the Panel configuration tool.

Buttons for your desktops appear on the panel in the Desktop Pager. Simply click on the tiles to move to a different desktop.

> **TIP** You can use the keyboard combination of the Ctrl and Function keys to switch desktops. For example, Ctrl-F2 will switch you from Desktop 1 to Desktop 2, Ctrl-F3 will take you to Desktop 3, and so on.

Viewing the Taskbar

The taskbar displays all running applications — both minimized and on the desktop.

Figure B-5. Applications on the Taskbar

You can maximize running applications or bring them to the front of your working windows by clicking on the associated item on the taskbar.

> **TIP** Another way to bring minimized or background windows to the front is to use the Alt and Tab keys. To pick an item from the taskbar, hold down Alt-Tab. To scroll through the tasks, hold down the Alt key, while pressing the Tab key in succession. When you have found the task you want to maximize and bring to the front, release both keys.

Adding Icons and Applets to the Panel

To further customize the Panel for your particular needs, you can include additional applets and icons (launchers).

To add an applet to the panel, click the Main Menu button and choose Configure Panel ⇨ Add ⇨ Applet. Choose the applet you want from the menu and it will immediately appear on the Panel. You can move the applet by clicking on the applet bar and choosing Move from the menu.

To add a new launcher to the Panel, click the Main Menu button and choose Configure Panel ⇨ Add ⇨ Button and choose the application or resource you wish to add to the Panel. This will automatically add an icon to the Panel.

Configuring the Panel

You can hide the panel automatically or manually, place it on any edge of your desktop, change its size and color, and change the way it behaves. To alter the default Panel settings, click the Main Menu button and choose Configure Panel ⇨ Preferences. The Settings window will appear, allowing you to adjust all Panel settings, or any one of the specific properties (Position, Hiding, Look & Feel, Menus, and so on).

Working with Konqueror

Konqueror is the file manager and Web browser for the KDE desktop. Konqueror allows you to configure your KDE desktop, configure your Red Hat Linux system, play multimedia files, browse digital images, surf the Web, and more, all from one interface. This section explains some of the ways Konqueror can help you work with and enjoy your Red Hat Linux system.

Managing Files with Konqueror

To start Konqueror for file management, click on your home directory icon. Konqueror will open up in a window on your desktop, allowing you to navigate through your home directory and throughout your Red Hat Linux file system. After exploring, you can return to your home directory by clicking the Home button on the toolbar.

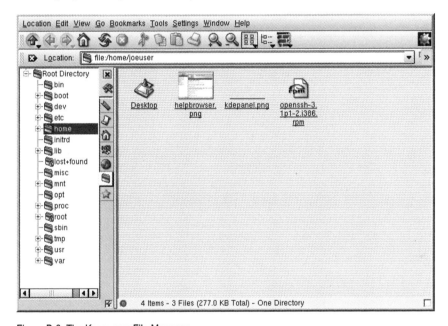

Figure B-6. The Konqueror File Manager

You can navigate through the file system by clicking on folders within the main window frame or through the hierarchical file system viewer on the navigation panel, as shown in Figure B-6. Files and folders in the main window frame can be moved or copied to another folder or sent to the trash.

TIP You can also delete files and folders by right-clicking on the desired item and choosing Delete.

Konqueror can also generate thumbnail icons for text, images, PostScript/PDF files, and Web files. You can even generate preview sounds from digital music files. From the toolbar choose View ⇨ Preview and choose the file types for which you would like to see thumbnail icons generated. Thumbnails will be immediately generated for any associated files in the Konqueror window.

The Navigation Panel

Another useful feature of Konqueror is the *navigation panel*, which appears on the left side of the Konqueror window by default. The navigation panel makes many of your personalized resources available to you in convenient tabbed icons. Figure B-7 shows the navigation panel.

Figure B-7. Working with the Navigation Panel

The navigation panel lets you access your Web bookmarks, browsing history, network resources, file system, and has a built-in media player for playing multimedia files without having to open a separate application. The navigation panel makes Konqueror an efficient solution for users who wish to have fast and easy access to all of their information.

Viewing Images with Konqueror

You can also use the Konqueror file manager to view images. If you chose KDE as your default desktop environment, click on your home directory desktop icon to access the Konqueror file manager:

Using Konqueror as an image browser works similarly to Nautilus (discussed in the previous section). To configure Konqueror to view image files within a folder as automatically generated thumbnail icons, choose View ⇨ Preview ⇨ Images. When you click on a thumbnail icon, the browser displays the image in its native size.

Figure B-8. Viewing an Image in Konqueror

To zoom in and out of an image within Konqueror, you first need to change the way it renders the image. From the top toolbar, choose View ⇨ View Mode ⇨ KView. This will re-display the image and allow for zooming in and out using the two magnifying glass icons on the toolbar.

Figure B-9. Zooming Buttons in the Konqueror Toolbar

You can also open the image with more advanced image viewers, as well as with The GIMP. To do so, right-click on the image and choose Open With . . . . A pop-up menu will appear allowing you to open the application you wish to use. To launch The GIMP, choose Graphics and scroll down the list of applications. Click on The GIMP icon and click OK.

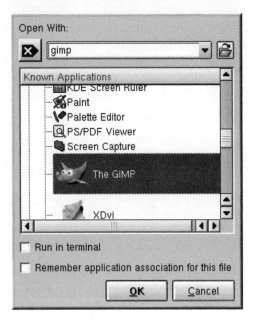

Figure B-10. The Open With . . . Dialog Box

Customizing KDE

KDE allows you to configure the desktop and your system to suit your needs. The KDE Control Center, available by clicking the Main Menu button and choosing Control Center, lets you customize the look and behavior of the desktop. The following list explains some of the configuration options in detail:

♦ *File Browsing* — This section lets you configure the Konqueror file manager and customize certain file operations. You can also associate files to applications that you prefer (for example, assigning all digital music files to open in XMMS instead of the default player).

♦ *Look & Feel* — This section allows you to customize the visual aspect of your desktop environment. You can customize background images and configure fonts, themes, icons, Panel elements, screensavers, and window header decorations. You can also customize mouse and keyboard events, which makes working with the desktop as efficient for your needs as possible.

> **NOTE** KDE features support for smooth (anti-aliased) fonts. However, not all fonts are smooth by default. In order to have smooth fonts for your entire desktop (whether you are reading text files, Web pages, or text in menus and icons), you must choose fonts that are designed to be anti-aliased, such as LucidaTypewriter or Courier).

♦ *Personalization* — This section allows you to set country and language options to your particular locale. You can also configure accessibility features such as audible and visual cues and keyboard/mouse customization. You can also configure your shell prompt settings via the Konsole option. Privacy and encryption settings can be configured via the Crypto option.

♦ *System* — This section is an advanced administration interface. You will need your root password to configure most of these options. This section allows you to configure system boot settings, Linux kernel configuration, printer settings, and install fonts system-wide. It is *strongly* recommended that you leave these settings at their default values unless you understand the consequences of changing them.

♦ *Web Browsing* — This section allows you to configure the Konqueror Web browser. You can configure options such as cache sizes, website cookies, plug-ins, proxy settings (if available), and enhanced browsing using keyword shortcuts.

KDE Keyboard Shortcuts

Table B-1 shows a few of the more useful keyboard shortcuts for KDE.

Table B-1: KDE Keyboard Shortcuts

Shortcut	What It Does
Alt-Tab	Walk through windows
Alt-Shift-Tab	Walk backward through windows
Ctrl-Tab	Walk through desktops
Ctrl-Shift-Tab	Walk backward through desktops
Ctrl-Esc	Show a table of running processes
Alt-F1	Access the Main Menu
Alt-F12	Emulate the mouse using the arrow keys on the keyboard
Alt-Left Mouse Button	Drag a window to move it
Alt-Print Scrn	Take a snapshot of the current window into the clipboard
Ctrl-Alt-Print Scrn	Take a snapshot of the entire desktop into the clipboard
Ctrl-Alt-l	Lock the desktop
Ctrl-Alt-d	Toggle hide/show the desktop

Finding Help

You can access a comprehensive set of documentation about KDE through the KDE HelpCenter. You can access the HelpCenter by choosing Help from the Main Menu.

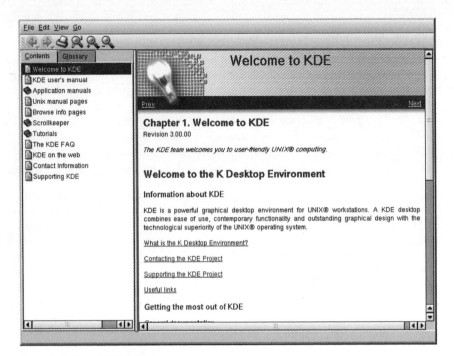

Figure B-11. The KDE HelpCenter

TIP To access HelpCenter from the desktop, right-click on the desktop and choose Help from the menu that appears.

The opening screen of the KDE HelpCenter browser will look like Figure B-11. From this main page you can view help documentation on topics such as using and configuring the desktop, working with the many applications included with KDE, and working with the Konqueror file manager.

The HelpCenter allows you to perform searches based on keyword entries and Web queries. To do this, click on the Search tab and type in a keyword, subject, or significant phrase in the Keywords field. Click on Search or press Enter to begin searching the Internet for your subject.

Logging Out of KDE

You can log out of your KDE session by using either of the following methods:

♦ From the Main Menu, select Logout.

♦ From the desktop, right-click on the desktop and select Logout from the menu.

Figure B-12. KDE Logout Screen

At the logout screen, KDE offers you the chance to save your current settings, which will preserve your Panel configuration and start any applications that you left open in your session.

If you are working in an application and you have not saved your work when you log out, a dialog will inform you that you will lose your unsaved material when you log out. When you see this dialog, you can simply select the Cancel button, save your work, then log out again.

CAUTION If you log out without saving your work, you will lose the unsaved data.

Appendix C

Configuring a Dual-Boot System

Sharing a computer between two operating systems requires dual booting. You can use either operating system on the computer, but not both at once (unless you're using a virtual machine such as Vmware; see http://www.vmware.com for more information). Each operating system boots from and uses its own hard drives or disk partitions.

This chapter explains how to configure your system to boot into both Red Hat Linux and another operating system. For clarity, we will assume that the other operating system is Microsoft Windows, but the general procedures are similar for other operating systems.

> **NOTE** If Red Hat Linux will coexist on your system with OS/2, you must create your disk partitions with the OS/2 partitioning software — otherwise, OS/2 may not recognize the disk partitions. During the installation, do not create any new partitions, but do set the proper partition types for your Linux partitions using fdisk.

If you do not have any operating systems installed on your computer, install Windows first and *then* install Red Hat Linux.

- If you are installing Windows 9*x* or Windows Me, you cannot define partitions during the Windows installation. Install Windows, and then see the "Partioning with FIPS" section later in this chapter for instructions on using FIPS to repartition your hard drive and create free space for Linux.

- If you are installing Windows NT or Windows 2000, you can create partitions of a specific size for Windows. Leave enough free space (space that is not partitioned or formatted) on the hard drive to install Linux.

> **TIP** While partitioning your hard drive, keep in mind that the BIOS in some systems cannot access more than the first 1024 cylinders on a hard drive. If this is the case, leave enough room for the /boot Linux partition on the first 1024 cylinders of your hard drive to boot Linux. The other Linux partitions can be after cylinder 1024.

See Chapter 1 to determine how much disk space to leave.

After installing Windows, see the "Installing Red Hat Linux in a Dual-Boot Environment" section later in this chapter.

If the computer you want to install Red Hat Linux on is currently running Windows (or some other operating system you have installed), you have an important decision to make. Your choices are:

♦ *Do you want Red Hat Linux to be the only operating system on your computer, despite the fact that you already have Windows on your computer?* If your answer is yes, you do not have to configure a dual-boot system. First back up any information that you want to save and then start the installation.

During the installation, if you choose to have the installation program automatically partition your system on the Disk Partitioning Setup screen, choose Remove all partitions on this system. If you choose manual partitioning with Disk Druid or fdisk, delete all the existing MS-DOS (Windows) partitions and then create your Linux partitions.

♦ *Do you want to install Red Hat Linux and then have the option of booting either Red Hat Linux or your other operating system?* A Red Hat Linux installation can be performed so that Red Hat Linux is installed on your system, but the other operating system is not affected. Because you already have Windows installed, you need to allocate disk space for Linux. Refer to the next section and then refer to the "Installing Red Hat Linux in a Dual-Boot Environment" section later in this chapter.

Allocating Disk Space for Linux

If you already have Windows installed on your system, you must have free hard drive space available on which to install Red Hat Linux. Your choices are as follows:

♦ Add a new hard drive.

♦ Use an existing hard drive or partition.

♦ Create a new partition.

For all three options, be aware that the BIOS in some older systems cannot access more than the first 1024 cylinders on a hard drive. If this is the case, the /boot Linux partition must be located on the first 1024 cylinders of your hard drive to boot Linux.

> **WARNING** Remember to back up all important information before reconfiguring your hard drive. Reconfiguring your hard drive can result in the loss of data if you are not extremely careful. Additionally, be sure to create a boot disk for both operating systems in case the boot loader fails to recognize either of them.

Adding a New Hard Drive

The simplest way to make room for Red Hat Linux is to add a new hard drive to the computer and then install Red Hat Linux on that drive. For example, if you add a second IDE hard drive to the computer, the Red Hat Linux installation program will recognize it as hdb and the existing drive (the one used by Windows) as hda. (For SCSI hard drives, the newly installed Red Hat Linux hard drive would be recognized as sdb and the other hard drive as sda.)

If you choose to install a new hard drive for Linux, all you need to do is start the Red Hat Linux installation program. After starting the Red Hat Linux installation program, just make sure you choose to install Linux on the newly installed hard drive (such as hdb or sdb) rather than the hard drive used by Windows.

Using an Existing Hard Drive or Partition

Another way to make room for Linux is to use a hard drive or disk partition that is currently being used by Windows. For example, suppose that Windows Explorer shows two hard drives, C: and D:. This could indicate either that the computer has two hard drives, or a single hard drive with two partitions.

In either case (assuming the hard drive has enough disk space), you can install Red Hat Linux on the hard drive or disk partition that Windows recognizes as D:.

> **NOTE** Windows uses letters to refer to removable drives (for example, a Zip drive) and network storage (virtual drives) as well as for local hard drive space; you cannot install Linux on a removable or network drive.

This choice is available to you only if the computer has two or more hard drives or disk partitions.

If a local Windows partition is available in which you want to install Linux, follow these steps:

1. Copy all data you want to save from the selected hard drive or partition (D: in this example) to another location.

2. Start the Red Hat Linux installation program and tell it to install Linux in the designated drive or partition; in this example, in the hard drive or partition that Windows designates as D:.

Note that Linux distinguishes between hard drives and disk partitions. Thus:

♦ If C: and D: on this computer refer to two separate hard drives, the installation program will recognize them as hda and hdb (IDE) or sda and sdb (SCSI). Tell the installation program to install on hdb or sdb.

♦ If C: and D: refer to partitions on a single drive, the installation program will recognize them as hda1 and hda2 (or sda1 and sda2 for SCSI). During the partitioning phase of the Red Hat Linux installation, delete the second partition (hda2 or sda2) and then partition the unallocated free space for Linux. You do not have to delete the second partition prior to starting the Red Hat Linux installation.

Creating a New Partition

The third way to make room for Linux is to create a new partition for Red Hat Linux on the hard drive being used by the other operating system. If Windows Explorer shows only one hard drive (C:), and you do not want to add a new hard drive, you must partition the drive. After partitioning, Windows Explorer will see a smaller C: drive; and, when you run the Red Hat Linux installation program, you can partition the remainder of the drive for Linux.

> **NOTE** Make sure to leave Windows enough room on your Windows partition to function properly.

You can use a destructive partitioning program, such as fdisk, to divide the hard drive, but doing so will require you to reinstall Windows. (This is probably not your best option.)

A number of non-destructive third-party partitioning programs are available for the Windows operating system. If you choose to use one of these, consult their documentation.

For instructions on how to partition with FIPS, a program that is on the Red Hat Linux CD-ROM #1, refer to the "Partitioning with FIPS" section later in this chapter.

Installing Red Hat Linux in a Dual-Boot Environment

After Windows is installed and you have free disk space ready for Linux, you can start the Red Hat Linux installation program. See Chapter 1 for instructions on installing Red Hat Linux.

At this point, the only difference between a Red Hat Linux installation and configuring a dual-boot system during the Red Hat Linux installation is partitioning the hard drive and configuring the boot loader. When you are at the Disk Partitioning Setup screen, return to this section.

Disk Partitioning

At the Disk Partitioning Setup screen of the installation program, you have a few options. Depending on which option you choose, the steps for configuring a dual-boot system vary. If you do not know how many Linux partitions to create, refer to Chapter 2 for a recommended partitioning scheme. If you choose:

♦ *Automatic partitioning* — Choose Keep all partitions and use existing free space. This option will leave your Windows partitions on the hard drive and partition the free space or additional hard drive for Red Hat Linux.

♦ *Manual partitioning with Disk Druid* — Do not delete the existing Windows partitions (they are the partitions of type vfat). Create your Linux partitions on the additional hard drive or in the free space you have reserved for Red Hat Linux.

♦ *Manual partitioning with fdisk* — This option is similar to using Disk Druid except you will not have the graphical interface. The basic procedure is the same. Do not delete the existing partitions of type FAT16, FAT32, or NTFS. Create your Linux partitions on the additional hard drive or in the free space you have reserved for Red Hat Linux.

Configuring the Boot Loader

When you arrive at the Boot Loader Installation screen during the Red Hat Linux installation, choose to install the boot loader. You can use a different boot loader to boot both Red Hat Linux and Windows.

Red Hat does not support alternate boot loaders. Thus, this section will discuss how to configure GRUB or LILO to boot both operating systems.

The Red Hat Linux installation program will usually detect Windows and automatically configure the boot loader (GRUB or LILO) to boot either Red Hat Linux or Windows. This can be seen on the boot loader screen of the installation program. An entry named DOS appears in the list of operating systems to boot.

Post-Installation

After the installation, whenever start the computer, you can indicate whether you want to start Red Hat Linux or the other operating system from the boot loader screen. Choose Red Hat Linux to boot into Red Hat Linux or choose DOS to boot into Windows.

If you did not partition all the free space on your hard drive for Red Hat Linux, you can partition it for Windows after installing Red Hat Linux. You can use `parted` or `fdisk` to create these partitions.

`parted` is easier to use than `fdisk` because of the interface and the commands used. For example, to view the partition table, you type **print** in `parted` instead of typing **p** in `fdisk`. For more information about `parted`, see the *Official Red Hat Linux Administrator's Guide* (Red Hat Press/Wiley, 2003).

> **WARNING** It is highly recommended that you use `parted` or `fdisk` to create partitions after installing Red Hat Linux. Other partitioning software has been known to change the partitioning table of the hard drive and move the Linux partitions. If this happens, the boot loader will not be able to find the Linux partitions and will not boot into Red Hat Linux.

To access the files on the Windows partitions while using Red Hat Linux, see Chapter 21.

> **NOTE** If you formatted the Windows partitions in NTFS format, this method will not work.

Partitioning with FIPS

As a convenience to our customers, we provide the FIPS utility. This is a freely available program that can resize FAT (File Allocation Table) partitions. It is included on the Red Hat Linux CD-ROM in the `dosutils` directory. If you are using NTFS partitions, FIPS will not work.

> **WARNING** Many people have successfully used FIPS to repartition their hard drives. However, because of the nature of the operations carried out by FIPS and the wide variety of hardware and software configurations under which it must run, Red Hat cannot guarantee that FIPS will work properly on your system. Therefore, no installation support whatsoever is available for FIPS: *use it at your own risk.*

With the immediately preceding warning in mind, if you decide to repartition your hard drive with FIPS, it is vital that you do two things:

♦ *Perform a Backup* — Make two copies of all the important data on your computer. These copies should be to removable media (such as tape, CD-ROM, or diskettes), and you should make sure they are readable before proceeding.

♦ *Read the Documentation* — Completely read the FIPS documentation, which is located in the `dosutils/fipsdocs` directory on the Red Hat Linux CD-ROM #1.

Should you decide to use FIPS, after FIPS runs you will be left with two partitions: the one you resized and the one FIPS created out of the newly freed space. If your goal is to use that space to install Red Hat Linux, you should delete the newly created partition, either by using `fdisk` under your current operating system or while setting up partitions during a custom-class installation.

The following instructions are a simplified version of the FIPS documentation file, `fips.doc`, which is located in the `/dosutils/fips20/*` on the Red Hat Linux CD-ROM #1. These instructions should apply in most instances. If you encounter any problems, see the documentation file.

1. From within Windows, perform the following steps:

    a) Do a full backup.

    b) Run `scandisk` to verify that the hard drive contains no bad clusters.

    c) Decide how to distribute the available space on the hard drive between the operating systems.

    d) Use Windows Explorer to see the free space on the drive. Make a note of the space (in megabytes) that each operating system will have.

    e) If you do not have one, create a Windows boot disk. The diskette will be formatted, and `COMMAND.COM`, along with the associated hidden files (`IO.SYS`, `MSDOS.SYS`, and `DBLSPACE.BIN`), will be copied to the diskette.

> **NOTE** Creating a boot disk varies between different versions of Windows. Consult the Windows documentation for instructions on creating a Windows boot disk.

    f) Copy the following files on the Red Hat Linux CD-ROM #1 to the DOS boot disk:

```
dosutils/fips20/fips.exe
dosutils/fips20/restorrb.exe
dosutils/fips20/errors.txt
dosutils/fips20/fips.doc
dosutils/fips20/fips.faq
```

    g) Defragment the hard drive so that all the data on the hard drive is located at the beginning of the drive.

2. Insert the Windows boot disk into the floppy drive and reboot the system.

3. Start FIPS (type **fips** at the prompt).

When FIPS begins you'll find a welcome message similar to the following:

```
FIPS version 2.0, Copyright (C) 1993/4 Arno Schaefer
FAT32 Support, Copyright (C) 1997 Gordon Chaffee

DO NOT use FIPS in a multitasking environment like Windows, OS/2, Desqview,
Novell Task manager or the Linux DOS emulator; boot from a DOS boot disk first.

If you use OS/2 or a disk compressor, read the relevant sections in FIPS.DOC.
FIPS comes with ABSOLUTELY NO WARRANTY, see file COPYING for details.

This is free software, and you are welcome to redistribute it
```

```
under certain conditions; again, see file COPYING for details.

Press any key.
```

When you press a key, a root partition screen will appear.

> **NOTE** If the computer has more than one hard drive, you'll be asked to select which one you want to partition.

When you press a key, details about the hard drive, such as the following, will appear:

```
Boot sector:
Bytes per sector: 512
Sectors per cluster: 8
Reserved sectors: 1
Number of FATs: 2
Number of rootdirectory entries: 512
Number of sectors (short): 0
Media descriptor byte: f8h
Sectors per FAT: 145
Sectors per track: 63
Drive heads: 16
Hidden sectors: 63
Number of sectors (long): 141057
Physical drive number: 80h
Signature: 29h

Checking boot sector ... OK
Checking FAT ... OK
Searching for free space ... OK

Do you want to make a backup copy of your root and boot sector before
proceeding? (y/n)
```

You should select **y** for yes to make a backup copy of your root and boot sector before proceeding with FIPS.

Next, you will be presented with the following message:

```
Do you have a bootable floppy disk in drive A: as described in the
documentation? (y/n)
```

Verify that a DOS boot disk is in the floppy drive and type **y** for yes. A screen similar to the following will appear, allowing you to resize the partition:

```
Writing file a:\rootboot:000

Enter start cylinder for new partition (33-526)

Use the cursor keys to choose the cylinder, <enter> to continue
```

```
Old partition              Cylinder           New partition
 258.9 MB                     33               3835.8 MB
```

The initial values allocate *all* free space on the disk to the new partition. This is not what you want, because this setting would leave no free space on your Windows partition. Press the right arrow to increase the size of the Windows partition and decrease the size of the new (Linux) partition; press the left arrow to decrease the size of the Windows partition and increase the size of the Linux partition. When the sizes are what you want, press Enter. A verification screen will appear.

If you type **r** (to re-edit the partition tables), the output shown immediately preceding the above paragraph reappears, allowing you to change the partition sizes. If you answer **c**, a confirmation screen like the following appears:

```
New boot sector:

Boot sector:
Bytes per sector: 512
Sectors per cluster: 8
Reserved sectors: 1
Number of FATs: 2
Number of rootdirectory entries: 512
Number of sectors (short): 0
Media descriptor byte: f8h
Sectors per FAT: 145
Sectors per track: 63
Drive heads: 16
Hidden sectors: 63
Number of sectors (long): 141057
Physical drive number: 80h
Signature: 29h

Checking boot sector ... OK

Ready to write new partition scheme to disk
Do you want to proceed (y/n)?
```

Answering **y** for yes completes the resizing operation. A harmless error message may occur, stating in effect that FIPS cannot reboot the system.

After a successful operation, the disk will have two partitions. The first partition (hda1 or sda1) will be used by Windows.

NOTE We recommend that you start Windows (remember to remove the boot disk from drive A:) and run scandisk on drive C:.

If you encounter any problems (for example, Windows will not boot), you can reverse the FIPS resizing operation with the restorrb.exe command that you copied to your MS-DOS boot disk. In case of any errors, read the FIPS documentation files (fips.doc and `fips.faq`), which describe a number of factors that could cause the resizing operation to fail. If all else fails, you can restore Windows with the backup you made.

The second partition (`hda2` or `sda2`) contains the space that the Red Hat Linux installation program will use. When the Disk Druid screen appears during installation, delete this partition (the installation manual explains how) and then proceed with Linux partitioning.

Appendix D

An Introduction to Disk Partitions

Disk partitions are a standard part of the personal computer landscape and have been for quite some time. However, with many people purchasing computers featuring pre-installed operating systems, relatively few people understand how partitions work. This chapter attempts to explain the reasons for and use of disk partitions so your Red Hat Linux installation will be as simple and painless as possible. This chapter also discusses the partition naming scheme used by Linux systems, sharing disk space with other operating systems, and related topics.

> **NOTE** If you are reasonably comfortable with disk partitions, you could skip ahead to the "Making Room for Red Hat Linux" section later in this chapter for more information on the process of freeing up disk space to prepare for a Red Hat Linux installation.

Hard Disk Basic Concepts

Hard disks (also called *hard drives*) perform a very simple function — they store data and reliably retrieve it on command.

When discussing issues such as disk partitioning, it is important to know a bit about the underlying hardware. Unfortunately, it is easy to become bogged down in details. Therefore, this chapter uses a simplified diagram of a disk drive to help explain what is really happening when a disk drive is partitioned.

Figure D-1 shows a brand-new, unused disk drive.

Figure D-1. An Unused Disk Drive

Not much to look at, is it? But if we are talking about disk drives on a basic level, it will do. Say that we would like to store some data on this drive. As things stand now, it will not work. There is something we need to do first, namely formatting the drive (as discussed in the next section).

It's Not What You Write, It's How You Write It

Experienced computer users probably got this one on the first try. We need to *format* the drive. Formatting (usually known as "making a file system") writes information to the drive, creating order out of the empty space on an unformatted drive.

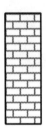

Figure D-2. Disk Drive with a File System

As Figure D-2 shows, the order imposed by a file system involves some trade-offs, as follows:

♦ A small percentage of the drive's available space is used to store file system-related data. This percentage can be considered overhead.

♦ A file system splits the remaining space into small, consistently-sized segments. In Linux, these segments are known as blocks.

> **NOTE** Blocks really *are* consistently sized, unlike our illustrations. Keep in mind, also, that an average disk drive contains thousands of blocks. But for the purposes of this discussion, please ignore these minor discrepancies.

Given that file systems make things like directories and files possible, these tradeoffs are usually seen as a small price to pay.

It is also worth noting that there is no single, universal file system. As Figure D-3 shows, a disk drive may have one of many different file systems written on it. As you might guess, different file systems tend to be incompatible; that is, an operating system that supports one file system (or a handful of related file system types) may not support another. This last statement is not a hard-and-fast rule, however. For example, Red Hat Linux supports a wide variety of file systems (including many commonly used by other operating systems, such as

FAT, which is used by Windows 9*x*/Me), making data interchange between different file systems easy.

Figure D-3. Disk Drive with a Different File System

Of course, writing a file system to disk is only the beginning. The goal of this process is to actually store and retrieve data. Figure D-4 shows our example drive after some files have been written to it.

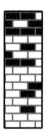

Figure D-4. Disk Drive with Data Written to It

As the figure shows, 14 of the previously empty blocks are now holding data. However, we cannot determine exactly how many files reside on this drive by simply looking at this picture. There may be as few as one or as many as 14 files, as all files use at least one block and some files use multiple blocks. Another important point to note is that the used blocks do not have to form a contiguous region; used and unused blocks may be interspersed. This concept is known as *fragmentation*. Fragmentation can play a part when attempting to resize an existing partition.

As with most computer-related technologies, disk drives changed over time after their introduction. In particular, they got bigger. Not larger in physical size, but bigger in their capacity to store information. This additional capacity drove a fundamental change in the way disk drives were used.

Partitions: Turning One Drive Into Many

As disk drive capacities soared, some people began to wonder if having all of that formatted space in one big chunk was such a great idea. This line of thinking was driven by several issues, some philosophical, some technical. On the philosophical side, above a certain size, it seemed that the additional space provided by a larger drive created more clutter. On the technical side, some file systems were never designed to support anything above a certain capacity. Even if the file systems *could* support larger drives with a greater capacity, the overhead imposed by the file system to track files could become excessive.

The solution to this problem was to divide disks into *partitions*. Each partition can be accessed as if it was a separate disk. This is done through the addition of a *partition table*.

> **NOTE** While the diagrams in this chapter show the partition table as being separate from the actual disk drive, this is not entirely accurate. In reality, the partition table is stored at the very start of the disk, before any file system or user data. But for clarity, we keep it separate in the diagrams for this chapter.

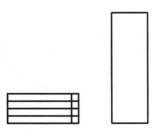

Figure D-5. Disk Drive with Partition Table

As Figure D-5 shows, the partition table is divided into four sections. Each section can hold the information necessary to define a single partition, meaning that this particular partition table can define no more than four partitions.

Each partition table entry contains several important characteristics of the partition:

♦ *The points on the disk where the partition starts and ends* — The starting and ending points define the partition's size and location on the disk.

♦ *Whether the partition is active* — The "active" flag is used by some operating systems' boot loaders. In other words, the operating system in the partition that is marked "active" is the partition that will be booted by default.

♦ *The partition's type* — The partition's type can be a bit confusing. The type is a number that identifies the partition's anticipated usage. If that statement sounds a bit vague, that is because the meaning of the partition type is a bit vague. Some operating systems use the partition type to denote a specific file system type, to flag the partition as being associated with a particular operating system, to indicate that the partition contains a bootable operating system, or some combination of the three. Table D-1 contains a listing of some popular (and obscure) partition types along with their corresponding numeric values.

Table D-1: Partition Types

Partition Type	Value	Partition Type	Value
Empty	00	Novell Netware 386	65
DOS 12-bit FAT	01	PIC/IX	75
XENIX root	02	Old MINIX	80
XENIX usr	03	Linux/MINUX	81
DOS 16-bit<=32M	04	Linux swap	82
Extended	05	Linux native	83
DOS 16-bit>=32M	06	Linux extended	85
OS/2 HPFS	07	Amoeba	93
AIX	08	Amoeba BBT	94
AIX bootable	09	BSD/386	a5
OS/2 Boot Manager	0a	OpenBSD	a6
Win95 FAT32	0b	NEXTSTEP	a7
Win95 FAT32 (LBA)	0c	BSDI fs	b7
Win95 FAT16 (LBA)	0e	BSDI swap	b8
Win95 Extended (LBA)	0f	Syrinx	c7
Venix 80286	40	CP/M	Db
Novell	51	DOS access	e1
Microport	52	DOS R/O	e3
GNU HURD	63	DOS secondary	f2
Novell Netware 286	64	BBT	Ff

By this point, you might be wondering how all this additional complexity is normally used. See Figure D-6 for an example.

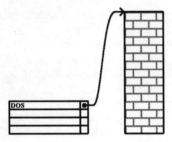

Figure D-6. Disk Drive with a Single Partition

In many cases, there is only a single partition spanning the entire disk, essentially duplicating the method used before partitions. The partition table has only one entry used, and it points to the start of the partition.

In the figure, this partition is labeled as being of the "DOS" type. Although it is only one of several possible partition types listed in Table D-1, it is adequate for the purposes of this discussion. This is a typical partition layout for most newly purchased computers that have a consumer version of Microsoft Windows preinstalled.

Partitions within Partitions — An Overview of Extended Partitions

Of course, over time it became obvious that four partitions would not be enough. As disk drives continued to grow, it became more and more likely that a person could configure four reasonably sized partitions and still have disk space left over. There needed to be some way of creating more partitions.

Enter the *extended partition*. As you can see in Table D-1, there is an "Extended" partition type. When a partition is created and its type is set to "Extended," an extended partition table is created. In essence, the extended partition is like a disk drive in its own right — it has a partition table that points to one or more partitions (now called *logical partitions*, as opposed to the four *primary partitions*) contained entirely within the extended partition itself. Figure D-7 shows a disk drive with one primary partition and one extended partition containing two logical partitions (along with some unpartitioned free space).

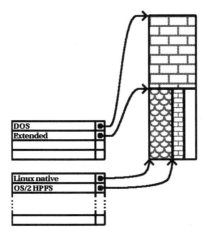

Figure D-7. Disk Drive with Extended Partition

As the figure implies, there is a difference between primary and logical partitions — there can only be four primary partitions, but there is no fixed limit to the number of logical partitions that can exist.

However, due to the way in which partitions are accessed in Linux, you should avoid defining more than 12 logical partitions on a single disk drive.

Now that we have discussed partitions in general, the next section shows you how to use this knowledge to install Red Hat Linux.

Making Room for Red Hat Linux

There are three possible scenarios you may face when attempting to repartition your hard disk:

♦ Unpartitioned free space is available

♦ An unused partition is available

♦ Free space in an actively used partition is available

The following sections look at each scenario in order.

> **NOTE** Please keep in mind that the illustrations in this chapter are simplified for clarity and do not reflect the exact partition layout that you will encounter when actually installing Red Hat Linux.

Using Unpartitioned Free Space

In this situation, the partitions already defined do not span the entire hard disk, leaving unallocated space that is not part of any defined partition. Figure D-8 shows what this might look like.

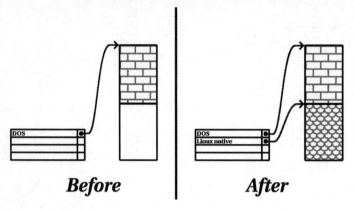

Figure D-8. Disk Drive with Unpartitioned Free Space

> **NOTE** If you think about it, an unused hard disk also falls into this category. The only difference in that case is that *all* the space is not part of any defined partition.

You can simply create the necessary partitions from the unused space. Unfortunately, although very simple, this scenario is not very likely (unless you have just purchased a new hard disk just for Red Hat Linux). Most preinstalled operating systems are configured to take up all available space on a disk drive (see the "Using Free Space from an Active Partition" section later in this chapter).

Using Space from an Unused Partition

In this case, maybe you have one or more partitions that you do not use any longer. Perhaps you have dabbled with another operating system in the past and the partition(s) you dedicated to it never seems to be used anymore. Figure D-9 illustrates such a situation.

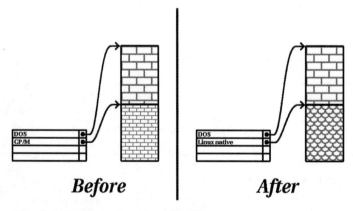

Figure D-9. Disk Drive with an Unused Partition

If you find yourself in this situation, you can use the space allocated to the unused partition. You will first need to delete the unused partition and then create the appropriate Linux partition(s) in its place using the reclaimed free space. You can either delete the partition using the DOS `fdisk` utility, or you will be given the opportunity to do so during a custom installation.

Using Free Space from an Active Partition

This is the most common situation. Unfortunately, it is also the hardest to handle. The main problem is that, even if you have enough free space, that space is presently allocated to a partition that is already in use.

If you purchased a computer with preinstalled software, the hard disk most likely has one massive partition holding the operating system and data.

Aside from adding a new hard drive to your system, you have two choices: destructive repartitioning and non-destructive repartitioning. The following sections discuss both of these choices in detail.

Destructive Repartitioning

Basically, destructive repartitioning involves deleting the single large partition and creating several smaller ones. As you might imagine, any data you had in the original partition is destroyed. This means that making a complete backup of any files that you don't want to lose is necessary. For your own sake, make two backups of important files, use verification (if available in your backup software), and try to read data from your backup *before* you delete the partition.

> **CAUTION** If there was an operating system of some type installed on that partition, it will need to be reinstalled as well (assuming you want to continue using that operating system, of course). Be aware that some computers sold with preinstalled operating systems may not include the CD-ROM media to reinstall the original operating system. The best time to notice if this applies to your system is before you destroy your original partition and its operating system installation.

After creating a smaller partition for your existing software, you can reinstall any software, restore your data, and continue your Red Hat Linux installation. Figure D-10 shows this being done.

> **NOTE** New computers often come with recovery disks so that you can restore your computer to its factory settings in case your operating system becomes corrupted. Using these recovery disks will undo everything you do with fdisk.

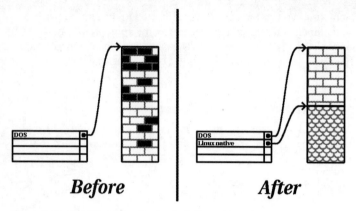

Before | *After*

Figure D-10. Disk Drive Being Destructively Repartitioned

CAUTION Again (we can't stress this enough), as Figure D-10 shows, any data present in the original partition will be lost without proper backup!

Non-Destructive Repartitioning

Here, you run a program that does the seemingly impossible: it makes a big partition smaller without losing any of the files stored in that partition. Many people have found this method to be reliable and trouble-free. What software should you use to perform this feat? There are several disk management software products on the market. You will have to do some research to find the one that is best for your situation.

While the process of non-destructive repartitioning is rather straightforward, there are a number of steps involved:

1. Compress existing data.
2. Resize the existing partition.
3. Create new partition(s).

The following sections look at each step in a bit more detail.

Step 1: Compress existing data

As Figure D-11 shows, the first step in non-destructive repartitioning is to compress the data in your existing partition. The reason for doing this is to rearrange the data such that it maximizes the available free space at the "end" of the partition.

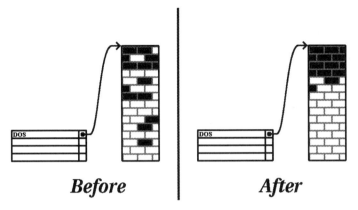

Before   *After*

Figure D-11. Disk Drive Being Compressed

This step is crucial. Without it, the location of your data could prevent the partition from being resized to the extent desired. Note also that, for one reason or another, some data cannot be moved. If this is the case (and it severely restricts the size of your new partition(s)), you may be forced to destructively repartition your disk.

For Windows operating systems utilizing the FAT partition type, the FIPS program can be used (after defragging the hard drive) to perform this step. See Appendix C for more details.

Step 2: Resize the existing partition
Figure D-12 shows the actual resizing process. While the actual result of the resizing operation varies depending on the software used, in most cases the newly freed space is used to create an unformatted partition of the same type as the original partition.

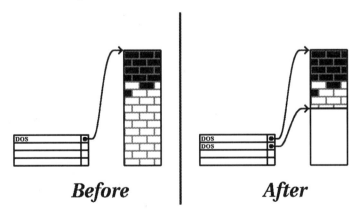

Before   *After*

Figure D-12. Disk Drive with Partition Resized

It is important to understand what the resizing software you use does with the newly freed space so that you can take the appropriate steps. In the case we have illustrated, it would be best to simply delete the new DOS partition and create the appropriate Linux partition(s) using the reclaimed space.

Create new partition(s)

As the previous step implied, it may or may not be necessary to create new partitions. However, unless your resizing software is Linux-aware, it is likely you will need to delete the partition that was created during the resizing process. Figure D-13 shows this being done.

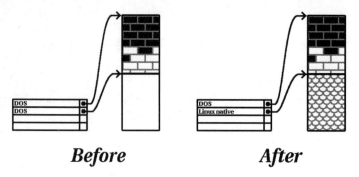

Before   *After*

Figure D-13. Disk Drive with Final Partition Configuration

NOTE The following information is specific to x86-based computers only.

As a convenience to Red Hat Linux users, the DOS FIPS utility is included on the Red Hat Linux CD-ROM #1 in the `dosutils` directory. FIPS is a freely available program that can resize FAT (File Allocation Table) partitions.

WARNING Many people have successfully used FIPS to resize their hard drive partitions. However, because of the nature of the operations carried out by FIPS and the wide variety of hardware and software configurations under which it must run, Red Hat cannot guarantee that FIPS will work properly on your system. Therefore, no installation support is available for FIPS. Use it at your own risk.

With the preceding warning in mind, if you decide to repartition your hard drive with FIPS, it is *vital* that you do two things:

◆ *Perform a backup* — Make two copies of all the important data on your computer. These copies should be made on removable media (CD writables, diskettes, or tape), and you should make sure they are readable before proceeding.

◆ *Read the documentation* — Completely read the FIPS documentation, which is located in the `dosutils/fipsdocs` subdirectory on Red Hat Linux CD-ROM #1.

After FIPS runs you will be left with two partitions: the one you resized and the one FIPS created out of the newly freed space. If your goal is to use that space to install Red Hat Linux, you should delete the newly created partition either by using `fdisk` under your current operating system or while setting up partitions during a custom installation.

Partition Naming Scheme

Linux refers to disk partitions using a combination of letters and numbers. This naming scheme can be confusing, particularly if you are used to the "C drive" way of referring to hard disks and their partitions. In the MS-DOS/Windows world, partitions are named using the following method:

1. Each partition's type is checked to determine if it can be read by DOS/Windows.

2. If the partition's type is compatible, it is assigned a drive letter. The drive letters start at C (A and B are reserved for floppy drives) and move on to the following letters, depending on the number of partitions to be labeled. The drive letter can then be used to refer to that partition as well as the file system contained on that partition.

Red Hat Linux uses a naming scheme that is more flexible and conveys more information than the approach used by other operating systems. The naming scheme is file-based, with filenames in the following form:

```
/dev/xxyN
```

Here is how to decipher the partition naming scheme:

♦ /dev/ — This string is the name of the directory in which all device files reside. Because partitions reside on hard disks and hard disks are devices, the files representing all possible partitions reside in /dev/.

♦ *xx* — The first two letters of the partition name indicate the type of device on which the partition resides. You will normally see either hd (for IDE disks) or sd (for SCSI disks).

♦ *y* — This letter indicates which device the partition is on. For example, /dev/hda (the first IDE hard disk) or /dev/sdb (the second SCSI disk).

♦ *N* — The final number denotes the partition. The first four (primary or extended) partitions are numbered 1 through 4. Logical partitions start at 5. So, for example, /dev/hda3 is the third primary or extended partition on the first IDE hard disk and /dev/sdb6 is the second logical partition on the second SCSI hard disk.

> **NOTE** There is no part of this naming convention that is based on partition type; unlike DOS/Windows, *all* partitions can be identified under Red Hat Linux. Of course, this does not mean that Red Hat Linux can access data on every type of partition, but in many cases it is possible to access data on a partition dedicated to another operating system.

Keep this information in mind; it will make things easier to understand when you are setting up the partitions Red Hat Linux requires.

Disk Partitions and Other Operating Systems

If your Red Hat Linux partitions will be sharing a hard disk with partitions used by other operating systems, most of the time you will have no problems. However, there are certain combinations of Linux and other operating systems that require extra care. See Appendix C for information on creating disk partitions compatible with other operating systems.

Disk Partitions and Mount Points

One area that many people new to Linux find confusing is the matter of how partitions are used and accessed by the Linux operating system. In Windows or MS-DOS, the naming scheme is relatively simple: each partition gets a drive letter. You then use the correct drive letter to refer to files and directories on its corresponding partition.

This is entirely different from how Linux deals with partitions and, for that matter, with disk storage in general. The main difference is that each partition is used to form part of the storage necessary to support a single set of files and directories. This is done by associating a partition with a directory through a process known as *mounting*. Mounting a partition makes its storage available starting at the specified directory (known as a *mount point*).

For example, if partition /dev/hda5 were mounted on /usr, that would mean that all files and directories under /usr would physically reside on /dev/hda5. So the file /usr/share/doc/FAQ/txt/Linux-FAQ would be stored on /dev/hda5, while the file /etc/X11/gdm/Sessions/Gnome would not.

Continuing our example, it is also possible that one or more directories below /usr would be mount points for other partitions. For instance, a partition (say, /dev/hda7) could be mounted on /usr/local, meaning that /usr/local/man/whatis would then reside on /dev/hda7 rather than /dev/hda5.

How Many Partitions to Create?

When preparing to install Red Hat Linux, you will need to give some consideration to the number and size of the partitions to be used by your new operating system. The question of "how many partitions" continues to spark debate within the Linux community and, without any end to the debate in sight, it is safe to say that there are probably as many partition layouts as there are people debating the issue.

Keeping this in mind, we recommend that you should create at least the following partitions:

♦ *A swap partition* — Swap partitions are used to support virtual memory. In other words, data is written to swap when there is not enough RAM to hold the data your system is processing. You must create a swap partition to correctly use Red Hat Linux. The minimum size of your swap partition should be equal to twice the amount of your computer's RAM or 32MB, whichever is larger, up to 1GB. A swap partition of over 1GB is typically not necessary.

♦ *A /boot partition* — The partition mounted on /boot contains the operating system kernel (which allows your system to boot Red Hat Linux), along with a few other files used during the boot process.

> **CAUTION** Make sure you read the next section — the information there applies to the /boot partition.

Due to the limitations of most PC BIOSes, creating a small partition to hold these files is a good idea. For most users, a 32MB boot partition is sufficient.

♦ *A root partition (/)* — The root partition is where / (the root directory) resides. In this partitioning layout, all files (except those stored in /boot) reside on the root partition. Because of this, it is in your best interest to maximize the size of your root partition. For example, a 1.2GB root partition may permit the equivalent of a workstation installation (with very little free space), while a 3.4GB root partition may let you install every package. Obviously, the more space you can give the root partition, the better.

Specific recommendations concerning the proper size for various Red Hat Linux partitions can be found in Chapter 1.

One Last Wrinkle: Using GRUB or LILO

GRUB and LILO are the most commonly boot loaders for Red Hat Linux on x86-based systems. As operating system loaders, they operate outside of any operating system, using only the Basic I/O System (or BIOS) built into the computer hardware itself. This section describes GRUB and LILO's interactions with PC BIOSes and is specific to x86-compatible computers.

GRUB and LILO are subject to some limitations imposed by the BIOS in most x86-based computers. Specifically, most BIOSes cannot access more than two hard drives, and they cannot access any data stored beyond cylinder 1023 of any drive. Note that some recent BIOSes do not have these limitations, but this is by no means universal.

All the data GRUB and LILO need to access at boot time (including the Linux kernel) is located in the /boot directory. If you follow the partition layout recommended above or are performing a workstation or server install, the /boot directory will be in a small, separate partition. Otherwise, it may reside in the root partition (/). In either case, the partition in which /boot resides must conform to the following guidelines if you are going to use GRUB or LILO to boot your Red Hat Linux system:

> **NOTE** Disk Druid, as well as automatic partitioning, takes these BIOS-related limitations into account.

♦ *On the first two IDE drives* — If you have two IDE (or EIDE) drives, /boot must be located on one of them. Note that this two-drive limit also includes any IDE CD-ROM drives on your primary IDE controller. So, if you have one IDE hard drive and one IDE CD-ROM on your primary controller, /boot must be located on the first hard drive only, even if you have other hard drives on your secondary IDE controller.

♦ *On the first IDE or first SCSI drive* — If you have one IDE (or EIDE) drive and one or more SCSI drives, /boot must be located either on the IDE drive or the SCSI drive at ID 0. No other SCSI IDs will work.

♦ *On the first two SCSI drives* — If you have only SCSI hard drives, /boot must be located on a drive at ID 0 or ID 1. No other SCSI IDs will work.

♦ *On a partition that's* completely *below cylinder 1023* — No matter which of the above configurations apply, the partition that holds /boot must be located entirely below cylinder 1023. If the partition holding /boot straddles cylinder 1023, you may face a situation where GRUB and LILO will work initially (because all the necessary information is below cylinder 1023) but will fail if a new kernel is to be loaded and that kernel resides above cylinder 1023.

As mentioned earlier, it is possible that some of newer BIOSes may permit GRUB and LILO to work with configurations that do not meet these guidelines. Likewise, some of GRUB and LILO's more esoteric features may be used to get a Linux system started, even if the configuration does not meet our guidelines. However, due to the number of variables involved, Red Hat does not support such efforts.

Appendix E

The X Window System

While the heart of Red Hat Linux is the kernel, for many users the face of the operating system is the graphical environment provided by the X Window System, also called simply X.

This appendix is an introduction to the behind-the-scenes world of XFree86, the open-source implementation of X that is provided with Red Hat Linux.

The Power of X

Linux began as a powerful, server-based operating system that excelled at efficiently processing complicated programs that require high CPU resources, as well as handling requests from hundreds or even thousands of clients communicating through network connections. Because of its open nature and stability, however, Linux has quickly developed into a popular GUI-based operating system for workstations, both at home and in the workplace.

In the Unix world, windowing environments have existed for decades, predating many of the current mainstream operating systems. The X Window System is now the dominant graphical user interface (GUI) for Unix-like operating systems.

To create this GUI for the user, X uses a client/server architecture. Specifically, an *X server* process is started so that *X client* processes can connect to the X server via a network or local loopback interface. The server process handles the communication with the hardware, such as the video card, monitor, keyboard, and mouse.

The X client exists in the user space, issuing requests to the X server.

On Red Hat Linux systems, the XFree86 server fills the role of the X server. As a large-scale open-source software project claiming hundreds of developers around the world, XFree86 features rapid development, a wide degree of support for various hardware devices and architectures, and the ability to run on different operating systems and platforms.

The X server performs many difficult tasks using a wide array of hardware, requiring detailed configuration. Luckily, most Red Hat Linux desktop users are unaware of the XFree86 server running on their system. They are much more concerned with the particular desktop environment in which they spend most of their time. The Red Hat Linux installation program does an excellent job of configuring your XFree86 server during the installation process, ensuring that X performs optimally when first started.

If some aspect of your system changes, such as the monitor or video card, XFree86 will need to be reconfigured. In addition, if you are troubleshooting a problem with XFree86 that cannot be solved using a configuration utility, such as the X Configuration Tool, you may need to access its configuration file directly.

The X Configuration Tool is capable of configuring XFree86 while the X server is active. To start the X Configuration Tool while in an active X session, click the Main Menu button and choose System Settings ⇨ Display. Or, to start the X Configuration tool from the command line (a likely scenario if you can't get X working), type **redhat-config-xfree86** at a command prompt.

After using X Configuration Tool during an X session, you will need to log out of the current X session and then log back in for the changes to take effect.

XFree86

Red Hat Linux 8.0 uses XFree86 version 4.2 as its base X Window System, which includes the various necessary X libraries, fonts, utilities, documentation, and development tools.

> **NOTE** Red Hat no longer provides the older XFree86 version 3 server packages. Before upgrading to the latest version of Red Hat Linux, be sure that your video card is compatible with XFree86 version 4 by checking the Red Hat Hardware Compatibility List at `http://hardware.redhat.com/hcl/`.

The X server includes many cutting-edge XFree86 technology enhancements such as hardware 3-D acceleration support, the XRender extension for anti-aliased fonts, a modular driver based design, support for modern video hardware and input devices, and many other features.

The Red Hat Linux installation program installs the base components of XFree86. You may choose to install any optional XFree86 packages.

The X Window System resides primarily in two locations in the file system:

- ♦ `/usr/X11R6/` directory — This directory contains X client binaries (in the `bin` directory), assorted header files (in the `include` directory), libraries (in the `lib` directory), and manual pages (in the `man` directory), and various other X documentation (in the `/usr/X11R6/lib/X11/doc/` directory).
- ♦ `/etc/X11/` directory — The `/etc/X11/` directory hierarchy contains all of the configuration files for the various components that make up the X Window System. This includes configuration files for the X server itself, the X font server (`xfs`), the X Display Manager (`xdm`), and many other base components.

Display managers such as `gdm` and `kdm`, as well as various window managers and other X tools, also store their configuration in this hierarchy.

XFree86 version 4 server is a single binary executable: `/usr/X11R6/bin/XFree86`. This server dynamically loads various X server modules at runtime from the `/usr/X11R6/lib/modules/` directory, including video drivers, font engine drivers, and other modules as needed. Some of these modules are automatically loaded by the server, whereas some are optional features that you must specify in the XFree86 server's configuration file, /etc/X11/XF86Config, before they can be used. The video drivers are located in the /usr/X11R6/lib/modules/drivers/ directory. The DRI hardware accelerated 3-D drivers are located in the /usr/X11R6/lib/modules/dri/ directory.

XFree86 Server Configuration Files

The XFree86 server configuration files are stored in the /etc/X11/ directory. The XFree86 version 4 server uses /etc/X11/XF86Config. When Red Hat Linux is installed, the configuration files for XFree86 are created using information gathered during the installation process.

While there is rarely a need to manually edit these files, it is useful to know about the various sections and optional parameters found in them.

Each section begins with a *SectionName* line and ends with an EndSection line. Within each of the sections, you will find several lines containing an option name and at least one option value, occasionally seen in quotes. The following sections explore the most useful sections of an XFree86 version 4 file and the roles of various popular settings.

To review the current configuration of your XFree86 server, type the **xset -q** command. This provides you with information about the keyboard, pointer, screen saver, and font paths.

> **NOTE** For more information, refer to the XF86Config man page.

Device

This section specifies information about the video card used by the system. You must have at least one Device section in your configuration file. You may have multiple Device sections in the case of multiple video cards or multiple settings that can run a single card. The following options are either required or widely used:

- BusID — Specifies the bus location of the video card. This option is only necessary for systems with multiple cards and must be set so that the Device section will use the proper settings for the correct card.

- Driver — Tells XFree86 which driver to load in order to use the video card.

- Identifier — Provides a unique name for this video card. Usually, this name is set to the exact name of the video card used in the Device section.

- Screen — An optional setting used when a video card has more than one head, or connector, to go out to a separate monitor. If you have multiple monitors connected to one video card, separate Device sections must exist for each of them with a different Screen value for each Device section. The value accepted by this option is a number starting at 0 and increasing by one for each head on the video card.

- VideoRam — The amount of RAM available on the video card in kilobytes. This setting is not normally necessary because the XFree86 server can usually probe the video card to autodetect the amount of video RAM. But because some video cards XFree86 cannot correctly autodetect, this option allows you to specify the amount of video RAM.

DRI

Direct Rendering Infrastructure (DRI) is an interface that primarily allows 3-D software applications to take advantage of the 3-D hardware acceleration capabilities on modern supported video hardware. In addition, DRI can improve 2-D hardware acceleration performance when using drivers that have been enhanced to use the DRI for 2-D operations. This section is ignored unless DRI is enabled in the `Module` section.

Because different video cards use DRI in different ways, read the `/usr/X11R6/lib/X11/doc/README.DRI` file for specific information about your particular video card before changing any DRI values.

Files

This section sets paths for services vital to the XFree86 server, such as the font path. Common options include:

- ♦ `FontPath` — Sets the locations where the XFree86 server can find fonts. Different fixed paths to directories holding font files can be placed here and separated by commas. By default, Red Hat Linux uses `xfs` as the font server and points `FontPath` to `unix/:7100`. This tells the XFree86 server to obtain font information by using Unix-domain sockets for inter-process communication (IPC). See the "Fonts" section later in this chapter for more information concerning XFree86 and fonts.

- ♦ `ModulePath` — Allows you to set up multiple directories to use for storing modules loaded by the XFree86 server.

- ♦ `RgbPath` — Tells the XFree86 server where the RGB color database is located on the system. This database file defines all valid color names in XFree86 and ties them to specific RGB values.

InputDevice

This section configures an input device, such as a mouse or keyboard, that is used to submit information to the system via the XFree86 server. Most systems have at least two `InputDevice` sections, one each for the keyboard and the mouse. Each section includes these two lines:

- ♦ `Driver` — Tells XFree86 the name of the driver to load to use the device.

- ♦ `Identifier` — Sets the name of the device, usually the name of the device followed by a number, starting with 0 for the first device. For example, the first keyboard `InputDevice` would have an `Identifier` of `Keyboard0`.

Most `InputDevice` sections contain lines assigning specific options to that device. Each of these lines start with `Option` and contain the name of the option in quotes, followed by the value to assign to that option. Mice usually receive options such as `Protocol`, `PS/2`, and `Device`, which designates the mouse to use for this section. The `InputDevice` section is well commented, allowing you to configure additional options for your particular devices by uncommenting certain lines.

Module

This section tells the XFree86 server which modules from the `/usr/X11R6/lib/modules/` directory to load. Modules provide the XFree86 server with additional functionality.

> **CAUTION** You should not edit these values.

Monitor

This section refers to the type of monitor used by the system. While one `Monitor` section is the minimum, there may be one `Monitor` section for each monitor in use with the machine.

> **WARNING** Be careful when manually editing values in the options of the `Monitor` section. Inappropriate values in this section could damage or destroy your monitor. Consult the documentation that came with your monitor for available safe operating parameters.

The following options are usually configured during installation or when using the X Configuration tool:

♦ `HorizSync` — Tells XFree86 the range of horizontal sync frequencies that are compatible with the monitor in kHz. These values are used as a guide by the XFree86 server so that it will know whether to use a particular `Modeline` entry's values with this monitor.

♦ `Identifier` — Provides a unique name for this monitor, usually numbering each monitor starting at 0. The first monitor would be named `Monitor0`, the second `Monitor1`, and so on.

♦ `Modeline` — Used to specify the video modes that are used by your monitor at particular resolutions, with certain horizontal sync and vertical refresh resolutions. `Modeline` entries are usually preceded by a comment that explains what the mode line specifies. If your configuration file does not include comments for the various mode lines, you can scan over the values (also called mode descriptions) to uncover what the mode line is attempting to do. See the `XF86Config` man page for detailed explanations of each mode description section.

♦ `ModelName` — An optional parameter that displays the model name of the monitor.

♦ `VendorName` — An optional parameter that displays the vendor that manufactured the monitor.

♦ `VertRefresh` — Lists the vertical refresh range frequencies supported by the monitor in kHz. These values are used as a guide by the XFree86 server so that it will know whether to use a particular `Modeline` entry's values with this monitor.

Screen

This section binds together a particular `Device` and `Monitor` that can be utilized as a pair and contain certain settings. You must have at least one `Screen` section in your configuration file. The following options are common:

♦ `DefaultDepth` — Tells the `Screen` section the default color depth to try in bits. `8` is the default, `16` provides thousands of colors, and `32` displays millions of colors.

◆ `Device` — Signifies the name of the `Device` section to use with this `Screen` section.

◆ `Identifier` — Identifies the `Screen` section so that it can be referred to by a `ServerLayout` section and be utilized.

◆ `Monitor` — Tells the name of the `Monitor` section to be used with this `Screen` section.

You may also have a `Display` subsection within the `Screen` section, which tells the XFree86 server the color depth (`Depth`) and resolution (`Mode`) to try first when using this particular monitor and video card.

ServerFlags

This section contains miscellaneous global XFree86 server settings. These settings may be overridden by options placed in the `ServerLayout` section. Among the most useful settings are these two:

◆ `DontZap` — Prevents the use of the Ctrl-Alt-Backspace key combination to immediately terminate the XFree86 server.

◆ `DontZoom` — Prevents cycling through configured video resolutions using the Ctrl-Alt-Keypad-Plus and Ctrl-Alt-Keypad-Minus key combinations.

ServerLayout

This section binds together a `Screen` section with the necessary `InputDevice` sections and various options to create a unified collection of preferences used by the XFree86 server as it starts. If you have more than one `ServerLayout` section, and the one to use is not specified on the command line when bringing up the XFree86 server, the first `ServerLayout` section in the configuration file is used.

The following options are used in a `ServerLayout` section:

◆ `Identifier` — A unique name used to describe this `ServerLayout` section.

◆ `InputDevice` — The names of any `InputDevice` sections to be used with the XFree86 server. Most users will only have two lines here, `Keyboard0` and `Mouse0`, the first keyboard and mouse configured for the system. The options `CoreKeyboard` and `CorePointer` refer to the fact that these are the preferred keyboard and mouse, respectively, to use with the XFree86 server.

◆ `Screen` — The name of the `Screen` section to use. The number to the left of the name of the `Screen` section refers to the particular screen number to use in a multi-head configuration. For standard single-head video cards, this value is `0`. The numbers to the right give the X and Y absolute coordinates for the upper-left corner of the screen, by default `0 0`.

Below is an example of a typical screen entry:

```
Screen 0 "Screen0" 0 0
```

Desktop Environments and Window Managers

The configuration of an XFree86 server is useless until accessed by an X client that will use it to display a program using the hardware controlled by the X server. X clients are programs designed to take advantage of the X server's hardware, usually to provide interactivity with a user.

You do not have to run a complicated window manager in conjunction with a particular desktop environment to use X client applications. Assuming that you are not already in an X environment and do not have an .xinitrc file in your home directory, type the **xinit** command to start X with a basic terminal window (the default xterm application). You will see that this basic environment utilizes your keyboard, mouse, video card, and monitor with the XFree86 server, using the server's hardware preferences. Type **exit** at the xterm prompt to leave this basic X environment.

Of course, most computer users require more features and utility from their GUI. Developers have added layers of features to create highly developed and interactive environments that utilize the full power of the XFree86 server. These layers break into two fundamental groups based on their purpose: window managers and desktop environments. The following sections describe each of these groups.

Window Managers

Window managers are X client programs that control the way other X clients are positioned, resized, or moved. Window managers can also provide title bars to windows, keyboard focus by keyboard or mouse, and user-specified key and mouse button bindings. Window managers work with a collection of different X clients, wrapping around the program, making it look a certain way and appear on the screen in a particular place.

Four window managers are included with Red Hat Linux 8.0:

- ◆ *twm* — The minimalist *Tab Window Manager*, which provides the most basic toolset of any of the window managers.

- ◆ *mwm* — The default window manager for the GNOME desktop environment, mwm stands for *Metacity Window Manager*. It is a simple and efficient window manager that supports custom themes.

- ◆ *sawfish* — This full featured window manager was the default for Red Hat Linux until the release of Red Hat Linux 8.0. It can be used either with or without the GNOME desktop environment.

- ◆ *wmaker* — *WindowMaker* is a full-featured GNU window manager that was designed to emulate the look and feel of the NEXTSTEP environment.

These window managers can be run as individual X clients to gain a better sense of their differences. Type the **xinit** *path-to-window-manager* command, where *path-to-windowmanager* is the location of the window manager binary file. The binary file can be found by typing **which** *window-manager-name* or by looking for the name of the window manager in a bin directory.

Desktop Environments

A *desktop environment* brings together assorted X clients that can be run together using similar methods, utilizing a common development environment.

Desktop environments are different from window managers, which only control the appearance and placement of X client windows. Desktop environments use an underlying window manager to enable advanced features that allow X clients and other running processes to communicate with one another. This allows all applications written to work in that environment to commonly integrate and be used in new ways, such as permitting drag-and-drop behavior with text.

GNOME is the default desktop environment for Red Hat Linux, and uses the GTK2 base widget toolkit and miscellaneous other widgets that extend the base functionality. KDE, another desktop environment, uses a different toolkit called Qt. GNOME and KDE both contain advanced productivity applications, such as word processors, spreadsheets, and control panel devices that allow you to have complete control of the look and feel of your user experience. Both environments can run standard X client applications, and most KDE applications can run in GNOME as long as the Qt libraries are installed.

When you start X using the `startx` command, a pre-specified desktop environment is utilized. To change the default desktop environment used when X starts, open a terminal and type the `switchdesk` command. This brings up a graphical utility that allows you to select the desktop environment or window manager to use the next time X starts.

Desktop environments utilize window managers to provide the consistency in appearance between different applications. KDE contains its own window manager, called `kwm`, specifically for this functionality.

For information on the customization of the GNOME and KDE desktop environments, see Chapter 6 for GNOME and Appendix B for KDE.

Runlevels

Most users run X from runlevels 3 or 5. Runlevel 3 places your system in multi-user mode with full networking capabilities. The machine will boot to a text-based login prompt with all necessary preconfigured services started. Most servers are run in runlevel 3, as X is not necessary to provide any services utilized by most users. Runlevel 5 is similar to runlevel 3, except that it automatically starts X and provides a graphical login screen. Many workstation users prefer this method because it never forces them to see a command prompt.

The default runlevel used when your system boots can be found in the `/etc/inittab` file. If you have a line in that file that looks like `id:3:initdefault:`, then your system will boot to runlevel 3. If you have a line that looks like `id:5:initdefault:`, your system is set to boot into runlevel 5.

As root, change the runlevel number in this file to set a different default. Save the file and restart your system to verify that it boots to the correct runlevel. See the *Official Red Hat Linux Administrator's Guide* (Red Hat Press/Wiley, 2003) for more information on runlevels.

Fonts

Red Hat Linux uses `xfs` (X Font Server) to provide fonts to the XFree86 server and the X client applications that connect to it. While it is possible to not use `xfs` and place the paths to font directories in your `XF86Config` configuration file, `xfs` has several advantages:

♦ *It is easier to add and remove fonts, including editing the font path.* The font path is a collection of paths in the file system where font files are stored. The `xfs` service keeps the font path out of the XFree86 configuration files, making it easier to edit.

♦ *Fonts may be stored on one machine acting as a networked font server and can be shared among multiple X servers over the network.* A common set of fonts can be maintained in one place and easily shared between all users.

♦ *More types of fonts are supported.* `xfs` can handle TrueType, Type1, and bitmap fonts.

The XFree86 configuration files know whether to use `xfs` or hard-coded font paths because of the `FontPath` setting in their `Files` sections. By default, the `FontPath` is set to `unix/:7100`. This tells the XFree86 server to connect to port 7100 using an inner-machine communication link. The `xfs` server listening on this port will respond with font information when queried by the XFree86 server.

The `xfs` service must be running when X is started. If it is not, you will be returned to a command prompt with an error similar to the following:

```
failed to set default font path 'unix/:7100'
```

Check to see if `xfs` is running using the `ps aux | grep xfs` command. By default, `xfs` is set to start in runlevels 2, 3, 4, and 5, covering all runlevels where you would run X. If `xfs` is not running on your system, you can start it as root using the `/sbin/service xfs start` command. Use the `/usr/sbin/ntsysv`, `serviceconf`, or `/sbin/chkconfig` utilities to force it to start at the correct runlevels. For more on configuring services for a particular runlevel, see the *Official Red Hat Linux Administrator's Guide*.

xfs Configuration

The `/etc/rc.d/init.d/` `xfs` script starts the `xfs` server. Several options can be configured in the `/etc/X11/fs/config` file:

♦ `alternate-servers` — Sets a list of alternate font servers to be used if this font server is not available. A comma must separate every font server in the list.

♦ `catalogue` — An ordered list of font paths to use that contain the font files. A comma must follow every font path before a new font path can be started in the list. You can use the string `:unscaled` immediately after the font path to make the unscaled fonts in that path load first. Then, you can specify the entire path again, so that other scaled fonts will also be loaded.

♦ `client-limit` — Sets the number of clients this font server will service before refusing to handle any more. The default is `10`.

- `clone-self` — Decides if the font server will clone a new version of itself when the client limit is hit. By default, this option is on. Set it to `off` to disable this feature.

- `default-point-size` — Sets the default point size for any font that does not specify this value. The value for this option is set in decipoints. The default of `120` corresponds to 12 point fonts.

- `default-resolutions` — Specifies a list of resolutions supported by the XFree86 server. Each resolution in the list must be separated by a comma.

- `deferglyphs` — Tells `xfs` whether to defer the loading of glyphs, which is an image used to visually represent a font. You can disable this feature (`none`), enable this feature for all fonts (`all`), or turn this this feature on only for 16-bit fonts (`16`), which are largely used with Asian languages.

- `error-file` — Allows you to specify the path and file name of a location where `xfs` errors can be logged.

- `no-listen` — Tells `xfs` not to listen using a particular protocol. By default, this option is set to `tcp` to prevent `xfs` from listening on TCP ports, primarily for security reasons. If you plan on using `xfs` to serve fonts to networked workstations on a LAN, you need to remove `tcp` from this line.

- `port` — Specifies the TCP port that `xfs` will listen on if `no-listen` does not exist or is commented out.

- `use-syslog` — Tells `xfs` to use the system error log if set to on.

Adding Fonts

When using `xfs`, adding fonts to your system is rather straightforward. Use the `chkfontpath -- list` command to see the font paths currently configured on your system. To add new fonts in a new directory, follow these instructions as the root user:

1. Create a font directory, such as `/usr/share/fonts` and place the fonts inside that directory. Be sure to set the permissions correctly; it is only necessary that the files can be read; no other permissions are necessary.

2. Type the **chkfontpath --add** *font-directory-path* command, where the *font-directory-path* is the full path to the directory holding the fonts. This will add this font path to the `xfs` configuration file.

> **NOTE** You must have a `fonts.dir` file in your new font directory for the `chkfontpath` command to work correctly. The creation of the `fonts.dir` file, as well as any other files used by `xfs` with these fonts, is beyond the scope of this book. Many font collections available for Linux include these files for you, so it may not be necessary to create them by hand.

3. Restart `xfs` using the `/sbin/service xfs restart` command. You will also need to restart your X session.

4. Typing the **chkfontpath --list** command will show the new font path. Any fonts you added will be available for use.

The Red Hat Support website contains more information on this subject; see the following URL for additional help documents:

```
http://www.redhat.com/support
```

Additional Resources

Much more can be said about the XFree86 server, the clients that connect to it, and the assorted desktop environments and window managers. Advanced users interested in tweaking their XFree86 configuration will find these additional sources of information useful.

Installed Documentation

The following documentation can be accessed from your Red Hat Linux system itself:

- ◆ `/usr/X11R6/lib/X11/doc/README` — Briefly describes the XFree86 architecture and how to get additional information about the XFree86 project as a new user.

- ◆ `/usr/X11R6/lib/X11/doc/RELNOTES` — For advanced users that want to read about the latest features available in XFree86.

- ◆ `man XF86Config` — Contains information about the XFree86 configuration files, including the meaning and syntax for the different sections within the files.

- ◆ `man XFree86` — The primary man page for all XFree86 information, details the difference between local and network X server connections, explores common environmental variables, lists command line options, and provides helpful administrative key combinations.

- ◆ `man Xserver` — Describes the X display server.

Useful Websites

See the following websites for more information on Xfree86:

- ◆ `http://www.xfree86.org` — Home page of the XFree86 project, which produces the XFree86 open source version of the X Window System.

- ◆ `http://dri.sourceforge.net` — Home page of the DRI (Direct Rendering Infrastructure) project.

- ◆ `http://www.redhat.com/mirrors/LDP/HOWTO/XFree86-HOWTO` — A HOWTO document detailing the manual installation and custom configuration of XFree86.

- ◆ `http://www.gnome.org` — The home of the GNOME project.

- ◆ `http://www.kde.org` — The home of the KDE desktop environment.

Appendix F

About the CD-ROMs

The two CD-ROMs that accompany this book contain the Publisher's Edition of Red Hat Linux 8.0.

To use the CD-ROMs to install Red Hat Linux, follow these steps:

1. Insert CD-ROM #1 into your computer's CD-ROM drive.

2. Boot (or reboot) your computer, making sure that your BIOS is set to boot from CD-ROM. The Red Hat installation Welcome screen appears.

> **NOTE** If you can't boot from the CD-ROM, you'll need to create a boot diskette. See Chapter 2 for information on creating a boot disk.

3. See Chapter 2 for full instructions on installing Red Hat Linux.

System Requirements

Make sure that your computer meets the minimum system requirements listed in Chapter 1. If your computer does not meet these requirements, you may not be able to install Red Hat Linux from these CD-ROMs.

Need Help?

If you have difficulty installing or using any of the materials on the companion CD-ROMs, consult the detailed installation and troubleshooting instructions in Part I.

If you still have trouble with the CD, please call the Customer Care phone number: (800) 762-2974. Outside the United States, call (317) 572-3994. You can also contact Customer Service by email at techsupdum@wiley.com. Wiley Publishing Inc. will provide technical support only for installation and other general quality control items.

Index

Symbols

* (asterisk) character, 303
. (dot) character, 303
.. (two dots) character, 303
| pipe, 155
    more command, 156
    redirection, 157
~ (tilde character), 303

A

-A option (mkisofs command), 140
About Myself option, 114
access
    Mozilla, 211-212
    Windows partitions, 295
        mounting automatically, 296
        mounting manually, 295
Accessibility option, 114
Accessories command (Main Menu), 172
Accessories menu commands, Archive
    Manager, 172
Account Creation screen, 57
Account Info tab (User Properties window),
    184
accounts
    configuration, 56-57
        root password setup, 57-58
        user accounts, 58-59
    root, passwords, 57-58
    user
        creating, 101-102
        names, 102
        passwords, 102
        setup, 58-59
active partitions, 367
    destructive repartitioning, 367-368
    non-destructive repartitioning, 368
        compressing existing data, 368-369
        creating partitions, 370
        resizing existing partitions, 369-370
Add command (Panel menu), 338

Add Partition dialog box, 43-44
Add to Drawer menu commands,
    Drawer, 116
Add to Panel menu commands,
    Launcher, 116
Additional Size options (Add Partition dialog
    box), 44
addresses, email, 218
Adobe Acrobat Reader, website
    for downloading, 198
Aisle Riot, 234
All Devices and System Summary report, 6
Allow Incoming option, 53, 259-260
Allowable Drives option (Add Partition dialog
    box), 43
alternate-servers option (etc/X11/fs/config
    file), 383
Apache-based httpd service, troubleshooting,
    94
apic command, 25
apm=allow_ints command, 25
apm=off command, 25
apm=power_off command, 25
apm=realmode_power_off command, 25
applets, 107
    adding to Panel, 116
    icons, 107
    KDE, 338, 340
    Taskbar, 107
    Workspace Switcher, 107
applications
    dragging across workspaces, 119
    email, 217-218
        Evolution, 218-221
        KMail, 223-225
        Mozilla Mail, 221-223
        plain text, 225-228
    starting, 294
Apply Theme command (View menu), 120
Archive Manager command (Accessories
    menu), 172
archives, 172
    File Roller, 172-174
    shell prompts, creating, 176-178
askmethod command, 25

GNU General Public License

Version 2, June 1991

Copyright (C) 1989, 1991 Free Software Foundation, Inc.

59 Temple Place - Suite 330, Boston, MA 02111-1307, USA

Everyone is permitted to copy and distribute verbatim copies of this license document, but changing it is not allowed.

Preamble

The licenses for most software are designed to take away your freedom to share and change it. By contrast, the GNU General Public License is intended to guarantee your freedom to share and change free software — to make sure the software is free for all its users. This General Public License applies to most of the Free Software Foundation's software and to any other program whose authors commit to using it. (Some other Free Software Foundation software is covered by the GNU Library General Public License instead.) You can apply it to your programs, too.

When we speak of free software, we are referring to freedom, not price. Our General Public Licenses are designed to make sure that you have the freedom to distribute copies of free software (and charge for this service if you wish), that you receive source code or can get it if you want it, that you can change the software or use pieces of it in new free programs; and that you know you can do these things.

To protect your rights, we need to make restrictions that forbid anyone to deny you these rights or to ask you to surrender the rights. These restrictions translate to certain responsibilities for you if you distribute copies of the software, or if you modify it.

For example, if you distribute copies of such a program, whether gratis or for a fee, you must give the recipients all the rights that you have. You must make sure that they, too, receive or can get the source code. And you must show them these terms so they know their rights.

We protect your rights with two steps: (1) copyright the software, and (2) offer you this license which gives you legal permission to copy, distribute and/or modify the software.

Also, for each author's protection and ours, we want to make certain that everyone understands that there is no warranty for this free software. If the software is modified by someone else and passed on, we want its recipients to know that what they have is not the original, so that any problems introduced by others will not reflect on the original authors' reputations.

Finally, any free program is threatened constantly by software patents. We wish to avoid the danger that redistributors of a free program will individually obtain patent licenses, in effect making the program proprietary. To prevent this, we have made it clear that any patent must be licensed for everyone's free use or not licensed at all.

The precise terms and conditions for copying, distribution and modification follow.

Terms and Conditions for Copying, Distribution and Modification

0. This License applies to any program or other work which contains a notice placed by the copyright holder saying it may be distributed under the terms of this General Public License. The "Program", below, refers to any such program or work, and a "work based on the Program" means either the Program or any derivative work under copyright law: that is to say, a work containing the Program or a portion of it, either verbatim or with modifications and/or translated into another language. (Hereinafter, translation is included without limitation in the term "modification".) Each licensee is addressed as "you".

   Activities other than copying, distribution and modification are not covered by this License; they are outside its scope. The act of running the Program is not restricted, and the output from the Program is covered only if its contents constitute a work based on the Program (independent of having been made by running the Program). Whether that is true depends on what the Program does.

1. You may copy and distribute verbatim copies of the Program's source code as you receive it, in any medium, provided that you conspicuously and appropriately publish on each copy an appropriate copyright notice and disclaimer of warranty; keep intact all the notices that refer to this License and to the absence of any warranty; and give any other recipients of the Program a copy of this License along with the Program.

   You may charge a fee for the physical act of transferring a copy, and you may at your option offer warranty protection in exchange for a fee.

2. You may modify your copy or copies of the Program or any portion of it, thus forming a work based on the Program, and copy and distribute such modifications or work under the terms of Section 1 above, provided that you also meet all of these conditions:

a) You must cause the modified files to carry prominent notices stating that you changed the files and the date of any change.

b) You must cause any work that you distribute or publish, that in whole or in part contains or is derived from the Program or any part thereof, to be licensed as a whole at no charge to all third parties under the terms of this License.

c) If the modified program normally reads commands interactively when run, you must cause it, when started running for such interactive use in the most ordinary way, to print or display an announcement including an appropriate copyright notice and a notice that there is no warranty (or else, saying that you provide a warranty) and that users may redistribute the program under these conditions, and telling the user how to view a copy of this License. (Exception: if the Program itself is interactive but does not normally print such an announcement, your work based on the Program is not required to print an announcement.)

These requirements apply to the modified work as a whole. If identifiable sections of that work are not derived from the Program, and can be reasonably considered independent and separate works in themselves, then this License, and its terms, do not apply to those sections when you distribute them as separate works. But when you distribute the same sections as part of a whole which is a work based on the Program, the distribution of the whole must be on the terms of this License, whose permissions for other licensees extend to the entire whole, and thus to each and every part regardless of who wrote it.

Thus, it is not the intent of this section to claim rights or contest your rights to work written entirely by you; rather, the intent is to exercise the right to control the distribution of derivative or collective works based on the Program.

In addition, mere aggregation of another work not based on the Program with the Program (or with a work based on the Program) on a volume of a storage or distribution medium does not bring the other work under the scope of this License.

3. You may copy and distribute the Program (or a work based on it, under Section 2) in object code or executable form under the terms of Sections 1 and 2 above provided that you also do one of the following:

a) Accompany it with the complete corresponding machine-readable source code, which must be distributed under the terms of Sections 1 and 2 above on a medium customarily used for software interchange; or,

b) Accompany it with a written offer, valid for at least three years, to give any third party, for a charge no more than your cost of physically performing source distribution, a complete machine-readable copy of the corresponding source code, to be distributed under the terms of Sections 1 and 2 above on a medium customarily used for software interchange; or,

c) Accompany it with the information you received as to the offer to distribute corresponding source code. (This alternative is allowed only for noncommercial distribution and only if you received the program in object code or executable form with such an offer, in accord with Subsection b above.)

The source code for a work means the preferred form of the work for making modifications to it. For an executable work, complete source code means all the source code for all modules it contains, plus any associated interface definition files, plus the scripts used to control compilation and installation of the executable. However, as a special exception, the source code distributed need not include anything that is normally distributed (in either source or binary form) with the major components (compiler, kernel, and so on) of the operating system on which the executable runs, unless that component itself accompanies the executable.

If distribution of executable or object code is made by offering access to copy from a designated place, then offering equivalent access to copy the source code from the same place counts as distribution of the source code, even though third parties are not compelled to copy the source along with the object code.

4. You may not copy, modify, sublicense, or distribute the Program except as expressly provided under this License. Any attempt otherwise to copy, modify, sublicense or distribute the Program is void, and will automatically terminate your rights under this License. However, parties who have received copies, or rights, from you under this License will not have their licenses terminated so long as such parties remain in full compliance.

5. You are not required to accept this License, since you have not signed it. However, nothing else grants you permission to modify or distribute the Program or its derivative works. These actions are prohibited by law if you do not accept this License. Therefore, by modifying or distributing the Program (or any work based on the Program), you indicate your acceptance of this License to do so, and all its terms and conditions for copying, distributing or modifying the Program or works based on it.

6. Each time you redistribute the Program (or any work based on the Program), the recipient automatically receives a license from the original licensor to copy, distribute or modify the Program subject to these terms and conditions. You may not impose any further restrictions on the recipients' exercise of the rights granted herein. You are not responsible for enforcing compliance by third parties to this License.

7. If, as a consequence of a court judgment or allegation of patent infringement or for any other reason (not limited to patent issues), conditions are imposed on you (whether by court order, agreement or otherwise) that contradict the conditions of this License, they do not excuse you from the conditions of this License. If you cannot distribute so as to satisfy simultaneously your obligations under this License and any other pertinent obligations, then as a consequence you may not distribute the Program at all. For example, if a patent

license would not permit royalty-free redistribution of the Program by all those who receive copies directly or indirectly through you, then the only way you could satisfy both it and this License would be to refrain entirely from distribution of the Program.

If any portion of this section is held invalid or unenforceable under any particular circumstance, the balance of the section is intended to apply and the section as a whole is intended to apply in other circumstances.

It is not the purpose of this section to induce you to infringe any patents or other property right claims or to contest validity of any such claims; this section has the sole purpose of protecting the integrity of the free software distribution system, which is implemented by public license practices. Many people have made generous contributions to the wide range of software distributed through that system in reliance on consistent application of that system; it is up to the author/donor to decide if he or she is willing to distribute software through any other system and a licensee cannot impose that choice.

This section is intended to make thoroughly clear what is believed to be a consequence of the rest of this License.

8. If the distribution and/or use of the Program is restricted in certain countries either by patents or by copyrighted interfaces, the original copyright holder who places the Program under this License may add an explicit geographical distribution limitation excluding those countries, so that distribution is permitted only in or among countries not thus excluded. In such case, this License incorporates the limitation as if written in the body of this License.

9. The Free Software Foundation may publish revised and/or new versions of the General Public License from time to time. Such new versions will be similar in spirit to the present version, but may differ in detail to address new problems or concerns.

Each version is given a distinguishing version number. If the Program specifies a version number of this License which applies to it and "any later version", you have the option of following the terms and conditions either of that version or of any later version published by the Free Software Foundation. If the Program does not specify a version number of this License, you may choose any version ever published by the Free Software Foundation.

10. If you wish to incorporate parts of the Program into other free programs whose distribution conditions are different, write to the author to ask for permission. For software which is copyrighted by the Free Software Foundation, write to the Free Software Foundation; we sometimes make exceptions for this. Our decision will be guided by the two goals of preserving the free status of all derivatives of our free software and of promoting the sharing and reuse of software generally.

NO WARRANTY

11. BECAUSE THE PROGRAM IS LICENSED FREE OF CHARGE, THERE IS NO WARRANTY FOR THE PROGRAM, TO THE EXTENT PERMITTED BY APPLICABLE LAW. EXCEPT WHEN OTHERWISE STATED IN WRITING THE COPYRIGHT HOLDERS AND/OR OTHER PARTIES PROVIDE THE PROGRAM "AS IS" WITHOUT WARRANTY OF ANY KIND, EITHER EXPRESSED OR IMPLIED, INCLUDING, BUT NOT LIMITED TO, THE IMPLIED WARRANTIES OF MERCHANTABILITY AND FITNESS FOR A PARTICULAR PURPOSE. THE ENTIRE RISK AS TO THE QUALITY AND PERFORMANCE OF THE PROGRAM IS WITH YOU. SHOULD THE PROGRAM PROVE DEFECTIVE, YOU ASSUME THE COST OF ALL NECESSARY SERVICING, REPAIR OR CORRECTION.

12. IN NO EVENT UNLESS REQUIRED BY APPLICABLE LAW OR AGREED TO IN WRITING WILL ANY COPYRIGHT HOLDER, OR ANY OTHER PARTY WHO MAY MODIFY AND/OR REDISTRIBUTE THE PROGRAM AS PERMITTED ABOVE, BE LIABLE TO YOU FOR DAMAGES, INCLUDING ANY GENERAL, SPECIAL, INCIDENTAL OR CONSEQUENTIAL DAMAGES ARISING OUT OF THE USE OR INABILITY TO USE THE PROGRAM (INCLUDING BUT NOT LIMITED TO LOSS OF DATA OR DATA BEING RENDERED INACCURATE OR LOSSES SUSTAINED BY YOU OR THIRD PARTIES OR A FAILURE OF THE PROGRAM TO OPERATE WITH ANY OTHER PROGRAMS), EVEN IF SUCH HOLDER OR OTHER PARTY HAS BEEN ADVISED OF THE POSSIBILITY OF SUCH DAMAGES.

END OF TERMS AND CONDITIONS